Truth's

Debt to

Value

David Weissman

Truth's
Debt to
Value

Yale
University
Press

New
Haven &
London

Designed by Deborah Dutton

Set in Janson text type by Maple-Vail Composition Service, Bing-
hamton, New York.

Printed in the United States of America by Vail-Ballou Press, Bing-
hamton, New York.

Library of Congress Cataloging-in-Publication Data

Weissman, David, 1936–
    Truth's debt to value / David Weissman.
        p.   cm.
    Includes bibliographical references and index.
    ISBN 0-300-05425-4 (alk. paper)
    1. Truth.   2. Values.   I. Title.
BD171.W44   1993
121 – dc20   92–43608
                                              CIP

A catalogue record for this book is available from the British Library.

The paper in this book meets the guidelines for permanence and du-
rability of the Committee on Production Guidelines for Book Lon-
gevity of the Council on Library Resources.

10 9 8 7 6 5 4 3 2 1

To my parents

Contents

Chapter Three   **The Cognitive-Affective**
Basis for Value   101

Chapter Six   **Rational Attitude and Desire** **297**

Acknowledgements

Many people have helped me during the writing and production of this book. Several deserve my special thanks.

I might never have coupled truth to value but for Robert Neville's insistence that they go together. We explain the connection somewhat differently. See his *Reconstruction of Thinking* (Albany: State University of New York Press, 1981).

Jonathan Brent, Lawrence Kenney, and Jean van Altena have been my editors at Yale University Press. Their moral and technical support has been unstinting. Linda Webster prepared the index.

My family tolerates my writing and sometimes even approves of it. Doing it would be much harder without them.

Introduction

All of us make a difference to one another and to the things around us; but none of us is a world-maker. Devising laws, educating ourselves, bending glass and steel: we do remake some parts of the world, but never all of it. World-makers condemn this modesty. No truth, they say, can resist our power to undo it. Ideologies, strong readings (or misreadings), values that are practical, aesthetic, or moral: these are the engines of contemporary world-making. Conceptual systems are its wheels: we differentiate and organize sensory data, sentences, symbols, and behaviors, creating the thinkable states of affairs, theories, texts, and conduct where these values are satisfied.[1]

The values impelling us may be the common objects of desire or the qualities, including simplicity and expressiveness, rated highly in discourse. Valuing power, we create a social order in which the behavior of the people ruled expresses the despotic authority of their rulers. Valuing simplicity, as Quine does,[2] we use quantifiers, variables, predicates, and relations to express the minimal set of theoretical notions required to organize whatever observation terms are admitted into our conceptual scheme. No matter the context, be it practical or discursive, we swallow our naturalist scruples, agreeing that there is nothing in reality—no political relation or logical form—that value-driven minds have not put there.

World-making is a romantic persuasion, one that blinds us to the places where we accommodate, stumble, or die. Worse, it is a dangerous persuasion. Oblivious to a world we have not made, we pollute it. Empowered by our technology, we alter the environment and ourselves, though we cannot foresee the consequences of doing either one. Craving authority, inventing slogans to which other people will march, we organize them for purposes of our own. World-making, as expressed in all these ways, is a celebration of desire, freedom, understanding, and power. This is our philosophic narcotic, one that would surely destroy us if criticism did not first expose its presumption. Here is a case where philosophical analysis might have some useful effect.

Many philosophers in our time are, nevertheless, committed to the idea that we make worlds. They say, with Kant,[3] that we use conceptual systems to create a thinkable experience: we are to believe that no property can be ascribed to any state of affairs if it is not anticipated as a predicate within the conceptual system used for schematizing our experience of that thing. The truth that something has one of these properties then depends on the logical apparatus, including quantifiers and inductive rules, introduced as part of the system for schematizing experience. These rules for determining the inferences permissible among sentences are conventions. They fix the evidence required before it can be affirmed that something has a particular property. What shall count as piety? How much piety is required for being pious? We set the minimum standard somewhere along the gradient from little to more. Having evidence of that much prayer and good works, we infer that our candidate is pious. The rules are made, then applied, with the consequence that reality is enriched by one pious man.

The content of this reality is a matter of dispute among contemporary Kantians, some of whom argue that words, sentences, symbols, or behaviors, not sensory data, are the matters schematized. This difference is incidental here, because the outcome is generically the same for all: using a conceptual system to schematize some *materiel*, we create a thinkable experience and thereby a thinkable world. It is also incidental to my purposes that defenders of Kantian world-making slight his distinction between transcendental and empirical categories. Kant supposed that the categories of quantity, quality, and relation are fixed for every thinker, but determinable. They achieve determination when a schema introducing specific predicates is applied to sensory data. Quality, for example, is expressed contingently as a specific color, sound, or taste, when an empirical schema determines that a category shall have this particular expression. We get a different experience and a different world depending on the rule used to schematize sensory data, symbols, or behavior. The Kantians of whom I shall be writing emphasize the variability — in literature, science, and daily life — of the schemas used to create an experience and world. This variability makes these thinkers indifferent, or averse, to the fixed status of the transcendental categories. But this is no diminution of what is Kantian in the view they endorse: that we use conceptual systems to schematize experiences and worlds.

My title, *Truth's Debt to Value*, is a précis of one dominant feature in this Kantian view. The use of schematizing conceptual systems is well known among Kant's readers. The relation of truth to value (of theory to practice, cognition to interest) is an equally decisive, if neglected, feature of his Critical Idealism. Value is the black hole, the unvoiced mover at the center of our alleged world-making.[4] Its importance is conspicuous only where Kant or his heirs suppose that values determine the choice of conceptual systems, hence the world or experience in which these values are satisfied. Hilary Putnam, for example, argues that "what counts as the real world depends upon our values."[5] Donald Davidson is more abstract, albeit equally determined that truth be founded in our valorizing attitudes and desires. As he writes: "The conceptual underpinning of interpretation is a theory of truth; truth thus rests in the end on belief and, even more ultimately, on the affective attitudes."[6]

What I shall be calling *values* are, more exactly, objects of desire and attitude. They are not intrinsic goods or evils, or even the instrumental relations invoked when we say, for example, that cow fever is bad for cattle. Value is bestowed, whenever anything, however ordinary, is either favored or scorned. It is always these mental intentions, not the object thereby made valuable, which energize the choice of whatever conceptual system is used to create the experience and world in which this passion is satisfied. Wanting excitement or peace and quiet, we create the circumstances realizing our aim.

There are, however, these ulterior questions: what factors determine our attitudes and desires? What is it that fixes our preference among conceptual systems? Answers of one sort are anthropological, historical, circumstantial, or psychological. Conceptualizations vary not only among cultures and epochs, but also among individuals distinguished by their situations and developmental histories. Another kind of answer emphasizes our freedom: prizing beauty and style, we discount pinched feet; wanting comfort, we find beauty in shoes that fit. These considerations sometimes conflict, as tradition may collide with circumstances. It is freedom, Kantians suppose, that enables us to supersede these conflicts. We choose one conceptual system over another because we suppose that an experience and world schematized by it will satisfy the attitude or desire which directs us. Being fishermen or farmers, we use a conceptual system and create a world appropriate to our values. Desire dictates the choice among conceptual systems, and we schematize a world having whatever discriminations and relations are prefigured in the chosen system.[7]

This relation of truth to value is often described below in a simple formula: thinkers of Kantian persuasion make truth a function of value. Value is the determining variable; truth is the variable determined. It follows that truth cannot be the correspondence relation of a thought or sentence to a state of affairs independent of it. That is so because thoughts or sentences are the parts or expressions of whatever conceptual scheme is used for creating experience: things discerned within experience cannot be hived off from this conceptual apparatus, then set against it as objects or referents satisfying the thoughts or sentences. That naturalistic, realistic hypothesis about representation is inappropriate here, where the relation of thought or language to the things signified is much more intimate. We are to assume that things signified, or *re-presented*, have no standing, as regards either their character or existence, apart from the conceptual system schematizing sensory data, symbols, sentences, or behaviors. The coherence of thoughts or sentences under inductive rules, not their correspondence to states of affairs independent of thought and language, is the notion of truth appropriate to this Kantian view of things. And always, the rule-governed coherence among thoughts and sentences is supported by the more fundamental coherence between a value or values and the conceptual system used to schematize the world in which they are satisfied: coherence, hence truth, in the relations of thoughts or sentences has no function but the one of creating the experience whereby some object of desire is realized.

Agitators for world-making typically assume that truth is a function of value, though the point is not much emphasized. Perhaps the lingering support for emotivism explains their reticence. Emotivism trivializes value, so a theory making value determining and truth derivative risks seeming bathetic. Better that the relation of truth and value be left to that obscurity where the force of values is not considered.

Fichte was more direct: "*In relation to a possible object*, the pure self-referring activity of the self is a *striving*; and as shown earlier, *an infinite striving* at that. This boundless striving, carried to infinity, is the *condition of the possibility of any object whatsoever:* no striving, no object."[8] But if no striving and no objects, then no truths.

One could hardly exaggerate Fichte's anticipation of current views about truth and value. If we too often ignore him, that is only because Kant had expressed similar ideas: "All of the soul's powers or capacities can be reduced to three that cannot be derived further from a common basis: the *cognitive power*, the *feeling of pleasure and displeasure*, and the *power of desire*."[9] The cognitive power uses conceptual systems to create schematized experience of the only worlds we can know. Desire is the valorizing expression of freedom: we create values by freely selecting the objects of desire. The cognitive power chooses its conceptual systems so that schematizing thought may create an experience and truths whereby desires are satisfied. Pleasure or pain is the feeling produced when a theory, interpretation, or plan succeeds, or not, in this objective. Kant thinks of us as artists at play: we imagine and paint a subject, all the while enjoying the work we do because of seeing our values realized within it.

How can we justify saying that value is the independent variable, truth the dependent one? Kant explains it by affirming that desire in its relation to value-fulfilling experience is transcendental. Understanding schematizes sensory data or behaviors. Its domain is the experience created. The domain of reason and will (desire) is, by contrast, supersensible. This is the "place" where mind or soul has immediate—not conceptually mediated—contact with itself. It is here that mind chooses, first, the purposes described by Kant as "final,"[10] then the conceptual systems used for realizing them. Freely choosing God, wisdom, or power as my ultimate aim, I organize my experience and world so that my purpose is realized. This is my pleasure.

Notice that Kant's order of priority, desire before understanding, value before truth, is not metaphysically innocent. Value-directed world-making is an expression of the psycho-centric ontology inherited from Descartes, then refined: everything credited with existence is either mind itself or one of its qualifications—for example, its desires, conceptual systems, or schematized experiences. Valorizing, schematizing mind is the subject and source of all being—or, at any rate, all the being we can know.

Notice too that this formulation is problematic for more than ontological reasons. That is so because desire operating supersensibly seems dangerously liberated: what limit or agency is there to restrict the choice of objects for desire? The obstacles encountered within experience have no effect upon it, because desire choosing its objects operates supersensibly—that is, before experience is schematized. There is, on this Kantian telling, only one opportunity for restraining attitude or desire. That is the place where desire, as will, is constrained by reason. Kant supposes that reason limits desire after considering what effects would result if some objective were universally desired and pursued: Is a contradiction entailed by willing that everyone in the actor's situation should behave in the way proposed? No desire is responsible, Kant supposes, if we cannot will its object without violating reason's demand for universalizability without contradiction.

Suppose that we test the desire to break promises. This is an aim that cannot be consistently universalized, because making promises is a reciprocal relation: one party promises, the other accepts the promise. Promises will not be accepted (the promising relation will not be established) if everyone expects promise-makers to renege. The desire to break promises undercuts itself when universalized.

This test for rational desires is, however, insufficiently subtle. Many things we desire are bad for us without failing Kant's test, as when refusing to do one's homework has consequences that are undesirable but not contradictory when universalized. Nor do we always wait on universalization to know that something is bad: insulting one's mother or friend may be egregious without regard for the effects that would result if the behavior were universalized.

Kant has made a strategic error: he proposes that desire be answerable to the categorical imperative, not to truths about our circumstances. This seemed plausible and safe, because the contingency of these truths could be set against the demand that we acknowledge the categorical imperative as a necessary constraint upon impulse. Still, Kant's test is too crude. We can determine that some things are bad without having to universalize. Some others are bad, even though they can be universalized without contradiction. Desire requires an additional constraint. Truth, meaning truths discovered, not made, is my candidate. Wanting to help others or ourselves, not wanting to damage one or the other, we justify a desire by citing truths about the likely consequences of our behavior.

Thinkers who favor world-making in our time do not agree that there are truths independent of our world-making to educate and limit values. Nor do they concede that the choice of conceptual systems is motivated by a value. The urge to make desire responsible is all the less common. Nietzsche justifies this lapse. There is, he said, no appeal beyond the will as it creates values; nothing additional to a desire is required for its justification.[11] William James is hardly more guarded than Nietzsche, as when he describes value and desire as the incitement to action.[12] James's remarks about desire are often little more than a celebration of the energy that directs our choice of conceptual systems and behaviors. The problem of educating desire, or making it disciplined because accountable to rational choice, is less important to him. Similarly, Rudolf Carnap distinguishes the semantics, syntax, and pragmatics of conceptual systems[13] but says very little about pragmatics as they motivate the formulation or choice of systems.[14] Why prefer physical object predicates to phenomenalist ones? Convenience. Why prefer convenience to subtlety? Carnap doesn't tell us.

The determining role of value is more commonly acknowledged among contemporary world-makers, as when Richard Rorty argues that literature is value-driven[15] and that science is a kind of literature.[16] But literature is not mere story-telling: "This is the culture which claims to have taken over and reshaped whatever is worth keeping in science, philosophy, and religion— looking down on all three from a higher standpoint."[17] This literary, textualist culture is to transform our understanding of thought and knowledge: "I think we shall best understand the role of textualism within our culture if we see it as an attempt to think through a thorough-going pragmatism, a thorough-going abandonment of the notion of *discovering the truth* which is common to theology and science."[18]

We get this result:

The strong textualist simply asks himself the same question about a text which the engineer or the physicist asks himself about a puzzling object: how shall I describe this in order to get it to do what I want?[19]

Taken in a strong and ironic sense, the claim that everything is texts can be read as saying: "It makes as much sense to say that atoms are simply Democritean texts as to say that Democritus is merely a collection of atoms. That is because both slogans are attempts to give one vocabulary a privileged status, and are therefore equally silly."[20]

The pragmatist reminds us that a new and useful vocabulary is just *that*, not a sudden unmediated vision of things or texts as they are.[21]

We are to use the vocabulary, I infer, to schematize an experience in which we "get what we want."[22] No matter that many things (cancer, poverty, Saddam Hussein) will not do what we desire. Textualism is the device enabling us to rethink the things that interest us until they behave as we require them to do.

Where every other cognitive activity is only a kind of literature, and where literature is the adroit use of words for creating the circumstances we want, all world-making is likewise value-driven. We may have supposed that the sciences represent disparate aspects of nature's intrinsic form; but there is, says Rorty, no such form to represent. Indeed, there is no "Beyond," nothing beyond experience that might be represented.[23] Accept this disclaimer, and we have liberated science from having to discover nature's form. But what is left for science to do and be? Confounded by the loss of its former aim, science needs a different one. Affinity to literature supplies the new purpose. Like literature, science should construct whatever ideas of the world, and presumably whatever worlds, satisfy our attitudes or desires. Nor should we press scientists too closely about their aims. No one asked Melville to justify the values that provoked his writing *Moby-Dick*. Equally, we might excuse scientists from having to identify and justify the values that direct their world-making. Yet science and technology, even more than literature, have consequences. This makes it incumbent that scientists and engineers should consider the effects of their world-making, even if their motives are of less concern.

Thrasymachus, Marx, James, and Freud have taught us that governments, economies, and personal behaviors are value-driven. Derrida and Foucault have sensitized us to the possibility that any thesis, technology, or social arrangement may express, even as it conceals, the interest of some world-making faction or mind. We seem always to have known that literature is value-driven. Only science seemed exempt. No longer: we have Putnam and Rorty insisting that it, too, tells only schematizing stories impelled by some value.[24] None of these disciplines is witness to truths it reports but does not make. What is the benefit of this discovery? Where is the counterweight to the skepticism it encourages? I can think of only one offsetting advantage: elemental respect for the integrity of the values directing our world-making is the populist, anarchic generalization of Kant's own altruistic views about the kingdom of ends: every citizen, scientist, or author, every free spirit, a world-maker, whatever his desires.[25]

Talk of world-making is, however, more than a way of exalting our affective and cognitive freedom; it is more than an intellectual conceit. This is also the grandiose description-cum-justification for a social practice. Behaving as though the world has no intrinsic form of its own, we organize materials in ways congenial to our purposes. It doesn't matter, then, if we are cavalier about this world and the materials from which it is made. A world having no character but the one introduced as we schematize sensory data, sentences, symbols, or behaviors seems to require no respect except as it has instrumental value for us. Too bad if we, in our self-concern, carelessness, and conceit, poison the world we have not made but do inhabit. Before, it was only kings and despots who affirmed their right to remake some part of the world to suit themselves. Now, all of us claim that right. Democracy as a form of political organization is superseded by the demand that each of us be free to create a world appropriate to a tribe, a faction, or to himself. Each of us claims an essential creative power and right to make an ambient world suited to his or her taste. Think of credit cards assigned at birth and accepted universally with no monthly bill. Value-directed world-making encourages this fantasy.

Where philosophic rhetoric justifies our self-deception, we need other ways to speak. I suggest the following naturalistic alternative. We speculate that the world has at any moment a decided form. Our vulnerability to the things around us makes it urgent that we know the truths about our situation, for we cannot successfully secure and satisfy ourselves without knowing who we are and where we stand in the world. No longer having a settled ecological niche, lacking the instincts that would qualify us for effective action in the environments we have made for ourselves, we require these truths if we are to accommodate ourselves to our circumstances. Desire is often oblivious to truth. Passion moves us, in anger or love, before reflection can divert us. Even where desire is constrained by the force of assumed truths, no set of them forecloses the choice of objects for desire; we may want or refuse things we are powerless to have or resist. But then it often happens that we have both a realizable interest and some control of circumstances and ourselves. These are occasions when reflection mediates between desire and the behavior it provokes. We supersede impulse by creating the space where relevant truths may limit the reasonable objects of desire. Where desire is educable, with truths to inform it, the Kantian priorities are reversed: what thing to desire is often, if not always, determined by truths about our circumstances. Lost in the snow, anxious and cold, we want safety. But this is not literature. Rewriting the story will not save us. We shall have to save ourselves if we are not saved by someone else. The last is a matter of luck. The former requires that we have relevant truths about our circumstances and skills to use them.

Philosophic thinking alone could not have promoted the idea that everything once ascribed to the world itself is the product of our value-driven ways of thinking. It took the evidence of everyday life to support this idealist conclusion. For it is not incidental that so much of our physical and social environment is our contrivance: many of us live in places that would not exist if we had not made them. Truth does seem to be the function of desire, or desire perverted, in every big city. There may be only dirty pigeons, a skeletal tree, and the sky above to remind us that a nature we have not made is everywhere within and about us. Our responsibility seems almost complete: we have made it, presumably, because we want it.

Nietzsche declared, in the spirit of Schopenhauer and his reading of Kant's *Critique of Judgment*, that desire shatters old truths, creating whatever new ones are required to satisfy it.[26] There are many cities and rivers, dumps and spoiled lands, where desire or its unexpected consequences have had this effect. Still, Nietzsche's isn't the last word. For just how naked should desire be? Never mind that his gloss of truth and value is grandiose and dangerous; it is also false. Desires are made reasonable, as regards both their content and their execution, as we consider our circumstances. What were the consequences of acting upon some candidate desire in the past? How were people and things affected? Passion may cause us to do many things that are unconsidered. But desires can be, and often are, made reasonable as we consider truths relevant both to the past and to the likely consequences of the actions proposed. Deliberation, on these occasions, is the effective use of truths about the past and present to limit the consequences of future behavior. We never foresee all the consequences; but we can refuse to do things which are foreseeably bad or the many others whose principal consequences are unknown.

Nietzsche wrongly described deliberation as the compensatory intellectual strength of those who are terrified by will and too feeble for action. Kant failed us even more grievously. He separated freedom and desire from understanding and its conceptual systems, so freeing value from the scrutiny of truth. Endorsing that separation and acting upon it, we would make worlds

on behalf of insufficiently considered values. We are happily saved this consequence, because Kant's program is flawed. No one makes worlds; all of us
deliberate about some of our values. Value-driven world-making, Kant's be-
quest to us, is a complex error. Correcting some recent formulations of this
error is my purpose here.

There are six chapters. Chapter 1 compares Peirce and James on the
subject of truth's relation to value. James is my paradigmatic Kantian. Peirce
speaks for the tradition of Plato and Spinoza, for truth as guide to desire.
Chapter 2 distinguishes constructive from hypothetical thinking, the one as
it makes things, the other as it formulates and tests representations. Neither
the existence nor the character of the things represented depends in any way,
I shall be saying, on the fact that they are represented: thinking of this hypothetical sort is not a way of making the things represented. It is mistaken,
therefore, when certain pragmatists suppose that thinking about the world
must invariably be an occasion for world-making.

Chapter 3 is an explanation and justification for the claim that thinking is always impelled by value. The self is something we do make, if only
within constraints founded in biology and our circumstances. This chapter
describes the cognitive-affective balance which develops as we accommodate
ourselves to the world. It is this balance which shapes our initiatives and
responses to our circumstances. I shall be saying that impulses expressing a
dominant affective style may be reconsidered in the light of information about
ourselves and the world. This is the point of describing the balance as *cognitive-affective:* we subordinate feeling to cognition (meaning hypotheses tested)
at the point where doing so is critical for our well-being.

Chapter 4 distinguishes some of the candidate notions of truth. It
argues that each of them fills the space made for it within a larger-scale
metaphysical theory. This compares to the more familiar claim that notions
of truth resemble pillars of salt, each one separable from the rest of theory
and self-sufficient. I shall also be saying that theories embedding notions of
truth are themselves motivated by values. Some of these values are generated
within the dialectic of philosophic reflection; others, like fear, are values closer
to the texture of everyday life. But always, I shall claim, the truth conditions
for these embedding metaphysical theories are distinguishable and separable
from the values motivating them. Their truth, were any of them true, would
not be a function of their motivating values. This fourth chapter considers
four notions of truth: truth as coherence, identity, redundancy, and behavior.

Each is located within a supporting metaphysical theory. Motivating values for each theory are cited and appraised.

Does any of these four notions of truth enable us to account for the critical role of truth in effective behavior? Plans signify the instrumental relations on which successful behavior is predicated: maps represent the circumstances where plans are enacted. Which of these four notions is appropriate to truths representing the causal relations and terrain salient to a map or plan? I shall say that coherence, identity, redundancy, and behaviorist versions are all deficient as explications of these truths.

This is a significant failure. We do not understand the accommodations enabling us to save, secure, or satisfy ourselves if we have no idea of truth adequate to the truths which orient and direct our behavior. Nor can we explain the use of truths in reflections where possible objects of desire are appraised. What would be good for us to do? What has happened when we or others have done things of this sort in the past? Truths about those consequences are vital to our deliberations, though none of the four notions of truth considered in this chapter has anything helpful to say about them. We deliberate about means and ends. Truths are vital to these deliberations. Let us have an idea of truth appropriate to the use made of particular truths.

Chapter 5 specifies a notion of truth adequate to this demand. It defends the claim that truth is correspondence. One reads that correspondence is incoherent.[27] We also read that extra-mental, extra-linguistic states serving as truth conditions have disappeared or were never there.

> The correct objection to correspondence theories is not, then, that they make truth something to which humans can never legitimately aspire; the real objection is rather that such theories fail to provide entities to which truth vehicles (whether we take these to be statements, sentences or utterances) can be said to correspond. If this is right, and I am convinced it is, we ought also to question the popular assumption that sentences, or their spoken tokens, or sentence-like entities or configurations in our brains, can properly be called "representations," since there is nothing for them to represent. If we give up facts as entities that make sentences true, we ought to give up representations at the same time, for the legitimacy of each depends on the legitimacy of the other.[28]

This passage may be intentionally paradoxical, for reasons important to its author, Donald Davidson. I suggest that we read his categorical assertions literally: we infer from Davidson's skepticism about "facts" in general that there are no particular dogs, cats, sentences, or brains serving as truth conditions for our claims about them. Chapter 5 specifies the entities Davidson ignores, and thereby referents for words and sentences.

My argument for correspondence proceeds in three steps. The first derives from J. L. Austin's defense of correspondence. The second supplies naturalistic referents for the truth by correspondence of thirteen kinds of truths. This diversity is an answer to critics who say that correspondence is sufficient only as a criterion for the truth of positive categorical thoughts or assertions—for example, "Snow is white."[29] Step three corrects the unsatisfactory or clumsy solutions of the second one. It argues that the referents for our thoughts and sentences are, in the first instance, simple or complex properties existing as logical, eternal possibilities.[30] Thoughts or sentences are true, this implies, when the possibilities they signify are instantiated.

Acknowledging these possibles allows us to improve the formulations of the second step. Readers unsympathetic to the metaphysics of eternal possibilities may, nevertheless, ignore it without considerable damage to my thesis. They may want to skip sections VIII and IX of this chapter. Even the stripped-down, naturalistic metaphysics remaining is a caution to those who declare that schematizing mind papers over an undifferentiated, unknowable thing-in-itself.

Chapter 6 mixes respect for the history of our practical successes and failures with the belief that technologically driven changes promise unforeseeable goods and horrors. Turning our back, digging in our heels, preferring the present or past to any thinkable future: these are not viable strategies. We are more effective when truths about the salient past are used to make educated choices for the future. Knowing who we are and where we have been; knowing, too, the consequences of what we have done: these are the essential preparation for choosing what to do. I shall be saying that truth is the required adjunct to desire.

This chapter describes the use of truths—that is, hypotheses confirmed—to discipline choice. It argues that pertinent truths establish a domain of objects appropriate to desire, without themselves determining which object should be desired. This leaves attitudes and desires, not only truths, to determine our choices. Attitudes and desires express the distinguishing cognitive-affective balance within us. More, they are educable insofar as truths about us, our circumstances, or the consequences of past behaviors inform attitude and desire. Rarely knowing the one thing that is surely best to do, we enhance the likelihood that we shall choose reasonable aims before acting on behalf of the things important to us. We care about truth, for these good, prudential reasons. This is, I shall be saying, truth's only debt to value.

Chapter One

C. S. Peirce, writing in the *Monist* in 1905, blessed the writers who had endorsed his pragmatism and then disassociated himself from them:

> (This) writer finding his bantling "pragmatism" so promoted, feels that it is time to kiss his child goodby and relinquish it to its higher destiny; while to serve the precise purpose expressing the original definition, he begs to announce the birth of the word "pragmaticism" which is ugly enough to be safe from kidnappers.[1]

Several thinkers espoused pragmatic ideas during Peirce's lifetime, but it was William James especially whose renegade formulation provoked this response. My concern is the difference between Peirce and James as expressed in their contrary views of pragmatism. My thesis is that James, not Peirce, established the framework for those pragmatic theories of truth and value which dominate today's philosophical claims about knowledge and objectivity. I shall say that James's "Will to Believe"[2] illuminates the narrow set of cases to which he first applied it, though the notion of truth formulated therein is mistaken when universalized: the truth of a sentence or theory is not usually a function of our values together with our determination to realize those values in belief or action. Peirce rightly separated himself from this way of characterizing truth. He is wrongly claimed as an advocate of the pragmatic, but idealist, consensus which dominates current rhetoric about knowledge and reality.

My argument makes this general assumption about philosophical thinking: detailed views are often formulated within a penumbra of conditioning, but unacknowledged, assumptions.[3] We assume the structure of some theory and then operate within it. Where commitment to a theory or interpretation is shared by several or many thinkers, discussion among them allows that important things may be left unsaid. This is sometimes an advantage, if we can exploit our assumptions without having to declare or justify them. There is, however, the risk of evasion: it may happen that few or none of the interlocutors can specify the form or constituents of their shared persuasion. Worst of all, consensus is too often a weapon used to enforce intellectual uniformity: anyone who challenges our assumptions makes himself unrecognizable to us. He is no longer one of us. Philosophy becomes ideology, so that we better understand the conduct of philosophers by studying the behavior of cults.

Nothing so extreme is relevant here. Though there is a circle of conditioning assumptions which is ignored by thinkers who assimilate truth to value in the style of James. These are people who do not usually concede— they may not realize—that their views reaffirm the gloss of Kant common to Nietzsche and James: thought, they suppose, makes experience, hence worlds, in service to value-driven will.

I Two Kinds of Pragmatism

Peirce and James disagreed about the focus for pragmatism, because of differences centering on their ideas about truth and value. James is dominated by his concern for value. Peirce is more detached, though he never doubted that each of us is motivated by personal and social interests or that beliefs and behavior express these concerns.

Both points are acknowledged in "The Fixation of Belief,"[4] where Peirce describes the sequence of methods for acquiring beliefs about matters of fact: namely, tenacity, authority, a priori intuition, and the making of hypotheses tested empirically. Every application of each method is suffused with value, as some of their names imply. Still, the methods differ with respect to this question: is value intrinsic to a method, or only the consequence of the desires or attitudes motivating its use? Consider tenacity and authority. These are methods shaped by our interests, the one as we persistently affirm a belief that was once useful to us, the other as we accede to the views

of whatever authority enforces the social cohesion that protects us. Both
methods endure because they defend interests we value. Each is superseded
when we distinguish self-interest from truth. Truths are vital to self-interest,
because they are critical for effective action; though self-interest is not sufficient to make truths of those beliefs which justify or defend it.

A priori intuition, as Descartes described it,[5] is a method of the other
kind. It separates truth from value, as when contexts of application are laden
with personal, ephemeral interests, while the content of the beliefs tested is
universal. Someone arguing with his or her neighbors about the lot-lines of
their respective properties may be indifferent to the fact that five times five
is twenty-five, though he cares intensely that the size of his garden be no less
than twenty-five square yards. Confirmation is similarly value-free. It occurs,
says Descartes, as we establish the necessary truth of an a priori claim either by
deducing it from axioms or by showing that its negation is a contradiction.[6]

Peirce was scathing on the subject of a priori truths intuitively confirmed. There is, he said, no power for self-inspection or intuition.[7] But
more, this Cartesian notion of truth has intolerable implications for our
knowledge of things independent of our minds. A priori ideas will have referents only if there is a preestablished harmony between the world and our
ideas of it or if there is direct apprehension of the things signified. Peirce
scorned both alternatives. He denied that we might know the world either
by intuiting the universal forms that operate within it or by turning upon
ourselves to examine forms present in the world as they are represented within
us, as innate ideas.

The method of hypothesis is superior, Peirce said, on all these counts.
It dispenses with the intuition of universals outside or within us, requiring
instead that we specify, then find, those empirical differences that would obtain if our hypotheses were true. We engage the world as natural creatures
dwelling within it. One crucial difference between us and most other natural
things is our ability to speculate about things distinct from us. We hypothesize, as stones, leaves, and probably beetles cannot, that some thing does or
does not exist, that it has or lacks certain properties, or that its existence or
character is conditioned by some thing that is its constituent, cause, or determining law. There is, we say, no Man-in-the-Moon to explain the look of
the moon; though seeing smoke, we speculate that there is a fire causing it.
Every such truth-claim invokes the presumed alignment of a sign and its
object, though the relation between them has three terms, not two: a thought

or sentence signifies its object only as there is a mind construing the one as sign of the other.[8] The thought or sentence is always particular. The thing represented may be a particular, localized in space-time (this fire), or the identity-making universal which constrains a class of represented particulars $(F = ma)$.

Peirce supposed that truth is the satisfaction of a thought or sentence affirmed or denied by the particular or universal it signifies. Things exist or not as declared, having or not the properties or conditions affirmed or denied of them. This is truth as correspondence. The signs used to represent matters of fact are only mental events, marks, or noises. They relate to their objects conventionally, having been construed as signs representing them. But then the world is or is not as these signs make it out to be.

Peirce does not say very much, in his theory of inquiry or elsewhere, about the concerns that provoke us to make hypotheses. He doesn't need to say much about them when describing the method of hypothesis, because he reasonably assumes that vulnerability and the desire for greater security dominate us as much as they did when tenacity and authority were our methods. Now, as then, concern for our well-being is the undisputed backdrop for those accommodations which secure us. Knowledge emerges in the midst of these reality-testing behaviors, where the proximate value of knowing is its utility. Sometimes, however, the well-being secured there liberates us for reflection of a different kind. What sort of place is the world? What beings are we, and where do we stand within it? Knowing what is true of the world and ourselves now becomes more urgent than using truths to determine the manner of our accommodation there.

What is value? Hume supposed that values are passions and, more exactly, secondary or reflexive impressions.[9] Having some first-order impression, we may also have an impression of liking or disliking its content or object. Remember now Hume's principle that anything distinguishable is separable[10] and its implication that first-order impressions are separable from second-order ones. Accordingly, valuings (in the form of second-order, reflexive impressions) are never more than incidental, on Hume's telling, to the character of the things valued—that is, the first-order impressions. This has two effects that are notable here: on the one side, first-order impressions do not derive any part of their character from these second-order ones; on the other, second-order impressions are never hidden or disguised by those which are first-order. Valuings can be noted and discounted, all the while leaving intact the things valued.

The notion of valuing common to Peirce and James has more affinities to Kant, Fichte, Schopenhauer, and Nietzsche than to Hume. These four suppose that values are the valorizing expressions of attitudes or desires; they are activities, not impressions. The valuings they describe may be distinguishable, but they are not easily separated from their objects. That is so because an attitude or desire is individuated and identified by having some particular object. Conversely, the identity of the things imagined and desired is not so plainly independent of these valorizing activities. There is, indeed, an inclination (James submits to it, Peirce resists) to suppose that attitude or desire posits or creates its objects while using them to disguise itself. Suppose, for example, that some person or party favors a particular social arrangement or law. Their motive is not identifiable apart from the result they prefer, so that the rest of us may ignore the motive while responding to the objective desired. We risk being manipulated and controlled as their idea comes to be the organizing force among us. Its valorizing attitude or desire may be all the while disguised, though it is only attitude or desire which supplies the energy propelling this ideology to its realization. It takes Marx, Nietzsche, Weber, or Freud, or, more recently, the Frankfurt school, Sartre, or Derrida to expose the self-interested attitudes and desires that are satisfied when these programs are successful. Those skeptics direct us to the joints and tensions of a social organization. We discover the ossified valuings of its sponsors in the arrangements that secure power for them while suppressing opposition and understanding in the people subjected to their regime.

This more engaged style of valuing is explicit where Peirce characterizes the relation of value to truth as regards the four methods described in "The Fixation of Belief." There is this difference among them: value is *constitutive* of truth when the method is tenacity or authority; value is *regulative* for inquiry but not constitutive of its objects when the method is a priori intuition or hypothesis.

Where values are constitutive, *truth is a function of value.* We get this result in several steps. First, value establishes our universe of discourse by determining which predicates may be ascribed to things. Believing, for example, that all illness is in the mind, we decline to use the medical vocabulary which assigns illness to the body. Second, our rules of inference express this same value as they determine what evidence shall count for or against the claim that someone is ill or well. Third, we apply these rules to candidate sentences: it is then true or false, given these rules, that someone is the one or the other.[11] But fourth, the truth or falsity of the claim entails that some condition does or does not obtain. Existence is a function of truth, hence, more remotely, a function of the values which have determined the choice of inductive rules. You are not sick, we declare, by our rules. And we may add: cling to that view of yourself or accept our authority as regards it.

Compare this use of constitutive values to the use of regulative values, especially with regard to Peirce's hypothetical method. He resists the inclination promoted in us when valuings are distinguishable, not separable, from their objects. The intimacy of this connection is reasonable when we consider that a desire cannot be specified without regard for its object. It is dangerous, however, when the constitution of objects is said to depend on our desires for them. For now there are the two readings of this last-mentioned notion. It is plausible that desire should express itself in actions which create the desired circumstances, thereby satisfying desire. It is not so plausible that the objects of desire should be created by the value-driven schematization of sensory data, sentences, or whatever.

Peirce resists the idea that the inseparability of desire from ideas of its objects might be an argument for the value-directed schematization of those objects. Value, Peirce supposes, must not dominate truth. He guarantees that it will not by restricting the domain of our valuings. Values are to be regulative, not constitutive: they direct the formulation and confirmation of truth-claims; they do not create those states of affairs which are truth conditions for these hypotheses. Wishing, we say, doesn't make it so.

Peirce is less detailed than he might have been regarding the differences among regulative values. They are, to start, *final* or *instrumental*. Value is final when, for example, all the rest of inquiry is organized so that we may learn the truth about some part of the world. Values are instrumental when they have utility for realizing a value taken as final. Instrumental values are *those appropriate to the conduct of inquiry*, or *contextual*. Values appropriate to the conduct of inquiry are *logical* or *practical*. Logical values include consistency and validity. Practical values (meaning practices valued) include truth telling, free access to information, and the repeatability of experimental results. Contextual values divide into those which are *motivating* and those which are *situational*. Motivating values may be *personal* or *social*, as pique is the one,

while the behavior encouraged of every citizen is the other. Situational values
are circumstances valorized; so a winning lottery ticket or flooded subway
acquires value for us as we strike some attitude towards it, for reasons that
are *current* or *historical*.[12]

These issues are better known in these other terms: are values *internal*
or *external* to the meaning and truth of hypotheses about the world? Do I
study beetles because I like them? That would be external. Do I tinker with
the predicate and relational terms of my language (hence with the range of
properties and relations ascribable to a world), then with relevant inductive
laws as they determine which sentences about beetles are true or false? That
would be internal. *Internal* is sometimes synonymous with *constitutive, external* with *regulative*.

Calling values regulative, hence external, is not meant to imply that
values are remote from their points of application. They are not remote from
either the inquiries wherein truths are formulated and confirmed, the truths
we think or speak, or the practices directed by truths. The proximity and
urgency of values are apparent in all three domains, but especially wherever
we humans control the things about us. Needing food or medicine, we do
whatever we can to establish the control that guarantees our access to them.
More subtly, we need this control for the purposes of empirical inquiry. We
experiment, for example, by opening our eyes, thereby observing the effects
predicted by tested hypotheses.

Shall we say that experimental control of our circumstances is a value
internal or external to practice and inquiry? Surely, both control and the
desire for it are internal to inquiry, there being no inquiry in the absence of
conceptual and experimental control. But now consider: I have said that values described as *constitutive* may equally be called *internal*. Does this stipulation oblige us to say that the desire for control is constitutive of the truths
formulated and confirmed within inquiry? It surely does not. Seeing an elephant requires that I open my eyes; but opening my eyes does not make ele-
phants. This is one of the cases justifying the qualification urged above in saying that internality is *sometimes* the same as constitutivity. Here is a case where
one value—namely, control—is internal but regulative. What satisfaction might
world-makers derive from this terminological consideration? None at all.
Control promotes access to the things represented by our hypotheses. This
power is the lever without which no hypothesis about the physical world would
ever be confirmed. It does not follow that inquiry, however saturated with

regulative values, is constitutive of the things about which we hypothesize.

Peirce is all the more insistent on distinguishing inquiry from the realities investigated because he recognized that value pervades every aspect of our thinking lives, inquiry included. We plausibly suppose that the ramifying hierarchy of contextual values (values that are motivating, hence personal or social, and situational, hence current or historical) is embodied in the attitudes and desires of every human being. This is plain in the case of motivating values (they are personally or socially sponsored attitudes and desires), but cogent too as regards situational values, whether current or historical, for I know something of my history and have attitudes appraising it. We are dervishes, spinning in all directions, valorizing everything that draws our attention. There are the attitudes and desires prefiguring our reactions to circumstances and those attitudes and desires (perhaps the same ones) which direct us as we secure and satisfy both ourselves and those others who are important to us.

Peirce would probably have accepted this characterization of us, though he would have asked that we be mindful of the difference between the regulative and constitutive use of values. Is there cold fusion in nature? We distinguish our interest in truth from our desire for cheap energy (a situational and motivating value). We do that for the practical reason that self-interest is best served by distinguishing truth from fantasy. We concede, as Peirce would likely have done, that contextual values, including motives, circumstances, and history, may very well do more than regulate the terms of inquiry. Those regulative values may define—that is, constitute—the personality of the inquirers. Still, the effective difference between constitutive and regulative values is preserved. Contextual values may regulate all my choices, to the point where these characteristic, persistent valuings are definitive of all I do. They may constitute the perspective from which I view the world. None of that justifies the claim that my values are constitutive of the reality to which I accommodate myself. Someone raised a Brooklyn Dodger fan was surely warped by this contextual value. It does not follow that the control exercised by a value is constitutive of the things studied. Attitude or desire may obscure our view of the things investigated; it may blind us to possibilities and properties significant for those things and cause us to misrepresent them. None of this entails that things studied are remade by the values which move the inquirer.

There is no conflict between these two claims: first, that contextual regulative values determine what we are and often what we expect to find when we examine the things about us; second, that our values are not constitutive of the things about which we report in the moment of representing them.[13] Inquiry as Peirce described it is a process of discovery and confirmation; it is not the process of imposing the biases or character of the inquirer on the subject investigated. Things do not become balding middle-aged men merely because they are studied by them.

Peirce supposed that inquirers can distinguish personal or factional desires and attitudes from their interest in knowing the truth about themselves and their circumstances. He was surely naive as regards the depth of our biases and the difficulty of discovering and discounting them. But he did acknowledge these attitudes: what he described as the methods of tenacity and authority are saturated with them. We are to progress beyond these methods so that we may take charge of our circumstances, at least to the point of freeing inquiry from the biases so patent in the two methods. More, we are to identify and discount our biases where doing so is a necessary step on the way to this more important objective. Peirce, like Plato, supposed that truth is a final value. Truth, absent its advantages or consequences, is for both of them an intrinsic good and the final cause of inquiry. Instrumental regulative values, excepting those appropriate to inquiry, are mostly assumed by Peirce without comment.

Compare James:

Our passional nature not only lawfully may, but must decide an option between propositions, whenever it is a genuine option that cannot by its nature be decided on intellectual grounds.[14]

James says this after acknowledging that his formulation is irrelevant to science and mathematics.[15] This might seem a dubious reservation; for why suppose that there are any propositions whose truth can be decided with finality on intellectual grounds alone? Someone wanting to press James's proposal beyond the domain in which he applies it might say there there are no truth-claims of the kind he exempts. Isn't it the point of Descartes' first *Meditation* that there are no propositions whose truth or efficacy can be decided on intellectual grounds only? This is alarming for its implication that we may be unable to adjudicate any truth-claim without recourse to attitudes and desires. James visibly shudders at this implication when, in "The Will to

Believe," he is most careful. It is only with respect to practical questions that our passional nature is said to create its objects.

Values work constitutively for James in the ways implied by the methods of tenacity and authority. In them, desire for the control of problematic situations determines both the content of thoughts or sentences and the affirmation that they are true: we want to believe that an old solution will work again or that some authority knows what to do. This is a consequentialist argument for the constitutive role of values: believe that something is or will be as you want it to be, and you will have that effect: "How many women's hearts are vanquished by the mere sanguine insistence of some man that they *must* love him! he will not consent to the hypothesis that they cannot. The desire for a certain kind of truth here brings about that special truth's existence; and so it is in innumerable cases of other sorts." [16] The suitor invents a plan to create the circumstances he desires. Actions directed by the plan transform a protean, determinable world in ways that satisfy the desire. This is tenacity in service to passion. An idea is made true as a consequence of the actions undertaken to confirm it.

Notice that James has extended the constitutive role of value in the direction of Kantian world-making. This happens when the suitor creates the state of affairs he desires by the plan he formulates and then applies: he remakes a certain region of the world so that differentiations and relations prefigured in his plan shall obtain there. The plan, like a recipe, prescribes the behaviors to be sequenced and the instruments to be used so that this change may be achieved. Where tenacity is only grim persistence, the suitor requires more than stubbornness if his desire is to be fulfilled: he must remake the world until it satisfies him.

James is quick to misconstrue the force of this example. This happens because of his answer to the question, how do we confirm that our belief has been made true? He tells us to do that by appraising the feelings we have when ardor provokes a response in the one adored. Are those feelings satisfactory or not? Do we feel good or bad, having been accepted or rejected? Feeling is the evidence confirming (or not) the belief that, yes, we are or shall be loved. More, feeling is the measure that we have achieved harmony with our circumstances, by realizing in them the thing desired. There is, however, a plain difference between a belief that is confirmed when action creates the circumstances which satisfy it—for example, winning someone's affection by insisting on one's own—and those beliefs having no coupled action that justifies the belief by creating the desired result. James makes his notion of truth credible with respect to the suitor, but not as regards our belief in God: feeling good about the idea of God is not a truth condition for the claim that there is a God. For there is no action coupled to believing in God such that we create God by our action, thereby confirming the belief. The attitude of a believer might change from pessimism to brimming hope, and this might alter his behavior—but not in a way sufficient to create a God.

There is, of course, this response available to James. He might say, in the manner of Kant, that every object credited to reality is one that mind creates by its schematization of sensory data. The idea of God might be used first to provoke, then to organize, our experience. *God* might be for us nothing more than this idea coupled to the experience it generates: namely, one of liberated energy, hope, and satisfaction. God would then be as much an object of experience and as much our creation as any other thing perceived. I suggest that this Kantian justification is the one to which James tacitly appeals. Where nothing is credited with reality if it is not discovered within experience, let us show that the idea of God is legitimate because it, too, has cash value there.

Do we hesitate before subjecting this idea to a Kantian reduction? This is not so much piety as the thought that a mind claiming to schematize the experience of God and, to that extent, God himself will not be much deterred by the burden of having to create the laws of motion and all the properties of light, matter, space, and time. Does James believe that minds driven by their passions can do all that? He equivocates in the way described above: sometimes he concedes that the choices left to passion are those which, unlike decisions in mathematics and science, cannot be decided on intellectual grounds. Other time, James extends the freedom and power claimed for thought allied to passion. "The world stands really malleable," he writes, "waiting to receive its final touches at our hands. . . . Man *engenders* truths upon it."[17] It is feeling that testifies to these truths, confirming the persuasion that there is a god's power within us.[18]

II Jamesian Pragmatists

Peirce supposed that liking and talking about things does not, by itself, create them. James disagreed, saying that action allied to our passional nature determines what thoughts and sentences shall be declared true. Richard Rorty is closer to James than to Peirce: "The question of what properties to assert, which pictures to look at, what narratives to listen to and comment on and retell, are all questions about what will help us get what we want (or about what we *should* want).[19] Hilary Putnam is more explicit:

> I'm going to rehabilitate a somewhat discredited move in the debate about fact and value, namely the move that consists in arguing that the distinction is at the very least hopelessly fuzzy because factual statements themselves, and the practices of scientific inquiry upon which we rely to decide what is and what is not a fact, presuppose values.[20]

> Truth itself gets its life from our criteria of rational acceptability, and these are what we must look at if we wish to discover the values which are really implicit in science.[21]

> 'Every fact is value loaded and every one of our values loads some fact.'[22]

These remarks have the conclusion quoted above: "what counts as the real world depends upon our values."[23]

> Rudolf Carnap expressed similar ideas in his more formal way:

> We take the position that the introduction of the new ways of speaking does not need any theoretical justification because it does not imply any assertion of reality. We may still speak . . . of "the acceptance of the framework" or "the acceptance of the new entities" since this form of speech is customary; but one must keep in mind that these phrases do not mean for us anything more than acceptance of the new linguistic forms. Above all, they must not be interpreted as referring to an assumption, belief, or assertion of "the reality of the entities". There is no such assertion. An alleged statement of the reality of the framework of entities is a pseudo-statement without cognitive content. To be sure, we have to face at this point an important question; but it is a practical, not a theoretical question; it is the question of whether or not to accept the new linguistic forms. The

acceptance cannot be judged as being either true or false because it is not an assertion. It can only be judged as being more or less expedient, fruitful, conducive to the aim for which the language is intended. Judgments of this kind supply the motivation for the decision of accepting or rejecting the framework.[24]

Rorty, Putnam, and Carnap agree that value determines our choice of conceptual system. But then their understanding of the relation between conceptual systems and values also has these other two consequences: first, that disparate worlds result as we use contrary systems to project differentiation and order onto sensory data; second, that correspondence must be the wrong notion of truth when there is no world independent of language to which sentences within a language might correspond. What could truth be? Only that property credited to sentences (or those relations of sentences) which satisfy our inductive rules: we affirm that there is rain when sentences describing the amount of precipitation satisfy whatever minimum standard is fixed by pertinent inductive rules. The choice of inductive rules in an expression of value, as Midwestern farmers disagree with Bedouin shepherds about the amount of precipitation which is to count as "rain," because of their different circumstances and motives. This is truth as a function of value.

These American pragmatists closely resemble some Continental thinkers who join existentialism to hermeneutics. Advocates of one view are often oblivious to the other, because of different styles and histories. These are, however, expressions of the same themes. Both formulations join social practice and moral individualism to metaphysical and epistemic idealism. Here, for example, is Michel Foucault writing of truth:

> Truth isn't outside power, or lacking in power. . . . Truth is a thing of this world: it is produced only by virtue of multiple forms of constraint. And it induces regular effects of power. Each society has its regime of truth, its "general politics" of truth: that is, the types of discourse which it accepts and makes function as true: the mechanisms and instances which enable one to distinguish true and false statements, the means by which each is sanctioned; the techniques and procedures accorded value in the acquisition of truth; the status of those who are charged with saying what counts as true.[25]

Truth, this says, is only the set of affirmations, principles, and procedures sanctioned by power and value. Gilles Deleuze and Felix Guattari agree:

Ever since philosophy assigned itself the role of ground it has been giving the established powers its blessing, and tracing its doctrine of faculties onto the organs of State power. Common sense, the unity of all the faculties at the center constituted by the Cogito, is the State consensus raised to the absolute. This was most notably the great operation of the Kantian "critique," renewed and developed by Hegelianism . . . it is not at all surprising that the philosopher has become a public professor or State functionary. It was all over the moment the State-form inspired an image of thought. With full reciprocity.[26]

Thought, I infer, is the tool of power, so that truth-claims too are its authoritarian expressions.

Rorty anticipates this convergence between Continental hermeneutics and his version of pragmatism: "On my view, James and Dewey were not only waiting at the end of the dialectical road which analytical philosophy traveled, but are waiting at the end of the road which, for example, Foucault and Deleuze are currently traveling."[27] This is a predictable convergence when we remember that the Jamesian assimilation of truth to value is also common to those Heideggerians who emphasize that man-in-the-world chooses the interpretation, the "fore-having," which directs his creation of a life-world.[28] Where language is the house of being (i.e., the basis for whatever is intelligible, hence thinkable, in the world), it is our values which are to decide what differentiating, organizing conceptual system each of us shall choose.[29]

We are also reminded of Nietzsche and Marx, the one as he emphasized that will is the source of value and the determinant of our conceptual perspectives,[30] the other as he taught that the material system realizing a conceptual system is an expression of value and an instrument of power.[31] Derrida can celebrate *différance* while half deploring the sequence of interpretations it generates.[32] Each of them is a coagulated expression of value, will, and power, every one affirming its own authority while casting doubt on the claims of the others. Every one reinforces a delusion, because each supplies a world obscuring the one real world, thereby making it inaccessible to thought. We are left to dream of that Heideggerian time before the beginning of philosophical time when being was simply present, undistorted by the subsequent history of obscuring conceptualizations, none of them truth-

worthy because each is inspired by self-interested or class-determined values.[33] *I think, therefore I am* has evolved. With Kant, Fichte, Heidegger, and
James providing the details, it is better restated, *I value, therefore there is a
world appropriate to my interests.*

Conversations among these world-makers will not be so edifying as
Rorty supposes.[34] They will often reduce to hermetic monologues, each of
the participants spinning a private world or begging tolerance for the right
to have one. We shall more likely hear babble than talk when each world is
unthinkable, hence invisible, to minds that do not share its sponsoring values.
We might hope to avert this result, because of supposing that intelligibility
is established at the place where words or acts, formation or inductive rules,
are introduced: the rules learned and applied by many speakers, not their
motivating values, might seem to be the basis for whatever is unthinkable.
This is, however, a mistaken impression if rules and their sponsoring values
are distinguishable but not separable. For consider the choice and application
of rules: semantic, syntactic, and inductive rules create a differentiated, organized experience, though any rule might be interpreted and used in infinite
ways. It is only values which fix the choice of rules, then their interpretation
and application, given this Jamesian, Heideggerian view. Each world is thinkable, they supposed, only in the terms fixed by its motivating values—from
which it follows that each of us is intelligible to others only as they perceive
our values.

How are they to do that? Consider the evidence before them. Every
speech is a performance. Each speaker exhibits his or her peculiar world as
though it were an ethnic mime or dance. Suppose that each performance is
sinuous and rhythmic. Observers are rapturous, but uncomprehending: What
does it mean? We observe the behaviors, sitting like tourists wearing leis or
funny hats, watching ceremonies we do not understand. Or we observe world-
makers talking at one another—no one understanding any other—in a language they nominally share. How shall they or we infer the bias of world-
shaping values from the words spoken when any particular use of a word or
rule might be sponsored by any of several values? The problem is com-
pounded if commonly used words, grammatical forms, or inductive rules disguise motivating values that are radically opposed. We get the fractured result that people of different values live within disparate worlds. We must
always worry that agreement about life-worlds is only tactical or cosmetic.[35]

III Thought as the Venue for Action

This radical version of James's pragmatism marks a sea change in our views about effective action. We normally suppose that actions engaging us in the world require the use of maps and plans. But plans won't work if the instrumental relations they propose do not obtain. Nor will maps direct us to the places where action is to be done if they do not accurately represent those terrains. Effective action requires, on this Aristotelian and Peircian view, that maps and plans be true—that they correctly represent both terrains and the instrumental relations possible in the places where action is considered. These are, moreover, truths we do not make, truths to which we contribute in only this limited way: we correctly represent things as they are.

Suppose, however, that the context is altered. Rather than speak of actions requiring that we engage a world we have not made, we cite only those actions accomplished within thought itself. There is nothing muscular here apart from tightening the jaws or suppressing motion in the larynx and tongue. This is thought as it invents stories, poems, proofs, and hypotheses; thought as it appraises, imagines, remembers, or calculates. These too are actions, even to the point of having aims that are satisfied when a conceptual performance requires the use of conceptual instruments for achieving a conceptual aim. Still, there is a difference between these cerebral actions and those considered above: success in telling coherent stories does not require that we engage a world that resists us. Imagination is never confounded by a world whose existence and character are independent of the ways we think and talk about it. Are you a novelist stymied because your story requires that its characters be in two places at once? Split them as circumstances require, merely announcing or implying that personal identity has special complexities in the world of your story.

Actions and worlds restricted to the domain of thought and language are special indeed. Whether performing or creating them, we are favored by this extraordinary exemption: we dispense with the maps and plans required for actions performed within the ambient natural world. We don't need maps or plans because we are no longer constrained by states of affairs that are alien and resistant. There is a world through which to find our way; but we require imagination, not the material truth of our representations, as we locate ourselves within it. Phenomenologists and pragmatists characterizing man-in-the-world have misdescribed the conditions for our presence there. They would have us rely on imagination, not truth of a material sort, as we furnish the world to our taste. We are to be novelists, not scientists; or science itself is to be a kind of literature—that is, a narrative about nature.

Literature has its values, including cogency, coherence, and sensibility. Even truth is a value for it, though the truth relevant to literature is not the truth of maps and plans. A story is "true" or "rings true," we say, because of having such properties as cogency, coherence, and sensibility. Still, we would not usually want to confuse this literary truth with the material truths required for engagements in the physical world. We may even suppose that we have a choice: to live where maps and plans need to be true if the actions they direct are to be successful or to live within a world contrived by thought, a world where *truth* has the literary, nor its material, sense. Which of these worlds should we prefer? Do we really have the choice of living in one or the other?

IV World-Making

Some writers think that there is no contest: all the world, they say, is the creature of imagination. Here, for example, are two passages from Richard Rorty:

> Pragmatism . . . does not erect Science as an idol to fill the place once held by God. It views science as one genre of literature—or put the other way around, literature and the arts as inquiries on the same footing as scientific inquiries.[36]

> (Dewey's) chief enemy was the notion of Truth as accuracy of representation, the notion later to be attacked by Heidegger, Sartre, and Foucault. Dewey thought that if he could break down this notion, if scientific inquiry could be seen as adapting and coping rather than copying, the continuity between science, morals and art would become apparent. We would no longer ask ourselves questions about the "purity" of works of art or of our experience of them. We would be receptive to notions like Derrida's—that language is not a device for representing reality, but a reality in which we live and move. We would be receptive to the diagnosis of traditional philosophy which Sartre and Heidegger offer us—as the attempt to escape from time into the eternal, from freedom into necessity, from action into contemplation. We would see the social sciences not as awkward and

unsuccessful attempts to imitate the physicists' elegance, certainty, and freedom from concern with "value," but as suggestions for ways of making human lives into works of art.[37]

Pragmatism of the sort that Rorty invokes disclaims an interest in shovels, saucepans, subways, or anything that might count as an implement appropriate to some physical behavior. This is a pragmatism having just one instrument and one aim. The instrument is a conceptual system. The aim has two sides.

Negatively, "The urge to make philosophy into Philosophy is to make it the search for some final vocabulary, which can somehow be known in advance to be the common core, the truth of, all the other vocabularies that might be advanced in its place. This is the urge that the pragmatist thinks should be repressed, and which a post-Philosophical culture would have succeeded in repressing."[38] We should worry about the invitation to "repress" thinking of any kind, but especially the thinking required to specify conditions for effective action and inquiry. Thinking about the truth of maps and plans is speculation of that sort: we reasonably ask for a general characterization of their truth conditions in advance of knowing specific truths (e.g., Rorty's "other vocabularies") that might be used within particular maps and plans. Repressing this inquiry subverts us: we are less effective if ignorant about the operation of instruments (i.e., maps and plans) essential to our well-being. Wanting to repress this information, hoping for the time when "a post-Philosophical culture" does repress it, is daft or dangerous. It is hopeful that "the pragmatist" to whom Rorty ascribes this view is never Peirce and only sometimes Dewey and James.

We get the positive side of Rorty's claim with this quotation from Sartre: "In reality, things will be as much as man has decided they are." Rorty explains:

> This hard saying brings out what ties Dewey and Foucault, James and Nietzsche, together—the sense that there is nothing deep down inside us except what we have put there ourselves, no criterion that we have not created in the course of creating a practice, no standard of rationality that is not an appeal to such a criterion, no rigorous argumentation that is not obedience to our conventions. A post-Philosophical culture, then, would be one in which men and women felt themselves alone, merely finite, with no links to something Beyond.[39]

Our accommodation to a world independent of us (the "Beyond") is only the nightmare and prejudice of ancient philosophical lore. Maps and plans would direct that accommodation, but we should not fear for their truth if there is no Beyond in which to locate ourselves. Sartre, writing in the shadow of Nazi victory and French collaboration, refused to accept the identity forced on him by these humiliations. Rorty would have us generalize from situations of this sort to the conclusion that there is no abiding human nature and no settled world in which to express it.[40] Accommodations founded in the real limits of things, accommodations impelled by urgent needs and directed by truths we confirm and apply, are a crippling myth.

What values should drive us as we create ourselves and our worlds? I infer that power is everywhere the principal value. Power, as energy, will be the force creating both our own character and that of the ambient world. This is the power of thought as it uses a conceptual scheme to create a differentiated, organized manifold. Included within this manifold will be a self-image, hence all of the self that is knowable in those who think. We shall be these two things: a raw originary power (the power of thought as described by Fichte[41] or the power invoked at the start of Hegel's *Logic*[42]) and that self-image which is an artifact of the conceptual system used for thinking a world and ourselves.

Other values will be subsidiary to this elemental, creative power. We value ourselves and our world, expressing this regard in our aesthetic and moral judgments. There are, for example, aesthetic vices and virtues. Is a world simple like a Bauhaus design or excessive like a Victorian lounge? Is it clumsy because it leaves things disconnected or impoverished because it has too little of everything? Ethical values also dominate our world-making. First among them is the mutual tolerance of world-makers, each one acknowledging the right and power of other thinkers for world-making. Though, equally, we might be contemptuous of the worlds manufactured by those who vie with us for dominance within the community of thinkers. Whose world shall establish the common standards for personal and social identity? Shall we be democrats, celebrating equal rights to an experience and world of one's own making, or autocrats, insisting that the vanquished live by the terms prescribed in the world surviving a contest of wills? We have the choice of mutual respect or servile deference, freedom or domination. This latter alternative is moral theory in the style of Thrasymachus and Nietzsche. We may tremble at the prospect or take this satisfaction: every world is, on this telling, a fantasy contrived in circumstances wherein neither we nor the world has an antecedently settled character; even victory and despotism might be only the dream of some feverish world-maker. Wake up to tell some different ent story, and you are liberated.

Two sorts of truth are cogent now, one corresponding to each of the political options mentioned above. Encouraging every mind to create a world congenial to itself, we prize the sort of truth expressed in the phrase *true to oneself*: we fulfill ourselves by making a world that satisfies both our needs and our aesthetic or moral sensibilities. Generalizing this result, we get a diversity of world-makers, each one a spider in its self-constructed web.

This first notion of truth is solipsistic; a mind that is true to itself may find other people's needs and their worlds unintelligible. The second option averts this implication by requiring that we live in the world created when all of us use the same conceptual system for thinking it. The rules of the system are normative. Anyone who ignores them passes out of our common world into the darkness of unthinkable nonbeing: he is alien and invisible. *Being in the truth*, this implies, is the condition for finding one's way out of limbo into the light of public recognition, hence into being.

Being true to oneself and *being in the truth* are useful notions of truth. Still, mind is doing too much: we don't really believe that accommodation to a world we have not made is a superstition superseded when mind takes up all the slack, inventing whatever world satisfies it. Probably Rorty, like James, would want to modulate the egregious idealism of his own least-guarded remarks. It isn't really supposed, we shall assume, that the only actions occurring are those performed within storytelling minds. This would leave no provision for bodily action or for those associations of bodies which secure and satisfy us within a nature where life is otherwise perilous and short. These are the inferences from which we shall need to defend ourselves if there is no "Beyond," including that part of the Beyond occupied by our bodies. We avert the idealism and solipsism so close to the surface of Kantian world-making by assuming that these implications would be denied. There would be no reason, otherwise, to believe that a storyteller hears any yarn or lives within any world but his own.

V Making a Social World

Let us do better on behalf of Rorty's world-makers. Rather than speak of truth by appealing to activities that occur only within minds, we acknowledge behavior that spills out of and beyond us. Conceding our engagement in a world having thickness and depth, one that includes the things and other people around us, we reinterpret Rorty's claim that there is no "Beyond" so as to acknowledge these things confronting us within experience. Pushing Rorty in the direction of Ryle[43] and Moore,[44] we say that there is nothing beyond our experience of people, things, and ourselves.

Consider the actions of someone who is willful but effective. Conceiving a plan of action, he carries on until his aims are achieved. Everything about the plan is consistent with this agent's values: he is true to himself while acting upon it. What is more, he lives within this truth, executing the plan while affirming its worth. Behaviors directed by the plan furnish this man's world with just those differences and relations which are pertinent to his aims. This project has effects that are psychologically rich and diverse: there is the mix of expectation, disappointment, and pleasure as the agent reflects or acts upon the plan. The project also satisfies aesthetic and logical values: it has a beginning, middle, and end, while being cogent, coherent, and economic in its use of resources. One moral value is also conspicuous: the agent perceives his own heroism, with its risk of tragedy, in the desire to set an agenda for himself. This self-reliance is, the person thinks (and we may agree), the archetypcal expression of moral strength when order and a world are created from the chaos or limbo into which we are "thrown."[45] We qualify for living within the truth because of being true to the selves we resolve to become.

This characterization is too rabidly atomistic. It needs socialization. Consider a dance, one whose every step is established by routine. Dancers learn the steps and perform them in the ways prescribed. Each one is coaxed and praised for doing the routine in the time-honored way. Where dancing serves a communal value (e.g., it is the traditional dance of a culture besieged), dancers do the steps with intense, reverential feelings. Each one is true to him or herself because of being in the truth.

Suppose that we look for these same features in a conversation. It too is a ritual of some kind, so there are prescribed utterances and responses, as happens in ritual chants and the rhetoric of political factions. The leader says one thing; the audience responds. Something important to the community is secured by these activities. Members feel that their communal lives are energized at the moment when a socialized, but individual, identity is achieved. Loyalty to the group, hence to oneself, is intensified. For personal identity is parasitic on social identity, while social identity is achieved as we learn and perform the tribal practices. The members, together, create or sustain a world whose properties, relations, and valences are known to everyone "in the truth." It may also be important to the members' identity that other people are excluded from the community: they do not dance or chant; they are not party to that intensification of feeling and aim experienced by those who participate. With no tribe of their own, these strangers may be unintelligible even to themselves.

The practices establishing this world require that interlocutors take up differentiated positions of authority and deference. Someone who speaks in the voice of any one position comes to regard him or herself as having particular prerogatives and obligations. Anyone abridging the rights or duties of one position while occupying some other one trespasses on that position and the person occupying it. The person usurped is violated. He is "true to himself" when acting to defend his position against the trespasser. He may do so with no sense that his own identity is separate from that of the position occupied. His social identity, his intelligibility to the others in the group, is established by whatever role is played within it. Abandoning the role or allowing others to take it for themselves is a kind of personal and social suicide. One is true to oneself by defending that place, including all its rights and obligations.

VI Some Notions of Truth

There are four notions of truth having application to the circumstances just described. First is the literary truth of a project that is coherent and cogent. Second is the satisfaction of each will's demand that one be true to oneself. Third is the demand that we dwell in the truth by fulfilling norms. Fourth is a version of warranted assertibility: I am justified in making this demand of you because this practice of ours establishes in me the right to make this claim upon you. There is also the simplification of these four into one: each of us declares that his or her conduct will be directed by those compatible practices that obtain among us. We may think of the assumption common to Aristotle, Kant, and Hegel that we humans are most like gods when we legislate for all the world, hence for ourselves. This is a portrait of the world-maker at peace with himself because of having made a world proportionate to his needs. His inner state is harmonious and coherent. He is in the truth and true to himself. The demands he makes of others and himself are warranted by his status as a member of the tribe.

Correspondence is not included among these four notions of truth, and purposely so. Nothing is said of a terrain correctly represented by a map: there is no appeal to the instrumental relations invoked and represented by a plan. There is no reason for having information of either sort if we discount two considerations that have usually seemed elemental. First, we humans are fragile and vulnerable, but able to secure and satisfy ourselves as we respond to our circumstances. Add that accommodations to our situations are problematic when all our information about the world is mediated by time and distance and by the causal path to thought and language through perception. This path is everywhere subject to distortion or interruption, so that hypotheses about our situation, together with proposals about the conduct likely to be effective there, are often mistaken. Error would be averted were we to have rational or sensuous intuitions of our circumstances, hence the opportunity for an unmediated, undistorted view of it. But there is no intuition of either sort. Action apart, we address the world by way of the percepts, thoughts, and sentences that are its natural or conventional signs. But now correspondence does seem apposite: thought-directed conduct usually fails to achieve the result desired if perception is not accurate or if conventional signs (e.g., sentences) are not true. What is the condition for their truth? Where thoughts and sentences signify possible states of affairs, each is true when the possibility signified is instantiated. The actual state of affairs (the possibility instantiated) satisfies one or more of them. They correspond to it, because they satisfy relevant conventions for description and reference.

Kant and James never worry that maps and plans may not be accurate representations of the terrain and causal relations vital to our engagement in the world. They can dispense with correspondence, because they never assume that accommodation to a world independent of us is the objective for thought-directed behavior. Kant and his successors make the very different claim that action creates a world congenial to our aims. James said—and contemporary pragmatists seem to agree—that the world is plastic and malleable. Making a world suited to our values, we are more like architects than geographers. The one represent a terrain correctly; the other create designs, then use them to direct carpenters and masons. Like architect-builders, we are to act on our plans, thereby creating whatever order and differentiation are discernible in our world. We are to have only this choice: create worlds that are more or less grand, worlds that satisfy us; or learn the plans and rules of others, taking care to live decorously in their worlds. Never suppose that there is a world of decided character, hence circumstances we shall have to represent correctly if we are to secure ourselves therein. Truth is not correspondence, but rather the function of value: we "no longer make the distinctions between Truth, Goodness and Beauty which engender such problems."[46]

Aristotle supposed that thinking about something is different from making it. Anyone who reads Kant, James, Carnap, Putnam, or Rorty (to name only a few) is to know better. For it is not the task of mind to know the world as it stands apart from mind. No matter that we propose knowing it by direct inspection (rational or sensuous intuition) or by way of testable hypotheses (abductions) specifying the causes of our percepts. Neither method is feasible, because the only thinkable world is the one created when we project differentiations and order onto sensory data, sentences, or behaviors. Nothing that is "beyond" them, hence beyond the ambit of thought, language, and experience, can be known or even thought to exist.

More, this discredited realism inverts the order of priorities: it supposes that nature, the "Beyond," has an intrinsic form of its own, one that we must know if we are to contemplate or accommodate to it. The superseding view of Nietzsche and James has this contrary emphasis: that reason is the slave of the passions and especially of value-directed will. Attitude and desire prescribe the sort of world that would suit us; thought creates the story or interpretation prefiguring that world; will moves us in ways that fulfill the promise of the story we tell. We make the world that suits us, enjoying both our power and its effects. There are only these two possible annoyances: something unthinkable forever intervenes, preventing realization of the world that would satisfy us; or there are several, contending wills, each making its own world while insisting that the rest of us accommodate ourselves to it. What would make these problems go away?

Difficulties of the first sort are ignored or denied: embarrassed by a recalcitrant datum with its intimation of something unforeseen, one may always, says Quine, plead "hallucination."[47] Impatient of strategies like this

one, Peirce describes an idealist drunk: he denies the existence of a world
other than the one we make or inspect before careening out of a bar into a
lamppost. One would never guess from Kant or James, Carnap, Quine, Putnam, or Rorty that obstacles of any sort might confound the schematizations
launched to satisfy our motivating values.

Conflict among wills and worlds is acknowledged more forthrightly,
though one solution is mostly ignored. Agents frustrated when schematization fails to produce the worlds desired might hypothesize that nature resists
us because of having a form intrinsic to itself. Those are features (e.g., the
laws of motion) exempt from our plans and desires. Acknowledge them, and
we concede that nature itself is reproof to despotic wills. I mention this possibility for the sake of completeness only: it was covered over when Kant
relegated the nature independent of mind to the status of negative noume-
non.[48] It was obscured another time when James supposed that we might
create the truth merely by acting on a plan. The world that might have
resisted our projects (Rorty's "Beyond") has disappeared and, with it, the
idea of truth as correspondence. Nothing is left to constrain the disparate
world-making wills. They have the choice only of destroying, confounding,
or subordinating one another. Alternatively, they may find the mutual respect (and fear) that will enable them to invent rules for imposing order on
themselves. Here is a survey of some constraints to which powerful wills
might defer.

VII Power and Respect among World-Makers

Power regulates diversity among world-makers when each one tries to dominate the others. This happens when one of them stifles the thought and
action of others, thereby aborting the worlds they might have created for
themselves. The powers used may be physical or cerebral. At one extreme,
people are murdered for daring to inhabit worlds expressing values different
from our own, including fantasy worlds and unfamiliar cultures. At the other
extreme are the worlds crippled or abandoned when their makers are persuaded to renounce their own values and stories for those of some dominant
power. This creates a circle of people (Nietzsche's "slaves" or "herd")[49] willing to live within the "truths" that an intimidating power prescribes for them.

One alternative is that respect among world-makers be founded on
recognition of the power common to them: each would acknowledge the

right of every other to create a world of his own. Or respect might be expressed as regard for the disparate worlds created. Each world-maker might then visit other worlds as one tours other countries or a street fair, strolling among the booths and exhibits, hearing the accents and sampling the food, then going home. There is, to be sure, the problem of translation: how is one to make sense of the differentiations and relations constituting some other world if one does not know the story and values which have directed its creation? We may be unable to imagine other worlds, let alone visit them, if we have not ourselves accepted their organizing stories, values, and behaviors. Every world other than one's own might be forever unintelligible, except perhaps by analogy to one's own. We might have to concede that no one who is not "in the truth," through having collaborated in making a world, has access to it. Mutual respect among world-makers would reduce, were this true, to respect for each one's power and autonomy. Like Nietzschean supermen, each would defer to the others from the safety of his own hermetic sanctuary.

Respect among world-makers might of course be expressed in this other way: each power might will the law or rule which establishes a kingdom of world-makers, each sovereign in his or her domain. More than recognition of differences among worlds alien to one's own (supposing them to be intelligible), this would acknowledge the inalienable right among world-makers to enjoy the worlds in which each sees his motivating values satisfied. Respect of this sort would be normative. It would demand that every center of power be acknowledged as having an inviolable integrity and that we be tolerant and respectful of the disparate worlds created when other thinkers use stories different from our own to create the worlds they inhabit. More than an inclination to tolerance, this would be our categorical imperative. Where previously there was only self-help and power, there would now be law. We might become a United Nations of differences, with Rorty's "conversation of the West" supplying the anxious test that our differences have not reduced us to a babel. We would be democratic, even to the point of encouraging our neighbors in behaviors that are unintelligible to us. Each one could be true to his or her nature as a world-builder, while having the respect of others and living within his or her own truth.

Suppose that respect among world-makers comes to have the foundation in law just described: we respect other thinkers, even though we understand little or nothing of their motivating values or worlds. Respect for their unthinkable worlds is, we concede, derivative: worlds that are unintelligible in themselves (because motivated by values and schematized by conceptual systems unknown or alien to us) are esteemed only in virtue of having identified, respected makers. Worlds not traceable to their founders do not earn our respect.

Now consider this implication: *nature*, meaning hierarchically organized structures and processes in space-time, is a world fallen into disrepute, then relegated to that limbo beyond the law prescribing respectful relations among world-makers. For nature is sometimes thought to be either of two things: a thing-in-itself, unthinkable and unknowable to every particular mind (e.g., Rorty's "Beyond"); or nature is brought into the circle of acknowledged worlds because of being credited to the world-making activities of God. Any world God makes may be as unthinkable by me as the worlds created by finite minds like my own. Yet, I may defer to God's world-making power, hence to the world he creates. What I do not respect is an alleged world having no origin in any mind that I respect.

We get this familiar consequence: world-makers devoted to the realization of their own values may be slow to value the worlds of other thinkers and oblivious to the value of any world not traceable to a value-driven will. Nature is an orphan of this sort: no finite mind could have made it; we no longer believe that a world-making God presides over it. Nature is no one's child, no one's creature. This excuses us for using it in whatever way is required by the stories or interpretations which direct our world-making. We may guiltlessly pollute, transform, or annihilate whole parts of it, always citing Kant as our rationale: nature, we say is unthinkable in itself, hence unsuitable as an object of moral regard. Nature is the un-thing that everywhere supports and impinges on us, only to disappear from intellectual sight when the properties and relations ascribable to it are only those projected onto sensory data by a schematizing conceptual system. With *my* truth or *our* truth, *in the truth* or *true to ourselves*, we are all the while mute about those other truths which mark out the domain of nature. Truths about nature vital to the satisfaction of attitudes or desires are assimilated without comment or they are redescribed as stipulations made to cohere with the other sentences of a useful interpretation. Truths incidental to our plans are ignored; they slide into noumenal shadows, beyond the circle of light which defines our interests. This is Kant and James turned to the purposes of self-obsessed, value-driven power. This judgment would be different if made from the standpoint of nature: our kingdom of ends is, from that perspective, the covenant of mutually tolerant vandals.

VIII Peircian Realism

Peirce may not have foreseen the rhetorical excesses to which James's view would be elaborated. But he was never at risk of believing such things as James's successors declare. Scotus had convinced him that nature has an intrinsic form of its own.[50] We discover and use that form to our advantage; we do not create it. James himself might have recoiled from so grand a "final touch" as his many successors promote; but Peirce had heard enough. Where is the evidence, he might have asked, that human desire determines what the laws of motion shall be?

Peirce separated himself from James, never bothering to declare that truth's relation to value and action was the issue between them. He may have believed that this difference was too plain for commentary; but in this, he was too casual. James's view might have seemed less compelling to the many thinkers who prefer it had Peirce spelled out the differences between them.

Certainly, the evidence against world-making is plain to see. *Most* of the states of affairs about which we report truly are not sponsored by a motivating value. The ardent suitor and James's belief in God, notwithstanding, there are myriad states of affairs to which attitude and desire are irrelevant, as the variety of beetles is no consequence of my interest in them. World-making requires that all the differences credited to the world should originate in our ways of thinking about it and, prior still, in the values impelling the choice of conceptual systems. Consider, however, those things (e.g., beetles, moles, and snails) which concern us little or not at all. Surely, there is nothing in them deriving from our desires and attitudes. Value has no constitutive role as regards these things; truths about them are not a function of values. Their existence and character are independent of the ways we think, talk about, or value them.

Equally relevant is the fact that desire for, or aversion to, an outcome is not a condition for correctly representing it. Indeed, isn't it usually the disinterested observers who report most accurately about a state of affairs? Victims may resist information about their circumstances, while victors may want the information suppressed. Journalists or passersby may be the more acute observers. We may agree that values are constitutive of, because causes of, the situations created to satisfy them. It does not follow that telling the truth about a situation is a way of endorsing or expressing the values which motivate the behaviors creating it. Someone reporting truly on cholera or tyranny does not usually want either of them. He reports what he sees or infers, not what he wants.

James could preclude these objections only by foreclosing the possibility that value-neutral observers may report on things in which they have no interest. Doing this would have required that he eliminate the standpoint from which observers report about things they have not made. What perspective is that? The spatiotemporal, physical one of people standing on a sidewalk watching an excavation. They gawk as others work. Kantian pragmatists must eliminate these disinterested observers. They must convince us that there are no extra-mental physical states of affairs available to observers having no attitude or desire to shape the objects thought or perceived. They would have us agree that nothing exists for us except as thinking has schematized it. Why think as we do? Only because of our attitudes and desires.

This is the position apparent already in James's defense of the belief in God. For God, too, is not assumed to be something we discover, then report. We are to believe in God, James says, because of the satisfaction created in us by the actions undertaken because of our belief in God. This belief might be construed in either of two ways. Emphasizing God's reality and transcendence, we affirm God's existence, though there is no evidence distinct from the successful consequences of the believer's behavior to confirm that God exists. Alternatively, and still consistent with James's view, we say that the meaning of a claim is the set of empirical differences it makes. The truth of the claim that God exists is identical with the fact that we are energized and pleased by the initiatives that we take because of believing it. The believer's own experience is, on this other reading, both the evidence for God's existence and the referent signified by "God." God, like every other object schematized, is to have no standing in reality apart from experience and the value-driven schematizations used to create it. God reduces to the believer's experience of his or her ample hopes and successful projects.

No one who is awed by his God or a thunderstorm welcomes the view that either one is the creature of desire. Nor do we concede that value-driven thinking is the productive power creating whatever there is of reality.

This claim achieves its *reductio* when James invokes God only by making us humans responsible for creating the God who inspires us. This would be faulted for the heresy of self-deification if world-making were not rejected for the better philosophic reason that this idealist thesis fails to explain the experience of things which resist, surprise, and confound us. Why should anything frustrate or disappoint us if everything present in the world is the product of our value-driven conceptualizations or behaviors? Should we explain frustration, error, and death as snares introduced into the world by self-subverting but preconscious wishes of our own?

We stop making ad hoc excuses for the thesis of world-making only as we tire of ignoring the fact that the Kantian argument does not identify or explain the conditions having these effects. That is a grave deficiency in theories purporting to inform us about the world and our place within it. For these are commonplace features of life, with no evidence that they are delusory. They do want explaining, and we reasonably ask about the conditions that need to prevail if there is to be birth, death, and error. There are some explanations for these phenomena congenial to James and Kant. Error, for example, might be an anomaly or incoherence in the system used to schematize experience or an effect of this distortion within experience itself. But this is feeble. Nothing in it explains the effect of stubbing a toe or driving off the road in the dark. A competent world-maker would avert doing either one, though we typically do as much or worse. Birth and death do not get even this much explanation in the story of world-making, unless we describe them metaphorically as turning on, then off, our personal film projector or closet light.

Kantian-inspired world-making is no more convincing when it speaks for the detail of our lives. Do we make all the books we read, the buses we ride, or the music we hear? Do we create space-time and the laws and constants of nature? Is all of the cosmos the product of value-driven conceptual systems? World-makers are surprisingly immodest: "The reduction of higher level concepts to lower level ones cannot always take the form of explicit definitions; generally more liberal forms of conception in reduction must be used. Actually, without clearly realizing it, I already went beyond the limits of explicit definition in the construction of the physical world."[51] Are we to believe, with these lines from Carnap, that the reconstructing of conceptual systems, scientific ones especially, is tantamount to constructing the physical world? That is, I suggest, too quick a shuffle from the formal to the material mode.

IX Putnam and Peirce

Putnam is close to Carnap, but remote from Peirce. As Peirce remarked: "That is *real* which has such and such characters, whether anybody thinks it to have those characters or not. At any rate, that is the sense in which the pragmaticist uses the word."[52] And again: "It appears that there are certain mummified pedants who have never waked to the truth that the act of knowing a real object alters it. They are curious specimens of humanity, and as I am one of them, it may be amusing to see how I think."[53] Compare Putnam: "It is necessary to have standards of rational acceptability in order to have a world at all."[54]

The differences with Peirce are amplified when Putnam elaborates[55] on a distinction introduced in Carnap's "Empiricism, Semantics, and Ontology."[56] Claims about the world as it exists independently of thought and language, Putnam's "metaphysical" (Carnap's "external") realism, are the incoherent appeals to a point of view that only a god could have. The only worlds we can think and know ("internal" realism) are the ones whose differentiations and relations are prefigured by the sentences of some well-formed theory: "*Fact* (or truth) and *rationality* are interdependent notions." "A fact," Putnam continues,

> is something that it is rational to believe, or, more precisely, the notion of a fact (or a true statement) is an idealization of the notion of a statement that it is rational to believe. 'Rationally acceptable' and 'true' are notions that take in each other's wash. . . . Being rational involves having criteria of *relevance* as well as criteria of rational acceptability. . . . All our values are involved in our criteria of relevance. The decision that a picture of the world is true . . . and *answers the relevant questions* . . . rests on and reveals our total system of value commitments. A being with no values would have no facts either.[57]

Peirce's genealogy of facts is different. He would have said that all or most of them are transformations of interacting physical states, without regard for criteria or desires of ours. Putnam disagrees. He thinks that value-driven thinkers use conceptual systems to create whatever facts there are, including presumably all the cosmos.

There is, this implies, no determinate reality standing beyond inquiry as a control upon true utterances and beliefs. "Metaphysical realism," says

Putnam, "Is, or purports to be a model of the relation of *any* correct theory to all or part of THE WORLD. I have come to the conclusion that this model is incoherent."[58] Why? First, because metaphysical realism contends that truth is "radically non-epistemic."[59] Truth is alleged to be the relation of something independent of thought and language to sentences or beliefs, so that tinkering with the rules for using thoughts or words, all the while ignoring extra-linguistic states of affairs, cannot be sufficient to establish the material truth or falsity of any thought or sentence. But second, why suppose that each of an infinity of possible languages (in the sense of *theories*) is not true of whatever world it signifies, when each of the theories has "operational utility, inner beauty and elegance, 'plausibility,' simplicity, 'conservatism,' etc," hence, the property of meeting all *"operational* constraints?"[60] As Putnam summarizes the argument, "The supposition that even an 'ideal' theory (from a pragmatic point of view) might *really* be false appears to collapse into *unintelligibility.*"[61]

Putnam's use of the words *unintelligibility* and *incoherent* may be more psychological and rhetorical than conceptual and logical; for there seems to be no difficulty specifying the sense in which a theory, "ideal" by the criteria listed, is false. We have many examples of theories that are useful in practice but false, including Ptolemy's astronomy with its prediction of lunar eclipses, and the work still done using Newtonian mechanics. Why are these theories false? Because they ascribe to the world properties and relations which it does not have. Why are the theories useful? Because they specify conditions sufficient to produce the effects observed, though these conditions do not obtain, or because their misrepresentations are close enough to the relationships actually obtaining. Theories of either sort may supply useful leverage as we predict what will be or act to produce some effect.

Putnam responds that obeisant references to THE WORLD do nothing to explain the success of our theories. Internal realism, meaning the thesis that ascribes to the world just such possible differences, entities, and relations as are signified by the chosen semantics of a theory, is sufficient to explain successful predictions and efficient behaviors. But is this so? Is there provision within internal realism for material truth? Putnam argues that there is: "Pick a model M of the same cardinality as THE WORLD. Map the individuals of M one-to-one into the pieces of THE WORLD, and use the mapping to define relations of M directly in THE WORLD. The result is a satisfaction relation SAT—a 'correspondence' between the terms of L and sets of pieces of THE WORLD—such that the theory T_1 comes out *true*—true of THE WORLD—provided we just interpret 'true' as TRUE (SAT)."[62] This is odd for its implication (contrary to the metaphysical realism denied) that we might map the relations of model, M, onto THE WORLD.[63] Disregarding this stray implication, but wanting clarification of the notion TRUE(SAT), we consider Putnam's footnote: "Here, if SAT is a relation of the same logical type as 'satisfies,' TRUE(SAT) is supposed to be defined in terms of SAT exactly as 'true' is defined in terms of 'satisfies' (by Tarski). Thus 'TRUE(SAT)' is the truth-property 'determined' by the relation SAT."[64] Putnam invokes this Tarskian notion of satisfaction when T_1, the theory at issue, generates true sentences such as this one: "If 'there is a cow in front of me at such-and-such a time' belongs to T_1, then 'there is a cow in front of me at such-and-such a time' will certainly *seem* to be true—it will be 'exactly as if' there were a cow in front of me at that time. But SAT is a *true* interpretation of T_1. T_1 is TRUE(SAT). So 'there is a cow in front of me at such-and-such a time' is 'True' in this sense—TRUE(SAT)."[65] We see Putnam invoking Tarski in defense of his claim that a true sentence has a referent, though we have yet to discover the sense in which truth of the sort Putnam describes—TRUE(SAT)—has a material condition.

We have a clue about that sense in Putnam's use of Tarski. For remember Tarski's rebuff to the critic who wanted to construe his semantic notion of truth in such a way as to make it a criterion of material truth:

> It has been claimed that—due to the fact that a sentence like "snow is white" is taken to be semantically true if snow is *in fact* white (italics by the critic)—logic finds itself involved in a most uncritical realism. If there were an opportunity to discuss the objection with its author, I should raise two points. First, I should ask him to drop the words *"in fact,"* which do not occur in the original formulation and which are misleading, even if they do not affect the content. For these words convey the impression that the semantic conception of truth is intended to establish the conditions under which we are warranted in asserting any given sentence, and in particular any empirical sentence. However, a moment's reflection shows that this impression is merely an illusion; and I think that the author of the objection falls victim to the illusion which he himself created. In fact, the semantic definition

of truth implies nothing regarding the conditions under which a sentence like (1):

(1) *snow is white*

can be asserted. It implies only that whenever we assert or reject this sentence, we must be ready to assert or reject the correlated sentence (2):

(2) *the sentence "snow is white" is true.*

Thus, we may accept the semantic conception of truth without giving up any epistemological attitude we may have had; we may remain naive realists, critical realists or idealists, empiricists or metaphysicians—whatever we were before. The semantic conception is completely neutral toward all these issues.[66]

Consider how little Putnam has advanced into THE WORLD when he establishes that 'there is a cow in front of me at such-and-such a time' is TRUE(SAT). This means, says Putnam's footnote, what Tarski says of it: "There is a cow in front of me at such-and-such a time" is true if and only if there is a cow in front of me at such-and-such a time. This is just the specification that *true* be defined as the relation between a sentence in the meta-language and one in the object language mapped or represented by its meta-language. The truth of sentences in the theories Putnam considers is, therefore, no evidence that we have advanced even a step into THE WORLD. To the contrary, "internal realism" of the sort that Putnam espouses is just what Carnap said it should be: we create a universe of discourse by the predicate terms introduced into a language; we formulate and then apply inductive rules, determining that sentences formulated in the terms of our semantics are true or not.

The cows of Putnam's example are never cows in THE WORLD; but they do have whatever properties we want them to have, hence whatever properties language or theory makes them out to have:

Suppose we include a sentence S in the ideal theory T_1 just because it is a feature we *want* the ideal theory to have that it contain S . . . assuming S doesn't make T_1 inconsistent, T_1 *still* has a model. And since the model isn't fixed *independently* of the theory, T_1 will be *true*— true in *the* model. . . . So S will be true? "S" is "analytic"—but it is an "analyticity" that resembles Kant's account of the *synthetic a priori* more than it resembles his account of the analytic. For the "analytic" sentence is, so to speak, part of "the form of the representation" and not "the content of the representation." It can't be false of the world (as opposed to THE WORLD), because the world is not describable independently of our description.[67]

It is no longer remarkable that a theory contrived in this way, without careful regard for THE WORLD itself, should have utility for anyone using the theory. Why? Because we *make* such languages and worlds (but not Putnam's THE WORLD) as suit us. Wanting cows in our world, we introduce, first, an analytic expression, or rule, into our semantic framework, then inductive rules interpreted in ways that confirm the presence here of cows. We live, thereby, in a world whose intelligibilities exactly suit our purposes.

Putnam wants to dismiss THE WORLD as "noumenal," with the implication that noumena are unthinkable in themselves. Sometimes the problem seems to be one of verification: we cannot stand apart from our languages or theories in order to see things as a god might do. Other times, the problem alleged for metaphysical realism is graver still: there are no properties left over for the world in itself if the only properties assignable to it are, more accurately, the predicates introduced into the several theories used for thinking a world. That leaves THE WORLD on the verge of nonbeing, thereby explaining the "unintelligibility" of the notion that truth is correspondence. For there is no possible correspondence of language to things if things do not exist.

Peirce was not nearly so sanguine as Putnam that we can arrange matters to our advantage, merely by introducing definitions into whatever semantic framework satisfies our desires. Peirce's fallibilism is just the inference, the abduction, drawn from error: there is something we do not make but can misrepresent. But equally, we do sometimes represent such things to whatever degree of cogency and accuracy is demanded for our purposes, whether intellectual or practical. We confirm our speculations if and when we have the sensory effects predicated by these representations.

Putnam seems less concerned about error, perhaps because he can exclude it by allowing no affirmation which is not protected from error by the semantic and inductive rules of the system. We are reminded of an explanation in Kant. Asked about the fact that "mere wishes are desires too, and yet we all know that they alone do not enable us to produce their object," Kant responds: "That, however, proves nothing more than that some of man's desires involve him in self-contradiction."[68] Speaking coherently, we invoke " 'the [analytic] forms of the representation'."[69] Speaking erroneously, (I speculate) we have fallen into contradiction.

Metaphysical realism explains error in this other way. It proposes three, linked hypotheses: first, that there is a world whose existence and character are independent of the ways we think and talk about it (Putnam's THE WORLD); second, that our thoughts or sentences signify possible states of affairs in that world; last, that the possibilities signified do not obtain. This external realism concedes that the confirmation of our thoughts and sentences is always incomplete, so that subsequent evidence or inference may force a revision of our first estimate. Peirce's realist agrees that the descriptive terms of an apparently confirmed sentence may be very crude indeed; hence the truths of one era seem barely cogent from the perspective of superseding descriptions. Truth, we say, is provisional, not only because the world may not remain as it is at any particular moment, but also because our standards of cogency and accuracy may change. The truths good enough for one time or purpose may not be sharp enough for others.

Nothing about this seems unintelligible or incoherent. Nor is it odd that we should formulate this hypothesis without the benefit of a god's-eye view of things as they are in themselves. Metaphysical realism is simply the best explanation we have for the continuity and regularity of experience, for the convergence of theories, for birth, error, truth, and death. Successful practice and the convergence of alternative theories, in practice and science, are evidence that we know who we are and something of where we stand within a world we alter but do not make.

Putnam is much exercised by the diversity of possible representations (i.e., of languages or theories). Peirce seems not to have anticipated this explosion of possible theories; but he could have acknowledged their variety without thinking that his metaphysical realism was compromised by it. For we quickly dispense with all but a tiny fraction of this multitude when having to represent any one state of affairs. Newton is celebrated for the particular interpretation of his laws, not for saying that there are an unspecified infinity of possible laws pertinent to motion. Nor is it especially salient that any single hypothesis, whether a sentence or a theory, might be interpreted in infinite ways,[70] when most or all those interpretations predict effects that are experimentally disconfirmed. The prodigious exfoliation of alternative theories and interpretations of theories is, therefore, no evidence that the world in itself disappears as the referent of true thoughts or sentences. This diversity is, so far, only so much flak introduced to obscure the relation between those states of affairs which do obtain in the world and the thoughts or sentences that correctly represent them.

The problem of multiple representations is severe only when differing hypotheses or disparate readings of some one hypothesis all make correct empirical predictions. For then we don't know which hypothesis or which reading of some one hypothesis is to be preferred. Why? Because truth is our concern; further, because correct predictions are the evidence of truth. A multiplicty of hypotheses or readings correctly predicting some one effect is an excess of good things. Notice, however, that Putnam misdescribes our situation. He infers from the diversity of confirmations that there is no singular fact of the matter: "If the picture as I drew it were correct, there would have to be a 'fact of the matter' as to *which* translation *really* preserves reference in every such case!"[71] But, says Putnam, the thesis that a representation might be uniquely correct is mistaken, so there is no extra-mental or extra-linguistic state of affairs. There are as many facts of the matter as there are coherent and established ways of thinking or talking.

We see what is faulty about this claim if we distinguish Putnam from Peirce as regards the activity and function of thought. Peirce supposed that our thoughts and sentences are abductions: we infer from something thought or perceived to its conditions, where conditions include constituents, causes, and laws. Seeing a flash of light, you say "Lighthouse"; I say "Shooting star." The sensory datum confirms either hypothesis, though both of them cannot be true (short of special circumstances: simultaneous flashes at the same point of the sky), and both could be false. There is, on this Peircian telling, a fact of the matter, a fact that is not reducible to the evidence of it. Putnam, however, has little interest in abduction. His view, like Kant's, requires that sensory data be taken up by a thought or sentences which projects differences and relations—hence identity—onto them. But then it is important that there be two or many ways of schematizing the same sensory data. For the object constituted when the data are schematized (differentiated and organized in accord with the description supplied by the sentences of a theory) is only what thought or language makes it out to be. A diversity of schematizations entails a diversity of identities: hence the conclusion that there is no unique fact of any matter for which there are alternative representations. (These points are elaborated in the next section.)

Consider now the finishing piece of Putnam's argument. He would have us consider "complete" theories, meaning those applicable and adequate to every empirical difference, including any that are past and future: "Language has *more than one* correct way of being mapped onto THE WORLD. . . . But now *all* grasp of the picture seems to vanish: if what is a *unique* set of things *within a correct theory* may not be a unique set of things 'in reality,' then the very heart of the picture is torn out."[72] This is the alleged result when theories are said to be equivalent and complete, because each comprehends every empirical effect. For now, any fact of the matter is constituted by whatever theory is used for thinking a world. There are no facts standing apart from theories as measures of their truth.

There is no difference in this respect between terms signifying particular kinds of things (e.g., 'dog', 'cat') and categorial terms — such as 'space', 'time', 'motion', and 'substance'. Every vocabulary offered as the compendium of differences present in a world is subject to the qualification that it applies only within the world schematized by its use. There is, therefore, no categorial description appropriate to THE WORLD. Putnam makes this point by arguing that we could never establish an order of preference among competing categorial descriptions, speculating that one or another is more likely to be the better categorial description of THE WORLD.

The supporting example he proposes is odd. Disputes about an ontology of lines or points[73] is germane to the axiomatization of geometry; but not to categorial descriptions of THE WORLD. That formalization may proceed from either basis does not confirm the alleged parity of these formulations as regards the material world. For who imagines that even a one-dimensional line can be generated from dimensionless points? Points are the objective to which we move asymptotically by forever dividing line segments, or they are the idealized intersections of line segments having length but no width. Line segments there are; but there are no dimensionless points in nature. Putnam's "sophisticated realists" suppose that we may have an ontology of points or lines, these being " 'equivalent descriptions.' "[74] But this honorific characterization, "equivalent," is question-begging: the equivalence lapses for the reason just stated at the moment when this example is extracted from geometry to illustrate the incompatibility of empirical theories. Sober realists reject this elaboration for what it seems to be: the use of an inappropriate example to imply both the irresolution of disputes between complete but contrary representations and the skeptical conclusion that nature has no unique, intrinsic form of its own.

Putnam might answer with an example more appropriate to a natural ontology. He might propose that we start with events, deriving substances from them, or the reverse; or he might argue the vacuity of debating the priority of rabbit parts, rabbit stages, or rabbits. But the "equivalence" of even these options is dubious if the adequate specification of natural phenomena requires the integration of some apparent contraries. So, rabbit parts and stages are derivative, for two reasons: first, because there is no way to identify relevant parts or stages except as they are the parts or stages of rabbits; second, because we say of parts and stages what is also true of points and lines: that we get them from rabbits, not rabbits from them. The whole supervenes, not for reasons that are mysterious, but only because atomizing talk about parts or stages ignores those static and dynamic relations without which there are no rabbits. It is the functioning stable system, the rabbit, that is prior ontologically to the parts or stages stripped or abstracted from it. Equally, an ontology of events is not opposed in dialectical perpetuity to one of substances; neither is good enough as an explanation of natural phenomena. We do better only by combining them. We speculate that events are the transformations or interactions of substances and that stability in a substance is the regularizing of the events (transformations or interactions) constituting it. Why do we reject Putnam's tolerant view that any choice among the available options is good enough? Because none of the apparent contraries is usually good enough, there being no adequate explanation for the phenomena at issue until we have integrated the emphases from two or more of the contenders.

X Opposed Ideas about Reality and Knowledge

It is plainer now that the disagreements between Peirce and Putnam turn upon their differing notions of *world* and *thought* or *knowledge*. These differences guarantee that any accord between them as regards knowledge and being could only be superficial.

For Peirce, the world ("reality") stands apart from, and is unaffected by, our knowledge claims. He supposes that knowledge is achieved when hypotheses are confirmed. Certainly, this is not knowledge of the sort promised by Plato and Descartes. But it is all the knowledge we can hope to achieve, given that we are fallible natural creatures, without innate ideas or a power for rational intuition. These hypotheses are abductions, meaning inferences from sensory data to their extra-perceptual, extra-conceptual, and extra-linguistic conditions. Seeing smoke and thinking fire is the act of specifying the possible cause at the moment of having evidence supporting the truth of our hypothesis. Being mistaken results from making hypotheses which misidentify the *conditions* for sensory data. Says Peirce, "A true proposition is a proposition belief in which would never lead to such disappointment so long as the proposition is not understood otherwise than it was intended." [75] That intending, or construing, is a way of reading the descriptive terms. They signify a possible state of affairs, which obtains or does not. Supposing it obtains and supposing we read the hypothesis in such a way as to designate this state of affairs, the hypothesis is true.

It is important to Peirce that intending is not understood in the sense of Brentano:[76] mind is not to be regarded as a theater in which mental lights play upon an object set before the mind's eye. Intending, for Peirce, is a sign process in which the "interpretant"[77] of a sign is itself the sign for a subsequent interpretant. This process has a dynamic of its own: signs are read and registered by successive interpretants in a (presumably branching and hierarchically organized) skein of associations.

Equally important is the idea that the relation of a sign (a hypothesis), its object, and an interpretant may be likened to the focusing of a microscope or telescope. The object in view may be large or small relative to the capacity of the instrument as, equally, we may have a sharp or fuzzy view of it. Things are viewed under these constraints, just as a thing signified is true (we are supposing) under the description supplied by the hypothesis. The existence and character of the object are independent of the sign and our way of construing it, though the truth of the hypothesis depends on conditions that include the existence or character of the object and our reading of the sign. "That's a rabbit" is false if directed at a rabbit when we read 'rabbit' as others read 'mouse'.

Putnam would not be satisfied, I think, by this modest acknowledgment that our way of reading signs is a condition for their truth (i.e., that truth is partly epistemic). This is hardly a concession, he might say, given Peirce's metaphysical realism. That realism is the more urgent target when Putnam renounces the idea of a world unaffected by our thinking about it; though doing so obliges him to understand the *conditions* for sensory data in ways quite different from Peirce. Peirce supposed that these conditions are extra-mental or extra-linguistic constituents, causes, or laws. Putnam demurs. He affirms, in the manner of Kant, that the objects of knowledge are constituted by the linguistic rules used to generate descriptions of those objects. This is the point of the passage quoted above which ends with the remark: "The world is not describable independently of our description." This would be a pointless tautology if we did not read it as, I believe, Putnam intends: what we call the world from within some particular language or theory has, and can have, only such properties as are prefigured by the semantics of the theory. And equally, the conditions for sensory data are just the ones responsible for making these data thinkable—meaning the semantic rules used to differentiate and organize the data.

It is less surprising now that the equivalence of complete theories should lead Putnam to conclude that all the heart is torn from the idea that THE WORLD might have some unique, decided character. Better, we misread Putnam if we suppose that his arguments have revealed some flaw in the realist account. For Putnam cannot take metaphysical realism seriously so long as his theory of knowledge requires that the objectification of the world is consequent upon the language used to schematize whatever objects are ascribed to it. Putnam has refuted metaphysical realism merely by endorsing a theory which argues, first, that THE WORLD cannot be successfully represented (there being no God's-eye view from which to validate our claims about it), and second, that we shall make as many worlds as there are schematizing theories. This is dialectical opposition, not dialectical refutation.

We have an example of this difference when Putnam deflates Peirce's notion of a theory's completeness only by stating his own. Putnam supposes that completeness is achieved when every empirical datum is brought under a schematizing theory. Completeness of the sort required by Peirce is different: for him, a complete theory supplies abductive explanations for every sensory datum. It specifies those conditions sufficient to produce all the sensory effects created in us by those extra-perceptual and extra-linguistic matters which include both our bodies and the circumstances in which we perceive and think. There are, in principle, many alternative theories able to explain all empirical data. Yet, we would not describe these theories as "equivalent," when the character ascribed to the world by any one of them may be different from, even exclusive of, the features ascribed to it by the others. One might be true, while all the others are false.

Notice that Quine's views on these matters are close to Putnam's, but antithetic to the ones of Peirce. Quine, following Kant and Carnap, also supposes that empirical data are taken up into theories so as to provide the differentiations and relations credited to the "objects" constituted by a schematizing theory.

> We find reification contributing to the logical connection between observation and theory by tightening up on truth functions. . . . It is this tightening that is achieved by subjecting the four-fold conjunction to existential quantification, thus:
>
>> Something is catting and is white and is dog-facing and is bristling, which is to say . . . An object has been posited, a cat.[78]

Here, as with Putnam and Carnap, the use of theory to constitute its objects is vital to our understanding of Quine's views about incompatible theories. Finding theories to be incompatible, Quine looks for a way to eliminate their mutual opposition:

> Take any sentence S that the one theory implies and the other denies. Since the theories are empirically equivalent [they schematize, hence explain, the same sensory data], S must hinge on some theoretical term that is not firmly pinned down to observable criteria. We may then exploit its empirical slack by treating that term as two terms, distinctively spelled in the two theories. S thus gives way to two mutually independent sentences S and S'. Continuing thus, we can make the two theories logically compatible.[79]

Incompatible theories are to be rendered compatible by stripping aside all theoretical language, leaving only the unschematized "stimulus meaning(s)"[80] or, better, the words first learned when they are associated with these data (as reactions to them).[81] This implies that the equivalence among theories reduces to the fact that the theories have the same raw empirical base.[82]

This is not Peirce's idea of what compatibility might be. He never supposed that the equivalence of theories might reduce to the empirical data used as evidence for and against our hypotheses. Theorizing requires that we supersede these data on the way to identifying their extra-empirical conditions (e.g., as the cat sitting a yard in front of me is the condition for the catlike effects occurring within me). Differing hypotheses regarding the conditions for some effect may not be compatible, as there are in principle an infinity of mutually exclusive, possible conditions for the same sensory effects. But then it does sometimes happen that two apparently incompatible theories predicting the same effects turn out to be inter-translatable. This compatibility is familiar in the case of theories having radically different mathematical formulations, without implications for ontology. More to the current point, it happens when hypotheses specifying apparently different conditions turn out to have the same object. Someone speculating about a light in the sky at dawn and at dusk hypothesizes that there are stars causing the effect. He calls them the "morning" and "evening stars" before discovering that both are Venus. We should not be dismayed, if we think as Peirce does, that the power of the hypothetical method is its inventiveness—that is, our ability to specify a diversity of mutually exclusive conditions for the same effect. Detectives do this as they reconstruct a crime. Physicists, garage mechanics, and internists do it too. More often than not, the theories they propose are not compatible.

Incompatibility is most problematic for Peirce, as for Quine and Putnam, when theories are incompatible but complete. For then we seem to have exhausted the devices for resolving their conflict: we exclude a difference of perspective as source of the incompatibility, while stipulating that there are no further empirical data that might be explained by one but not the other. Should we then infer that the world has no decided, intrinsic character of its own? Peirce's answer is different because his notion of *completeness* is different. Putnam and Quine suppose that a complete theory is one that explains (by schematizing) all sensory data. Here as before, *schematization* implies that the data are subsumed by a theory, with its semantics, quantificational machinery, and inductive rules. All the relations—even perhaps the distinguishing qualities—of the data are supplied by it. Peirce objects: a theory is complete, he supposes, if it identifies conditions sufficient to produce all the sensory data. Alternative schematizations of sensory data are not the same as hypotheses specifying alternative systems of conditions for the data. One wraps the data in a conceptualization; the other makes inferences to their conditioning causes and laws.

Do these alternatives have the same practical effect when we cannot see beyond the data schematized or explained abductively to tell what the world is in itself? Don't we risk skepticism either way? Peirce would likely reply that skepticism is not the same as agnosticism. Suppose that physicalism and phenomenalism are the theories available to us. Both are complete, because each explains all the sensory data. Should we infer that the world is the one way or the other depending only on our willingness to use one theory or the other for thinking about sensory data? This seems evasive when we notice that the two theories differ radically in what they say of the world: one supposes that everything actual is the state or activity of some physical system; the other alleges that everything is either a qualification of mind (including activities, sensory data, and conceptual systems) or the mind that knows itself by inspecting its qualifications.

The world itself might be either way, or neither. With no additional empirical evidence on which to base our estimate, we need to consider the coherence of these options. Phenomenalism, in a finite mind or the Absolute, is monadic solipsism. Is that a plausible theory? Does the theory say enough about the structure and functions of mind to support its claim that being in its entirety is constituted by a mind and its qualifications? One may doubt that this phenomenalist ontology is sufficiently articulated or even coherent.[83] Compare the physical world postulated by the other hypothesis: can we tell how it achieves self-sufficiency? We can, even allowing such doubts as theologians may raise about the self-sufficiency of a physical system whose existence is contingent. We have, I suggest, these dialectical procedures to help us choose between incompatible but complete theories. Agnosticism is less tempting now. We, like Peirce, can disavow the skepticism disguised as internal realism.

Going one step further, confirming that one theory is true and the other false might forever elude us. But then it does not follow that "all grasp" of the realist story "seems to vanish." Granted that we operate within one theory or the other, using all its semantic and logical resources for describing our experience, it does not follow that we cannot step back from that representation saying that it may be false to the world. Something like this happens often enough when a person concedes the peculiar warp of his neurotic fears while despairing that he will ever shake them. The world is probably not, he says, as scary a place as his anxieties make it out to be; though he cannot now see it otherwise.

Oppositions like that between physicalism and phenomenalism are rare. More often, we have to choose between hypotheses and theories which are not complete. There will yet be, we suppose, some empirical difference, predicted by one but not by the other, which will enable us to decide. Or we apply one or another of the good explanations already available for oppositions which are less than global. There are, for example, the different perspectives of people describing a state of affairs (having a toothache or observing someone else who does); the different scales appropriate for describing the same phenomena (as pianists and piano-tuners describe the same effects). There are many ways to represent the same things. We who lack a god's-eye view of the world may often fail to detect the object common to these variant descriptions, though we do not say if we agree with Peirce, but not Kant, Carnap, Quine, Putnam, and sometimes James, that THE WORLD has fallen into limbo. We know that it has not, because our various thinkings, however disparate from one another, bring us into direct, practical contact with the world itself. Tapping with a cane, feeling with the tips of one's fingers, and seeing with one's eyes are also three different kinds of access to the world. We do not say, as parity of reasoning would force these Kantians to do, that we address a different object in each modality. We find ways to correlate these behaviors so as to make each a test of the others. We approach that limit about which Peirce speculated, not as a boundary condition remote from any current state of our understanding and being, but rather as the ambient reality everywhere present, about and within us. This is the world in which we participate but only partly understand.

XI The Transcendental World-Maker

Which should we prefer, "metaphysical" realism or the "internal realism" that Putnam and Quine inherit from Kant and Carnap? The one acknowledges that we live, act within, and speculate about a world we have not made. The other supplies only as much reality as we get by formulating and organizing the sentences that render, within themselves, a thinkable world. The one identifies that world whose established character would explain all or most of what is supporting or confounding in life. The other leaves us mystified by error, frustration, and death. Is each of them just an unfortunate twist in the theory used to schematize sentences, hence experience? Is Putnam himself merely a figure created in one of the internally realist stories he tells? Could he tinker with those procedures to the point of concluding truly that he does not exist? Would he be satisfied if either or both results were shown to be a function of his own valuings? How would we understand Putnam were his nonexistence (internal to a consistent conceptual system) to satisfy the values of the Putnam who makes and uses the system?

Putnam anticipates this embarrassment:

Let me close with a last philosophical metaphor. Kant's image was of knowledge as a "representation"—a kind of play. The author is me. But the author also appears as a character in the play (like a Pirandello play). The author in the play is not the "real" author—it is the "empirical me". The "real" author is the "transcendental me". I would modify Kant's image in two ways. The authors (in the plural—my image of knowledge is social) don't write just *one* story: they write many versions. And the authors *in* the stories are the *real* authors. This would be "crazy" if these stories were *fictions*. A fictitious character can't also be a real author. But these are true stories.[84]

Kant would surely reject the cosmetic suggestion that his distinction between empirical and transcendental egos is an "image." For this is not merely a rhetorical feature of the first and second Critiques: one cannot explain anything that matters to Kant, including the unity of experience, moral freedom, and the allegedly synthetic but a priori character of metaphysical and mathematical necessity, without it.

More important is the intimation that Putnam has begged the question. He recoils from having to apply to himself the implications of his internal realism: the consequences of doing so (those suggested above) would be "crazy." Let this be Putnam's puzzle: why is it that a real author writing himself out of his own play does not thereby undo himself? Putnam has a choice: suffer this consequence, with implications for his own nonbeing; or concede that internal realism commits him to the ontological foundationalism he shares with Carnap and Kant. There are, they imply or declare, the many world-schematizing languages or theories and that transcendental agent who creates and applies them.

Everyone who supposes that conceptual systems might be used to make thinkable worlds nevertheless resists this inference emphatically. Carnap tries to avert it in a way reminiscent of Kant's arguments against the dialectical uses of reason:

Ultimately, all knowledge goes back to my experiences, which are related to one another, connected, and synthesized; thus, there is a logical progress which leads, first, to the various entities of my consciousness, then to the physical objects, furthermore, with the aid of the latter, to the phenomena of consciousness of other subjects, i.e., to the heteropsychological, and, through the mediation of the heteropsychological, to the cultural objects. *But this is the theory of knowl-*

edge in its entirety. Whatever else construction theory states about the
necessary or the useful forms and methods of construction belongs to
the logical, but not to the epistemological, aspect of its task. The
theory of knowledge does not reach beyond what has just been indicated. How cognition can proceed from one object to another, how,
in what sequence and in which form the levels of a system of cognition can be formulated, — all this is contained in the indicated material. The theory of knowledge cannot ask any further questions.[85]

Why can there be no question about the agent responsible for using a conceptual system to create thinkable objects? Only, we surmise, because this
would be a metaphysical, not an epistemological, question. Epistemology
specifies the semantic, syntactic, and inductive rules required for constructing
thinkable objects. Metaphysics is an expression of reason in its dialectical
uses:[86] it is *"a transgression of* (the) *proper boundaries"*[87] established by a con-
structional system. Those systems define the limits of intelligibility, so that
nothing occurring on the other side of their semantic boundaries, including
the agent who formulates and uses a system, is describable within it.

How could we gain access to this transcendental agent? The first
Critique argues that there is no direct way of addressing it: every attempt to
specify the transcendental subject requires our use of the schemas (in Kant's
terms) or theories (in contemporary terms) that schematize sensory data or
the words or observation reports signifying them. Their application to things
noumenal, including things-in-themselves and the noumenal subject, would
violate Kant's strictures against the dialectical uses of reason. This is also the
answer given by those contemporary Kantians who think that they might
evade responsibility for their commitment to a transcendental world-maker:
we could specify that agent only within one or another language, with the
implication that anything so described would be a construct of the system,
hence nothing transcendental.

This evasion is transparent. What is more, it is false both to the architecture of all that is Kantian in the views of Carnap, Putnam, and like-
minded thinkers and to Kant's own method.[88] It was plain to him that we
can infer from what is done to the functional powers of the agent who does
it. Is experience unified? This would presuppose a unifer who is the ground
for that unity. Are sensory data (sentences or symbols) differentiated and
organized within our experience? If so, there is the schematizer whose existence and activity are the logically necessary conditions for this schematiza-

tion. Kantian pragmatists, no less than Kant himself, have inferential access to the transcendental ego from within experience or language. Like Kant, their characterizations of it point to an external source for the unity, differentiation, and order within experience and language. Constructing thinkable objects by using one or another conceptual system, we presuppose the agent who formulates and then chooses among these systems before using one of them to create a thinkable world.

Does this argument beg the question? It assumes that we can think our way out of, or past, the constructions supplied by languages merely by using one of the inferential formulas common to some languages. Perhaps it is only certain languages which make it thinkable that activity presupposes an agent, hence that experience is the effect of some maker. The idea of a transcendental ground for experience might not even be formulable in other languages, though nothing about the extra-mental reality of this agent would be established even were it true that this inference is sanctioned by every single natural language, real or possible. Why? Because the things constructible within experience (whether sensible, linguistic, or conceptual) or inferred from aspects of it have no demonstrable reality in any other place. Thinking otherwise is, as Carnap has said, "a transgression of the proper boundaries."

Still, the question is not settled, because Carnap, Putnam, Goodman, Quine, and others make no secret of their musings as they consider the choice of languages to be used for constructing thinkable worlds. How should we interpret these reflections? There are only two possibilities: talk about, or the implication of a standpoint above or apart from, language is always a fiction, perhaps a heuristic or careless fiction, but always an ontologically harmless fiction; alternatively, the inference is essential to the architecture and integrity of this essentially Kantian view. The first strategy is an evasion, one that requires kicking the ladder away lest one be asked to climb it. Only the second alternative speaks to the import of this Kantian view. There are, consequently, these two possible standpoints from which to characterize the transcendental world-maker: we infer to the schematizer from within the experience schematized, or we stand apart from an actual or prospective experience while considering the conceptual system that will be used to make it. Rather than infer to the transcendental perspective from within a language, we rise to the transcendental attitude, looking down, as though from a distance, on the languages that could be used for making worlds. Which one will be made? Let desire decide. It determines the formulation or choice of that conceptual system best calculated to produce a world in which our interests or passions are satisfied. Forsaking inference, we discover the transcendental thinker by turning upon our volorizing selves.

The difference between these two procedures—the one inferential, the other a self-intuition—is chronicled in the shift from Kant's first Critique to his second and third Critiques, also in Kant's own anticipation of that move in the section of the first Critique entitled "The Canon of Pure Reason."[89] These sources catalogue our unmediated access to the transcendental ground of our thinking. We achieve this self-perception, says Kant, by turning from questions of cognition to those of interest and practice. We escape the limits of a conceptual system, thereby recovering the transcendental standpoint, merely by considering the attitude or desire impelling our use of the system. The transcendental attitude is, this implies, everywhere immanent and accessible if only we turn from the exigencies of cognition to the interests of practice. Equally, and in terms more familiar to the linguistic expressions of Kant's views, we may ascend from the material to the formal mode: rather than use a language, we consider its semantic, syntactic, and inductive rules as they govern the formation of sentences expressed in the material mode.[90] But now we are poised on that boundary which divides the empirical from the transcendental. Looking one way, we see an empirical world biased by the prominence given to certain interests. Looking the other way, we discover that this world is created when a transcendental subject makes and uses a conceptual system in ways calculated to satisfy its attitudes or desires.

No striving, no reality, said Fichte. Kant agreed, while reporting all that he could learn—by inference or self-inspection—of the transcendental striver. This subject, more than an "image," is the ground for every claim, by Kant, Fichte, or their successors, that the world is thinkable and known. Annihilate the transcendental subject, and there could be no experience or world, because there would be no agent to construct or enjoy it.

Critical idealists embarrassed by the idea of a transcendental subject are reasonably perplexed: should they admit to having a world if this presupposes a thinker who grounds or creates the world by thinking it? Is this really a choice? Can we plausibly deny having experience of a world? Concede that this is so, and our choice, as Kantians, is forced. Admitting that a thinkable world exists (if only in experience), we commit ourselves to the transcendental subject who has made it.

Peirce had an instinct for puzzles like this one: "Dismiss make-believes."[91] The paradox to which Putnam commits himself is the consequence of one such fantasy: namely, that we create whatever realities there are by using conceptual systems to schematize worlds from percepts, sentences, other symbols, or behaviors. Think of Putnam himself: he is the author of his books, not a character in one or several of them. Peirce explains Putnam's authorial integrity by saying, as quoted above, "That is real which has such and such characters, whether anybody thinks it to have those characters or not." The existence and character of things are independent of the ways we think, talk about, or value them. One might read this either as dogmatism or as the presumption that we might step outside thought, language, or perception to see things as they are in themselves, perhaps as a god might do. This would be a misreading. Peirce's realism, like his every other claim about any state of affairs is, on his own terms, a hypothesis. Realism is, he would say, the best explanation we have for the phenomena that invite explanation. We have a ready test for this hypothesis: does it save Putnam from the paradox of having to suppose that his existence is an artifact of the conceptual system which some value motivates him to apply? It does.[92]

XII Must Truth be the Function of Value?

No one denies that we engage nature in ways that change it. Everyone should deny that worlds are made so that attitudes and desires may be satisfied. Some truths are the effects of desire, hence of value. The truth that I have a place to live is an example, that truth being the consequence of a need, hence a desire. Still, this causal relation between values and truths is not the issue. Our concern is the much tighter ("logical") relation between truth and value, the one allegedly established when the differentiations and relations projected onto sensory data or behaviors are sponsored by the values satisfied when a desired experience is schematized. This is the relation signified by the claim that truth is everywhere a function of value.

Sidney Hook, writing of Dewey, observes that "the preeminent subject matter of philosophy has been the relation between things and *values*."[93] Philosophers recommend that we think about the world in one or another way, though the theories they propose always embody their author's values. Hook is not saying that thinkers neglect to scourge their views of suppressed bias. His point is stronger: philosophy, he says, is always ideology. This claim about philosophy might generalize to all out thinking: every true claim about the existence and character of anything will be the function of our values if the Kantian arguments shared by James and Dewey are correct. For then every matter of fact will be the product of some value-driven conceptual system.

Is that so? Must truth be the function of value? Why not make this other hypothesis? Suppose that the existence and character of many things are independent of our thoughts, words, or percepts. Acting on the information supplied in one of these three ways, we might change some part of the world; but just now, as we think, talk about, or perceive it, the world has an existence and character independent of us. There might be an infinity of truths representing these mind-independent states of affairs. Correctly representing them is always problematic; but there is no necessary reason, on this hypothesis, for saying that everything is the creature of our values just because values motivate our thought, talk, or perception of it. Why make this hypothesis? Because this realist proposal, better than the one of Kant, identifies the likely conditions for our engagement in the world. "A little gleam between two eternities," Thomas Carlyle said of life. One might read this as a Kantian or as a realist—but with this difference: the realist makes abductive inferences citing conditions for events occurring before, during, and after the gleam. The Kantian has nothing to say of the two eternities, while having only this single explanation for everything that happens in between: mind does it.

Blowing the idealist cobwebs from our eyes, we should consider the possibility that material truth is not the function of value. Nature is not our product, though many changes made within it express our attitudes and desires. Motivating values are not constitutive of truth, though regulative values appropriate to inquiry are essential for determining which hypotheses are true. Material truths are confirmed, not made, when hypotheses representing things discovered or made are formulated and tested. Contextual values distorting hypotheses about these things may be identified and purged. We struggle to see beyond our attitudes and desires. There is always something to be seen. Sometimes, we see it.

Chapter Two

I Two Kinds of Thinking

Thinking, Kant supposed, is the use of rules to schematize some content. We are draughtsmen, cooks or artists, musicians, architects or poets. These tasks are constructive. The thinking appropriate to them requires that something be differentiated and organized, as when the mind schematizing sensory data makes experience. There is no place here for the representational side of thought: there are rules for making things, but no ideas of or about them. This is a grave omission, for no one walks safely across the street in full sunlight or through a dark house at night without maps and plans representing both these terrains and the instrumental relations appropriate to them. Granting Kant his constructive applications of thought, we insist that hypothesis be given its due: making designs, music, and proofs, we also make and test representations.

Thinking of both kinds, hypothetical and constructive, directs behavior: we use maps and recipes too. Overt behaviors are, however, irrelevant to this discussion until section VII. It is only the intrapsychic use of hypothesis and construction that is critical until then. Value is also peripheral to most of this chapter, though hypothesis, as much as construction, is usually (or always) motivated by attitudes or desires. There is little to tell of value until section VIII, when value-neutrality in the formulation and testing of hypotheses becomes the issue. I shall say that value never makes any false sentence true, or the reverse. We often discover successive layers of distorting interest while considering our hypotheses, but rigorous self-scrutiny can often eliminate a bias. Alternatively, we let those valorizing attitudes and desires stand, taking care to set them apart from the hypothesis being formulated and tested. Or, like referees and reporters, we defend ourselves against the personally distorting values of those who participate in an activity by appraising hypotheses formulated for purposes and activities in which we do not participate.

Purging ourselves of values, or merely identifying and separating them from our hypotheses, is problematic. Have we identified all the relevant valuings? Should we be most alert to bias when we seem most detached? There are potholes and deceptions everywhere; but sometimes we do seem to isolate hypotheses from those values which obscure, rather than focus, our understanding of things. We achieve that limit where hypotheses are sanitized (e.g., as when $F = ma$ is assumed to be a hypothesis about, not the definition of, a natural law). Having any single example of a hypothesis set apart from the values motivating it, we wonder if each and every claim about matters of fact may not be reformulable in ways that distinguish its representational content from the values impelling it.

Ernest Nagel was considered naive for saying this in *The Structure of Science*.[1] Nagel understood that the descriptive terms of a science may disguise fathoms of bias. He nevertheless affirmed that the value-neutrality of the physical sciences is not in doubt: thought does not create nature by using conceptual systems to schematize sensory data or sentences; all the less does value-driven thought have that effect in the moment when some hypothesis is affirmed. Values that regulate inquiry, and even those which motivate it, are not constitutive of the things investigated. No wonder Nagel seems obtuse to readers who assume that physicists as much as sociologists and urban planners are ideologists and world-makers.

Nagel was guilty only of charity toward his actual and potential critics. He seems not to have foreseen that they would confuse inquiry with its objects or would suppose — gratuitously, it would have seemed to him — that inquiry creates its objects. It was plain to Nagel that having values, even to the point of making value-warped hypotheses, is not the same as constructing the objects of inquiry. That we make and do many things for some valued aim is not disputed. That thought cannot be successfully representational — values stripped from our hypotheses for this purpose — should be vigorously denied. For why bother to confess our values or to emphasize that inquiry is reflectively self-correcting if we are not concerned that hypotheses distorted, because value-driven, should be reformulated? Ideologists don't have this privilege. They cannot admit to value-sponsored error: more than misrepresenting some state of affairs, they have made and will now have to unmake it.

This chapter, like the previous one, argues that values operate regulatively within inquiry without being constitutive either of truths or the things they represent. Thinking, I shall be saying, is as often hypothetical as constructive. We often make or alter a social order so that our values are realized within it: parents, coaches, and politicians are forever doing that. But equally, we speculate about the world, the social world included, without creating the states of affairs that satisfy our attitudes and desires. Hypothesis is different from construction.

Thought does both, and sometimes at once, as in the case of mathematical proof. For we construct the proof while hypothesizing that it applies to some relationship independent of it. There are, for example, proofs in Euclidean geometry representing relationships within a flat space. But equally, a proof may misrepresent its domain, as would happen were we to allege having proof that a circle can be squared or an angle trisected. This is the vulnerability of all hypotheses: they may say of an extra-conceptual state of affairs that it is not as it is or that it is as it is not. Proofs are different only for the remarkable fact that we may formulate notions of extra-conceptual things with an accuracy that enables us to determine such additional properties they must, or cannot, have.

I shall not be concerned in this chapter, or elsewhere in this book, with the places where construction and hypothesis converge. This chapter describes only their difference.

II The Motive for World-Making

James sometimes agreed that the claim of world-making is not appropriate to the truths of mathematics and science. Why does Kantian orthodoxy require that there be no exceptions? What consideration obliges us to say that every truth about any world has no standing apart from our determination to use a theory or story to schematize a thinkable experience? I suggest this answer: idealists are skeptics. Denying that we might ever have confirmed access to a world existing apart from our minds, they prefer to make do with a world that is everywhere accessible to mind. How is accessibility guaranteed? By (re-)presenting the world, meaning schematized sensory data, sentences, or behavior, for inspection: mind creates a differentiated, organized manifold, while setting this content before itself. Turning upon ourselves, we discover a world. This schematization and presentation has the effect of making correspondence dispensable. For there is no gap between mediating thought and its objects: we have no reason to speculate about the accuracy of our representations when the only thinkable phenomena are those set plainly before our inspecting minds.[2]

Let us start with those details of the argument which are pertinent to contemporary versions of Kant's views. We consider first the skeptical arguments, then the talk of world-making as it fills the space vacated when correspondence is repudiated as our idea of truth.

One objection to correspondence emphasizes the difficulty of establishing fixed referents for words designating things in the world. How can we fix the meaning of *gold* so that it signifies the same things or the same set of properties when used by different speakers, some of whom are separated by time, culture, or language? There is also the problem of establishing stable inductive rules for interpreting the evidence of things. Do alchemists and modern chemists use the same rules for construing the evidence that some change has been produced? Why assume that the same thing is observed then and now if the predicates and inductive rules applied then and now are different?

These quandaries are symptoms of a deeper problem. We fear that access to the objects of our truth-claims is uncertain and suspect. For we never exceed the barrier of mediating thought, language, or perception so that thoughts, sentences, or percepts may be compared with their referents or causes. Truth may be attained—we may correctly represent some part of the world—though we can never know that this is so, because we cannot step outside ourselves to compare the vehicles of belief to things allegedly represented.

Skepticism overwhelms us when we are unable to determine which of our representations, if any, are true. At first, these doubts are only methodological: we cannot put aside our possibly distorting conceptualizations or percepts to check truth-claims against the things themselves. Later, skepticism becomes despair for a world lost to us. We may defer to the world for a time, calling it the ground and referent for experience; but deference is soon renounced as a pious but empty habit: for there is, we say, no world independent of thought and experience for its existence and character; or none we can know. The idea of the "Beyond" has become a chronic delusion, an "idea of reason" having no referent.

Experience is made, Kant said, when sensory data are schematized by the application of categories operating as rules.[3] These categories are the determinable forms of experience, as any experience must have quantity, quality, and relation. The categories require further determination, since there is no generic experience of quality, but only the experience of specific qualities (e.g., of red or green). Empirical schemas are rules for supplying that more determinate form which is lacking in the transcendental categories.[4] There are, for example, empirical schemas for thinking of dogs or cats. They organize sensory data so that we may see this cat or that dog, each one a particular, qualitatively determinate, perceptual object. There is, however, no ascertainable similarity, and perhaps no similarity at all, between the data schematized and the noumenal ground of experience. Properties or changes in the dog or cat stretching just now in front of me may not correlate to anything within that noumenal ground.

The chasm between experience and things-in-themselves is deeper still, for the difficulty of knowing the extra-mental world is more than the problem of verifying our claims about it. That is so, because sensory data are assumed to be atomic prior to their schematization.[5] This implies that all the relations present within experience (e.g., all the spatial and temporal relations introduced by schematization) are thought's product. It may be a delusion, therefore, if we suppose that the coherence-making relations within experience have their parallel in something external. The differentiation and relations used for schematizing sensory data may not apply beyond the forms of intuition—space and time. Using them transcendently, to think of extra-mental noumena, we address the void. It may not be empty; but none of our resources qualify us for thinking of it.

Accordingly, things-in-themselves (if such there be) exercise no thinkable effect on the character of our sensory experience: they provide its content, though all the character and relations present in experience derive from the rules used in schematizing the data, not from the data themselves. The actual posture of noumena is irrelevant, consequently, to our experience-creating schematizations. Cats only twist or stretch within experience.

Such noumena as there may be cannot be thought to move in either way, nor is it thinkable that there are cats among them.

The inaccessibility of the noumenal world, coupled with mind's self-sufficiency as synthesizer of experience, has a notable consequence: we must introduce some other notion of material truth when the idea of beliefs or sentences satisfied by circumstances independent of thought and language is rejected. What alternative ground for truth might there be? Three plausible alternatives are close at hand: namely, experience, the rules used to schematize it, and the mind that applies the rules to make the experience. Kant invokes all three: rules determine the form of truth,[6] while mind applies these rules to the schematization of sensory data by way of making objects for thought. Mind also reflects on its achievement. It thinks about (re-presents) the things made, thereby satisfying the classical formula: truth consists in "the agreement of knowledge with its object."[7] Finally, mind confirms these truth-claims by observing the "things" set before it.

There is still the problem of telling how it is that disparate minds schematize the same objects. This would be no problem if minds were located within a stable physical world, each one perceiving the same things. It is problematic if those extra-mental things are eliminated from consideration because of being noumenal, hence inaccessible or nonexistent. The difficulty is exacerbated when Kant's insistence on each thinker's autonomy implies that each of us is free to make an experience suited to him or herself, subject only to the constraints of general logic and the categorical imperative. How, then, shall we explain the contrary evidence of experiences that cohere with those of other thinkers because of having the same objects? What remains to explain this community of objects and truths in the absence of a stable, common material environment? Kant seems to rely on an extra-mental material world for this shared environment when he describes a ship moving downstream; but then he quickly locates the stability common to our individual experiences in the rules we severally apply: "In the perception of an event there is always a rule that makes the order in which the perceptions (in the apprehension of this appearance) follow upon one another a *necessary* order."[8] This response is, however, deficient, because incomplete: it does not tell us the basis for the rule establishing uniformity among schematizers.

Kant finds this ground in a contingency that is implied, more than detailed. We infer from purposes "contingently occasioned (the number of which cannot be foreseen)"[9] that there are many different rules. Yet Eskimos differentiate among kinds of snow, while Bedouins have little to say of snow but many ways of schematizing camels. Notice the implied source of this difference: each culture chooses those experience-determining schemas which express its distinguishing values. Each culture creates a world congenial to itself. These stable values, differing from culture to culture, are the secure basis for a culture's inductive rules, hence for its truths.

There are, of course, some things still unexplained, as Kant never tells how it can happen that transcendental egos take their direction from empirical egos immersed in a culture before regularizing their schematizations in ways that sustain the culture's rules. (Perhaps Kant believed that cultures are created transcendentally; though again we might ask about the regularizing communications among transcendental egos.) Nor does he explain the equally mysterious determination that occurs when transcendental egos schematize coffee rather than yak's milk or beer for thirsty empirical egos: how decide to do one or the other when there is no rule? It is crucial to these uncertainties that we establish what relation there is between empirical and transcendental egos; but here again, the issue is confused. Kant sometimes intimates that transcendental and empirical egos are the two aspects under which a thinking subject experiences and knows itself.[10] There are other places in the first Critique where the transcendental ego has all the power while the empirical ego is disparaged as the mere feeling of sameness, mine again, that persist through experience.[11] Perplexed by these uncertainties, we learn to settle, as Kantians, for the less detailed claim that the particular character of any experience, hence of any world, is determined by the values of the schematizing mind. We locate that mind within its native culture, perhaps seeing variant schematizations as idiosyncrasies within the normal range of the culture's world-making.

It is important to our reading of James and his effect on our time that Kant's formulation, with its emphasis on the synthesis of sensory data, was extended in the nineteenth century to include the synthesis of social realities: we create "life-worlds" by selecting and sequencing the behaviors that make us recognizable to one another. Marx, for example, can be read as saying that workers and capitalists live in different worlds because of their opposed, experience-organizing behaviors. Marx would surely have resisted the monadic isolation of social classes, especially as it ignores the common world where material conditions provoke these different ways of organizing life. We are, nevertheless, easily distracted from Marx's realism by the idealism of Kant and Hegel. It is, Hegel said, some Idea that dominates a culture, determining its behaviors by organizing the experience, hence the life-worlds of its people.[12] The Idea might be expressed as an organizing style of thought, but equally as a style of behavior.

It is the behavioral versions of this Kantian view that are most familiar in our century, especially in Wittgenstein's remarks about "forms of life" and "language-games."[13] These phrases signify behaviors, hence experiences, schematized by rules. Agents create their worlds by acting in certain ritualized (rule-governed) ways, as we may live within the life-worlds of commerce or the university. We dress as they prescribe, observing their routines, acquiring whatever status, manners, and expectations they encourage. Each of these routines engages and possesses us until our idiosyncrasies are all but extinguished. Each of us is made familiar and predictable to others. We are, on this telling, creatures of the forms (the rules or Ideas) we enact.

This extrapolation from schematizing sensory data or sentences to schematizing behaviors is problematic for Kant's distinction between experience and noumena. For where do behaviors stand? They are experienced; yet they occur, we assume, beyond the circle of mind, hence among the "things" which should count as noumenal. Kant has argued that knowledge does not extend beyond the plane of phenomena schematized. It follows that we should be incapable of knowing either these behaviors or their significance for the agents performing them. Here we are favored with some additional evidence, for we ourselves perform these same acts using such rules as we have learned. Doing only what the rules prescribe, knowing that I do it, and knowing the significance of these behaviors, I know as well what any actor applying these rules would do and know of him or herself. Accordingly, knowledge of my behavior does not violate the prohibition against knowledge of anything noumenal: I am always and only in reflective, intuitive relation with myself.[14]

III Textualism

Consider now that Jamesian pragmatists and Continental hermeneuticists dwell together in Kant's long shadow. They agree that minds impelled by their values create the life-worlds which are, for every Kantian, all that reality can be or (more cautiously) all that it can be thought and known to be. This is ample reason for believing that twentieth-century versions of this Kantian argument are not so original as their practitioners suppose. Rorty hopes to fracture that continuity. Textualists, he agrees, are "the spiritual descendants of the idealists";[15] but then he emphasizes their distance from the philosophic tradition:

> In the last century there were philosophers who argued that nothing exists but ideas. In our century there are people who write as if there were nothing but texts. . . . Some of these people take their point of departure from Heidegger, but usually the influence of philosophers is relatively remote.[16]

I have been saying, first, that idealism and textualism have in common an opposition to the claim of science to be a paradigm of human activity, and, second, that they differ in that one is a philosophical doctrine, and the other an expression of suspicion about philosophy. I can put these two points together by saying that whereas nineteenth-century idealism wanted to substitute one sort of science (philosophy) for another (natural science) as the center of culture, twentieth-century textualism wants to place literature in the center, and to treat both science and philosophy as, at best, literary genres.[17]

I can sum up by saying that post-Kantian metaphysical idealism was a specifically philosophical form of romanticism whereas textualism is a specifically post-philosophical form.[18]

Textualism is the view that nothing of life or being is intelligible outside whatever text is used to make it articulate. It results from the application of Kant's views about schematization to literary texts, though now we have a double schematization. First is the novelist. Using words (where Kant assumed perceptual data), he organizes them to create a fictive world. Second is the literary critic. He interprets the novelist's sentences, paragraphs, and chapters, thereby schematizing them. He says of these words what Kant assumed of sensory data: that they have no intrinsic differentiations and relations of their own. (This is, I take it, a claim about sense or significance, not about words on pages or their grammatical relations.) Imposing his own "strong reading," the critic achieves a new interpretation of the novelist's words and a new fictive world. These two worlds, the novelist's and the critic's, might co-exist; but equally, one may supersede the other, as New York is imposed on New Amsterdam.

Is textualism post-philosophic? Or is it merely the application to literature of a doctrine incubated and declared within philosophy? Is every application of Plato's ideas equally post-philosophic? Or should we say, more accurately, that philosophic ideas are frequently borrowed and applied by people who use them without regard for their implications and assumptions. Nothing in the history of these ideas is misrepresented when we say that the relation of idealism to textualism is the instance of a philosophic lineage. Rorty seems determined to erase this history, hence the opposition he alleges between textualism and Hegelian idealism. But that is a false opposition, proving only that the textualist roots are independent, somewhat, of Hegel. Indeed, they have a common origin. Hegel's Absolute idealism, no less than textualism, is a version of Kantian world-making. Both are inspired by Kant's acknowledgment that disparate empirical schemas (e.g., alternative Ideas or interpretations) are required as we supply more determinate expressions for the determinable categories quality, quantity, and relation.

Rorty obscures this common source by misdescribing it:

> There . . . are two ways of thinking about various things. I have drawn them up as reminders of the differences between a philosophical tradition which began, more or less, with Kant, and one which began, more or less, with Hegel's *Phenomenology*. The first tradition thinks of truth as a vertical relationship between representations and what is represented. . . . To understand Derrida, one must see his work as the latest development in this non-Kantian, dialectical tradition—the latest attempt of the dialecticians to shatter the Kantians' ingenuous image of themselves as accurately representing how things really are.[19]

These remarks are curious, for Kant did both these things. He reduced "things as they really are" to unthinkable things-in-themselves. Ideas, he said, are not signs related "vertically" to their objects; they are rules for differentiating or organizing sensory data. Derrida's opposition to Kant is dissolved when Kant's own view is plainly stated: the languages celebrated as products of *différance* are just the instances of Kant's experience-making rules of understanding. Schematizing rules make worlds, there being nothing thinkable beyond them. Derrida and Rorty can invoke this idea, almost without fear that a realist will answer, because Kant explained and justified it.

IV The Dependence of Existence on Truth

Each of us has some desires that are never realized. It is hard squaring this fact with the romantic celebration of world-making. Why tolerate frustration if world-making is so easy? Why not make a world where desire is satisfied?[20] Am I being too literal in reading the many claims that there is nothing outside language, texts, or inquiry that might confound us? We might regard talk of this sort as a kind of harmless play, but that would be too easy: first, because the claims about world-making are not intended so frivolously; second, because revoking a thesis at the moment when its strong implications prove awkward is only evasive.

Perhaps we can blunt the dialectical edge by remarking that some part of the urge to world-making has an ethical motive. Most of us suppose that life would be fairer if each of us could have the life he or she desires, up to the limit where the conduct of one person does not adversely affect the experiences of any other. Suppose that experience is rechristened as *world*, so that each of us is impelled by the desire that we be *free from* the worlds of others, yet *free to* have a world of our own. This is the hope that we might choose all the furnishings of our lives, the hope that each of us should be the measure of all that is and is not within that world centered on ourselves. Kant and James justify and satisfy this regard for the integrity of each one's experience. Perhaps their idealism is only the metaphor affirming this democratic, pluralist aspiration. Too bad that this way of excusing Kantians their idealism is decorous, but vain: serious world-makers don't ask this exemption. They stand by the implications of their idealism: every differentiation and relation ascribable to the world is, they say, the consequence of whatever conceptual system is used to satisfy our desire.

This is the claim having dramatic consequences for our notion of truth. We were to seek an alternative ground for truth when skeptical arguments convinced us that a reality independent of thought, language, and experience does not exist or cannot be known. Correspondence, this implied, could no longer be our principal notion of truth. Kant, Fichte, Hegel, and Schopenhauer have provided the bits and pieces for a substitute ground: Kant as he described the role of the transcendental ego in making the only world we can know; Fichte as he emphasized the role of imagination in creating schematized worlds; Hegel for his emphasis on the role of Ideas in creating distinctive cultures; Schopenhauer for crediting will as the originary, moving force within us. James assimilated these emendations and emphases. We inherit, or merely repeat, his contention that value-directed will is the substantial basis for each person's truths. Value, we allow, originates in personal preference or social norms; either way, our power for making experience is the substitute ground for truth when noumenal reality and the idea of correspondence are rejected.

This solution is vague. For what is truth if it is not the relation of a state of affairs to the sentence or belief affirming it? What other relation can stabilize truth-claims? The familiar answer is that truth is a coherence relation: sentences are counted as true if, deductively, one is derived from others by entailment relations; or, if, inductively, there are rules for affirming or denying one sentence when others are denied or affirmed. So "It's cold" may be true when sentences already accepted affirm that bare skin and water do or would freeze. We assume that these already accepted affirmations and denials have also been tested for their coherence, even with sentences or beliefs like the one now considered for its coherence with them. This adjusting of mutually tolerant affirmations and denials goes back and forth, or sometimes in a circle, always requiring that conflicts and anomalies be minimized as we create a system of internally harmonious claims covering an ever larger range of phenomena.

Nor is it only sentences that are made to cohere: *being in the truth* is an existentialist expression of this coherentist idea. It calls for making oneself intelligible to all those citizens-actors-agents-persons with whom we make and share a life-world. They know and live by the same rules that articulate and organize our lives. We are to do the things that will make our behaviors predictable to them. This is a counsel of uniformity, one that permits only as much spontaneity as may be interpreted by our fellows in a rule-preserving way. Improvising musicians know this point as they exploit a margin of freedom within established limits. The language-game, the dance, the courtship ritual: all allow some measure of openness and variation, while establishing boundaries for mutual understanding. We get a margin of tolerance mitigating a uniformity that may narrow to repression.

Truth as coherence also has this other, quite astonishing implication: that existence is made conditional on truth. This result, so vital to the claim of world-making, follows in three steps. First, sentences are formulated and organized in ways sanctioned by grammatical and inductive rules, so that some of them are declared true. But second, there is no extra-linguistic world to which these truths conform; so that, third, existence claims are sanctioned, or not, by our inductive rules. Existence is made parasitic on the convention that these rules are the standard of truth.

This dependence of existence on truth is intimated whenever a material truth makes an existence claim: saying that a sentence is true, I imply that some state of affairs, positive or negative, obtains. Consider the truth "He is lucky" as it couples with the fact that someone has good luck. How is this state of affairs established? It happens when we apply the relevant inductive rules. They permit us to infer that someone is lucky when we have already affirmed sentences or thoughts alleging that events of a certain character and number befall him (e.g., he twice wins the lottery, survives a crash, is happily married). These inductive rules set the minimum evidence required for making the inference, with these two effects: it is true that someone is lucky, implying that there exists a lucky man.

More technically, we say in the formal mode that a sentence is true, given some inductive rule or rules, thereby entailing that a sentence in the material mode is true, hence that some state of affairs obtains. "Your hair is long" satisfies inductive rules, from which it follows that "Your hair is long" reports truly that your hair is long. Existence shadows material truth, which is in turn prefigured by the determination that inductive rules are satisfied. This is world-making with a vengeance. What explains this startling result? Just our power to fix the rules determining what shall count as luck, honesty, length, or whatever.

High rollers and corporate traders may set the rules so that many things need to go one's way before it is truly said that "He is lucky." The rest of us may set the standards lower, with the result that people using these different rules disagree about the relevant existence claims. They live, we say, in different worlds. We might repair this breach by agreeing to a stipulation telling how much luck is to count as good luck. But equally, we can imagine circumstances that defy this accord. Religious fundamentalists will not agree with freethinkers about what shall count as blasphemy, since affronts intolerable to the former are invisible to the latter. There is no middle ground. We might anguish about this difference or celebrate the remarkable authority claimed for world-makers: the right and power to make the rules determining what is assertible, acceptable, and true in a world of discourse is also, they suppose, the power to determine what shall exist in the world prefigured by these rules.

Putnam, who writes of *rational acceptability* in place of *truth*, is forth-right in this regard: "We must have criteria of rational acceptability to even have an empirical world. . . . In short, I am saying that the 'real world' depends upon our values."[21] Putnam's *rational acceptability* is Dewey's *warranted assertibility:* a thought or sentence is acceptable or assertible if it co-heres with those other thoughts or sentences which have already satisfied our inductive rules. The choice of rules depends on our values: what is mist to a farmer surveying his parched fields may count as rain in the Gobi desert. "It is raining" will be false to the farmer, but true in the desert; there will be no rain in the one place, though it rains in the other. There might be some other standpoint from which we measure precipitation in these two "places," determining that the amounts are equal; but this implies only that there might be a third set of inductive rules (hence a third universe of discourse) different from the ones sanctioning those other inferences. There will be three worlds, hence three domains of existence, not two "ways of speaking," set against our correct assessment of the "objective" circumstances.

This plurality of truths and worlds is one result of making the "em-pirical world" dependent on the "criteria of rational acceptability." This re-lation is odd in another way too: it offends a sensibility bred on the positivist distinction between that which belongs to the world and that which belongs to logic. The rigid distinction between the synthetic and the analytic has broken down. No longer separate from logic, the empirical world is made dependent on it. Putnam evokes a time when logic was motivated by some-thing quite different from our contemporary concern for the rigor and clarity of formal systems. Nineteenth-century idealists made logic the science of those principles which are constitutive of being.[22] Logical truths were said to be synthetic, not analytic and tautological. Principles, including noncontrad-iction, excluded middle, and identity, were described as truths applying in all possible worlds; they are, on this telling, the principles necessary for con-structing any world. More specific rules, including those of inductive logic, are rules for constructing particular worlds. These nineteenth-century ideal-ists supposed, as Putnam may also do, that worlds are generated by applica-tion of these two kinds of rules, one applying in all possible worlds, the other determining the differentiations and relations constitutive of particular worlds.

Why was it important to idealists that logical rules be synthetic? Be-cause Leibniz's Plotinian hope, that all apparent diversity might derive from the law of identity, $A = A$,[23] seems mistaken. The complexity of a deductive argument may derive from one or a few axioms. It seems unlikely, however, that the differences and orders apparent in our world might have emanated, as though deductively, from one simple property or relation. Why don't we think so? Because of our inability to reverse direction, thereby showing that all the complexity of our world reduces to a simple beginning. It follows that relations within the logic used for world-making cannot be analytic if 'analytic' means empty. Relations within a world must be synthetic, we conclude, wherever diversity does not collapse into tautology. As Putnam has said, " 'S' is 'analytic' — but it is an 'analyticity' that resembles Kant's account of the *synthetic a priori* more than it resembles his account of the analytic." [24]

It is less paradoxical now that world-makers should want to describe the generating rules of a world as "logical." For this is a reversion (conscious or not) to the cosmological logic of Kant and Hegel: the rules used by a schematizing ego are the rules of a *transcendental* logic. Our finite minds, no less than the infinite mind of God, create worlds by using the rules of a *synthetic* logic. These include, as above, construction rules applicable to every possible world, but also those inductive rules of practice and science required to differentiate and organize content (e.g., words or sensory data) in a particular world.

This is the idealist dream: we who make and apply the rules of logic exhibit thereby our power for world-making. We are the efficient causes; logic (our logic of synthetic principles) is the formal cause. We use its rules for thinking the world, thereby generating its constitutive differences and relations. We who create worlds have our distinguishing interests and desires, so that every "real world" depends on its maker's values: world-generating rules are contrived and applied to satisfy them.

V World-Making as Psycho-centric

Remember the status claimed, or presumed, for the mind that uses rules or schemas for making worlds: mind, with its logic, is "transcendental." This is Kant's word for the status of an agent presupposed by the experience it makes. Neither this agent nor its acts appear within its product, except for that empirical trace of itself known within experience as a sense of familiarity and continuity, as each of us says, "Me again" or "Still me" as experience carries on. This phenomenal expression of the experience-making ego is powerless; all the differentiations and order present within experience are the work of the schematizing transcendental ego. One may nevertheless confuse the transcendental and empirical egos, as Carnap does when he presupposes a transcendental ego choosing conceptual frameworks to make thinkable worlds while insisting that ego is the construct of empirical psychology.[25]

Every spokesman for world-making is as much responsible as Carnap for telling what relation mind has to its world-making logical rules and to the worlds made when sensory data, symbols, or behaviors are differentiated and organized. Surely, this world-maker cannot be a mere incident within any of its worlds. Neither is it characterizable in terms native to any particular conceptual system, when the predicates of a system apply only to the "things" schematized, not to world-making mind. This is a mind that rides free and clear of alternative logics and the worlds schematized. This is a transcendental mind in exactly the respect that Kant intended. Making synthetic logics and making worlds, it is exempt from both of them.[26]

Putnam has said that our choice of "real worlds" depends on our values. I infer that the "our" of "our values" is an allusion to the society of transcendental egos. Each of them chooses its logical rules, then creates a world satisfying its desires. There is, however, something more to explain when conceptual systems are used to make worlds. For thought is engaged in only these two activities: it formulates the rules used for making worlds, or it applies these rules to some content. Thought as the instrument of attitude and desire has no role in choosing an ego's values. What is left to decide them? Only the attitudes and desires themselves; or, more generically, only the will.

Kant required that will should satisfy the demands of reason: namely, universalizability and consistency.[27] This is Kant's pietism, his preference, rather than our necessity. Nothing entails that we be scrupulous and spartan in the ways he recommends, especially when there are alternative logics available to us, some of them dispensing with universality or even with consistency. And anyway, there are Schopenhauer and Nietzsche to tell us that will is denatured by too much reason.[28] Will is essentially despotic; thought is its instrument, not its governor or judge. All the order projected into any of the worlds we make has no purpose but that of satisfying some pre-rational lust. None of this would be news to Thrasymachus.

The conceptual pragmatists who speak for world-making in our time may describe themselves as "naturalists," or even as "physicalists." But this is a conceit, for what could these words signify? Only that these thinkers are motivated to use a language whose predicates are natural or physical rather than spiritual. Mind itself is not to be characterized either in naturalistic or in physicalist terms, for its ontological status is best understood in contrast to the languages it uses and the worlds it makes. They are derivative; it is necessary, meaning not that its nonexistence is a contradiction, but rather that its activity is a necessary condition for the existence of its languages and worlds.

This is the psycho-centric ontology inherited by conceptual pragmatists, including Carnap, Quine, Putnam, and Rorty, Derrida, Gadamer, and Foucault. We wait for them to supply a narrative tracing the progression from values mobilizing a transcendental ego through its choice of conceptual systems to the schematized life-world where these values are satisfied. But, of course, we never get this ample description of a will-impelled ego. Why is this transcendental synthesis so rarely described?

One explanation is the embarrassment of too much candid talk about world-making: why tell how we do it if no one will believe it is done? There is also the consideration that questions about a value-driven mind are more prominently political and moral than metaphysical or epistemological. If transcendental egos are little gods, each claiming an inalienable right to create its own world, then each one's values are that ego's own business, with no one inclined to inquire too deeply into their origin or efficacy. Insisting on privacy and the right to a life-world adequate to our values, we turn discretely from the values and worlds of everyone else. Philosophy, too, is appropriately discrete: it goes mute at the place where these democratic assumptions are shared, with the result that self-declared pragmatists are excused from having to tell how value-driven egos create their self-fulfilling worlds.

Claims for world-making may have seemed well motivated. Impelled by skepticism about a world independent of thought, then by the aspiration that each of us be free to make a life of our own choosing, we have dared to accept total responsibility for everything that is done in the name of our values. Enthusiasm falters only when world-making commits us to that bizarre psycho-centric ontology which it presupposes. For who will speak in the name of the transcendental ego? How shall we characterize this agent upon whom all world-making depends? There is an extraordinary silence, but for Kant.

He alone tried to fill this space. The *Critique of Pure Reason* is careful
to provide, in the limited way that Kant thought possible, a characterization
of the functions performed by the transcendental ego. Unable to speak of
this schematizing subject in the terms used to describe the experiences it
makes, we are very circumscribed in the claims that might be made for it.
We say that "something" has used a conceptual system to schematize and
unify experience, though we cannot say a single word about this agent or the
manner of its operation. Rather like the lady who speculated "It's turtles all
the way down," we have little to say about the condition upon which world-
making depends. There is the more elaborate account supplied when Kant
described, in the *Critique of Practical Reason*, the free use of reason to shape
the will. Still, we never overcome the suspicion that an agent responsible for
making worlds from a position outside them is a curious agent indeed.

We get this divided view: worlds are made when conceptual systems
are used to schematize sensory data, sentences, or behaviors, though speculating about world-makers is illegitimate. Certainly those who favor world-
making avert every reference to its conditions: those inferences are illegitimate, or they create a mere "image." This attitude, a mixture of defiance
and defensiveness, is common to thinkers embarrassed by whatever is profli-
gate in their theories. Stop the argument is their response. Don't tell us our
commitments; ignore them, and they may go away. This doesn't happen,
because we already have Kant's explanation that his idealism, and theirs, is
founded on the postulation of an ego which uses conceptual systems to make
worlds.

It would be good to endorse Kantian world-making while avoiding
its ontological baggage, but that can't safely be done. One pays for this scrupulous agnosticism when every claim about world-making is left to hang in
the dialectical void. What is a world-making transcendental subject? How do
transcendental egos relate to their worlds and to one another? Talk about
world-making is incoherent and fragmentary without those transcendental
inferences or self-descriptions which characterize and explain the extraordinary powers claimed for these thinkers. Questions about it do not go away,
however vigorous the assertions that they cannot be asked.

The transcendental ego, without causal links to anything, acting
spontaneously outside space and time, is an unattractive ontological posit. Its
introduction might never have been considered were it not supposed that

this is the rendering in a finite mode of the properties sometimes claimed for God. Indeed, the idea of "world-making" is most revealing for implying our unashamed presumption to godhood: God is not dead if each of us can have a place within the kingdom of ends by making a world suited to him or herself. We may lather this fantasy with the romance that we are frontiers-men expelled from some finished world in order that we may create one of our own. We may search the environments we make for confirming evidence that we are gods. But where do we get the panoply of assumptions justifying this exalted view of ourselves? They are supplied by Kant (that experience is schematized by the transcendental ego), by Hegel (that the world known to members of a culture exhibits the Idea used to schematize it), and by Scho-penhauer (that will achieves immanence for the signature Idea of a world). Imitating God, we integrate knowledge and power in our world-making, act-ing all the while for high moral purpose. What purpose? Only, perhaps, the one of satisfying a personal or social attitude or desire.

All this is paradoxical on its face. It requires that we claim divine power, though we know both our finitude and the frustration of being stym-ied by a world we have not made. Recoiling from this absurdity, we ask if it is not a figurative way of expressing some less scandalous notion. Is "world-making" only a metaphor celebrating our autonomy and freedom? We do make cities and remake the countryside, all by way of creating an environ-ment congenial to us. There is, even, a moral argument for this figure of speech, as each of us has the right to a life-world fulfilling our aims.

Being friendly to democracy is easy for those who enjoy its benefits. But it does not follow that an ontology of world-making egos should be the price of our commitment. It is incidental that this be democracy as a political system or democracy as the recognition that each person's experience has an irreducible integrity and worth. Neither the politics, the morals, nor the psy-chology of democracy requires or encourages this baroque ontology. Having the one incurs no obligation for keeping the other.

VI Thought as Hypothesis

The idea of world-making requires the sustained confusion of two kinds of mental activity. One is the activity of constructing plans, then directing be-havior so that we may achieve whatever objective motivates us. The other is the activity of making and testing representations, better called *hypotheses*.

The idea of world-making exploits the first kind of thinking while sometimes acknowledging the second. But while it may acknowledge hypothesis, it understand hypotheses as plans or directives for construction. It ignores hypothesis as representation, declaring that representational thinking is not possible. We are to believe that there is no way of testing hypotheses against the things represented. For doing that would seem to require that we stand outside thought and language, the better to escape the mediating effects of perception, thought, and language as we compare representations to their objects. But of course, no one has that unmediated view of things, so verificationism alone should justify dispensing with the idea that hypotheses are representations. I shall be saying that hypotheses work well enough as representations, and that we know they do, despite this impediment.

Thought as hypothesis recalls Aristotle's threefold distinction between thinking, doing, and making. Thinking, in one of its expressions, is a way of representing possible or actual states of affairs, without making the things represented: thinking of Cairo is not my private way of affecting it. We also conceive and act on plans for realizing the possibilities that thought has represented; but this is construction, not hypothesis. It is a kind of *doing* that is instrumental to *making* the thing represented. Also relevant is Aristotle's claim that *knowing how* and *knowing that* are both expressions of reason. Knowing how is the capacity or qualification for doing something. Knowing that is the disposition for, or the act of thinking about, a state of affairs. Dispositions of both sorts, together with the acts for which they qualify us, may be localized within our minds or heads, so that thinking of both sorts is distinct from the overt behavioral doings and makings directed or informed by thought. Architects draw maps of the sites where buildings are to be constructed: that is representation. They also create detailed plans of prospective buildings: that is construction. Both sorts of thinking are different from the activity of using the plans to make the buildings.

No one has worked harder than Kant to eradicate the idea that thinking is representational. His first Critique is the principal source for the view that thought is only construction, never hypothesis. We think otherwise, because of having a mistaken conception of our own ideas. We suppose that thoughts and words are signs of things existing apart from them, though thoughts and sentences are not "about" anything and are never other or more than rules for organizing sensory data. Subsequent Kantians extend the list of things organized to include behaviors and symbols, but their point is the same: no extra-mental object is, or ever could be, represented by a thought or sentence because thoughts and sentences are either rules for organizing some content or the products of organizing rules. No wonder that nothing is represented: nothing in mind qualifies to be a representation when all thinking reduces to doing and making. What does thinking accomplish? We apply our rules (transcendental and empirical) to sensory data, symbols, or behaviors. What do we make? First, the rules (the empirical schemas), then the experiences schematized.

Someone wanting to argue with Kant and his successors must challenge this conflation of thinking with making, of hypothesis with construction. Let us do that in steps, starting with a plainer characterization of the difference between them.

Hypothesis is the activity of proposing that states of affairs did, do, or will have the characteristics ascribed to them by our thoughts or sentences. The thoughts and sentences are representations of these putative matters of fact. 'There are crows in the corn' is a sentence of this hypothetical, representational kind. The individual words satisfy semantic and syntactic conventions, as 'crow' might have signified alligators rather than crows. The words together are a well-formed sentence, though here, too, the grammatical criteria for well-formedness are conventions that vary among languages.

The existence and character of the states of affairs represented are independent of the conventional signs (thoughts or sentences) used to represent them. This is apparent when sentences uttered in Mandarin or an African click language have little in common with a sentence in English, though all three affirm that the speaker's feet hurt. Granted that speakers fluent in one language only cannot confirm this identity of reference. Granted that the relevant word or sentence in one language may have a greater range of signification (e.g., it links pain to the weather) than the words in the other two. These are difficulties for communication and translation; but they are incidental here, where representation is the only point of contention. Differences among signifiers, like differences among the things signified, are no bar to representation.

Suppose that one or more sentences (from the same or different languages) represent a possible state of affairs. What condition need be satisfied in order that these sentences be true? A sentence is true, I propose, if the possibility signified is instantiated:[29] "There are crows about" is true if and only if there are crows about. The sentence is true or not, irrespective of our interests or desires. Nor is any sentence or thought barred from truth merely because the possibility represented is inimical to us; no prospective benefits can make a false sentence true. The suitor of James's vignette declares that he shall be loved, then acts accordingly. Yet, it may have been true that the woman he favored did not love him at the moment of his declaration. His ardor changes her mind; but not that painful truth.

Hypothesizing thought is impotent at the very moment of its greatest risk. Nothing is committed when we mull the possibilities, taking care not to choose among them. We risk error and foolishness only as we affirm that one or another possibility obtains. For mind, at this speculative moment, is powerless to assure that the possibility represented is, was, or will be instantiated. Certainly, there are things we may do to alter the circumstances in ways that would make a false sentence true. But that is separate from the act of hypothesis: we make ourselves responsible for the hypothesis we declare, even though we have no control at that instant over the states of affairs that need to obtain if the hypothesis is to be true. This is so, even when I who make the hypothesis set out concurrently to realize the possibility signified (e.g., by raising my hand when I have predicted that I shall do so). I might always fail to do the thing predicted; and anyway, doing it is different and separable from representing it. Only in special cases does it happen that thinking hypothetically creates its own truth conditions, as saying "They may riot" may *later* cause a riot. Certainly no one creates the laws of motion by wishing that nature would be organized so economically.

Hypothesis is different from construction in just this respect: the one represents, the other (*thought, not only behavior*) creates its objects. Thought as constructive invents tunes and mathematical proofs; it designs buildings, constitutions, recipes, and contracts. These things may be written down or merely imagined. Either way, construction is accomplished by assembling parts (e.g., words or ideas) which may or may not have been created for their place within these conceptual structures. Constructions often serve as models or directives for other things that might be made, as cakes are baked and houses built using recipes and architects' drawings. These subsequent acts of direction or construction are, nevertheless, incidental here, because they require that thought be turned to action, though our focus is thought itself.

The only issue before us is the one of distinguishing representational from constructive acts of thought and language. Only the making, not the implementation, of laws, designs, agreements, and plans concerns us now.

The difference between hypothesis and construction (always as they occur within thought or language) may seem fragile and easily compromised. This is because every representation is constructed: we make the sentence before construing it as a representation. This is a further complication of Aristotle's threefold distinction, for every act of representation presupposes both a doing and a making, hence a constructive act of thought. We assemble the parts of a thought or sentence (a making) before or while construing the thought or sentence as a sign (a doing).

Why not say that there is a single generic activity having these two steps? We make conceptual structures; and they are subsequently used, within thought or beyond it. Some are used as directives to action; others are construed as representations (by locating them within networks of associations, not by taking them up as the objects of mental lights). Both representations and directives are constructed at the first step, the difference between them arising only because of the use made of them at the second step. Isn't this the more accurate way of formulating the issue, at no cost to the point that some conceptual structures are used to represent possible or actual states of affairs?

I concede, but ignore, this simplification. Hypotheses are made; that is agreed. Parts are assembled, and the whole is construed as the sign of a possible state of affairs. We nevertheless risk losing the point at issue if we describe thought comprehensively and essentially as a kind of making: representing will again be absorbed into construction. Averting this result is important, because Kant was mistaken: some thought structures are rules used for organizing phenomena or behaviors; others are used as signs.

VII Distinguishing Hypothesis from Construction

Someone committed to the idea of world-making is likely to resist the notion that thought is ever representational. There is nothing separate from us to be represented if all reality is made by our thinking it. More cautiously, why acknowledge mental representation when there is no way of slipping outside thought or language to compare our representations with their objects? It is pointless to speak of signs if we cannot track their objects in ways establishing that conceptual or linguistic structures bear some systematic relation to the things represented. The one objection denies reality to anything that is not set before our inspecting minds. The other despairs that we cannot establish the relatedness of signs and their objects if the application of truth-claims is not limited to the domain of things present within our life-worlds. There may be no way of turning idealists into realists; someone convinced that reality is created by a self-sufficient world-spinning mind will not gladly acknowledge a natural world in which we participate as natural creatures. The merely despairing skeptic is reformable, however. He or she may be convinced that representation is possible and testable.

Suppose that we are free-market ideologists hired to change some aspect of a society from its bad, old ways to ways we recommend. Like building contractors with an architect's blueprint and detailed buildings plans, we know what to do and how to do it. There comes a time, after we have started, for asking about our progress. Is the building made to specifications? Has the economy been reorganized in the ways specified by our plan? It is too late now to invoke "the will to believe" or the values directing thought and action. Is the job well done or not? Does the altered reality satisfy the plans used to create it? These are questions of fact, not merely of value, though we may value both the answers and the state of affairs represented.

Consider, too, this altered example. A free-market economist discovers our newly created market and asks (while knowing nothing of this market's history) if his hypotheses about free markets are confirmed by this economy. Those hypotheses are, by chance, the very ones used by the contractors who established this market, though the visiting economist does not know this. Nor does he care, for this man is a scientist, not an ideologist. He is a hypothesizer, not a social engineer. He does not want to make or remake things. The man is naive: he doesn't know that social realities are made as often as they are discovered. He wants to confirm only that markets work as he speculates they do. He formulates his hypotheses carefully, revising or replacing them until he is convinced that his claims are true of the matters that concern him. This interest in the accurate representation of economies is, of course, a value. It drives this thinker to study economies, not to make them.

Could it happen that Jamesian pragmatists confuse mind's activity in making hypotheses with its force in making economies, raising children, or writing poetry? There is a degree of similarity between hypothesis and construction. Hypotheses themselves are constructed, as mind makes signs for representing putative matters of fact. Makers of both are motivated by values, just as farmers speculate about the identify of birds on a fence because of wanting to protect the corn. We remark these similarities without ignoring salient features distinguishing constructions from hypotheses. Sentences, as much as designs, are made; but nothing in the use of sentences entails that sign-making creates the states of affairs that make sentences true or false. Thought does sometimes complete itself in a performance, as when we prove a mathematical theorem or imagine a tune and enjoy the imagining. Hypothesis is different, because thought alone is powerless to complete the representational relationship. We may daydream, this savor of exotic places and deeds being all we need of them. We cannot equally establish our self-sufficiency by representing a possibility. Being a millionaire is a possible state of affairs, though hypothesizing that I am a millionaire does not make me rich. The world has to cooperate; something there (something other than thought) must create the actual state of affairs that would make the hypothesis true. Hypothesis is speculation. We propose that the world is as we represent it, though often it is not.

Construction controls its products as hypothesis never controls the states of affairs represented. Idealists are closet skeptics; they fear losing touch with the world. Certainty or control are for them the measure of their contact with the world, hence the evidence of their security. Let Descartes be our example. Certainty was evidence to him that mind's grasp of its subject matters is complete. Nothing was to be unavailable for inspection; nothing was to mediate between mind and those contents. Control is the analogous virtue, because total control implies that mind is answerable to nothing but itself. Total control in making its life-world is, therefore, the measure of a mind's autonomy. This is mind as world-maker, our human minds as gods. Kant makes this idea credible to some idealists by supposing that mind might make experience, hence the only world known to us. Jamesian pragmatists reproduce this inclination, though not the detailed argument to support it. Hypothesis is dangerous, because it cannot guarantee to Kant or James that mind achieves contact with the world by correctly representing the things present in it. This explains the assimilation of hypothesis to construction: we redescribe hypothesis as the plan directing activity—that is, as the schema differentiating and organizing some content. Don't risk speculating about

things whose character and existence you cannot guarantee, if you can make
and grasp the thing itself.

My claim—that thinking is sometimes hypothetical and representational—violates this conservative instinct. But is my proposal even thinkable?
Can we justify replacing the Kantian view that ideas are rules for schematizing sensory data, symbols, or behaviors with the alternative view that thoughts
and sentences are signs representing, but not creating, their referents?

An argument for this realist, representationalist alternative is proposed
in my *Eternal Possibilities* and *Hypothesis and the Spiral of Reflection*.[30] The argument makes several claims. Ideas (e.g., thoughts, words, and sentences), it
says, are not merely rules for organizing some content; they are signs having
objects whose existence and character are independent of thought and language. The objects of our signs are, in the first instance, simple and complex
properties existing as possibles. Thoughts and sentences are true when the
possibilities they signify are instantiated. These instantiated possibilities are
states of affairs in space and time. Making a sensible difference, they are
perceived. Accordingly, our access to the world is secure: eternal possibilities
are the referents of our signs; instantiated possibles supply both truth conditions for our thoughts and sentences and sensory effects to confirm our
predictions about things in space and time. One might, of course, prefer a
physicalist realism, without the backdrop of eternal, logical possibilities. Either
way, we have an alternative to Kantian idealism, one that promotes hypothesis, rather than construction, as the basis for our knowledge of things.

It is less mysterious now that maps and plans should be effective or
not, according as they represent or misrepresent our circumstances. Indeed,
maps and plans are prototypic representations. Maps represent spatial and
sometimes temporal relationships. Plans represent functional—usually causal—
relations. Where the truth of maps and plans is unaffected by values, so is
truth free of values when the representations at issue are the sentences or
theories of science or metaphysics. There are, of course, some differences
between theories and maps or plans. Scientific theories may be probabilistic
as maps and plans are not; maps and plans may represent particular things
and relations, whereas the sentences of a theory are typically general in their
application. These are tendencies, however, not rigid differences, as there
are scientists who study the Moon or the singularity from which our cosmos
was generated. More critical than any difference among these representations

is the fact that scientific or metaphysical representations may apply to things in just the literal way promised by cookbooks which say that their recipes specify instrumental relations repeatable at home. Bad theories misrepresent the variables and relations pertinent to a domain, just as cookbooks are deficient if they misrepresent the procedures for making bread.

I suppose that one or the other of the realist theories sketched above (one assuming eternal possibilities, the other not) is required for explaining thought's efficacy as it directs the behaviors which secure and enhance our lives. For why does it happen that some maps and plans work when others do not? One reason for ineffective maps and plans is their logical inconsistency or incoherence: they prescribe that we should and should not do the same thing or should do in sequence things that are anomalous. It might also happen that a plan calls for instrumental relations that violate some law of nature, or that a map and a plan are mismatched, as when the plan requires instrumental relations not applicable in the domain of the map. Some maps and plans fail for these reasons. Many more are defective because they misrepresent salient features of the world. Misrepresent the terrain where action is to be performed or the instrumental relations obtaining there, and action is confounded. We are hamstrung, or lost.

Suppose that we withdraw from our defeat, asking this more detached question: how should be explain the notion of *misrepresentation*, as when maps and plans fail because they misrepresent either a terrain or the instrumental relations that might obtain there? Those who speak for world-making cannot explain it. For why should anyone acquiesce to circumstances that resist him? A logically consistent plan should be, on the Kantian telling, one that we can use to make a world congenial to our desires. If there is no other mind and will to frustrate us—and it is not plain how other wills could intrude on the world-making Kant describes—then there should be no obstacle to making the world prefigured in a logically consistent plan. Every consistent plan should work, as does not happen. What other explanation could there be for these failures of representation? We discount the possibility that there might be an arbitrary, evil demon who frustrates our world-making in ways that are obscure and unpredictable. What is left to explain it?

Only this: plans go wrong when they or the maps coupled to them misrepresent the relevant instrumental relations or terrain. Plans express our desires; but maps and plans are also hypotheses about our circumstances. When the hypotheses are mistaken, maps and plans misdirect us. This is an error in our representations, not a failure of our world-making. We recall this difference among the things made by thinking mind: sometimes control is total because mind makes, then uses, some thing (e.g., a rule); at other times control is imperfect, as when mind uses hypotheses to represent states of affairs it has not made. Fantasy is a pleasure and a relief, because we turn our backs on things we cannot change. But no one lives all the time in a dream. All of us are obliged to do those things which effectively secure and satisfy us. We acknowledge the difference between thoughts unencumbered by their relevance to our circumstances and the maps and plans representing those situations.

James has fudged the difference between thinkings that establish control of a content and its functions and makings which require the cooperation of a world we can never dominate altogether. He sometimes agrees that the world has a form of its own, one that resists us. This is, he concedes, a world that scientists know by way of the hypotheses representing it. But James also dotes on the stubborn lover and implies the malleability of all things. His successors are more careless than he was. They never concede that there might be something to confound our world-making. Anything that might frustrate it would exist in the awful "Beyond." But that place is a realist myth, so there should be nothing "out there" to limit our power. Imagination should be free to construct whatever worlds satisfy us. The good democratic politics obtaining throughout the kingdom of ends should guarantee that every mind is free to live within the world of its choice.

Which is the better explanation, the one invoking fallible hypotheses or the one exalting our powers for world-making? Surely, the evidence important to answering this question includes the fact that plan-directed behaviors are frequently stymied. Kant, James, and their successors cannot explain these occasions, except perhaps as failures of will or as consequences of disguised contradictions in schematizing conceptual systems. The idea that representations are powerless to create their referents is, by comparison, a successful explanation: error, frustration, and defeat are exactly what one would expect if maps and plans misrepresent our circumstances. Pianists cannot use a score which requires that they play six octaves above and below middle C. Builders want to know the geological features of a site and the load-bearing properties of their heavy steel before working to an architect's designs. They, and all the rest of us, may resist doing anything until we have evidence that our maps and plans are appropriate to our circumstances.

World-making is a romantic conceit. The prudence learned in failure guarantees that no one hopes to exploit it, however much it appeals to skeptical epistemologists. Can we nevertheless save the appearance of world-making by displacing it from minds to cultures? For culture is mind turned inside out. It enfolds us within itself, showing us a world by teaching us to think and act in the formulaic ways it prescribes. We discover artifacts and behaviors and learn to differentiate, value, and integrate them by our understanding of their significance for us. We dwell within the worlds that cultures create, transparent to one another, but alien or invisible to everyone else. Foreigners are shocked by us until they learn our practices, even to the point of being swallowed and remade by them. Culture is no fantasy. It exists apart from us, though we help to make and sustain it. Within it is the mix of construction and accommodation required for anyone hoping to save the idea of world-making.

Let us agree that cultures are complex, stylized accommodations to the world, that the look and feel of life differ among cultures, and that culture cures our isolation by teaching us an identity that is intelligible to other people. Consider, too, that *knowing how* requires *knowing that* as its complement. Do clothes vary from culture to culture? Then surely, all of them are appropriate to the bodies of human beings, not dragons or fish. Are local habits suited to a people who live by fishing not farming, commerce not mining? Is it aspirin or angel dust that cures their headaches? Foreigners observing a culture may ignore the reality-testing hypotheses and behaviors implied by these questions. It may be only the dances and songs that excite them. But no culture survives for more than a generation if its members ignore the character of those things it has not made and cannot change. Too crude an emphasis on the constructivist side of thought, joined to skepticism about the hypothetical mode, gambles that a culture will survive its incompetence. But only novelists can save the characters of a story by making the circumstances congenial to their interests. Waking up in a book, we find the world remade to suit our every desire. Life is not that sort of novel. No one, idealist reveries apart, fails to distinguish the fantasies we make from the facts we suffer. Grit and desire (James) allied to action may overcome some of the obstacles before us; *différance* (Derrida), alternative linguistic frameworks (Carnap and Quine), story-telling (Rorty), or theory-spinning (Putnam) never, by themselves, do as much.

VIII Hypotheses are Conventional Signs

How shall we respond to the objection that every map and plan is replete
with values, because the choice of things represented, the objectives for action, and the means chosen for achieving them are value-determined? The
point is conceded, but extraneous, because the question of truth is different.
Does this or any other map or plan represent the pertinent terrain or instrumental relations obtaining in this part of the world? We grant the conventionality of our signs, their stylistic idiosyncrasies, and the fact that representation is selective (only some things being represented). None of this distracts
us from the question at issue: do matters stand as we say they do? If 'dog'
might have been used where 'cat' is used, and vice versa, it remains the case
that we use them in familiar ways, so that someone saying "Dog!" of the
creature now baring its teeth is right or wrong.

It is irrelevant to this standard of rightness that someone may read
the conventional signs in which maps and plans are written or uttered in
some nonstandard way. Their truth-bearing character is not altered if, for
example, we read a New York subway map as though it represents the Paris
metro. Such a reading would be complicated; but there is, in principle, no
reason why one couldn't successfully use the New York map in Paris. With
"Grand Central Station" signifying Montparnasse, "Grand Street" signifying
Odéon, and so on throughout the system, we could use the one as a map of
the other, never affecting the question of truth: do the several lines and
stations stand to one another and the rest of the city in the ways schematized
by the map as we read it? Either map may be more or less accurate as it
represents the several lines. Small curves and sidings may be ignored in both
maps. Still, we use maps to supply information about the systems represented. This information is correct or not. If my reading of a map requires
that there be a station where none exists, then this map on my reading is
mistaken. It doesn't matter that dozens of people read the map as I do, or
that all our readings are conditioned by the fact that there was a station in
the place where none is present now. The map is mistaken: the statements
that express our reading are false.

We may be annoyed by a bad map, one that systematically misleads
us under a reading that is standard and appropriate to our circumstances.
We are careful that truth is not overwhelmed by our interest in its consequences. Alchemy and cold fusion promise results that all of us favor; but we

distinguish their truth from these benefits, investigating the one, while deferring the other. We do not hope to create the facts that would support our desires merely by choosing predicates, grammatical forms, and inductive rules sufficient to make truths. This may be all that a novelist requires for contriving his or her illusions; but where are the engineers willing to affirm that alchemy and cold fusion are or might be verified merely by tinkering with conceptual systems? Surely, the alchemists would have had no patience for this conceptual legerdemain. It was usually clear to them that hypothesis alone, however careful, does not make theories true of the states of affairs they represent. This is because hypotheses signify possibilities which may or may not be instantiated. The speculations are true if the possibilities are instantiated, false if not.

There is only this exceptional case: hypotheses never create their own truth conditions apart from trivial self-reflexive cases, as when the hypothesis "I can make a sentence" is its own truth condition. The rest of being is not so easily invoked.

IX Hypotheses Motivated by Values

How should we settle the dispute between those who argue that every truth-claim is suffused with value and those who demur? By agreeing that attitudes or desires invariably motivate us when we hypothesize about the possibilities instantiated within and about us, then by adding that some hypotheses — that the first note of a piece is C♯ do seem to be stripped clean of motivating values.

We may weight our language with emotive baggage, favoring some things, scorning others. The first, we say, are "graceful," "reliable," "sincere." The others are "clumsy," "foolish," "dumb." These biases may sometimes disable us for distinguishing the evaluative from the narrowly representational content of a thought or sentence. And of course, some egregious examples of bias may go unexamined for centuries, some of them introduced, then covered over, by the eddies of social, scientific, and religious change. We are never far from the discovery of one or another previously unsuspected bias; but how many others twist our thinking?

These discoveries sometimes have only the effect of substituting a new distortion for an old one. At other times, we purge our talk of values, taking care to use only words that are value-free. Mathematical language is exemplary in this respect. If 'large' and 'small' may be value-laden, 'one' and 'ten' need not be, and usually are not. There are other advantages to mathematical representations; but it is no small advantage that its words cannot easily be made to seem value-laden. For there is always this simple question averting attention from whatever values motivate us: do matters stand as a hypothesis affirms? Is the hypothesis true or false?

One imagines a critic saying that the road to hell is paved with good intentions. For what is the point of eliminating some value-distorting nuances from language if our ways of using words are always warped by values, conscious or not. Isn't our situation reminiscent of the one Berkeley described when he argued that nothing but an idea is like another idea. Similarly, nothing but a different value can free us from some previous thought-distorting value. We never confront the things themselves (Berkeley) or sanitize thought or language so that all our representational vocabulary and rules become value-free (these critics).

We express this same point in another way of recalling the two sorts of regulative values, final and instrumental. Suppose that it is truth as correspondence which is the final value for inquiry. Inquiry, we say, formulates and tests hypotheses about a reality whose existence and character are independent of our hypotheses. Other regulative values are instrumental to this aim. Some are motivating: they are desires and attitudes driving and directing inquiry. Other instrumental values discipline the inquiry: inquirers should deal honestly with one another; experiments should be repeatable, and information shared. These values critical for the success of inquiry are indifferent to particular motivating values. But we do need discipline and incentive as we formulate and test hypotheses. Where material truth is our aim and empirical inquiry our way of getting it, these two are its practical conditions.

Now step back from this analysis to observe that appealing to this ensemble of intrinsic and instrumental values is, itself, a regulative idea. It is a hypothesis about values, one that prescribes the framework within which we are to understand the role of value as it determines the conduct of inquiry. Notice too the tensions within this model of inquiry: one side commits us to formulating hypotheses which are true of a world they represent but do not make; the other acknowledges that the thoughts or words used for expressing hypotheses are sponsored by attitudes or desires. There is no question to answer, hence no responding hypothesis, in the absence of these motivators. They determine the objective for inquiry and even its conduct.

We may grant that inquiry's aim is a value-neutral characterization of things. Still, there is no chance of stripping our hypotheses of value-distorted words. For how could value be incidental to inquiry when it is desires or attitudes which determine both the objective for inquiry and the words appropriate to its hypotheses? Every hypothesis is co-opted and tainted when a motivating attitude or desire determines the choice of its constituent thoughts or words. Every word stripped of some previous distortion is rightly suspected of a new, perhaps currently invisible, bias. Witness the features of language accepted as neutral in the past but now rejected for what they express of attitudes to race or gender.[31] Is there any defense against this corruption of our hypotheses? Four come to mind.

First is our sensitivity to the idea that thoughts and words may be distorted by a personal or social interest, as when children describe a brother or sister's behavior. Most important to this self-scrutiny are cases where distortions are apparent to no one, because the values motivating their use are so nearly universal and unexamined.

Second is the fact that we do have thoughts, words, and sentences — paradigmatically, mathematical ones — where value-impelled distortion is absent or more easily discerned and reduced. The misuse of statistics does not entail that number words or the rules for well-formed formulas are value-ridden. There is also the example of the physical sciences, whose vocabulary has been incrementally sanitized of its value-affected words and formulas. Anyone of the sciences may yet be shown to disguise a previously unsuspected bias, as medieval medicine explained mental pathology as the struggle of good and evil. There is no evidence, however, that any of these biases must remain invisible and unrevisable. Is 'considerate' a nominally descriptive word used plainly as a recommendation? Allay that charge by distinguishing this word's descriptive content from our favorable attitude to people who exhibit the behaviors specified.

Third is our response to the allegation that value-impelled discriminations are distorting because the thing signified is altered, because abstracted, if only in representation, from its circumstances. Holists warn us not to abstract anything from its context lest we mutilate it — though bodies are not much damaged for being measured and weighed, or heads by haircuts.

Is it true, fourth, that the language of our hypotheses is irremediably distorted by our aims? Having a cold, wanting hot tea, I boil water. Is the water boiling? It is, or it is not. Seeing the one or the other, I report accordingly. I may report this state of affairs with relief or impatience; but there is no obstacle in principle to distinguishing those value-loaded feelings from the words used to signify the state of affairs perceived. It often happens that we seem incapable of formulating a hypothesis that is neutral as regards our objective. But this is by no means a universal or necessary fact about representational language: laziness or intensity of feeling are enough to explain it. We dare to be flagrant in the words used to signify things remote from us; we learn to neuter the hypotheses important to our security and satisfaction. It is no good calling ketchup a vegetable in the name of feeding the undernourished if it has no food value.

These four considerations make a single point: hypotheses are not properly testable when overlaid by distorting biases. Realizing our bias, understanding that misdescription of our circumstances will not satisfy our interests, we find more neutral words. Nothing in this implies that we repudiate our attitudes and desires: only that we become sober and effective in their pursuit.

X Conclusion

We concede that thought and action are drenched in value. Thinking of every sort, hypothetical or constructive, expresses the perspectives and priorities that evolution, society, or personal interest establish in us. Value-free science, as much as value-free practice, is a delusion, because science, as much as practice, is always conducted from a perspective, with an interest. Still, all this is penumbral, not essential to the truth or falsity of hypotheses made in pursuit of an aim. We can and often do purge our deliberations of the values which motive them. Companies submitting bids on military contracts are specific in their proposals and scrupulously bland in their characterizations of efficiency. No one who makes bombs is oblivious to the uses made of them, though tests of a design are conducted without regard for those motivating values. This distinction is obligatory for anyone who cares that the bomb should work.

The context of experiment and confirmation is not perfectly sanitized: motivating values intrude there, as when the control so vital to mastering our circumstances is also critical for the experiments used to test hypotheses. This, however, is no basis for saying that the more specific values warping our ideas about nature, gender, economic class, or political power do, and must, intrude into the formulations and tests of every hypothesis. The most ardent stockholders in Alchemy, Inc., cannot make alchemy work merely by intruding their values into the experiments testing its claims. That hypotheses confirmed are used to satisfy someone's values, good or bad, is a different point.

James spoke for thought in its constructive mode. Enlivened by the pleasure of his initiatives, supported by the energies of his people and time, he insisted that we convert a determinable world to our purposes. This was forward-looking. Compare to it the time wasted when boring truths are tested for their correspondence to matters of fact. Confirmations of this sort would have been for James too much like sorting through dusty books to confirm an opinion. One imagines the Teddy Roosevelt of Emerson Hall, his impatience barely restrained. This edginess—his desire to get on with it—is harder to imagine in those contemporary thinkers who appropriate James. One doubts that any of them is devoted to building a continent or determined that raw America should be civilized by its thinkers and doers. James is invoked for his devotion to the Kantian idea that freedom is our *telos*. If God is dead, then we humans shall be gods, at least within the circle of individual conscious or social experience. James, not Peirce, is our favorite pragmatist only so long as this persuasion is not frustrated by a world we can pollute or improve but never make.

Chapter Three

I Spinoza on Desire

Why are so many of us persuaded that values shape our
beliefs, hence our worlds? Because everything we do to secure or satisfy ourselves propagates value into the world
around us. Value, not truth, is our efficient cause. Goading
or impelling us, it mediates all our relations to other people
and things. Think of Spinoza:

> *Desire* is the actual essence of man, in so far as it is
> conceived, as determined to a particular activity by
> some modification of itself.[1]

> By *good* I here mean every kind of pleasure, and all
> that conduces thereto, especially that which satisfies
> our longings, whatsoever they may be. By *evil*, I mean
> every kind of pain, especially that which frustrates
> our longings. For I have shown that we in no case
> desire a thing because we deem it good, but, con-
> trariwise, we deem a thing good because we desire
> it: consequently we deem evil that which we shrink
> from; everyone, therefore, according to his partic-
> ular emotions, judges or estimates what is good, what
> is bad, what is better, which is worse, lastly, what is
> best, and what is worst.[2]

The development and effects of valorizing desire are described in this chapter. I shall be exploiting these results
and their corollary: that value is always incidental to material truth. For if truths are formulated because of the interests propelling action, then confirmed under force of the

regulative values that discipline inquiry, none of this implies that truths or the states of affairs they represent are manufactured by the values directing action and injury.

II Truths Valued for their Efficacy

We humans are fragile creatures, vulnerable to the things about and within us. We alter these things to our advantage, or we accommodate ourselves to them. Is the sun too hot for bald heads? Is the kitchen floor too cold for bare feet? These are facts about us rooted in our animal nature and our circumstances. Truth is vital to us, but vital especially as we represent some aspect of the world to whatever degree of accuracy is required for securing and satisfying ourselves. Some few of us may dote on truths as others collect butterflies; but that is rare. Most of us never learn to enjoy truths for truth's sake; we value them for the efficacy of behavior directed by cogent truths. Well-being is our aim; truths are a prerequisite for getting it. I am supposing that action is more than physical behavior. Knees jerk when tapped by a hammer; hands draw back from hot stoves. These are neurological and muscular reactions, not actions. The difference is more than verbal, as spinal reflexes are different from the behaviors shaped and directed by attitudes and desires. These behaviors are paradigmatically intentional; they are launched and sustained in pursuit of an aim. My concern is the fact that actions are conceived and performed within a matrix of directing, constraining values.

Height and gait qualify us, but so does a learned, idiosyncratic valuational stance. Our attitudes, desires, feelings, principles, habits, and practices express this distinguishing posture. We may struggle to identify and control particular attitudes and desires. But more often, we are moved along, bent, and directed by our distinguishing ensemble of values. Like shipwrights changing plates or planks on a ship at sea, we employ some few values to change a different one, sometimes (though rarely) changing all of them. But this is a ship at sea; it is subject at every moment to wind and waves, responding to them in ways determined by the configuration of its parts. We do something analogous when values mediate our relations with other things, and even with ourselves. Heidegger makes a similar point when he argues that "ready-to-hand" is prior to "present-at-hand."[3] We may repress utilitarian valuations for the sake of more detached reflection; but this disengaged curiosity is usually cultivated only where we are safe to indulge it, as happens when we listen to music or read books. Otherwise, valuation is the first expression of reactive alarm. What is going on? What is the safe, securing, appropriate response for me or us?

Why and how do we acquire this tangled, constraining network of values? Later on, out of concern for the possibility of altering values, we shall want to ask if values are separable from one another (like sentences distinguished by their truth conditions) or mutually defining (like the inter-animating sentences of a theory). Just now, it is only the prior questions that occupy us. What are values? Why are we obliged to have them?

III The Objective and Subjective Bases for Value

Values are either created by our appraisals or founded in things themselves. Objective values of an intrinsic sort, as Milton's poems are said to be good in themselves, are moot and not at issue here. Instrumental values are also incidental, though the evidence for their objectivity is conceded. Education is good for people who work better because of having had it; polluted air is bad for every creature that breathes it. These things having utility occur naturally; or they are created for the good or bad they do. There is a point to saying that these utilities are objective: they exist in the relations of things independent of any interest or thought of ours. This sets utilities founded in the instrumental values of things apart from the values originating, subjectively, in our appraisals.

This difference between subjectivity and objectivity, between things happening within thought or consciousness and those standing apart from us, is nevertheless misleading if we infer that 'objectivity' can have no other sense. For it does have a common, but different, sense that is useful here. The valuings important to this chapter are rooted in our nature as sentient creatures, hence in the ways that we relate to our circumstances. They might be described as subjective, because of having their inception in us, especially as we feel, think about, and react to our circumstances. There is, however, a certain objectivity, a fact of the matter, to our valuings. Examine these attitudes and desires, and we discover something fundamental about the character of our engagement in the world.

The values that concern us here are only those having their inception in our valuings. These are of two sorts: *topical* (I shall also describe them as objects of interest, hence as *interested*) and *normative*, as when I prefer coffee to tea just now, always drinking my coffee black. Normative values are typically expressed as attitudes, principles, habits, and practices. Thoughts, feelings, and desires can be the expressions of either topical or normative values. This taxonomy of intrapsychic differences is sometimes less important than the acknowledgment that valuings of either sort are appraisals of our circumstances or ourselves. For each person has opinions about the pertinent, effective, good, or bad thing to do at any moment. Attitudes and feelings are favorable or opposed; thought and habit determine that we should effect the result preferred among all that are possible. Each of these postures takes the measure of some activity or thing. Each one is a judgment or perspective on what is more or less important, good or bad.

Is there any mental activity that is not valorizing, whether topically or normatively? There are not many. The retinal excitement caused by a flash of lightning is one of those exceptions, because its visual effects dissipate before we can attend to their cause. Many other unexpected effects linger. Attending to them is an expression of topical interest, hence of value: this is important to me, we imply. Both hypothesis and construction, on this telling, are valorizing: both are expressions of interest, however tepid.

Are some values slighted by this emphasis on attention, selection, and prescription—aesthetic values, for example? There is nothing odd about them if we suppose that ascriptions of beauty are findings or claims that there is a mix of properties, including proportion, contrast, diversity, and integration, in the objects or activities judged beautiful. The variables themselves are aesthetic virtues. They satisfy the rubrics of interest and normativity described above: we look for, and require, them in music, fiction, and dance. Logical values might also seem exempt from an analysis emphasizing valuation, as consistency and completeness do not depend on any perception of ours. This is correct if we think of these logical values as instruments on a par with rakes and hoes, as good for arguments as these implements are useful for gardening. Yet this cannot be the whole story about logical values, for we have still to explain their appropriation and use. Consistency, coherence, and completeness must be prized before they can be learned as norms for organizing and appraising thoughts and sentences. This first estimate is the judgment of their worth and the decision that they be applied.

Pleasure and pain are a test of this account, because their goodness and badness are thought to be intrinsic, hence unconditioned by attitudes or habits. But pleasures are not essentially good or pains essentially bad: the valuings of both are relative to the context of judgment. A diabetic may learn to dislike the pleasurable taste of sugar; someone told that pain will be the first evidence of his recovery from severe illness may, for a time, override the hurt by calling it a good. That pleasure is pleasurable and pain painful is not contested. Still, the goodness or badness of either one is a matter of judgment—that is, of interest and norms. There may be no value on the side of thought and action that is not the expression of an appraising, prescribing judgment.

IV Vulnerability and Security

Interest is shown and norms are applied as we solve a problem common to every living thing: namely, the opposition between vulnerability and security. Because our situation is precarious, we construct nested, interlinked defenses. We build houses to protect us from storms, then we organize fire departments and buy fire insurance. We secure ourselves from myriad threats in disparate ways, both individually and collectively; but then we risk forgetting that every response to threatening circumstances is only provisional, there being, usually, several or many effective substitutes. Where dancing propitiates our gods, we embellish the costumes and steps, telling myths about the beauty and strength of revered dancers. Dancing becomes the special province of a cult, with access reserved to people of special status. Derivative values attach to the social behaviors and organizations thought to secure us, though any connection between these activities and their original purpose is obscured. Having come to value dance as a good in itself, we forget that singing or praying would do as well. Only let some disaster break upon us, and these embellishments are ignored. We demand that our dancers save us. No more indulgences if they do not.

Suppose that vulnerability and security define our choices. How do we respond? How is value founded in the diversity of our responses?

V Submission and Control: Self-Sufficiency and Dependence

Each of us learns to cope in ways that are idiosyncratic, but stable for him or her. We position ourselves in thought, action, and feeling somewhere along two independent axes. One axis has submission and control as the alternatives for action: we submit to the flood, letting it carry us away, or we resist the tide, struggling to save ourselves by this exercise of self-determination. The other axis is that of self-sufficiency and dependence: we respond to a vulnerability by taking up a position of more or less self-sufficiency, less or more dependence.

These two axes may seem parallel to the point of being indistinguishable, as when someone is self-sufficient and controlling or submissive and dependent. This happens when a relationship turns on rejection or the fear of it: one party is self-sufficient and controlling, while the other fears rejection to the point of turning submissive and dependent. We are less likely to confuse the two axes when we notice that the frequency of their convergence expresses the intensity of our concern for those social relations where this doubling occurs. We prize the axes apart by noting the many cases in which the relation of the axes is reversed, as when control of our circumstances is achieved by co-ordinating our behaviors, thereby creating mutual dependence.

The difference between the axes is also obscured because the options they present are decided at once, not separately. Faced with a bear, I stare him down or run. There is control or submission, but also self-sufficiency or dependence: I confront him alone or with the support of a dog and a gun. My response expresses this amalgam of considerations, so that some degree of abstraction is required when the axes are characterized separately. But they are not separable, merely distinguishable: no one who is subject to the option of self-sufficiency or dependence is not also self-directing or submissive.

We take up positions along both axes as we act to reduce vulnerability by enhancing security. We also want something more than security: namely, satisfaction and well-being. But these are additional, sometimes extravagant demands. We simplify the issue by ignoring satisfaction and well-being until later. Security is the more fundamental interest. It is the most to be hoped for and sought by people in bleak circumstances. It is never less than a first priority for all of us, as people doing perilous things take care to protect themselves.

The two axes differ as regards the accommodations they prefigure. Submission and control are alternatives throughout the range of possible accommodations to a situation; we control our circumstances or submit to them. Control is appropriate when driving a car, but submission is the better policy for someone stopped in traffic. Why this shift? Because the risk has changed.

The threat of a crash is superseded by that of apoplexy. Here, as in many cases, submission and control are strategies for enhancing security by reducing vulnerability.

Notice this ambiguity in the idea of *submission*. Submitting to the reality of a traffic jam is the better way of controlling one's frustration. This is a kind of self-control, hence the very opposite of the submissiveness opposed to self-control. Compare situations in which submission expresses the despair of having no power, no control. People who are sick, starved, or terrorized are submissive in this way. They concede having no way of reducing their vulnerability, no hope of securing themselves. Dependence and self-sufficiency, too, are strategies for reducing vulnerability, but with this difference: their range of application is narrower than that of the other axis. All the behaviors on this axis express the desire for control. This is confusing when dependence converges with submission, self-sufficiency with control. There are, however, some clarifying distinctions, starting with the following three kinds of dependence.

First are co-ordinated, mutually dependent behaviors, including team sports and bridge building. Dependence of this sort is plainly a style of control. Second is the control achieved when someone feigning weakness captures the sympathy and support of another whose power makes him or her useful to the manipulator. Dependencies of this kind may be more passive and nearly hopeless, as when someone in terrible need attaches him or herself to a possible savior. These are, nevertheless, dependencies having control as their aim: they are calculated, however feebly and desperately. Dependencies of the third sort are not calculated. They occur without the active desire of the one who is dependent, as someone unconscious is dependent on doctors and the machines sustaining him. This third kind of dependence is not relevant here, where the question concerns the strategies that each of us undertakes to reduce vulnerability and enhance security. (The dependence of the unconscious victim is not so much undertaken as it is enforced.) We do of course go voluntarily into surgical procedures that will make us dependent in this third way; but that is the consequence of a decision expressing our control. It is not the helpless dependence caused by an accident. Only the first two kinds of dependence concern us. They, with self-sufficiency, are tactics serving the strategic interest of control. There is, accordingly, this simple schematic relation among the strategies for reducing our vulnerability: we submit to our circumstances, wanting a favorable outcome while fearing something less; or we try to control a situation, either by mastering it ourselves or by co-ordinating our efforts with those of other people.

Consider again the person who is either self-sufficient and controlling or dependent and submissive. He or she struggles to reduce vulnerability by way of self-sufficiency or mutual dependence. Hunters typically do the one, coal miners the other. Calculated submissiveness has this same effect: we reduce our vulnerability by going along with a mob or tide that would be much more dangerous were we to resist it. There are also religious people who are submissive to their God. They are not craven. They believe that submitting to God is an affirmation: they say that every human power must bend before the greater power and right of their God. This too is an expression of control; one gets the drift of things before calculating the behavior that is least risky. Now compare these last-mentioned expressions of submission and dependence with the submissiveness of a people inured to poverty and disease. They are submissive and, when someone offers help, despairingly or stoically dependent. This is submissiveness or dependence in circumstances where there is no hope of control.

It is plainer now that the dominant axis, control and submission, defines the range of alternative strategies for empowerment in the struggle to reduce vulnerability. We redescribe this dominant axis, saying that power and the lack of it are synonymous with control and submissiveness. Each of us has habits or resources that locate us somewhere along this axis, first as regards situations of specific kinds, then in some more global, aggregate sense. We are ineffective in situations of particular kinds, though more often we control circumstances to our advantage; or we are typically inept, but surprisingly capable in situations of one or a few kinds. Each of these constellations locates us somewhere along this axis of empowerment. We are more or less capable of securing and satisfying ourselves, though we can never be as safe as we might like to be. We struggle or submit, sometimes conceding that nothing we do will save us. The cost of our vulnerability may be slight, as it is if we submit to drenching rain; or it may be catastrophic, as happens to civilians in war and to everyone in a famine. Some of us are powerless most of the time; all of us are powerless some of the time.

VI Cognitive-Affective Balance

Each of us locates him or herself along these two axes as we cope more or less effectively with the circumstances about us. We learn behaviors and acquire habits that express a bent toward submission or control. We strike some balance on the side of control between self-sufficiency and dependence. Successive failures disrupt our tentative adaptations, pushing us toward greater passivity or greater initiative. Submissive in one sector, we learn to be controlling in another. Sometimes wanting to ignore our circumstances, we are obliged to consider them because of elementary interests and needs requiring satisfaction wherever we find ourselves. Each of us acquires a personal and characteristic style for satisfying our needs in the circumstances available to us. We are more controlling or more submissive, but never, we hope, merely passive, inert, and powerless. The development and plasticity of this style differ from person to person, but this is the intrapsychic, behavioral fingerprint that differentiates us.[4]

This set of distinguishing habits and practices has several constituents. First are the behaviors which exhibit our submissiveness or control, our self-sufficiency or dependence. Second, and less visibly, are intrapsychic cognitive behaviors and feelings. One's thinking may be conservative or bold, confused or coherent, simple or complex. Or thinking, whether hypothetical or constructive, may be daring and precise in one sector, predictable and confused in some others. These intrapsychic cognitive behaviors are charged with feeling. Fear dominates when the conduct sponsored by plans is usually frustrated; optimism when conduct is usually successful. Feelings, as much as needs or desires, count among the things that motivate us, even to the point of impelling well-organized, sustained behavior, as one may be driven by anger or fear. These feelings are themselves the more or less confused judgments of our earlier initiatives and prospects; more accurately, perhaps, they are reactions to those judgments. The judgments may pass unnoticed, or they may be buried out of reach of consciousness. The feelings, insofar as we have access to them, express these judgments by reacting to the facts they acknowledge. This has a curious effect. We expect that incompetent planning will be altered so that we might respond more effectively to our circumstances. An excess of feeling may, however, provoke the contrary result: we may be so rattled and anxious as to be incapable of revising either our intrapsychic cognitive behavior or the conduct it sponsors. Ineffectual before, we resist the changes that would make us more effective later. The plans we make and the manner of our planning are more inflexible and predictable as these feelings are more intense. We get the opposite effect when someone judges his or her behavior more favorably: optimism about the success of future initiatives makes him or her more flexible, hence better able to use new information or learn new skills. Optimism (but not grandiosity) is enabling, as anger and fear are (usually) incapacitating. Are we rigid and predictable or adaptable but steady? Feeling is both the symptom and the cause of being one or the other.

This mix of strategies, appraisals, and feelings has a corporate identity. Each of us establishes a balance on the side of submission or control, self-sufficiency or dependence. This posture, which I call a *cognitive-affective balance*, is an intrapsychic achievement.[5] It embodies the successive transformations that occur as an agent initiates behavior or responds to circumstances before reacting affectively to the judgment of success or failure. There are, of course, many sectors in which we may be simultaneously or successively engaged. Each one's posture is sensitive to some or many of these disparate situations.

This balance is a product and a power. It is the product of accommodations achieved across the range of situation to which the agent responds. It is a power for doing the things which stabilize and conserve this intrapsychic equilibrium. Why try to sustain it? Because this posture has become tolerably effective and familiar over the course of our developmental history. This is the only style we know. Our capacities and defenses are embodied within it. Here, too, is a fund of information about our circumstances and information pertinent to our interests, whether discovered and generic (e.g., social peace) or acquired and personal (e.g., stamp collecting). Our only freedoms are those prefigured by this balance. Acting in the ways it sanctions, we satisfy our needs in predictable circumstances we somewhat control; or we struggle to keep our footing in circumstances that were neither predicted nor desired. Accordingly, this balance is dynamic and defensive, never merely stable because inert. Change is possible in the midst of terrible failure or great success; but it is ever more rare as we move beyond pliable childhood into rigid middle age.

Calling this posture a *balance*, I do not mean to imply that all conflicts among the disparate sectors of our behaviors, thoughts, and feelings are resolved. No one has balance of that sort. Fully harmonized desires would soon be disrupted by circumstances in which one desire is satisfied at cost to the others. But worse, we never achieve even that temporary harmony. There is always competition among contrary interests (which cannot be simultaneously satisfied) or interests that are imperfectly evolved (hence uncertain as regards the circumstances that would satisfy them). There are also those assaults which occur when interests are ridiculed, squashed, or ignored by other people or one's circumstances. Irresolution, stunted growth, and conflict guarantee that a balance idealized is both a fiction and the mechanical rabbit pacing our developmental history from the moment when it turns self-conscious.

This compares to a working balance. One of these is achieved in early childhood by nearly everyone. This balance evolves. It incorporates interests, cognitive powers, information, obligations, and feelings never imagined by the child. Integrations are more complicated than before, inflections more subtle; stability is usually enhanced. Still, this is a working balance, not the perfect balance of synchronous parts. Frustration, anger, and impatience are symptoms that the balance is not perfect. These irritations measure the gap between desire, expectation, or demand on the one side and accommodating or controlling behavior on the other. How effectively do we master or accommodate our circumstances in the ways prescribed by our plans? How successfully do we resolve internal conflicts between our inclinations to security and risk? Development is scrappy and imperfect. Behavior, thought, and feeling are never joined harmoniously to one another and our circumstances. But we cope, suppressing feelings that would disrupt behaviors perceived as urgent, parceling out resources to competing and frustrated interests. We compromise, thereby securing a consistent, effective accommodation to our circumstances, invigorating and sustaining the wobbly gyroscope that defines us.

VII Pathologies

Are some postures normal, others pathological? That is so, if 'normal' means 'effective', not 'typical'. For then a posture is normal if someone having it can secure himself to some useful degree within his circumstances. This is a tolerant, not an empty standard, for there are adaptations which are perverse, not merely ineffective. Burning down the house in a cold winter is an example. Doing that is pathological, meaning conspicuously inappropriate to the situation, given all that one does or could be expected to know in the circumstances. This is a cognitive pathology: someone is unable to evaluate his or her situation correctly, to perceive danger, or plan to avert it.

There are also affective pathologies. Someone may be immobilized by chronic conflicts of desire and guilt or delight in taking risks to the point where life comes to depend on contingencies that are not planned (e.g., the haystack into which one falls after jumping heedlessly from a window). Other pathologies concern the equilibrium achieved when various interests and needs are made to square with one another. Some needs may be repressed, while others dominate our conscious thought, resources, and behavior. The needs repressed may be vital to well-being, so that their repression provokes emotional and cognitive, then physical disorder. Thinking ourselves fat, we give up eating, turn anorectic, and risk death. There is, finally, the development of this balance. It, too, can be a site for pathology, as when a child fails to learn from his or her initiatives that certain behaviors do or do not work for him or her. The child doesn't learn to cope, so that his accommodating behaviors become ever more feeble or frantic. Is this failure cognitive or affective? Is it a failure to perceive and interpret the results of action? Or is it the want of feelings appropriate to the risks taken and the success achieved? It could be either. Disorders of this fourth kind are consequent on one or more of the preceding three, though failures of integration are only discernible within the context where equilibrium is itself the point of reference.

Some of these disorders may be cured by reeducation; some others may be irreparable. But always the call for therapy must not be construed or justified as the demand for uniformity. Nothing in this survey supports the idea that there might be one right way to integrate the feelings, thoughts, and habits that direct or appraise our behavior. There are many different solutions to the task of securing and satisfying ourselves. Some of them are more effective than others. Some encourage greater reciprocity among people wanting to co-ordinate their behavior. But one is neither mad nor defective if one organizes one's life in ways that are hermitlike or unintelligible to people whose cognitive-affective postures are different.

My emphasis on cognition and affect is not meant to exclude other considerations—including culture, race, or gender—that might influence our developmental history. I assume that reality testing is everywhere a condition for survival, hence well-being. I speculate that a cognitive-affective balance is the more or less stable basis for each person's accommodations to his or her circumstances. But then each one's equilibrium is tinctured by the effects of engaging the world as a man or a woman, or as a person of a particular color or culture. These behaviors and the responses to them are incorporated in this evolving balance. This is so, paradigmatically of gender and sexuality, because they intensify our vulnerability while they promise well-being. Knowing our desires and fears while having strategies for controlling them (e.g., by satisfaction or repression) is manifestly one of the urgent tasks that fall to the cognitive-affective balance. It directs all the behaviors undertaken to satisfy or express us in our relations with other people and things. We should expect that pathologies relating to these particular factors—sexuality, for example—will conform to the fourfold rubric suggested above. There will be cognitive, affective, and developmental pathologies, together with those which turn upon some failure to achieve an effective equilibrium.

VIII Freudian Themes

Some Freudian themes are applicable here. What Freud called the "ego"[6] is close to the functional organization which I am describing as a cognitive-affective balance. Freud may be read simplistically as saying that the ego is a distinct agent who directs behavior after weighing the competing demands of passion and the social world of inhibiting laws. This way of entifying the ego, perhaps on the model of Descartes' *cogito*, is, however, implausible and unnecessary. It seems more likely that the ego is an internal, empowering equilibrium that reconciles the demands of passion and the external world on the way to securing and satisfying us. Freud would probably agree. Still, he was too much preoccupied with sexual development, too little concerned with our global interest in reducing vulnerability by enhancing security. We are vulnerable in many ways: sexuality is only one. Blindness, dyslexia, superior agility or intelligence may be equally critical for the development of a cognitive-affective balance.

Freud also described some other considerations vital to the achievement of a working balance. They include mechanisms like repression, frustration, the sublimation of desires too dangerous to express, the mutual determination of conscious and unconscious mental processes, and the opposition of animating passions to the thinking which controls their expression. Each is significant for the development or application of a cognitive-affective balance. All five are engaged when the economy of an effective balance requires repression of a conscious desire, as happens if we believe that the actions provoked by a desire would be dangerous to ourselves or other things.[7]

IX Differences and Affinities among Cognitive-Affective Balances

I have been emphasizing that each person achieves a cognitive-affective balance that is unique to him or herself. (I assume that differences of temperament, developmental history, and current circumstances make it overwhelmingly likely that there will be myriad expressions of the possibilities stretching along the two axes described above.) The differences among us may be subtle, but they are real; there are unlikely to be any psychologically identical twins.

There are, however, many offsetting affinities. We are physiologically variant only within narrow parameters. Our situations and developmental histories are often similar. We live within cultures that prize and reward uniformity. Each of these factors helps to regularize the balances achieved, though variations within each factor are decisive for the complexity and tilt of any particular cognitive-affective posture. Some illustrations help to make the point.

Situations are regularizing because they supply a common backdrop to our struggles against vulnerability and for security. This is apparent when all of us are bothered by great heat or cold, whatever the differences among our cognitive-affective postures. There are a relatively small number of successful accommodations, so that most cognitive-affective postures are altered as we learn one or another of these standardized behaviors. Developmental histories are regularized by our common physiology, by the likeness of our circumstances, and by child-rearing practices that are taught and sanctioned by the community. These histories, like cognitive-affective balances themselves, are appraised for their instrumental value: does some particular style of child rearing create adults whose adaptive behaviors are more effective? These learned ways of engaging the world are identified and taught, with the result that many of us behave in standardized ways. We infer from these uniformities to shared habits, feelings, and beliefs.

Physiology, too, is regularizing, though its effect is complicated by the two sorts of conditions that it establishes within us. Some, like height, bone structure, and blood type, are specific and determinate at any moment.

Height may change, but one is always some particular height. Some other physiological conditions—and this includes all or most of those important to a cognitive-affective-balance—are determinable: we shall speak some language, but which one will it be? Each of us will grow to have some degree of agility, though how much of it depends on genetic inheritance and the contingencies of diet and activity. Thought and feeling are equally determinable, with any particular expression depending on the many contingencies of place, inheritance, motivation, and practice. Each of us achieves a particular solution for these biological constants.

Culture, after situation and physiology, is the last of these regularizing factors. Its relation to individual cognitive-affective postures is like that of physiology. Again, we have determinable constants achieving determinate expression in single persons. English speakers differ in their use of particular words. Dancers do standard steps in variant ways. Cooks may be scrupulous in their use of recipes; though more typically, each one learns the standard formulas before creating favored variations. Culture, like physiology, reminds us that every cognitive-affective balance is the particularized expression of generic constraints. Each of us incorporates the determinables of our animal kind and those of a culture in ways that are unique.

There is also this salient difference between physiology and culture: physiology observes all the laws of nature as they stretch beyond us to cover everything in space-time; cultures are local. What is more, a culture has no reality, artifacts and behaviors aside, apart from its internalization within the cognitive-affective balances of its members. From the standpoint of culture, we really are world-makers, meaning culture-makers and -sustainers.

Our inventiveness is disciplined by uniformities observed in the behavior of our fellows. We shall be unrecognizable to them if we deviate too far from the standards prescribed in diet, language, architecture, clothing, and moral sensibility. We learn to do and approve what other people teach us to do and approve, though we may differ in our interpretations of the lessons taught: the moral directives I set for myself may not be identical with those adopted by anyone else. This difference is another instance of a relation we might describe as idiosyncrasy-in-identity. Here again, the relation is explained by way of the distinction between determinable generalities and their determinate applications. Culture teaches us the determinables, leaving us to decide the exact details and bias of their expression. There is a continuum of expression. It runs from determinable practices for which there are narrowly variant determinate applications (e.g., the behaviors enforced by traffic laws) to those determinables for which determinate expressions vary considerably (e.g., choosing one's clothing or decorating one's home). Slack between the determinables and their determinations permits these variations. It also encourages disputes regarding contrary determinations, as we argue the virtues of Chinese or French cooking while agreeing that nutrition of some kind is vital to health.

Discord is most ferocious as it turns on our self-conception and social relations. Shall I think of myself as free in the ways anticipated by John Stuart Mill's three regions of liberty[8] or as defined by the duties and opportunities falling to me because of my place within a well-defined system of relations? Are my social relations voluntary and contractual or the products of a biology and traditions I cannot alter? What distribution of opportunities, duties, goods, and services is appropriate and just? Cultures differ from one another and within themselves about these moral questions. Yet there are invariably some regularizing habits and rules that enhance co-ordination and minimize discord. Members of a culture incorporate these standards within themselves, first as they are taught, later perhaps because of rationalizing conviction. But always the rules and habits—or doubts about them—allow or encourage deviations from the declared norms. Or the standards are vague, so that personal interpretations are required whenever a rule is applied. We get diversity in practice, however definite and simple the rules seem to be.

Some cultures tolerate this diversity, calling it a moral prerogative. Others are terrified, then ferocious, in their aversion to anything that is not uniform. Ethnic and religious diversity are presumed subversive. So is every cognitive-affective balance, hence every person, dangerous because of its singularity. Each of these postures, with its private languages, plans, and morals, is to be forcibly socialized. But there is no way to eradicate the differences among cognitive-affective postures. Cultural norms will often have disparate expressions, because they are determinables, and because the development and dynamics of each cognitive-affective posture are unique. This is no problem when the rule calls for driving on the left or the right; uniformity in such a practice is easily taught and enforced. There are, however, many ways to be. Determinate expressions of cultural determinables exhibit this variability: they differ subtly in some cases, dramatically in others.

Diet, gods, sexual behavior, the books we read, our ways of making and using money: how much variability among these material and moral goods shall a culture tolerate? There might be a system of punishments and rewards calculated to reduce variability within the cognitive-affective balances of its people. There are many extant cultures that do this effectively. Still, the variability persists, because of being almost guaranteed by the essential determinability of many cultural norms. It is the individual, with his or her distinctive cognitive-affective balance, in his or her peculiar situation, who decides (by acting, not always consciously or intentionally) what his or her expression of a determinable shall be. The range of acceptable determinations may be narrow. It can be narrowed to a single expression if we are willing to exterminate alternative variations while overlooking the clumsiness of having a single determination for disparate purposes. But then, when the demand for uniformity is relaxed even a little, diversity breaks out again. Like weeds in the cracks, our differences will not go away.

This variability may seem dangerous or merely annoying to someone who thinks of us as standardized computer hardware programmed in uniform ways. But that analogy is false is circumstances where each of us learns determinate but more or less idiosyncratic expressions for determinable cultural norms. Consider the physiological, developmental, and otherwise circumstantial differences among us. Remember that each of us is distinguished from infancy by his or her cognitive-affective balance. Now ask how likely it is that we shall have identical solutions for all the determinables that a culture supplies. We get the one in the many from a many who will not be one. There is imitation and introjection, but also stubborn difference, in each of us.

X Pleasure

I have emphasized that development of cognitive-affective postures is a response to the opposition of vulnerability and security. This ignores the part of our lives devoted to pleasure and satisfaction.

Pleasure might seem to have been implicit all along. For if vulnerability implies the risk of pain, and pain is contrary to pleasure, then someone emphasizing pain reduction or avoidance must be implying that pleasure is our aim. Not so. Vulnerability does imply the risk of annihilation and pain, but relief from it is rarely a sufficient condition for pleasure. One might give chewing gum to a starving child; and the child might, for a time, forget his need for food out of pleasure; but these are separate objectives, not a single one. The difference is plain when we cultivate pleasures in ways or at times distinct from conduct that reduces vulnerability. Think of gulls or dolphins who seem to like gliding or swimming for its own sake. They do fly or swim to get food; but then when feeding is done, they do these same things, apparently, for the pleasure of it. What is more, the pleasure they enjoy may be contrary to boredom, not pain, with this implication: the opposition of pleasure to boredom may be separate from the opposition of security to vulnerability and pain. This distinction is obscured sometimes, as when pleasure is a lure to the things that secure us, food being an example. This doubling nevertheless confirms the separability of pleasure and security. One is an inducement to the other when the same behavior may give us both. Yet often we seek the one without thinking of the other. What is more, we may have either without the other. My description of the cognitive-affective postures developed as we learn to reduce our vulnerability is, therefore, incomplete. There must also be provision within each one's equilibrium for doing whatever supplies that person's favored pleasures.

One might reply that the convergence of security and pleasure is already anticipated: there are all the times when the work that secures us is also the thing we enjoy doing. Or we imagine someone who gets pleasure from riding a bicycle along the edge of a cliff, every moment using his wits to keep from falling. People who do this feel pleasure in the challenge of avoiding catastrophe. The separability urged above is inverted in them, as if the best pleasures are those occurring when security is at risk. Many people savor the pleasure of pushing this limit. But no one starves himself to the point of death in order to savor his dinner. Nor is every pleasure the direct or inverse measure of our security. Some things are done only for the pleasure they give us, far from anything risky, and not for any reason more prudential. Fly casting is an example. It is rarely dangerous and has little to do with feeding one's children. It might be alleged that activities like this one are pursued for the security they promote, insofar as doing them reduces stress. This is sometimes a motive for them, though many other people turn anguished only as they are denied the chance to do something they enjoy. They especially are the ones for whom my emphasis has been too narrow. Pleasure is vital to the economy of their lives. The attitudes and skills required for getting it are essential to their cognitive-affective postures.

XI Holism

Cognitive-affective balance is the motor for all that is prudent, moral, pur-posive, or satisfying in thought and action. This balance is *psyche*, the ani-mator. Each thinker's stance is the record of all that he or she has learned to value or reject. Each stance is defined by its distinguishing mix of attitudes and desires, habits, and principles. Everyone projects a distinguishing pattern of values onto the ambient world, thereby foretelling or prescribing the world anticipated by this stance. *World-making, or the illusion of it, starts here.* We adopt the maps and plans appropriate to our values, creating by thought or action an experience that satisfies them. Nothing in this, but the Kantian sense of "world-making," is surprising or excessive.

Each of us addresses the world from the perspective of this apprais-ing, prioritizing, self-interested, and culturally invested standpoint. These engagements are value-driven in two respects: first, as perception, thought, attitude, desire, feeling, habit, and practice are valorizing, each of them be-stowing value by its choice of objects, emphasis, or aim: second, as each is affected by its role within a cognitive-affective balance, thereby making each valorizer, hence each value, conditional on some or all of the others. The relation of these constituents is parallel to that of sentences within a theory:[9] a fulfilling or frustrated action, like a sentence tested empirically, may ramify to some depth within the system of valorizers. It may not be plain which desire or attitude requires alteration or replacement; changing one may re-quire that we alter or adjust the relations of several or many others.

One might be dubious about this holism as it is said to apply invari-ably to the relations of thoughts or sentences, each of them meaningful be-cause of signifying a possibility which would, if instantiated, be its truth con-dition. Each sentence might be true or false accordingly as the possibility signified is instantiated or not,[10] irrespective of the other sentences with which it is associated in a theory or story. Requiring a skein of thoughts or sen-tences for the inferences we draw, we may, nevertheless, discover that ma-terial truth conditions for individual though coupled thoughts or sentences are mutually independent. A bogus alibi is like that: the bits and pieces hang together as a coherent narrative, though truth conditions for the parts that are true are independent of others which are false.

The holism of valuations is altogether more plausible. For nothing set against valuations separates them from one another in the way that thoughts and sentences are separable because they signify distinct possibilities. Valuations, by contrast, are mutually conditioning in the way that the pieces of a jigsaw puzzle interlock. Wanting work, leisure, health, or status, we want some or all the things entrained and presupposed by them. This linkage among our valuings implies a complementary linkage among the thoughts, attitudes, desires, feelings, and habits organized as a cognitive-affective balance: expressing one of them, we express one or many others too. From which it follows that our engagements with the world are the analogue to a full-court press: we fasten on to things at several or many places. Each one is valorized as we grasp, confront, or respond to it; and always the valuing of any one is linked to the valuing of one or many others.

How tightly do values cohere as they issue from a developmental history? Granted that thoughts, habits, and feelings are distinguishable, are they also separable? These questions are important, because there can be no significant changes within a cognitive-affective balance if the linkage among values precludes changing one without changing all the others.

The likely answer is that relations among beliefs, feelings, attitudes, and habits (the states or activities bestowing value) are looser in childhood than they are in later years. It is also likely that some mature beliefs and habits are a tightly related core of valuings. Certainly, there are not many who forsake their values as a molting bird sheds its feathers. The core of mature, rigidly held values is expressed in thoughts, attitudes, and conduct of all sorts. These biased readings and behaviors are conspicuous everywhere, from situations perceived opportunistically to experiments organized to confirm a prejudice.[11] We are engaged (nearly) full-time in projecting, justifying, or exploiting our values. And this is no surprise when the thoughts and behaviors they impel have either of these two effects: they secure us from a perceived vulnerability or generate our pleasures.

This apparent rigidity is nevertheless misleading. Valuings and the links among them are more fragile than might be inferred when people are observed from a distance in the rituals of work, play, and family life. Taking a closer look, we see that valuings shift, so that linkages and priorities also change within a hierarchy that is stable in form but quickly changeable in its details. Some valuings have stable positions within the order, as saving one's life, honor, freedom, or wealth might have priority. Others may pass in and out of focus or into differing but successive patterns, like the pieces in a turning kaleidoscope, when we amend our estimates of risks and opportunities. Sitting on the porch, chatting or reading quietly, we forsake all that if someone yells "Fire" or merely if the telephone rings. We face the world, in thought, action, and feeling, in a posture that is never quite settled, never so frozen (short of terrible debilitation) that we cannot alter our priorities.

XII Hypothesis

It is less mysterious now that truth should seem to be the function of value. Aren't we dedicated already to the project of making an environment that supports our values? Idealist claims about "world-making" may be only the grandiose and exaggerated descriptions of this behavior. The cognitive-affective balance in each of us struggles to create circumstances congenial to itself. There is, however, something still missing in my description of this posture. This is apparent if we consider that no one could satisfy any attitude or desire if the only values impelling him or her were the self-interested ones just described. It is vital to our interests that we have maps and plans appropriate to the circumstances wherein we secure or satisfy ourselves. But maps and plans do not work unless they are sensitive to both the terrain on which a plan is to be enacted and the instrumental relations possible in these circumstances. *Cognitive* in the phrase *cognitive-affective balance* must signify something additional to the schematizing of sensory data, symbols, or behaviors on behalf of desire. Inferences from effective action to its conditions suggest that this balance must also provide for making and testing those hypotheses which correctly represent the situations (terrain and possible instrumental relations) where plans direct behavior. Wishing for security and satisfaction will come to nothing if we do not also value these accurate representations.

There is, we infer, provision within cognitive-affective postures for skills appropriate to making hypotheses. Complementary to this power and vital to the confirmation of hypotheses is our esteem for the skills and procedures required for testing them. These are the regulative, logical, and practical values described in chapter 1 as values appropriate to the conduct of inquiry. They include the requirements that well-formed hypotheses be internally consistent and consistent with one another and the demand that hypotheses be testable by way of the empirical differences that would obtain if the hypotheses were true. We require too that experiments be repeatable by separate agents, thereby reducing the likelihood that self-interested investigators will appraise their experiments in ways that satisfy only their personal interests.

There is also this other consideration mentioned in chapter 2: that the interest valorizing some content or object does not thereby alter the thing valued. Arithmetic is not captured and warped by the fact of having some valued consequence within the economy of a cognitive-affective balance. Rather like parents who worry that caring too much for children will ruin them, we needn't fear that anything taken up for our purposes, or only represented by our hypotheses, is thereby altered. Addressing the world from a standpoint replete with values does not entail that the world so addressed is thereby transformed. That it is or may be altered, we concede. That contending projects and values should color or taint everything they touch is odd. How should we explain, were that true, that all the many human agents, each with its idiopathic cognitive-affective balance, struggle for security and satisfaction in what appears to be the one world constraining all of them?

We expect that claims about the world will often express the opposed interests of, say, tobacco-makers, smokers, and insurance companies. We suppose that making a difference suitable to these interests requires that we take the measure of the circumstances within which we operate. We also suppose that there is a place for the values and procedures essential for reality testing within each person's cognitive-affective balance. Why should that be so? Because no one thrives if he cannot distinguish his desire for security and happiness from the representations required for operating safely and effectively in the world. No one, however self-interested and reckless, survives a day's freedom if there is no place within his cognitive-affective balance for those regulative values whose only function is the formulation of true hypotheses. Value still pervades all that we think and do; but now the values essential to navigating within the world are set apart. We distinguish the values appropriate to inquiry, if only for emphasis, from the values and activities that remake our circumstances for the purpose of satisfying our desires.

This last point is the crux of Peirce's alienation from James. James supposed that truth cannot be set apart from the personal interests that drive action, because, he thought, there are no disinterested tests for truth. Our views of the world are only those available as we defend an interest or press an advantage. Our cognitive-affective postures have no function, in the terms of this chapter, but that of projecting us into the world on the terms prescribed by our desires.

This Jamesian formulation subverts itself. No one can ever satisfy desires requiring some altered state of the world (rare accidents apart) if the maps and plans directing his behavior are not testable, true hypotheses. The actor will trip and fall while pursuing his aims—he may hurt himself—if the truth of his representations does not control the pursuit of his aims. It does not matter that we cannot escape thought, language, perception, or action to get a look at the world as it is in itself. No one requires that unbiased view of the things about us so long as he or she can infer from the mutually implicative results of disparate experiments to the existence and character of the things themselves. There are always alternative possible conditions for the same experimental results. We never eliminate the possibility that our speculative identification of a thing is mistaken. But usually there is evidence, apart from the desires motivating action, for thinking that some particular hypothesis is the true one. We never suppose that the ambient world might drop away, leaving us *carte blanche* for creating any world that suits us.

There is, however, this caution. For there is a way to avert having to concede that the skills and regulative values necessary for reality testing have a place within each person's cognitive-affective balance: we deny that the actions required for satisfying our desires need carry beyond thought into a world we have not made. Thought, we say, is the only action. The only worlds where thought operates are, we insist, the ones that thought has made. This, it seems to me, is a very strange persuasion. It leaves no space for the skills and values required to formulate the maps and plans used for testing a reality we do not make. It precludes or leaves unexplained the possibility that we might effectively co-ordinate our plans and behaviors with other people. We are reminded that conceptual systems, including systems of rules, are the only instruments important to the Kantian idealists described in chapter 1; making the world obviates having to test hypotheses about a world we have not made. The only cooperation, this implies, is transcendental: we participants in the kingdom of ends agree to respect the autonomy and worlds of our fellow world-makers. I recall their view for comparison: there are the imagined worlds we make and the natural world where humans live as natural creatures. Everyone who thinks that we live in the natural world will want to acknowledge that the regulative values important to reality testing do, and must, have a place within each person's cognitive-affective posture.

What must truth be on those occasions when we test our maps and plans, asking if they accurately represent the circumstances where action is intended to secure or satisfy us? The next two chapters consider the options.

Chapter Four

I Is Truth Simple and Separable?

Some philosophical problems give the impression of standing alone. They may be considered and solved without regard for collateral issues. Beauty, entailment relations, and the existence of God come to mind as topics of this sort. Is truth like them? The simplicity of the word, coupled to the role of truth as final cause of inquiry, enforces the impression that here, if anywhere, is a topic that earns its claim to separate analysis. Is this impression accurate? Can we satisfy ourselves about truth while ignoring every other topic?

I doubt that any philosophic question is resolvable apart from integrated solutions to an assortment of related issues. The impression of separability as regards truth dissolves as we observe two things: first, that every notion of truth is embedded in a metaphysical theory of greater scope; second, that every supporting theory satisfies its motivating values. Theories and these values are often hidden or disguised; or they may seem too ordinary to require justification. But values do energize our philosophic attitudes; and we create such metaphysical theories and notions of truth as will satisfy the demand that our values be made articulate. Truth is not singular or simple. It has this layered character.

Supporting theories and the values animating them are, nevertheless, incidental or invisible to some philosophers curious about truth. These are thinkers for whom *separable if distinguishable* is an article of faith. Truth, they say, is distinguishable and separable: standing alone within the circle of analytic light, it is "pure" and "adequate." [1] We are encouraged to discover this separability in either of two ways: procedurally by way of an analysis or "perceptually" by attending to individual ideas as they stand alone before the mind's eye. Let us consider these alternatives, while remarking that they sometimes converge.

Where analysis distinguishes and separates, there should be no better device for confirming the separability of truth. What kind of analysis should this be: ordinary language analysis, Husserlian eidetic reflection, or the formalization of conceptual systems with its forced division into axioms and theorems?

Ordinary language analysis isolates the notion of truth by imagining the many contexts where 'true' or 'truth' may be used. Successively altering the context of their use enables analysts to observe the uniformities and changes in usage across the backdrop of differing contexts. More than being the catalogue of its usage, this montage of uses exposes the "logical geography" of a term. We discern the rule, the normative standard, for its use. Notice, too, that this rule is distinct form the rules for using other words. The separability of 'truth' is to be just the fact that the "grammar" of 'truth' is different from the grammar of every other word.

Husserlian analysis also promises to expose the contours of truth, though now it is an inspectable essence or *noema*, not a word, that concerns us. Here, too, we explore an idea by varying its context, thereby revealing the invariant, essential features. Analysis culminates as we perceive (apprehend, grasp) a fully elaborated, distinguishable and separable essence. Axiomatization achieves separation in a different way, as when a theory of knowledge is formulated by stipulating notions of truth, proposition, and state of affairs before deducing from them a theorem characterizing knowledge. Because the axioms of a formalized theory should be mutually independent of one another, separation is achieved if the axiom specifying truth is consistent with, but not derivable from, the other axioms.

Each of these three procedures—ordinary language analysis, eidetic reflection, and formalization—may be used to justify the claim that truth is distinguishable and separable from other notions. We err, however, if we infer too quickly from the distinguishability of truth, established by all three modes of analysis, to its separability from other words or notions. For the want of separability is plain from the analyses themselves. Ordinary language uses of 'truth' vary with context, including circumstances and the other words used. Eidetic reflection does not isolate truth from the reciprocal effects of other essences, each one having ineliminable implications for some others: truth is implied by knowledge, while vehicles for truth and truth conditions are presupposed by truth itself. Formalization does not guarantee that truth must always be an independent axiom, never a theorem deducible within a formalized system. None of the three styles of analysis confirms the separability of 'truth' or truth.

Is its separability better confirmed when we pass from analysis to the intuitionist claim that there is an isolable idea of truth? We ask this question while ignoring that ordinary language analysis and Husserlian reflection already assume that the separability of a rule or essence is discovered by an inspecting mind: mind intuits a grammatical rule by surveying its uses, or it perceives invariances within an idea whose context and accidents are freely altered within imagination.

Let Plato, rather than Austin or Husserl, be our sample intuitionist. He was emphatic about the separability of Ideas in dialogues that attend unrelentingly to a single Form. His *Sophist* and *Parmenides* justify this procedure: sameness and difference relate the Forms to one another without compromising their essential separability. Descartes is also important to this program. His *more geometrico* gives formal expression to the alleged independence of ideas—as complex ideas are derived from simple ones. Simple ideas, including those of mind and extension, are distinguishable and separable. Each may be entertained clearly and distinctly without regard for other simple ideas. Hume is relevant too. He formulated the principle of separability— separable if distinguishable—after applying to sensible intuition the claims that Plato made for rational intuition: impressions, like Forms, stand before our inspecting minds, so that each can be noticed and compared to the others.

These three intuitionists are pioneer analysts. They have demanded that obscure complex ideas should be subjected, first, to differentiation, then to clarifying perception of their constituents. This was Descartes' point when he required that obscure ideas be reconstructed from simple ideas that are clear and distinct. Analysis as formalization is the contemporary expression of this Cartesian (and Euclidean) idea. It, too, may be conducted in ways that satisfy Descartes' intuitionist demands for clarity and distinctness—in our terms, for self-consistency and independence. (I do not imply that analysis cannot be purged of its intuitionist origins.)

Notice, however, that intuitionists never present or try to present a separable idea of truth. None of them supposes that truth is self-sufficient, simple, or "pure." Truth, for Plato, is the identity of knower and known achieved when mind participates in the Forms. Hume is an evocation of Plato: ideas are true as they embody a difference exhibited already by impressions, so that the mind having a true idea is infused with the property or properties signified. Truth for Descartes is the adequation of an idea to the essence it expresses. None of these three paradigmatic intuitionists lifts truth cleanly from circumstances where it presupposes other rules or ideas and all the apparatus of mental activity and truth conditions. Remembering that the analysts do no better in proving truth's self-sufficiency, we say that there is, so far, no evidence for the separability either of truth or any other philosophic notion.

This conclusion is justified by the inventory that follows. I shall be arguing that there are several notions of truth, each embedded in a metaphysical theory where it coheres with, because it answers to the demands of, the theory's other notions. I shall also say that each notion of truth is shaped, more remotely, by the value or values motivating its embedding metaphysical theory. It is apparent from this survey that the nuances of our several ideas of truth vary with the other claims of their embedding theories and with the values that drive these theories. Truth is, in all these cases, distinguishable, but not separable, from its cognitive, valorizing context.

One issue still blocks the way to this survey of candidate notions of truth: it will seem that the direction set in chapters 1 and 2 has been reversed. I argued there that James was mistaken in thinking that the truth of our hypotheses is a function of the values motivating thought and action. The truth of thinking one is loved may depend on the determination to win that love; but nothing I desire, think, say, or do will alter the speed of light or the Carolingian succession. These states of affairs, as well as true sentences or beliefs about them, are exempt, I have supposed, from the determining force of the believer's values. But then it is odd that particular truths should be exempt from value, though our notion of truth is the product (by way of an embedding metaphysical theory) of a motivating value. Why should our notion of truth, any more than its instances, be the effect of a value?

The issues dissolves when we distinguish particular truths and the generic character of truth from our ideas about truth. Value may be incidental to truths about arithmetic or the weather and also to the generic character of truth, though a notion of truth may be very much affected by the value or values motivating the metaphysical theory in which that notion is embedded. Values motivate our thinking (pursuant to chapter 3) even to the point where theories are shaped by the desire for their truth or implementation. It does not follow that individual truths or truth generically is the creature of our motives, more than the sunny day I have wanted is the product of my desire. Our notions of truth, like the theories in which they fit, are hypotheses. Values motivating hypotheses are not typically included among their truth conditions. Wanting to be loved is one of the exceptions only because subsequent behavior eventually supplies the truth condition that satisfies the truth-claim. Desiring that some notion of truth shall be true is not equally potent.

Five notions of truth compete for philosophic allegiance: truth is coherence, identity, redundancy, behavior appropriate to its context, or correspondence. These are, generically, the viable theories. The claim that truth is a property of thoughts or sentences is not viable, since it is only misleading to say, by analogy, that being an aunt, a spouse, or a brother is a property when these, like truth, are barely disguised relations. All five of the notions considered below assume that truth is relational, though in two of them the relation collapses into identity. The idea of truth as holistic is denied a separate place, provision being made for it in several of the other notions. Four of the five notions are considered in this chapter; correspondence is deferred to chapter 5.

II Truth as Coherence

Truth as coherence implies that we have answers to this short list of questions: Granted that many things may cohere, which ones are true because of cohering? Where is coherence achieved—out of mind or only within it? What are the criteria for the presence or lack of coherence among the things for which truth is claimed?

A. Things Counted True because they Cohere

Truth may be identified as coherence throughout the domain of thought and belief; ideas, thoughts, beliefs, propositions, sentences, and arguments are some principal examples of things whose truth is alleged to be their coherence — as sentences cohere under rules with other sentences. It is curious that truth is not claimed in some other regions where coherence is a significant property. Music and architecture are coherent; strategists in war and in chess demand it too, though we don't say that a masterful battle, building, or game is true. Why this restriction? Is it the mental origin of thoughts and sentences that qualifies them for coherence-as-truth? This cannot be a sufficient reason when emotions are acknowledged as coherent without also being counted as true.

Why this difference between things in and out of mind and even among things occurring within it? Because ideas, thoughts, beliefs, propositions, and sentences are attitudes regarding, or the representations of, things other than themselves. Believing that something is the case or representing it as the case, we affirm that these attitudes or signs are appropriate to their objects or referents. They are, we say, true. Thoughts and sentences are generated, then construed, as signs by or within minds. That is reason for supposing that truths originate within minds, not outside them. Only as true thoughts are recorded (e.g., as sentences in books) do we extend the domain of truth beyond mind to other places where representations are stored.

This way of distinguishing truth-making coherences is, however, problematic for those who favor coherence as the appropriate notion of truth. For we are encouraged to favor coherence over correspondence as our notion of truth because we want to be rid of the idea that words or sentences signify something beyond themselves. Invoking representation to differentiate among coherence-makers should, therefore, be anathema. The appeal to representation is nevertheless the only plausible basis for differentiating the coherences that make for truth from those which do not. We reduce the anomaly a little by saying that thoughts and sentences (merely) *seem* to be representations, while coherent feelings do not. Still, the idea of coherence is strangely parasitic on the mapping of thoughts or sentences onto states of affairs independent of them. This is not the last time that representation, or the appearance of it, is required for making sense of coherence.

B. The Empirical Basis for Coherence

Things that cohere are often homogeneous; they are, for example, thoughts or sentences. Sometimes, however, the things that cohere are heterogeneous, as when religious beliefs are declared true because of cohering with certain values. The Jamesian thesis considered in chapter 1 implies that truth-making coherences are heterogeneous: the truth of thoughts or sentences is said to depend on their coherence with an attitude or desire, then with the action launched to satisfy it. The complexities ramify: thoughts or sentences cohering with one another are true only as they also cohere with values and the actions they impel; further, cohering thoughts or sentences are true because they cohere with values and actions only if (possibly) multiple values or actions cohere with one another, then if the actions cohere with the values. Truth might founder at any of the places where heterogeneities disrupt the coherence of feeling, thought, and action.

Notice that these heterogeneous cases are the principal site for the error that preoccupied us in the first three chapters: the values motivating a belief are not, I argued, its truth conditions. Thoughts or sentences are not true merely because they cohere with the values provoking them or with these values and the actions they provoke. Hardly anyone gets to be ten years old without conceding this point. Adoring the idea of Santa Claus, wanting and getting presents, we discount the story that Santa Claus has brought them because of our desires and conduct. Truth, we realize, has nothing to do with desire, attitude, or action, except that the latter alter our circumstances so that false beliefs are made true or true beliefs made false. Mere coherence with them would not make thoughts or sentences true. Supposing now that attitude and desire are irrelevant to truth (except as they alter states of affairs, hence the truth-values of thoughts and sentences representing them), I shall give no further attention to these heterogeneous cases.

More often, the domain relevant to coherence and truth is homogeneous: only relations among thoughts or sentences count for truth. What are the criteria used to determine whether coherence does or does not obtain?

Such criteria as we have are often more impressionistic than exact. We say confidently that the details of a story hang together; we are quick to notice that a suspect's alibi does not cohere because it implies that he has moved from place to place faster than the speed of light. We make these judgments about particular coherences, but usually without being able to tell what criterion is applied. We fault the alibi for being contradictory, but we are less sure of the rule satisfied when a story is judged coherent.

The criteria are hard to specify, because they are founded in experiences that are usually not articulated. I mean that noncontradictory beliefs, theories, and stories are judged coherent when they mimic the coherences of the world about us. A novel is coherent if it describes people and events in relationships like those of everyday experience. Even the coherence of scientific explanations trades on this parallel, causal explanations being said to cohere if, for example, the antecedent and consequent in an if–then sentence track the relations of cause and effect. Spatial, temporal, and causal relations are the principal bases for coherent experience. They are familiar to all of us, so familiar as to provide everyone with standards for the coherence of the narratives or theories which evoke them.

Negative examples make the same point. Abstract painting was once hard to understand, because its coherences did not mimic in evident ways the coherences of ordinary perception. Conventions for interpreting the new art were formulated; but not until most patrons had been mystified by the difference between the world they observed and the painters' renderings of it. Even this delayed acceptance would have been more hesitant if the new standards for coherence did not originate in the coherences perceived, as relations of space, color, and shape survive, however stripped down and transformed, in the paintings of an Ernst or a Kandinsky.

This criterial use of experience is apparent wherever representations are appraised for their coherence. There are, for example, films which cut in and out of their characters' lives, often in ways which have no equivalent in our perceptions of ourselves or other people. We learn to integrate these altered perspectives, never objecting that experience is deformed beyond recognition until some director passes too quickly among his characters, supplying too little information about them. It also happens that characters and circumstances are introduced in ways having no apparent relevance to the action, or that events are mixed in ways that violate the normal sequence of time, place, or cause. We lose track of the people or the plot; the film (or novel or play) is incoherent.

We make these judgments easily and often, though we have little to say when asked to specify the coherence-making criteria that are violated or satisfied. It resembles experience, we say, when nothing more specific comes to mind; though surely the issue is sometimes too pressing for this informality. Someone about to be hanged insists that his alibi is coherent. We want to ascertain if this is so. Having plainly stated rules for the coherence of thoughts or sentences might be urgent to the point where handbooks listing them should be available everywhere. But there are no books and almost no rules that might plausibly be described as coherence rules. Criteria for coherence are mostly tacit. Appeals to experience—is the narrative a recognizable extrapolation from your experience?—are the principal test. Imagination too is permitted its variations. Some of them are elaborated until we can recognize coherences remote from everyday experience: compare Bartok quartets to bird song. More often, we stay close to the coherences of everyday experience.

Someone defending a standard more rigorous and universal, less impressionistic, will protest that there are rules for appraising the coherence of theories and arguments. They include the inductions that generalize from our observations of causal regularities in nature, as we find a story coherent when it reports someone being hurt in a fire. We notice that relations such as *to the left of* and *after* are transitive; we then find relevant sentences coherent or not as they do or do not satisfy the rules generalized from these observations. We begin to explain the rules invented for interpreting abstract art: they explain some, at least, of the elementary symmetries, transitions, and contrasts perceived.

Rules that mimic experience are the objective pole for our assessments of coherence. Topicality is the subjective pole, as thought or talk is judged coherent if one subject—Mars, for example—is the focus throughout. Topicality is the looser standard, as we strain to detect the focus of a conversation that moves from ducks to politics to stamp collecting. We may give it focus by the use of repetition or by some vaguely agreed notions of relevance. Still, conversations of this sort verge on free association. Here—and well short of it—there are no rules for the coherence of thought, attention, or conversation.

Equally, there are no rules for the coherence of a complex narrative, theory, or argument. Many subject matters fall between the idealizations of subjective and objective poles. So *Moby-Dick* is coherent, but not because it satisfies any rule that we could state. There are, no doubt, various experience-mimicking rules and topics that give this impression of coherence, but nothing, however complex, that could be abstracted from the text as its coherence-making rubric. Coherence rules for large-scale narratives elude us.

C. The Stability of Coherent Systems

We may begin to doubt that coherence is the basis for truth. How could it be if associations mimicking those of experience or embroidering topics of conversation are the principal bases for judgments about it? Inductive generalizations provide for coherence within the fragments of thought and language; but there are, typically, no additional rules to supply coherence to the theories, arguments, or conversations created by aggregating the fragments. Are the bits and pieces true because coherent, while the wholes are neither true nor false? Equally, topicality explains the coherence of some conversations; but how many of them depend for their presumed focus on the mutual tolerance of the speakers?

There are also doubts about the stability of coherences, hence of truths. For suppose that the focus of thought or conversation changes quickly. It follows that coherences deriving from topicality cannot be the sufficient basis for truth unless we say that the truths of one moment have evaporated when thought or conversation changes direction, or that truths then are falsehoods now, merely because our focus has changed. We don't say either. Someone full of insight, spinning a succession of pointed observations suddenly changes subjects with hardly a pause; surely the truths just uttered survive this change. How could they survive if truth is only the coherence established by a focus now dissolved?

Inductive truths would be equally unstable if the observed regularities supporting inductive rules were to come unstuck. For then the rules would have lost their authority, with the effect that coherences resulting from their application would no longer count as truth-making relations. Nor is this far-fetched. For granting that phenomena are more stable than Heraclitus supposed, they are not inert. Dramatic changes discrediting the old rules would deprive us of the old truths. The absence of some other coherence-making rules—those invoked as we withdraw from any one conceptual system in order to comment upon or compare systems—would create a certain amnesia: we would be unable to say truly within a successor theory that the old truths are no longer true.

We want our truths to have more stability than is promised by topicality or inductive rules. Some do have it, for there are truths—those of mathematics and logic—which survive changes of focus and nature too. Neither topicality nor observation-mimicking coherences are relevant explanations for them. Indeed, coherence seems fuzzy and precarious as a basis for their truth until we remember that there is a way of founding mathematical and logical truths, if no others, on coherence of a different kind: namely, the coherence rules for formal systems. They supply rules for generating systems of thoughts or sentences, as geometry is coherent because any last sentence derives from its antecedents in ways determined by the system's rules of inference. Notice too that the deductive rules used to generate coherent arguments may also be used criterially to assess the coherence of other people's theories or arguments: do their conclusions follow demonstrably from their premises? These two uses, for generation and appraisal, are reason enough for saying that demonstration is the preferred expression of coherence. But there is more. Coherence is not an incidental feature of thought, when thinking that lacks it hardly counts as thought. Nor is incoherent thought communicable. Deductive form meets both requirements, assuring coherence to thought in a form that makes for efficient communication.

Can we use it, too, to save some other truths? Coherence-making inductive rules are precarious, as just remarked: we may formulate generalizations appropriate to our experience, only to be confounded by subsequent events. Hume could be right: the very next crocus might sing *Rigoletto*. How shall we defend the coherence of thought against the possibility that familiar regularities might dissolve? All our established inductive rules would then be useless as generators of, and criteria for, coherence. Nor can we look for security in topicality. That is no answer when the focus of thought and conversation so often shifts unpredictably. Deduction saves us these embarrassments. Why not reconstruct every more fragile coherence so that it satisfies this firmer standard?

Anyone believing that truth is coherence may hurry to reestablish impressionistic coherences on this firmer ground. There is, however, a prior question. What takes priority? The desire that inductive rules should shadow the relationships of space, time, and causality observed in the world or mind's power for controlling relations among its thoughts by ordering them in accordance with deductive rules that mind invents? On the one side is the empiricist commitment to those fragments of thought and speech which achieve coherence because they signify things of a sort observed as connected in the world. On the other is the holism achieved when all our thoughts or sentences are organized deductively. One mimics relationships observed in the world; the other achieves comprehensive relatedness within a formalized system. We may, of course, use procedures of both sorts to generate the coherences in thought. Starting with inductive generalizations, we may go on to formalize the results. Suppose, however, that we are forced to choose between the two, or merely to tell which one is favored. What reasons could we give for preferring one or the other?

Wanting thought about the world to echo the world itself, we prefer coherences derived from inductive rules. That is the prudent choice of natural creatures who have to secure themselves in circumstances where safety depends upon the ability to accommodate themselves to states of affairs they only partly understand. Determined to represent our circumstances as accurately as efficient behavior requires, we risk the incoherence of thoughts turned irrelevant by unforeseen changes in the order of things. Everyone convinced first by Descartes' views about mind's priority in thought and being, then by Hume's skepticism, will opt for the other side and favor mind's power to establish, then apply, a system of ideas and rules for creating a stable, thinkable experience. Despairing at unexplained alterations of the world order, wanting to maximize our autonomy, we prefer the coherences that we ourselves guarantee.

D. Coherences Guaranteed by Formalization

Someone wanting to secure the coherence of his or her ideas will quickly take the point: deduction will be favored over induction as the basis for coherence. We might express this preference by dismissing inductive rules from any responsibility for thought's coherence. Or we do the thing suggested above: we reformulate inductive rules, organizing them deductively. The following four steps have this effect.

First, renounce the idea that we might learn about the deep structure of nature by generalizing from our observations. Nature, we say, does not have an essential, uniform-making structure. There is no reason, intrinsic to the things observed, for these regularities, hence no reason to suppose that the experiences supporting inductive rules will not come unstuck. Dogs may no longer bark; the future may or may not be like the past. We are obliged to find some other, less contingent basis for the coherence of our thoughts and sentences.

Second, let mind be active rather than passive as it formulates its inductions. Don't wait for nature to show us whatever conjunctions happen to obtain there: stipulate the couplings we shall acknowledge. What we call *nature* is better described on the analogy of forms perceived in billowing clouds: an elephant here, head and shoulders there. The clouds change, but we don't mind, for the clouds themselves are essentially formless; the only forms significant to us are those we project onto them.

Third, we shall need to organize these disparate stipulations as they project order onto phenomena presented for schematization. What order shall this be? Just that of deduction. We need axioms and rules of inference. Highest-order, stipulated laws are to be the axioms. Lower-order sentences are to be derived from these highest-order ones by applying the rules of inference adopted for the purposes of the system.

Fourth, we give this uninterpreted formal system an empirical interpretation. We do this because coherence is so far only a syntactic property. Sentences related in this coherence-making, syntactic way must also be made to say something about the world. This is accomplished by affirming these three things: that highest-order sentences of the calculus are the most general inductive laws of a theory, whether of practice or science; that lowest-order sentences signify empirical differences (e.g., red or gray); and that the theoretical terms of the higher-order sentences are introduced or defined by way of the observation terms occurring in the lowest-order sentences. A calculus satisfying these three requirements is interpreted as, hence suitable for, a deductivist treatment of inductive rules: lower-order rules can be deduced from those of higher order. Saying that "Humidity over 95 percent is rain," that "Rain is good for barley," and that "Humidity is currently 97 percent," it follows that "Current humidity is good for Dad's anxiety," since all his income comes from barley, his only crop. All this, including the missing premises, can be trussed and expressed in deductive form.

Coherence, after these four points, is just he *validity* of lower-order sentences deduced from those which are higher-order. *Confirmation* reverses the direction of inference: it moves from lowest-order test sentences to the higher-order sentences from which they are deduced. Test sentences signify the differences that should be observed, given our acceptance of the higher-order sentences. These are our predictions. Their confirmation is also confirmation of the sentences for which they are deduced. The idea of *truth* has become a nearly irrelevant vestige. We speak only of validity and confirmation (or of warranted assertibility), where both are syntactic, coherence-making relations.

What is the benefit of reformulating inductive rules to satisfy deductivist scruples? Just the one mentioned above: to show that thought does not have to come unstuck, losing its coherence, just because the world lacks the intrinsic form which would guarantee uniformity. We stipulate what differences and relations are to be ascribed to the world. We then exploit coherence-making deductive rules to guarantee the coherence of the thoughts and sentences that express these stipulations.

Not so quick, you say; confirmation as described two paragraphs above is not a syntactic relation only. Two sorts of confirmation were mentioned there: higher-order sentences are confirmed by lowest-order test sentences deduced from them, while test sentences are confirmed or not by the empirical data. The one relation is syntactic, the other semantic and representational. Are we obliged to admit, within the context of this apology for coherence, that the truth of observation sentences is correspondence? This does seem to be the case where "This is red" is true only if this is red.

Is it a good or a bad thing that we have averted this implication? For that is the effect of supposing that the truth of observation sentences does not depend on the fact that they correctly represent matters of fact independent of thought and language for their existence and character. We say instead that mind stipulates the predicates to be used in characterizing experience and the occasions for using any particular one of them. Carnap embellishes the point:

> After deciding to choose an autopsychological basis for our system (i.e., the acts of consciousness or experience of the self), we still must determine which entities from this general domain are to serve as basic elements. . . . We realize that in this case we do not take the given as it is, but abstractions from it (i.e., something that is epistemically secondary) as basic elements. It must be understood that constructional systems which proceed from such basic elements are as much justified and practicable as, for example, systems with a physical basis. However, since we wish to require of our constructional system that it should agree with the epistemic order of the objects, we have to proceed from that which is epistemically primary, that is to say, from the "given," i.e., from experiences themselves in their totality and undivided unity. The above-mentioned constituents, down to the last elements, are derived from these experiences by relating them to one another and comparing them (i.e., through abstraction). The more

simple steps of this abstraction are carried out intuitively in pre-scientific thought already, so that we quite commonly speak, for example, of visual perceptions, and simultaneous auditory perceptions, as if they were two different constituents of the same experience. The familiarity of such divisions which are carried out in daily life should not deceive us about the fact that abstraction is already involved in the procedure. This applies a fortiori to elements which are discovered only through scientific analysis. The basic elements, that is, the experiences of the self as units . . . we call *elementary experiences.*[2]

Carnap is saying that pre-analytic experience is a blooming, buzzing confusion, much too rich to pin down in any final way. Instead, we label experience in familiar, stable ways, until we come to mistake the differentiations which we project onto it for differences which are independent of us. But they are not: the differences we find are just the ones that we have imposed. Accordingly, the truth by correspondence of observation sentences is not the complement to the truth by coherence of a theory's more abstract sentences. Truth (on this telling) is only coherence. What is that? Just the syntactic relation of sentences (moving down or up) within an interpreted, formalized, conceptual system.

E. Quine and Kuhn on Coherence

It seemed for many years that the foregoing deductivist analysis was our best hope for analyzing truth as coherence. Impressionistic responses to the coherence of an argument or theory could be superseded by this more rigorous, formally testable account. This persuasion was shaken by Quine, then by Kuhn.

Quine challenged the distinction between analytic and synthetic truths, with its implications for correlative differences such as form and content, syntax and semantics.[3]

Coherence is defined above in syntactic terms: sentences cohere if one is entailed by another. Set against this appeal to deduction and syntax is the assumption that there is a categorial difference between syntax and semantics, especially as regards their truth conditions. Truth conditions for synthetic sentences are factual but contingent states of affairs, as the truth of claims about the weather is conditioned by extra-linguistic matters of fact. "Red!" is used prescriptively to focus attention on the redness of the percepts or things perceived; yet this situation is not quite an invention, because the things perceived are so brimming with qualifications as to provide a basis for this ascription. The truth conditions for analytic sentences originate, by contrast, in the mind's power for making rules: sentences may be true or false (necessarily true or contradictory) for any comprehensive substitution of truth-values for their variables. Nothing is uncertain about the entailment relations legitimized by these rules: they obtain or not.

My suggestion above was that coherence among sentences is firmly established only as sentences are organized so that they relate deductively, every last sentence in a proof being true because of its derivation from those above. Before, coherence had seemed to depend on synthetic, inductive rules or the merely contingent aggregation of claims considered topical. Now, with deduction as our point of reference, coherence seemed more secure. This solution is moot when Quine denies that there is a categorial difference between the analytic and the synthetic, syntax and semantics. This is the result when Quine's appraisal of the evidence for the analytic–synthetic distinction is joined to his Kantian, pragmatic view of language.

We get the first point when Quine asks us to assume the perspective of an anthropologist. He or she understands the verbal behaviors of some alien tribe by speculating about the rules used by its members. The anthropologist is reduced to hypothesizing about these rules, because of having no access to the private, intrapsychic intentions of native speakers. It is no advantage to him or her that the rules might be plainly articulated by and for these speakers. The anthropologist can observe only their applications, meaning the uses made of sentences. What he or she sees and hears is a statistical pattern of behaviors, one that is sensitive to two variables: circumstances provoking a verbal response and patterns of relatedness among locutions. Some utterances are responsive, principally, to circumstances, while others are sensitive to the relations obtaining among previous locutions. This is not, however, an all-or-nothing affair. The anthropologist observes that any locution may be somewhat sensitive to both considerations.

Paired to this claim about the evidence is a claim concerning the principal use of language. This is the site of Quine's pragmatism: his view that rules and the sentences they sponsor are taken up within the fabric of words used to make experience intelligible. There is, he supposes, nothing in linguistic practice so rigid as the traditional distinction between logical and empirical truths. Rather, we spin a coherent fabric of sentences, connecting them to one another with an eye to values of two sorts: first, the logical values of simplicity and consistency; second, the values (Carnap's pragmatics) that motivate us as we organize experience. The idea of sentences having truth conditions that are only empirical or only logical is, therefore, merely an idealized opposition. Actual sentences fall somewhere in between, closer to one or other end of the spectrum, but never so far to one end that considerations appropriate to the other one are irrelevant.

This analysis is dangerous to coherence. For remember the contingent and impressionistic coherences devolving only on the aggregation of inductive claims. Things joined spatially, temporally, or causally in previous experience may have formed an objective basis for the coherence of sentences representing them; but these things may have been joined only accidentally; or, if joined causally, they may no longer be connected. The coherences of words and sentences representing conjunctions once observed depend in that event on nothing stronger than our powers of association. This makes coherence the product of memory and imagination only. Every coherence is at risk of collapsing into topicality, with nothing but habit and focus to hold it together. This is too idiosyncratic and contingent a basis for the claim that the truth of thoughts and sentences is just their coherence. Deduction was to be the more secure foundation for coherence, but Quine subverts the reasoned basis for this difference, that being the effect of making syntactic truths only somewhat more resistant than semantic truths to the force of context. We are reduced again to coherences grounded by induction and topicality.

One might have some incompatible reactions to this outcome. Positively, it was never plausible that we might soon have a deductivist reconstruction of all our well-formed thinking about the world; there was nothing but hope to support the dream that every particularity and qualitative difference might be predicted and signified by observation sentences deduced from the highest-order theorems of a formalized system. That all truth should wait on the coherences in some version of this system defers, perhaps eternally, the attainment of many truths already available to us, as it is a truth for which secondhand memory is my only evidence that January 3, 1936 was a Friday.

Negatively, Quine's objections to the analytic–synthetic distinction do not prove either that there is no distinction to be made or that what real difference exists here is of no use. Consider the position of his anthropologist. He or she may be unable to distinguish analytic from synthetic relations in the speech of some alien tribe; but it does not follow that members of the tribe cannot tell the difference in particular cases or specify generically what the difference is. A Martian anthropologist might find that our uses of 'bachelor' diverge in some way from our uses of 'unmarried male'. They might also discover that many high school geometry students cannot prove the Pythagorean theorem or that they prove it by drawing crude triangles. It does not follow that Euclid's theorems are true only synthetically, or that we have not formulated deductive rules (e.g., those of geometry) commonly applied to myriad proofs and procedures.

Quine's anthropological myth is the expression of his verificationism. Deductive rules are suspect because we cannot confirm what rules are used or how they are interpreted. But this is odd when we consider that computers programmed with the rules of a deductive system perform in the ways predicted. Suppose that computers once programmed cannot be reprogrammed or opened for examination. Should we refuse to infer that a machine is operating in the ways prescribed by deductive rules just because we cannot tell how the machine "interprets" its program? But, of course, machines do not "interpret" the rules any more than a mechanical adding machine interprets its rules. Perhaps we humans also have no margin for interpreting deductive rules once the rules have been learned. Perhaps we apply them in some way analogous to machines. That would make inferences about the conditions for our behaviors (e.g., those of adding and subtracting) no more problematic than inferences concerning machines. We might reasonably say that either one, human or machine, may apply deductive rules without provoking, first, verificationist reservations, then the conclusion that the distinction between syntax and semantics is never more than contextual, pragmatic, and provisional.

Anyone rejecting this view is free to invoke the deductive rules we learn or invent, then apply. Acknowledging these rules does not commit us to Cartesian ghosts. It does enable us to distinguish between the analytic and the synthetic, syntax and semantics, form and content. We say that truth conditions for the one devolve only on the rules used for organizing thoughts or sentences, whereas truth conditions for the other are the states of affairs signified by our words. But now, as before, the coherence of sentences reporting these states of affairs is contingent, impressionistic, and often merely aggregative. Quine notwithstanding, this makes deductive relations our preferred standard for coherence.

A different reason for misgivings about deductivist formulations of coherence and truth is the historicist, sociological turn in our thinking about science. Talk about formalized scientific theories is displaced by historicized, sociological analyses. Thomas Kuhn gets credit for this sea change, though his views about paradigms founded in a culture, epoch, or metaphor[4] evoke Hegelian themes prominent in Continental thinking since the early nineteenth century. Hegelian Ideas, like Kuhn's paradigms, work holistically: the Idea is like a pattern, with thoughts or sentences shaped, then fitted, to the spaces it provides. Patterns of this sort are not fixed in stone. They are more like the gestalten of perception, as the picture of a rabbit looks like a duck when turned on its side. What cohered before still coheres, though to a different effect. Or we embroider the pattern, altering it beyond recognition. The old pattern and the coherences it sponsored seem fragmentary now, or merely invisible.

Coherences founded in patterns remind us of novels and poems, each of them a network of coherence-making relationships. Where truth is coherence, it depends, first, on the constitution of parts, then on that calibration of parts which realize the whole. The coherence established by each play or narrative, novel or poem, is, however, unique. This makes coherence fragile, since there is no criterion for the coherence of the thing except the thing itself. If a story is true because it hangs together, in the way of a gestalt, then it is equally true, though different, when one or more of the relations is altered to create some different coherence. But then it follows that every consistent story is true from the standpoint of someone claiming to see a coherence-making pattern within it. This is unsettling, because it relegates coherence, hence truth, to that private place where each of us discerns (or not) coherence-making wholes.

Coherences established in a hypothetico-deductive system are, by comparison, testable by everyone who knows the inference rules for moving up or down within it. We don't wait or depend on the lucky chance that some interpreter will make his own sense of the relations set before him. Quine and Kuhn agree, however, that this deductivist solution is objectionable. And they are right, though for psychological reasons having nothing to do with objections either to the analytic–synthetic distinction or to the exaggerated emphasis upon formal systems once current among philosophers of science. For we do not construct and apply one or another deductive system as we face and interpret the world. Consider, therefore, this alternative solution. It acknowledges the difference between stipulated or discovered necessities on the one side and empirical contingencies on the other. Still, it de-emphasizes this difference, while establishing coherence, hence truth, on grounds that mix experience with logic.

F. The Coherence of Inter-Animating Thoughts or Sentences

Suppose that we decline to found coherence, and truth, on fixed deductive relations. How shall we avert truth's slide into impressionism, topicality, privacy, and variability? Our solution is the one that Quine proposed as an alternative to the rigorously deductive systems sanctioned by the analytic–synthetic distinction—namely, his fields of inter-animating sentences. This is an alternative midway between the rigor of deduction and the fragile coherences of a novelist's imagination. Fields of sentences are responsive to change and augmentation while sustaining coherence by way of relations previously established. Individuals might differ as regards the system that each uses to create a thinkable world; but equally, socialization might require that all of us learn similar versions of one system.

This solution would have been congenial to Hegel, for he supposed that individuals integrate their thoughts or sentences uniformly when each of them expresses the dominant Idea taught and enforced by their culture. You will see what I see if we have been taught to perceive this thing in the same way. Still, these culturally sanctioned Ideas or forms are not exempt from variations that occur as Ideas are invoked by people having subtly different interests and circumstances. Worse, Ideas are no defense against incoherence and discord when interpreters are fractious and the paradigms come apart. These are the occasions that Kuhn describes as revolutionary, the times when paradigms are confounded, then scuttled, and replaced. Old coherences disintegrate; new ones, hence new truths, are established. How shall we defend against the risk that socially established truths may become variable or passé? Probably, there is no defense when old and new ideas are radically opposed, as slavery and freedom are antithetic. There is to be no place for one in the presence of its opposite. There is, however, no reason for the panic which anticipates the ultimate dissolution of every paradigm or Idea. Many endure, with their truth-making coherences, for a long time.

Notice that Quine's inter-animating thoughts or sentences are the substance of Kuhn's paradigms. This seems mistaken if we think that paradigms are the schematic expressions of things (e.g., Abe Lincoln as the paradigmatic president); but that use of paradigms is irrelevant here where Kuhn is appealing to schematic ideas expressed by linked thoughts or sentences (e.g., to mechanism or organicism). An implication inimical to Kuhn's emphasis is also relevant. He writes of the cycle that recurs as normal and revolutionary science succeed one another. This is a story about the substitution, exploration, embroidery, breakdown, and replacement of successive paradigms. It ignores the possibility that multiply connected sentences might have an inertia or persistence which defends them against the revolutions that occur when one paradigm displaces another. For there may be no reason to jettison everything we have accepted as true if our revision of some part of a field of sentences enables us to alter the pitch or bias of the whole. Given a succession of pictures showing the same face from childhood to old age, we get a radically different face at the end after subtle, repeated alterations to the constituent features. Radical alteration of a paradigm might also be achieved by transforming constituent sentences and their relations. Revision, not replacement, might be the order of the day. Hegel and Kuhn have emphasized replacement. Duhem, writing of thermodynamics, makes as good a case for the persistence, through revision, of established truths.[5]

Suppose that a system of inter-animating thoughts or sentences[6] survives shifts in conversation and empirical observations too, all this by way of evidence that we are determined to endure changes among the sensory data by insistently using this system of linked notions to order and differentiate the data. No matter, then, if things change in many ways, for slack in our conceptual system is sufficient to accommodate both the changes predicted and many that are not. Why this resilience? Because thoughts and sentences are typically under-determined by empirical data, meaning that the data may be construed in many, perhaps an infinity of, ways. Conversely, data that seem to confound a system may be reconstrued in ways congenial to it. We might change conceptual systems as often as we change socks, though there is no reason but boredom to do that if our system effectively interprets the data, come what may. Having a system that secures and satisfies us, we keep it. Indeed, it is this stable value (better, this complex valorizing attitude) that explains our enduring commitment to any particular effective interpretive system.

We get this effect: a system of stably linked thoughts or sentences is the cognitive side of the cognitive-affective posture evolving within each of us. These are the expectations with which we face a shifting world. There are other effective ways of addressing the world; but each of us learns some particular complex interpretive system. The system is elastic, but stable. It has a long developmental history, with a myriad practical applications and a facility for integrating disparate revisions and discoveries. With truth and understanding founded in this conservative but accommodating system, we no longer fear that the coherence of our thoughts or sentences must rely on either topicality or our facility for mimicking (in thought or language) the coherences in nature.

Remember that we are concerned to reduce the opposition of sentences that differ because they are true empirically or syntactically. Using a disguise that is transparent but rhetorically useful, we say that the truth of thoughts or sentences linked within a system or field is, for all of them, *probabilistic.* The probabilities may run, we suppose, from 0 to 1. Where truth has the probability value 1, it depends only on the syntactic relations linking some thought or sentence to others. Every thought or sentence having a probability value between 0 and 1 is sensitive, as syntactic truths are not, to empirical data.

Relations among thoughts or sentences might go in the following way. A is linked to E, P, and W; B to F, Q, and X; C to G, R, and Y; and D to E, Q, and Y. There are, we suppose, associative rules, appropriate to differences in the probability values of these links. A's linkage to E, for example, may have the probability of 1, while its links to P and W may have a value of less than 1. The rules appropriate to linkage having a probability of 1 include classical rules of inference such as *modus ponens.* Rules appropriate to linkages having a probability of less than 1 are inductive, since it is an inductive rule which sanctions the inference from "There is smoke coming from the windows" to "Your house is on fire."

The probability value of linkages within a field may fall off smoothly from 1 in the direction of 0, with successively weaker links all the way down. But equally, there might be a plateau of probability, say at 0.5, with most inductive links at this level or above and with a gap in the range of, say, 0.1 to 0.5. There is, in this case, empirical support for the linkage of A to P and W no less than half the time, but little or no empirical support for A's associations to other thoughts or sentences.

Where every link between the sentences of a set is probabilistic, it is only probable that the link inferred from some other linked pair obtains (e.g., as we might infer from the link of A to P and A to W that P is linked to W). Sometimes the probability of an inferred link is high to the point of having the value 1, as when one geometrical inference justifies a train of other inferences. Other times, probabilistic inference does not guarantee that a sentence will be true in the respect that it follows from, hence coheres with, a skein of other links. There is, we suppose, only the greater likelihood of a coupling—of P to W when both are linked to A.

We easily formulate sentences that contradict one another (as we express by saying that the probability of a linkage between them is 0). This is a limiting case, one that marks the point where a linkage among sentences is precluded. Sentences for which there is the somewhat greater probability of an empirical link may also fall outside a set of inter-animating sentences. That happens in our example when the probability of a link is greater than 0 but less than 0.5. There is, we assume, no logical relation and little empirical evidence to support inferences between sentences in and outside of the system having this lower boundary for its probabilistic connections. The logical limit and empirical threshold are barriers setting the various sets of cohering sentences apart from one another: probabilistic relations having higher values are the peaks marking sets of linked sentences, valleys of low probability are the evidence of gaps among these sets. Still, probabilistic truth-making relations do come to be established between sentences of disparate sets. That happens often as we learn to couple sentences in previously unexpected ways with links sanctioned empirically or syntactically: think of metaphors turned literal.

The systems we create resemble those established by phone companies: callers within one system can dial every other phone in that system, and some of them can dial numbers in other networks, though many or most callers in one system may be unable to dial most numbers in other systems. What is more, there are numbers within a system which some two or more cannot ring at the same time; there are party lines such that a call to one makes that caller or receiver more available to other callers; and there are bridges such that parties who cannot call one another can both call or be called by an intermediary. There are, finally, moving thresholds of impedance and facilitation, as the link between two subscribers makes one or both of them more or less resistant to calls to or from other subscribers.

Identifying the bases for these linkages requries that we do better than metaphor. But now, even that rhetorical disguise suggested above seems flimsy and maladroit. For we shall not make the distinctions appropriate to material truth as long as we refuse to differentiate among the links described probabilistically. There is, I mean to say, more than the degree of probability to distinguish links having a probability of 1 from those having a lesser degree of truth-supporting probability. This difference is the one invoked when we distinguish the synthetic or semantic from the syntactic or analytic. There are two things to notice.

One is the consideration that some coherence-making links among sentences related probabilistically are only syntactic, as we infer $-p$ from *if p then q* and $-q$ with a probability of 1. Inferences of this kind are sanctioned by rules, not by anything that might count as an observation. Certainly, we can imagine p without q, though not when we have construed 'then' as implying *q if p*. Quine implies that pragmatic interests or empirical differences might make some difference to connections that are typically thought to be logical only, though one strains to imagine what empirical difference would make one relinquish such logical rules as that of identity, $A = A$.

The other consideration is relevant here; for suppose that the formal, syntactic spine is only part of a conceptual system. The truth of some thoughts or sentences derives from coherences established syntactically; but there are other thoughts or sentences for which the coherentist truth relation is material—synthetic—rather than syntactic. Even syntactic truths might also be true because they cohere in ways that satisfy the conditions for material truth. But what supports material truths when no truth has any basis but the coherence of thoughts or sentences? First is the calibration of observation sentences with other sentences by way of inductive rules. More remote are the empirical data themselves. Probabilistic inference tells us that there is a chance, say, of 0.5 or better that one thing will be correlated with another (perhaps because one is cause of the other or because both are effects of the same cause). Observation tests the prediction, while sentences reporting an observation enter the network of inter-animating sentences. There they support or reduce—under the force of inductive rules—the strength of links among associated sentences, including sentences that are valid because of their syntactic links to other sentences. This is critical support for a coherentist, material truth when we do not accept its alleged truth on syntactic grounds alone.

Wanting to bypass disputes about the analytic–synthetic distinction, I proposed that we explicate the coherence of thoughts or sentences by way of links having a probability value: necessary truths would have the value 1, contradictions 0, contingencies some value in between. More plainly now, this cosmetic disguise merely obscures the important difference between syntax and semantics, form and content. Sentences that are true because of their relations to other sentences are not, on that count alone, true of the world. Truth of the material sort requires that sentences be linked to observation reports, directly or by way of intermediary sentences. Those linkages are never better than contingent and conditional; their probability values are always less than 1.

It is less consequential now that Quine's fields of inter-animating sentences fulfill only one of their two promises. For never mind that the analytic–synthetic distinction reemerges in an insistent way, making it hard to imagine that we might ever supersede the difference between syntactic and semantic truths (e.g., *modus ponens* versus any claim about the weather). Overriding this distinction would have been significant, but maybe not urgent. For that is not so critical *here* as the fact that systems of linked thoughts or sentences do supply a stable, resilient basis for every claim whose truth devolves only upon its coherence under syntactic or inductive rules with other sentences of a system. We are not reduced to truths deriving only from their topicality or from mimicking spatial, temporal, or causal relations in nature. Confident of a theory which has survived empirical confirmations and practical applications while evolving to include theoretical extensions and revisions, we say that coherentist truth is all the truth that anyone might require.

G. Holism

Coherence entails holism. For holism is the consequence of our demand that the truth of a claim should derive from its composability with others. It is not required that each sentence entail or be entailed by every other; only that every one is connected to some others, so that each relates to every other, however attenuated the connection. It might happen, for example, that all the people in a town are related. That would be so not only if all were descended from one person, but also if A and Z were related by way of N, their cousin, while sharing no bloodline. This loose holism compares to the tight holism of sentences ordered deductively. Either way, we get a tissue of sentences that are true because of their links to one another.

Why not have islands of coherence, each one having no relations (whether inductive or deductive) to some or any others? This does happen within societies and individuals: archaic systems of belief survive because of their isolation. But then the "truths" declared within these islands are suspect. Economy and cohesion impel us to mend the ruptures by establishing implicative relations among the disconnnected sectors of thought, even to the point where old truths are jettisoned.

Holism serves a metaphysical interest, for assume that we want access to the world, though we are skeptical that there is a knowable world existing independently of us. Assume, too, that it is true (because systematically linked) ideas, thoughts, or sentences that are the proximate objects of awareness, all objectivity made available to us by them. How shall we confront the world they present: in ways that are piecemeal or all at once? Think about the world bit by bit, and we have the problem of integrating the bits. That is averted if we comprehend all the world at once. But how are we to do that? Imitating Descartes, we grasp the entire system of linked thoughts or sentences, all its articulations set before us, in a single perception. Yet this Cartesian dream is not easily satisfied, if the system inspected is applicable and adequate to all being. For that is a lot to comprehend at once, even if we deflect the objection that Goedel's theorem precludes the completeness of deductive systems of the sort that Descartes envisaged. We deflect this point by saying that links among the sentences of our comprehensive system are probabilistic, not deductive, though some of the probabilities have the value 1. We suppose, in addition, that the system uses a small number of theoretical terms to represent all the myriad differences and relations within experience. Indeed, we do everything we can to make it plausible that a whole system might be thought at once, as anyone hearing a seamless melody understands the motive for wanting all the linked elements of an idea or theory to pass before him, nothing hidden, no stray part uncounted. Thinking or perceiving all of it at once (perhaps in an extended moment), seeing all the truth-making coherences, we would comprehend the world as gods do.

Holism is the shadow cast by the demand that all of being should be comprehensible at once. Mind is to be either the unifier of conscious experience, whether empirical or propositional, or the medium in which a unified world is presented (e.g., either as schematized data or as a conceptual system unified by its inter-animating sentences). It is only a psycho-centric ontology that gives credibility to this notion of being, for nothing else has the power to quash skepticism while making the world accessible to knowledge: we guarantee the world's existence and character, bringing it into noetic light, by entertaining or by making it. A god would have comprehensive knowledge of the world in all its ramifications, nothing out of place. We have it, too, if the coherences making sentences true are the implicative (internal) relations binding thoughts or sentences within a single, comprehensively inspectable network of thinkable differences.

H. Maps and Plans

The system of linked thoughts or sentences is stable and resilient. Predictions are confirmed and initiatives are successful when we use this system to address the world. There is, nevertheless, something quixotic in the idea that coherence might be a sufficient condition for the truth of thoughts or sentences. It does not matter to this point that thoughts or sentences are related deductively or as items within one of Quine's fields. Both characterizations locate truth in our ability to create a web of coherent thought or speech. This cannot be the whole story when action is more than the invention and use of conceptual systems for schematizing sensory data. Action of this bloodless sort is nicely suited to literary imagination, but not to fixing leaky roofs or caring for sick children. We are reminded of those pragmatists who suppose that conceptual systems are the only instrument required for accommodating ourselves to the world: why should we need any other tool if minds create experiences and worlds merely by using these systems to interpret sensory data? But we do not create our worlds, as anyone tripping on a stair or splattered by a pigeon knows. Error, frustration, confusion, and death give us pause. We do not control all the world around us; we have not made it, although we are obliged to find our way in it.

We do so only as we have accurate maps and cogent plans. Their coherence is partly the consequence of their topicality—that is, of our current focus and the style of our representations. Topicality is not sufficient, however, for directing the behaviors that secure and satisfy us. Maps and plans must also be true of the world, where truth is correspondence, not the mere coherence of thoughts or sentences. Firemen who share a mythology of danger and salvation also organize themselves to fight real fires. They use maps that represent their situation and plans that anticipate the instrumental relations obtaining there. Some firemen write or tell stories about fires. Some of those stories are true because they represent actual events; but others are fiction, however much the sentences cohere. For storytelling does not create either fires or truths about them, even when the stories are so vivid that we recoil in terror from the fires imagined. Firemen who start fires are better called arsonists than novelists. They do with matches what coherent thoughts and sentences can never do.

I. Truth is not Coherence

The failure to provide within our system of linked sentences for maps and plans should make us suspicious. Granted that the system's predictions are confirmed and that the conduct directed by it is successful, have we identified the factors that explain these successes? How do we explain them if there is no provision within the system for accurate representations of our circumstances? There seem to be just these two alternatives: either there are accurate representations within the system, however disguised and unacknowledged, or the successful predictions and behaviors credited to the system are make-believe. We use the system for predicting effects or directing behavior; but then we construe the evidence in ways that are favorable to the system, when a closer look would confirm that the predictions were falsified and the behavior ineffective. Remember what Quine said about protecting a system confounded by the data: plead hallucination. We do better than that if we suppose that differentiations and relations credited to the data are merely projections of differences and relations prefigured in our words or ideas. For then the data have only the character that we project onto them, not some alien, resistant character of their own. Nor must we suffer inconvenient truths if the inductive rules used to sanction truths are merely our stipulations. For then the power to declare truths or falsehoods is the power to make these stipulations. Where truth (declared in the formal mode) prefigures existence (expressed in the material mode), we needn't tolerate the inconvenient states of affairs that disconfirm our predictions or frustrate our plans. Resilient and stable, our system of linked sentences may be testimony only to our facility for constructing the sustained delusion that we are in touch with a world miraculously congenial to our desires.

We risk turning perpetually in a dialectical circle. We infer from our experience to its conditions, including the terrain represented by maps and the instrumental relations significant for plans. Or we distrust the coherences based on these inferences, either because we are unable to confirm them beyond a shadow of doubt or because we fear that nature may come unstuck in the way that Hume described. We then turn our backs on nature, preferring that semantic and inductive rules be used prescriptively to establish the linked thoughts or sentences (linked deductively or probabilistically) which supply the basis for stable experience. It is no matter now what the world tells us of itself, for we decide the differentiations and order that are to be constitutive of experience. We move from naive realism to Humean skepticism to Kantian prescriptivism and constructivism, then around another time.[7] We are propelled ever forward when each step is subjected to dialectical criticisms for which it has no perfect defense.

J. The Metaphysical Basis for Truth as Coherence

Two questions about coherence remain. What metaphysical theory supports the notion that truth is coherence? And what values provoke us to invent this theory, including its notion of truth?

It is important to the first question that metaphysical theories point two ways: on one side to the world, on the other to the dialectic of contending theories. Any particular theory may be responsive to both considerations, as we want a specification of the world's categorial features that is better than the theories currently available. Equally, a theory may be formulated principally or only to satisfy one of these aims. The metaphysical theory supporting the idea of truth as coherence is a theory of this latter sort: it is dialectical and reactive. Its origins are somewhat as follows.

Behaviors directed by maps and plans succeed or fail, and we infer that the world has a character of its own, one that stands against us as we try to alter it in ways that suit us. This is a character we see, hear, and touch, one that is represented more accurately as we infer abductively from perceptual evidence to its conditions (e.g., from smoke to fire). Stable and recurring percepts, confirmed hypotheses, and behaviors that satisfy our aims convince us that our natural and conventional signs are a window onto the world. Perceiving, then thinking and talking, about matters of fact, we suppose that we can see through these signs to the states of affairs they represent. Confidence erodes only as some representations prove inaccurate or false. Always fearing distorted representations, we become skeptical about every one: perhaps all our beliefs, thoughts, and sentences misrepresent the world. We begin to doubt that there are any safe inferences from successful action to the character of the world encountered. Apparent successes may be only chimerical or accidental. We despair of confirming any single belief beyond the possibility of error. Before, we hoped and expected that we might accurately represent things as they are in themselves. Now, skepticism turns us hostile to the very idea of a world existing independently of mind, thought, or language. No longer supposing that thoughts and sentences are a point of access to the world, we come to regard them as a barrier forever separating us from things represented. Having no way of confirming our beliefs about the noumenal world, we go these two steps further, doubting, then denying, the very existence of things apart from thought and language.

Sobered as only failure can make us, we consider our circumstances and resources. We seem to know many things about the world. But what is there to generate content and objects for this knowledge when a world independent of mind is no longer their plausible source? Could they originate in thought and language, hence in mind? Perhaps individual minds, or minds co-ordinated, create all that is differentiated and organized within experience. Perhaps the world is nothing additional to or beyond our experience of it. Knowledge, we come to say, has no aim but that of comprehending the things which are set before the mind, without need for mediating representations. These inspectables may be perceptual objects schematized when mind organizes sensory data, rules discerned in the logical geography of their uses, formalized theories set before comprehending minds, or a network of socialized behaviors such that actors know by self-inspection the rules governing everyone's conduct, hence the predictable outcome of ritualized behaviors.

This program for knowledge derives from the specification of our resources, though we now inherit the new problem of explaining mind's constitution of a thinkable world. This new problem has two sides. First, how do we provide within the experience that mind sets before itself for everything that was once thought vital to the world? Were there objects, causes, necessities, and laws credited to it? Then provision shall be made for them within the world reconstituted within experience. Second, what is mind itself, and how could it do all this?

Mind's sense of itself is vastly changed in the course of this reflection. Before there was modesty out of reverence for a world we have not made. There was also naiveté about mind's own powers. Now these two are superseded by mind's self-assurance: it will do everything for itself. Before, we were tentative. Now we inspect the world arrayed before us without fear of error. For there is no distorting space, no gap, between the things in space and time and our knowledge of them. The world is only what we declare it to be. Its character is the function of whatever predicates are used for describing it. The existence of things within it is a function of the inductive rules used for determining that the sentences affirmed are true because they cohere with other sentences already accepted. So there is white snow because "The snow is white" is true: the sentence in the object language satisfies the rules for using this sentence in conjunction with others sanctioned by our inductive rules. Yet the coherence of sentences in the object language under inductive rules has this obscured, deeper, probably transcendental beginning: thought or language in the material mode is the constituting shadow projected by thought or language in the formal mode. There is nothing in the world that we have not put there, as we determine in our meta-language (transcendentally) how to think and talk about the world.

Skeptics might have been satisfied by any number of positions short of this idealist extreme. We might have settled somewhere in the middle, saying with Leibniz[8] that the coherence of beliefs and sentences is not truth itself, but only evidence that the network of our thoughts or sentences represents states of affairs whose existence and character are independent of them. Warranted assertibility, this implies, is not truth, but only the evidence of it. Too bad that this middle view is unstable: it is pulled from left and from right, from realism on the one side, idealism on the other, the one as it demands recognition of the things we do not make, the other as it insists that there is no knowledge of anything but the things we do make. The dialectic of realism and idealism drives us inevitably to these limits. Saying that truth is only coherence, we express this opposition on the idealist side.

K. Coherence, Identity, and Redundance as Variations on the Same Metaphysical Theme

Notice that coherence is one of three notions of truth suited to a metaphysics generated by the skeptical response to representational realism. Truth may be identity, redundancy, or coherence when the fear of mistaken representations is a principal motive for our metaphysical thinking. The metaphysical theories embedding these alternate notions of truth may differ significantly from one another, though the psycho-centric ontology of Descartes and Kant is congenial to all three of them. Contemporary disputes often turn among these three notions of truth and within the metaphysical theory they share. Identity and redundancy are considered separately below; but the exposition will be clearer if we start by locating them within the generic meta-physical theory they share with coherence.

Coherence is the notion favored when knowledge is alleged to be propositional — that is, when the content and objects of knowledge are thoughts or sentences said to be true because of their logical relations (whether deductive or inductive) to one another. Identity is preferred when thoughts and sentences are rejected as the medium for truth because of their lingering reputation as signs. Knowledge requires presentation of the things known, without the mediation of entities whose only relevance to knowledge is their use as representations. Skepticism and mind's powers for world-making have stripped thoughts and sentences of this representational function. Still, thoughts and sentences never lose the opprobrium of having been stand-ins for something other than themselves. We can do without them, says the reading that favors identity: knowledge is to be achieved by direct perception of its objects. This is Plato's claim, that *nous* merges itself with the Forms, and also the claim of Berkeley's phenomenalism, that sensory data are qualifications of the mind apprehending them. There is also Kant's affirmation that schematizing mind grasps as part of itself the experience it has made.

Mind achieves identity with the objects of knowledge in each of these cases by incorporating or merging itself with them. The gap between knower and known where error breeds is eliminated. Descartes (though not Plato) might have expressed this point in the following terms. I am a thinking being, one whose existence is confirmed only as I perceive it. Yet I cannot think of myself if I am not thinking also of something else: empty my mind of every other content, and I lose myself. I who exist by virtue of my thinking think both these mental contents and myself in the same act: I see a thing as red in the moment and on the condition that I am aware of myself seeing it as red. Direct and infallible awareness of myself under qualification is assured, there being nothing to mediate or distort my self-perception. And equally, there is no possibility that I might be mistaken about the existence or character of something (however accidental and ephemeral) qualifying me. The truth of my claims about it, hence my knowledge of it, is assured. This is not to say that a mind distracted or deceitful cannot misdescribe its own qualifications; this often happens. The present claim is the narrower one that a mind turned upon itself apprehends its qualifications, thereby itself.

Truth as identity entails truth as redundancy. For suppose I apprehend myself suffused with the sound of a bell. Adding that I truly hear the sound is otiose, if the manner of my hearing it (by self-inspection) precludes error.

Redundancy, identity, and coherence are variations on a theme. The theme is complex, with four complementary parts. One is the idea that the objects of knowledge are not alien and remote, with the implication that access to them is mediated, distorted, and partial. Second is the contrary idea: that mind has an unmediated, undistorted, and comprehensive view of everything set before it. There is no gap between us and the things inspected, hence no mediating space to distort mind's view of its objects. These comprehensively inspectable things are, third, the proper objects of knowledge, so that, fourth, the contents of knowledge are merged with its objects. Ideas, percepts, sentences, or theories: each is grasped as it qualifies awareness. These things are inscribed in consciousness: we know them as we know ourselves.

Redundancy as the outcome of identity is not so familiar as the thesis that truth is "disquotational." Disquotational versions of redundancy are considered below. It is important to these preliminary points only that redundancy is seen to share its skeptical roots and supporting ontology with the notions of truth as coherence or identity. There will be time later on to answer the objection that disquotational versions of redundancy do not imply the psycho-centric ontology common to coherentist and identity notions of truth.

L. Some Implications of Truth as Coherence

Coherence is still the notion that occupies us. Mind is its centerpiece and condition. For mind is more than witness to the coherence among its thoughts, beliefs, or sentences. Coherence is created as judgments are made in accordance with rules that mind lays down for itself: mind finds the world intelligible in just the terms that mind has itself prescribed. Mind is responsible even for the existence of whatever is present in the world it has made, *existence* being only a word for expressing in the material mode what is affirmed in the formal mode.[9] Embellishing Tarski's semantic conception of truth, we say that snow is white—these last three words being a sentence in the object language—on condition that this sentence is true by virtue of its relations, under inductive rules, to other sentences. The presence of these rule-determined relations is not always evident, as when snow looks white while, independently, the sky seems blue or gray. Their apparent separability is untrustworthy, however, for we cannot declare that these features are mutually independent until we have determined that the thoughts or sentences prefiguring them are not related by inductive rules within our schematizing theory or interpretation. Holism says that there are no sentences so remote from one another in a consistent theory as to have no implications for one another. Mind is to enjoy the whole seamless weave, each part bound to and affected, directly or mediately, by every other.

All the world has mind as its only site, minds themselves being free-standing and self-sufficient. Thinking, perhaps by generating sentences, is their way of being. It is vital, too, that these world-makers are self-conscious, each one seeing the world schematized as a qualification of itself. Each mind's access to itself is, moreover, exhaustive, every articulation exposed, nothing hidden to mind's self-conscious gaze. Mysteriously, because no one ever tells exactly how it is done, these self-transparent, self-sufficient agents co-ordinate themselves with one another, thereby making a world they share. We get the intersubjectivity of Hegel rather than the hermetic, monadic subjectivity of Leibniz. Either way, this notion of mind is that of Descartes' *cogito* reconceived as Kant's transcendental ego, then elevated to the authority whereby it, like Hegel's God, fills all being with successive schematizations rooted only and always in itself.

No thinker who locates him or herself within the analytic, positivist, or naturalist tradition acknowledges this fantasy of transcendental world-making. But this is our heritage and burden when skeptical arguments drive us out of the natural world into the posture of making worlds for ourselves. We may want to reconsider the view that the truth of thoughts and sentences is their relation to one another, never the relation to their extra-mental, extra-linguistic truth conditions. It begins to seem less likely that truth might be nothing but the coherences secured by rules of inference or the ephemeral topicalities of conversation or attention. We see the good sense of distinguishing representational, hypothetical thinking from the thinking that is making.

M. Values that Motivate the Metaphysical Theory which Supports Truth as Coherence

Six desires—that is, six values—motivate this idealist result. First is the antipathy to realism: we shall never be able to prove that things have the character imputed to them by our signs; and anyway, there may be no world beyond the veil of percepts, thoughts, and words. Next is the desire for knowledge invulnerable to the uncertainties entailed by mediating signs. Coherentists want to set all the world, but, more urgently, all the apparatus for schematizing worlds, before our inspecting minds, nothing excluded, every thought or sentence in its place but connected to the rest. That would be a subject matter worth knowing. These first two values express the arcane preferences stirred by philosophical dialectic. No one unfamiliar with those disputes is likely to be moved by them.

A third value motivating truth as coherence resonates throughout our social and emotional lives, in art and religion. This is the desire for harmony. Harmony is opposed to conflict, with its implication of runaway violence. We are reassured and pleased when parts cohere, in machines and in social relations. We also prefer harmony in the relations of thoughts and sentences, because conflict is a sure sign that some of our judgments are partial or mistaken. Conflict in them, with its risk of bungled plans, is an intimation of danger. Coherence, like a smooth sea, feels safer.

But is coherence a sufficient test for truth? How could it be when stories about the Easter rabbit are not true for being well-knit? Coherentists have an explanation for examples like this: a story that seems ample, all its parts cohering, may not be long enough, for only as the story is extended does it encounter the thoughts or sentences with which it conflicts. Even a very long story may need to be extended through denumerably infinite additions before we can be sure that there are no irresolvable conflicts in it. It is these conflicts which expose the errors in a mistaken narrative that had seemed coherent. Accordingly, harmony in a story is evidence of its truth only as we assume that the story is infinitely extended.

Suppose this is done (though only a god could do it), and that there are no conflicts in a story of denumerably infinite length. The story is coherent, hence true; but, we ask, true of what? The answer, we have learned, is that nothing is external to the narrative, all objectivity being constituted within it. Truth is a property only of the system, not the relation connecting the system to something beyond itself. Every question about the truth of the system, as against the truth of parts co-ordinated within it, is the residual but empty gesture left over from realism and its notion that truth is correspondence.

Even this phantom disappears when we consider the fourth value: namely, the desire for a power sufficient to control the terms of our engagement in the world. Like gods, we want the power to make, then live within, a world suited to our attitudes and desires. We have that power if mind can establish truth-making relations among its thoughts and sentences. For there is to be an existing state of affairs for every truth. If a rule prescribes that nothing is to count as baked if it is not burnt, then we never say, "It is baked but underdone." But it is baked if "The dough was placed in the oven, and kept there until burnt" is true. Our worlds are to be detailed and populated in ways appropriate to our stories about them. This is power indeed. No god could do more.

The fifth value directs each mind as it considers using its power. What sort of world do I want? Is my ideal world ascetic or indulgent, one that values liberty or the corporate state? This preference might be a desire unique to myself or one favored by all members of a culture, though differences in content and origin are incidental to the fact that self-sufficient mind is free to direct its world-making in any consistent way and for any reason it chooses. We are reminded of Hume's dictum that reason is and ought to be the slave of the passions: we tell such coherence-fulfilling stories, thereby constructing such worlds, as satisfy particular attitudes or desires.

There is finally this sixth value: the conviction that there is a right to dwell in the world of one's choice. This is an extrapolation from the idea of democracy: the idea that people in their collectivity should be self-governing. We extend the application of this idea beyond politics, affirming each person's right to determine the character of his or her experience. For there is no expression of self-governance purer than the act of creating the world in which one lives. This is a right common to everyone dwelling in the kingdom of ends. Every rational being qualifies for membership in that kingdom by virtue of having the power to contrive a world for him or herself. Pluralism and tolerance are additional virtues required of ends when this kingdom has a membership larger than one, though these two qualities are already implicit in the idea of being an end. For anyone subordinated to the desires of other world-makers is a means, not an end. It is therefore a condition for each one's freedom that he or she acknowledge the right of every world-maker to make and live in the world he or she chooses.

There are, summarily, two requirements to meet if a world-making story is to be declared by a world-maker who achieves thereby his or her autonomy: a story can objectify a world only if it is coherent, hence true; the story must also satisfy this world-maker's desires. We are to believe that each of us can meet these conditions; and that each may respect, from the distance of his or her own world, the autonomy, experience, and world of every other world-maker.

N. Value-Driven Cognitive Systems

The three factors described above—namely, the coherentist notion of truth, its embedding psycho-centric metaphysics, and the values motivating the theory—have a corporate integrity for which we lack a word. Calling them a "theory," we ignore the role of motivating values. Speaking only of the values, we ignore the differentiating, schematizing systems whose creation they impel. The diversity of these elements should not blind us to their reciprocity or to the integrity of the systems in which they are the parts. Wanting a plausible neologism, but settling for a clumsy phrase, I describe these complexes as "value-driven cognitive systems." The name is important only for defending the corporate identity of these systems from a dissolving analysis. There is no notion of truth without an embedding metaphysical theory; and neither of them without the particular values motivating their formulation. We know the integrity of these complexes by their stability. Philosophers in the tradition of Kant and Fichte, including all or most of those who speak for world-making in our time, repeatedly invoke or assume all three elements. That these philosophers sometimes ignore the metaphysical complexity of their idealism is a different point.

III Truth as Identity

The idea that truth is identity, like the emphasis on coherence, originates in the fear that claims about the world will not be confirmable if mind is separated from the world by its percepts, ideas, or sentences. They might be a barrier to our knowledge of things, not the clear medium through which those states of affairs are apprehended. There is, however, a difference in the metaphysical positions promoting identity and coherence as our notions of truth. Preferring the coherence of thoughts and sentences, we emphasize the vehicles for representation past the time when their function as signs is eliminated by our suspicion that their referents cannot be known. Emphasizing identity, we express a desire to exceed representations on the way to grasping the things themselves. Let there be no mediation, we say: let us address things as they are. More, let us close the gap between them and ourselves, thereby eliminating the space that distorts our view of them. We do that by merging ourselves with the objects for knowledge or by taking them into mind as its qualifications. Knowledge is the consequence. It requires that we achieve identity with the things known, knowing them by virtue of knowing ourselves.

A. Intuitionist Versions of Truth as Identity

Plato's claim about the relation of *nous* to the Forms is one variation of this idea. Active intellect (rational intuition) grasps the Forms, not as a hand grasps things, but rather as an infinitely protean matter takes on the character of the thing qualifying it.[10] *Nous*, as Plato describes it, is the rational anima suffusing all Being. It is not a particularized Cartesian self-consciousness which affirms that its intuition of the Forms is, at the same time, a self-intuition: we do not have Plato saying, "I know that I am by virtue of apprehending myself as I think of the Good." Still, *nous*, however depersonalized, might be credited with a power of self-reflection enabling it to observe its qualification by the Forms, hence its identity with them. Self-consciousness of this sort is implied to at least the extent that acquaintance with the Forms is remembered.

The intuitionism common to Berkeley and Hume[11] is similar to that of Plato, though with this Cartesian difference: mind is receptive and particularized, not active, in relation to the things which fill and qualify it. There is also the difference that our powers of intuition are reduced to those of empirical, not rational, intuition; the phenomena infusing mind are sensory data, not ideas or Forms. There are, however, pertinent similarities between Plato, Berkeley, and Hume as regards intuition and identity. Each supposes that the content or objects of knowledge are present within mind as its qualifications, so that a mind aware of itself knows them. It is also striking that Hume, like Plato, does not credit mind with awareness of a distinct self, finding nothing of mind except the things that fill it; though Hume, after Plato, does seem to agree that awareness implies, and perhaps requires, a decentered self-consciousness, meaning consciousness of our receptivity without the particularized consciousness that it is I who am aware. Awareness of qualifications carries with it (and maybe presupposes) recognition that awareness is qualified by its contents.

We are also reminded of the phrase so often reiterated within the tradition of Humean empiricism: namely, *sense certainty*. Minds possessing their data cannot be mistaken, it is said, in their judgments that awareness is qualified, except in the trivial respect that one could misuse language, perhaps using 'red' to report that the qualifying datum is yellow. What is it about these judgments that eliminates the possibility of error? Just the fact that there is no gap between awareness and its object: mind has turned on and perceives—hence knows—this qualification of itself. Hume writes within the tradition of those psycho-centric ontologies in which nothing is real but mind and its states. Plato defied this skeptical view of things, arguing that *nous*, transcending its embodiments, grasps Forms whose existence and character are independent of finite bodies. This difference is striking, but incidental when knowledge for both Plato and Hume is the state or attitude of a (self-less) consciousness aware of its qualification by some content. This point of accord joins them to Berkeley's more Cartesian view. All three secure our access to the world by supposing that subject and object are one at the moment of knowledge: mind knows the world by knowing itself.

B. Behaviorist Versions of Truth as Identity

There is also a different notion of truth as identity, though now the tidiness of my organizational scheme is compromised, because this other idea of truth as identity could as well be introduced as one of the behaviorist notions. It addresses the social world of people who achieve social identity by learning rules, roles, rights, and duties. The metaphysics supporting this version of truth as identity is sometimes the physicalist account which explains behavior as the selective, learned response to physical cues, though equally, the emphasis on learned behaviors may be coupled to a rich sense of psychic interiority and to skepticism about the reality of anything existing apart from minds. The consequences of these opposed metaphysical views are considered below. Just now, we care only that truth as identity is sometimes alleged to be the outcome of socialization.

We are to say that appropriate behavior requires just what Wittgenstein said of it when he described the "forms of life" learned by players in language-games. You do it; I do it after you. Both learn the same rule, as we confirm when each does the same thing when responding to circumstances which provoke the behavior. How you feel about a prospective activity may or may not be important to performing in ways that are socially anticipated and approved; the first of the supporting metaphysical theories cited above denies, as the second affirms, that feeling or reflection is a necessary condition for the behavior. We have only this much accord between these views: the physicalist theory avers that behavior is the necessary and sufficient condition for achieving social identity; the psycho-centric metaphysics affirms that behavior (occurring within a mind or as an activity shared with other minds) can only reinforce the social identity achieved when a mind reflects on, grasps, and affirms a principle.

The truth ascribed to agents who learn regularized behaviors is well expressed by the phrase *being in the truth*. This is the learned ability for doing what society requires of us. Why emphasize these learned uniformities? One reason is neutral between these two metaphysical theories: societies function better when the business of work, education, family, and civic life is coordinated, stable, and predictable. We get this result when learned behaviors are performed competently but almost thoughtlessly in familiar circumstances, or, as psycho-centrists may prefer, when there is consensus about the principles to be affirmed and applied.

A different worry about these regularities interpolates the mediating, appraising mental space of the second theory into the physicalist agent of the first. There is, we remark, a certain uneasiness in each of us. Am I one of the group? Are my clothes, ideas, or accent right? Are my responses cogent, given our learned expectations for conduct in these circumstances? We make every speaker-actor responsible for public standards of behavior. Everyone is made to understand that there is no place among us for those who do not satisfy these normative expectations. We notice and wonder when behaviors are odd: are you (am I) a slow learner, a clumsy visitor, an impostor? You (I) haven't performed as we would do (as you would have me do). You are (I am) not in the truth; you are not one of us. We may tolerate you; or you (I) may disappear into the isolation and limbo of unintelligibility. Exile was long equivalent, in some countries, to a sentence of death. It assured the person's exclusion from all the rituals which were vital to membership in the community: he could not be in that local truth. With no one to employ him and no source of food, the exile might starve. Certainly, isolation and local contempt would nearly kill him.

Inclusion, not punishment, was the aim when ordinary language philosophers sought the grammatical rules for their corporate identity as English speakers. Analysts would defer reverentially to the behaviorism of Wittgenstein and Ryle while sitting about, eyes half-closed, affirming that meaning is use while imagining how they might use some linguistic expression. It was not required that the imagined circumstances be visualized, merely that the ordinary language analyst tell how he or she, a competent speaker, would use an expression. The analyst would consider the word as it might be used in various contexts, identifying and discounting features such as word order that might be incidental to a use. Such accidents would be distinguished from the rule-governed features essential to using the word correctly. Ordinary language philosophers sometimes agreed that their procedure might be characterized as "transcendental"; it was never to be described as inductive or sociological. After Husserl, with his odium for psychologism, they insisted that their discoveries were the stuff of logic. Analysts mapping the "logical geography" of a term would perceive its logical form by surveying the variety and relations of its possible uses. They would attain thereby an a priori view of whatever differentiations and relations are introduced into our universe of discourse by ascertaining the rules for the word's use.

Participants in a seminar would test their intuitions about the proper uses of a word by employing it in contexts for which they would provide sketchy descriptions. Other participants would approve or not, suggesting variations of their own. Each auditor would learn from the succession of examples and commentaries that he was or was not in the truth, that he did or did not have the well-formed linguistic dispositions of the community. This was frequently an exercise in bonding, each participant confirming his identity as an English speaker before the others, for himself. I know what I am, he might have said; or (probably as he would not have thought to say) I am in the truth. Punishment was subtle: one who could not banter in the stylized ways of the common room would know that his intelligence and identity were coarse or uncertain. He might feel intimidated and stupid. He would feel excluded.

Ordinary language philosophy would not admit to being simultaneously the inductive study of linguistic behavior and transcendental self-analysis. This rift, which set a rhetorical behaviorism against a deeper commitment to *verstehen*, guaranteed its instability. Suppose, however, that we are committed to the idea that truth is the identity of knower and known and, more particularly, that truth requires whatever activity is necessary for being in the truth. How is this idea to be explicated when the two notions joined in ordinary language analysis—that is, behaviorism and self-inspection—are distinguished? We do this best by emphasizing one side while appropriating elements of the other.

Behaviorism explains identity as the learned habits of a body that responds to circumstances in rule-governed ways. The rules are prescriptions and criteria. As prescriptions, they direct our behaviors; as criteria, they are formulas used to interpret what others of our kind are, or should be, doing. We might be no more adept at voicing these rules than a spinning top can know the physical laws exemplified by its motion. Still, we humans can do this one thing that tops cannot: we can see what other people are doing and the situations that provoke them, all the while assaying what we would do. These are the abilities that put us in the truth: we prove who we are by what we do and by expecting others to do it too. One reads that his own defense attorney demanded the death penalty for one of the officers charged with the 1944 plot to murder Hitler. This was behavior confirming to the attorney and relevant others that he was in the truth. The rest of us accommodate ourselves to fashions of every sort, though usually without complicity in anything so vile.

The metaphysics of *verstehen* also cares about behavior, especially behavior that is regularized and distinctive, as dances and wedding ceremonies are different among cultures. This other theory supposes, however, that behavior is an imperfect expression of mind: that it is one or more steps removed from mind's grasp of the principles which determine the shape that conduct is to have. Nothing else counts as knowledge of the rules, for it is only a mind turned upon itself that perceives these rules as they are abstracted from the particular circumstances where we have more or less thoughtlessly learned them. Only as they stand before our minds do we see rules as general principles having normative force throughout the domain of their application. The rules come to possess us. Rocks and rabbits are, at least partly, identical with their disposition; but neither of them strives to alter its conduct so that it may better align itself with principles that define and direct its moral sense. We humans often do that: we find our bearing and identity in those standards of behavior that are refined and idealized as we struggle to articulate them for ourselves, the better to apply them correctly.

But are we socialized, however consistent and uniform our conduct, however secure our identity? For there are these two notions of *socialization*. One formulation implies that socialization is the act of bringing one's will under a law. It is only mildly surprising that this idea requires us to stop at red lights in the middle of Utah, where one can see from horizon to horizon that nothing else is moving in any direction. Nor does it matter that one dwells all alone in a world one has made. Why call it socialization when acting on or accepting a rule does not bring one into contact within anyone else? Because bringing oneself under a universal is, on this view, the necessary and sufficient condition for socialization. No matter that other thinkers living in remote places or walled away in their private worlds do not will the same law; that is incidental. Social identity is achieved merely by affirming the law, for the obligations it implies are now my own. Here is a case where I may be in the truth and know that I am without regard for the confirming views of other thinkers.

The alternative formulation makes interaction a condition for socialization. It requires that we engage other people in ways that are sensitive as much to them and the rules directing us as to ourselves. We get hermetic isolation on the first view, but reciprocity on this other one. Skeptics make no sense of this interaction because of their hostility to naturalism and realism. But then it is odd that one should so fiercely desire to be socialized for the identity it bestows. Why should the skeptic care to have an identity socialized in this second way if mind is all alone in the world it has made? Perhaps for the reason that one shares laws and the world with one other person, at least: namely, a divine, moral being. Reciprocal relations among finite beings are secondary if one's first partner is God.

One thinks of Kant's categorical imperative. This is a rule founded in reason, as it is reason to which consistency and universalizability are essential. Reason as a faculty has a teleology which expresses itself as a rule: achieve consistency and universality in your thinking, whether theoretical or practical. The sociality achieved by affirming or acting on a maxim that satisfies the categorical imperative is just the expression of reason fulfilling its obligation to universalizability. Sociality of the reciprocal kind is derivative by comparison, for Kant supposes that each of us would be committed to the generalization of our private maxims were we alone in the world. There would be no occasion, then, for worrying about the mutual effects of people interacting or about their co-ordinated, rule-governed behaviors. Kant did, nevertheless, suppose that each of us does have a companion—namely, the God who is reason's purest expression and the source of our rationality. It is this affiliation, first with our rational nature, thereby with God, that puts us in the truth.

Being in the truth has, it appears, this simple condition: each of us must realize his or her own nature—as determined by a culture or the character of rationality. It follows that truth as identity is or ought to be close at hand. We have only to discover what we ought to be, then how to use it. *True Romance* is the name of a magazine, but also the demand for something genuine. Identity is genuine when the demeanor visible to the world, like that known to oneself, expresses one's identity, not some disguise. The doting midwife, the committed father, the pickpocket who likes his work, the defense attorney seeking his client's death: each sees his or her *telos* realized in the work done. Each is at one with him or herself and true to that self, if at times all the more culpable for that.

C. The Values that Sponsor Truth as Identity

What values direct us as we espouse the idea that truth is identity? Is there a single value or set of values common to these three notions of truth as identity: the personal, social identity achieved by someone who is in the truth; Platonic *nous* as it actively acquires identity by incorporating the Forms; and Berkelian, Humean sensibility as it accepts qualification by the data impressed upon it? That there are differences among the values impelling these three notions is plain. Plato's realism is moved by the desire that we recognize and accommodate ourselves to a world we have not made. Compare skeptics like Berkeley and Hume: they do whatever is required to establish the world within something that mind does or makes, then inspects. The value moving them is their antipathy to realism. These differences are incidental, however, to the point at issue: whether there are values common to these metaphysical alternatives, values satisfied by the claim that truth is identity.

Two values qualify. One is the epistemic fear that we may lose contact with the world. This anxiety pervades Western thinking about knowledge and its conditions. For we may be everywhere deluded, thinking we have knowledge of the world, all the while having no touch with things as they are in themselves. We are vulnerable and want to secure ourselves. Knowledge of the things around us seems desperately important to the actions that make us safe. But can we have it?

The other value is authenticity. We suspect that knowing mind is incomplete in itself and that it achieves completion only by grasping things as they are. Only this engagement with "the things themselves" is fulfilling. How shall we capture and possess the objects of knowledge so that they cannot be taken from us, thereby precluding error? We do this in a simple, albeit primitive, way: things to be known cannot escape us if we become, or incorporate, them. The knowing is now unproblematic, for we know the things possessed merely by turning upon them as they exist within us: I know Forms or sensory data because I know them as I know myself when they are a part of me. Think of Descartes' ruminations: I am, I exist. What am I? A thinking thing. For how long do I exist? As long as I think. Of what do I think? I think of myself, by way of the things that qualify me. All knowing is self-knowledge.

Truth as identity founded in social participation and acknowledgment is only a little more complicated: I know myself as others know me, while all that I find intelligible and acceptable in others is an expression of the same principles and properties that are constitutive and acceptable in myself. Once uncertain of my own identity, peering after others so that I may imitate them, I now demand that they acknowledge me as a model for themselves.

This last version of truth as identity almost suffocates us. The right haircut and manners, fervor in religious beliefs and practices, zeal for the right causes or team: all this is evidence to observers and to the actor himself that he belongs. But why this ferocity in the demand that individual identity be nothing but social identity? Could it be that socialization, *being in the truth*, is especially vital to groups or nations having unsettled practices, no secure history of mutual reliance, fear of isolation, fear of hostility, or too little conviction that regularizing ideals are shared by all the members? One or another of these considerations makes the idea attractive to soccer fans, nineteenth-century German philosophers, and everyone addicted to fashion. The rest of us look for ways to defend ourselves from the imperative that we acquire an identity that may not fit us. One strategy is the exposure of "hegemonic discourse"—meaning the revelation that every way of thinking or ruling disguises the interests of those who profit from it. "Post-modernism" saves us this abuse by exposing whatever power structure is immanent in the language and rules of a literature or social order, though Thrasymachus, Hegel, Marx, and Nietzsche said as much: that we too often learn to be true to ourselves by accepting someone else's rules.

There is also this other response. We say that no one can evade the opposition between these two poles of authenticity: the one as other people affirm that we are recognizable and safe because we are like them; the other as we acknowledge that the cognitive-affective balance in each of us is never the clone of any other. There is the many in the one: social identity coheres with individual differences. This implies a politics of difference, coupled and complementary to a politics that sponsors uniformity only to the point of making us predictable, efficient, productive, and safe.

IV Truth as Redundancy

Truth as redundancy is the idea that 'is true' adds no information when used in sentences such as

>"*Snow is white*" *is true, if and only if snow is white.*[12]

Eliminate the italics and the quotation marks, dispense with the phrase 'is true', and affirm only the sentence expressing the alleged state of affairs. The content of that sentence is the only pertinent information conveyed by this otherwise redundant formula. This is the notion of truth known as *re-dundancy*, or *disquotation*. It is advocated by Ramsey, supported by Tarski, Davidson, and Quine, and rechristened *minimalism* by Paul Horwich.

We usually suppose that this idea of truth has its inception in twentieth-century discoveries in language, as even the language used to express it seems to imply: we say that the first appearance of *Snow is white* in the definition above is a sentence in the meta-language for natural language; its second appearance a sentence in the object (the natural) language. We elaborate, observing that the truth ascribed to the sentence in the meta-language is not conditional upon there being an actual state of affairs (e.g., snow being white). For this is a claim about the relation of these two sentences. What claim? Only this: the sentence in the meta-language is a (logically proper) name if and only if there is a referent for the name; while conversely, there is a sentence in the object language appropriate to its name if and only if there is a name for it. The predicate 'is true' signifies this naming relation, nothing more.

What is the status of the sentence affirmed in the object language? Is it true, by correspondence perhaps, of something existing apart from language (snow being white)? The idea of truth as redundant has nothing to say of this extra-linguistic truth condition. Tarski's definition applies only to the relation of the two sentences, not to the relation between one of them and something that is not a sentence. Shouldn't there be an answer to this other question? Certainly, there should be one, though truth as redundancy does not provide it. Why does redundancy currently receive so much attention, when it is restricted explicitly to the relation between sentences, while saying nothing of the relation between a sentence and its extra-linguistic truth condition? The answer I propose requires that we examine this notion of truth as it originates in Kant's *Critique of Pure Reason*.

A. Kantian Origins

All experience, Kant argued, is created by the transcendental ego as it applies the categories of understanding to sensory data. The categories by themselves prescribe that every schematized experience shall have some quality, quantity, and relation (e.g., as a shade of color has magnitude and relation to some shape: it is round or square). They cannot decide more specifically what determinate expressions these categories shall have within experience. It is the empirical schemas (e.g., the rules for schematizing the experience of snow or camels) that supply this finer grain. These schemas differ, however, with time, place, and situation, so that epochs, cultures, or factions sharing the same transcendental categories differ as regards the more determinate rules used to schematize experience. There are the alternative forms of literature, science, and politics and the different experiences schematized when one or another of these forms is used to differentiate and organize sensory data. Our experiences of dogs and cats, and even of colors and sounds, vary as one or another empirical schemas supplies more determinate expression for the categories of quantity, quality, and relation.

Empirical schemas are learned, rather than innate, though the manner of their learning is obscure. We might think to identify them with generalizations about the extra-mental, natural circumstances where procedures are tried and revised; but this would be false to Kant's view that the experiential world we inhabit is the consequence of our schematizations, not their condition. It is closer to the spirit of his view that a people more or less spontaneously elaborates schemas having a certain grain and complementarity, as Eskimos have schemas of one sort, Bedouins of another. We learn to organize experience to the point of saying that we see dogs and cats; other minds, given these same data, might see wombats or the phoenix. Isn't it just a question of fact, answered yes or no, that dogs, cats, and other things exist? This way of putting the question is too categorical for Kant. Dogs and cats exist for us who have schematized them: Kant's theory goes only this far in the direction of naive realism and empirical learning.

Two refinements are required as we extend this sketch to cover the idea that truth is redundant. First is the claim that every particular episode or patch of experience (e.g., seeing one's hand) is the product of a judgment. Judgments are made when mind restricts itself to some particular schematization. For no matter that there are, in principle, an infinity of ways to schematize any sensory data, nothing is schematized if mind does not use some one of them to differentiate and organize the data here available to it. But more, every particular schema is variable in its applications, so that mind enforces its self-restriction by choosing a specific interpretation of the schema. Why accept these successive restrictions on our freedom? I infer that some purpose directs us: we think the world we want, as an artist uses plastic materials under specific constraints to make a desired object or effect.

The other refinement is commentary on this fact about the content of judgment. Suppose we have a hissing, arch-backed cat before us. What is this cat? Is it an entity whose existence and character are independent of our thinking about it, the thing itself being represented in our experience by its sensory effects? No, this cat is only the distribution and sequence, current and prospective, of these sensory impressions. The cat known to us is, more accurately, the cat-schematized-by-an-act-of-judgment. It exists only by virtue of occupying one of the phenomenal patches woven into our experience. Anything alleged to exist apart from experience is, Kant argued, an unknowable, unthinkable thing-in-itself. We habitually interpret experience as though things perceived exist in the space beyond us; but this is merely the naive, unconsidered view of our natural attitude. For judgment is not the finding that extra-mental objects exist, or exist in some way; but rather, the productive activity of introducing schematized data, hence the re-presentations of dogs and cats, into experience.

What could Kant mean by the *truth* of a judgment? He cannot mean that a judgment is true if it affirms of what is that it is or of what is not that it is not. This would imply, contrary to Kant's views, that the truth of a judgment is conditioned by matters independent of judgment, as the man judged before a court has an existence, character, and history independent of the jury. This is the point remarked above: Kantian judgment is not the finding of a spectator who weighs evidence as regards some matter separate from him. Truth, for Kant, is never disinterested or disengaged, however much he sometimes struggled against this implication.[13] Judgment creates its own truths by creating the objects of which we would say in the natural, unconsidered attitude that truths apply. For of course, the judgment "There is a cat before me is true" if I have, by dint of this judgment, created the experience-of-a-cat. Calling a judgment 'true' is, therefore, pleonastic: *there is no need to mention the truth of a judgment when judgment is the experience-creating act which fulfills its own truth conditions.*

The issue may seem confused; for doesn't it often happen that we make erroneous judgments, as when something heard in the night is misidentified. Surely, this misidentification has not created its object. This might seem to be evidence refuting Kant; but it is not, for there are two judgments at issue. One is the transcendental judgment of synthesizing mind, the one made "transcendentally," "outside," or "prior to" experience. This is judgment as it lays down a network of objectifying relations. Truth-claims about its work are redundant. The other judgment is made within experience. Truth or falsity in its case is the function of its coherence with the other empirical judgments we do or would make. "It's a burglar," he says. "No," she corrects him, "only Roger closing the refrigerator."

Transcendental judgments are made with unconditional authority, though Kant does not suppose that there are, typically, reports about them — it is enough that we experience the effects. Empirical judgments are declared, though tentatively. These reports express a spectator's appraisals of the things encountered or inferred. Can one be a mere spectator within the tide of experience one has created transcendentally? We do seem to make these detached, fallible observations all the time. Yet this must be something of a puzzle given the fact that transcendental judgments are constitutive of the phenomena occurring within experience. The only phenomena experienced are the ones we have made; hence misidentification is a curious lapse, one resulting from some discontinuity between the transcendental perspective whence things are made and the empirical one from which we observe them.

The relation between acts of the transcendental and empirical ego is not fully detailed in Kant's first Critique. We are left to invent some of the theory's necessary details. What is the mutual bearing of these two orders of judgment, one transcendental and productive, the other empirical? Contemporary linguistic philosophy specifies their relation (usually without explicit reference to Kant) by introducing its distinction between the *formal* and *material* modes of speech. The formal mode corresponds to the activities called "transcendental" by Kant. The material mode signifies the products of transcendental synthesis. Saying that there is a cat before me, I express myself in the material mode. Saying *"There is a cat before me* is true," expresses this same point in the formal mode.

The distinction between the material and formal modes was introduced by Carnap, with help from Quine. Each of them emphasizes mind's power for fixing the rules of language, hence the conventionality and relativity of linguistic rules and systems. Their bias is set against Kant's transcendental (but arguably still psychologistic) account of mind's faculties and his insistence that every possible experience presupposes the same categories of understanding. The affinities are also remarkable, for common to them and to Kant is the emphasis on mind's power for using rules to create a thinkable world. It matters considerably that the rules organize words or sentences rather than percepts; but this difference is incidental to mind's autonomy when choosing rules and to its power for using them to create a thinkable experience by schematizing some content—whether sentences or percepts.

Accordingly, sentences in the formal mode express mind's freedom to determine the shape of its experience, as *Three is a number* might be a rule in a semantic framework used to schematize an experience, hence create a world. Live within the world where this rule applies, and you will see some things in groups of three. Busy as you are with life's details, you will be content to report your observation, not wondering about its conditions. You will live, unselfconsciously, using the material mode of speech. There will be little or nothing calling your attention to that level of world-making where *Three is a number* expresses mind's determination to create a world using this schema as one of the rules organizing experience.

It follows that truth's redundancy is neither mysterious nor the invention of twentieth-century ingenuity. It fills a well-marked place in Kant's theory of mind and knowledge. Frank Ramsey introduced Kant's notion, or one very much like it, into twentieth-century linguistic philosophy:

> It is clear that the problem is not as to the nature of truth and falsehood, but as to the nature of judgments or assertion, for what is difficult to analyze in the above formulation is "he asserts *aRb*." It is, perhaps, also immediately obvious that if we have analyzed judgment we have solved the problem of truth; for taking the mental factor in a judgment (which is often itself called a judgment), the truth or falsity of this depends only on what proposition it is that is judged, and what we have to explain is the meaning of saying that the judgment is a judgment that *a* has *R* to *b*, i.e., is true if *aRb*; false if not. We can, if we like, say that it is true if there exists a corresponding fact

that *a* has *R* to *b*, but this is essentially not an analysis but a peri-phrasis, for "The fact that *a* has *R* to *b* exists" is no different from "*a* has *R* to *b*."[14]

I don't know that Ramsey detailed his affinities with Kant; but why would someone be attracted to Kant's theory of truth, with its intimations of re-dundancy, coherence, and identity, if he were not also drawn to Kant's the-ory of mind and his metaphysics of experience? Certainly, writers who favor disquotational notions of truth in our time are squarely Kantian. After Car-nap, and like Putnam, they share his belief that the world in itself is unknow-able, all the differences and relations within experience resulting from the rules employed for differentiating and organizing experience. Redundancy is here the notion of truth filling the space defined by a metaphysical theory structurally homologous to Kant's own.

B. Quine on Disquotation

Quine is one of those who favors disquotation:

> Yet there is some underlying validity to the correspondence theory of truth, as Tarski has taught us. Instead of saying that
>
> *'Snow is white' is true if and only if it is a fact that snow is white*
>
> we can simply delete 'it is a fact that' as vacuous, and therewith facts themselves:
>
> *'Snow is white' is true if and only if snow is white.*
>
> To ascribe truth to the sentence is to ascribe whiteness to snow; such is the correspondence, in this example. Ascription of truth just cancels the quotation marks. Truth is disquotation. So the truth predicate is superfluous when ascribed to a given sentence; you could just utter the sentence.[15]

This cannot be the whole story that Quine wants to tell about truth, since we might infer from his example that the truth of any one sentence about a contingent state of affairs is unconditioned by the truth of any other. That would violate Quine's strictures favoring inter-animating sentences and his claim that the truth of any sentence is a function of its relations to the other sentences acknowledged within a field. Indeed, Quine's holism might require our saying that the only uncontroversial truth, from the standpoint of a the-ory, is that very long and grammatically complex sentence expressing the entire field of inter-animating sentences. Disquotation would then yield the equally complex state of affairs expressed by canceling the quotation marks around this sentence.

Quotation marks are, this implies, a semaphore: they announce that we have moved to the formal mode from the material one; or the reverse. This is a move to the transcendental conditions for experience, or from the rules used for making it to experience itself. Quine, himself, describes the prior of these moves as "semantic ascent":

> The strategy of semantic ascent is that it carries the discussion into a domain where both parties are better agreed on the objects (viz., words) and on the main terms concerning them. Words, or their inscriptions, unlike points, miles, classes and the rest, are tangible objects of the size so popular in the marketplace, where men of unlike conceptual schemes communicate at their best. The strategy is one of ascending to a common part of two fundamentally disparate conceptual schemes, the better to discuss the disparate foundations.[16]

Quine says elsewhere that "Semantic ascent serves also outside of logic. When Einstein propounded relativity, disrupting our basic conceptions of distance and time, it was hard to assess it without leaning on our basic conceptions and thus begging the question. But by semantic ascent one could compare the new and old theories as symbolic structures, and so appreciate that the new theory organized the pertinent data more simply than the old."[17] Semantic ascent is invaluable for the view it gives us of the rules for organizing the pertinent data. This perspective, in Kant's language, is transcendental.

We have this choice. We can move, with disquotation, from the formal mode to the material one; or we can reverse directions, going from the phenomena constituted by rules to the standpoint from which the rules are applied, if only for the purpose of comparing alternative conceptual frameworks. Disquotation is just the contrary of semantic ascent. Both are testimony to the nearly pure vein of critical idealism that Quine inherits from Kant.

C. Tarski's Semantic Definition of Truth

Kant's influence is also plain in the ideas of some others who favor the idea that truth is redundancy. Most prominent (and Quine's point of departure) is Alfred Tarski's definition of truth: *"Snow is white" is true, if and only if snow is white.* Tarski defends his definition with these remarks:

We should like our definition to do justice to the intuitions which adhere to the *classical Aristotelian conception of truth*—intuitions which find their expression in the well-known words of Aristotle's *Meta-physics; To say of what is that it is not, or of what is not that it is, is false, while to say of what is that it is, or of what is not that it is not, is true.* If we wished to adapt ourselves to modern philosophic terminology, we could perhaps express this conception by means of the familiar for-mula: *The truth of a sentence consists in its agreement with* (or correspon-dence to) *reality.* (For a theory of truth which is to be based upon the later formulation the term "correspondence theory" has been sug-gested.)[18]

And later, "The question has been raised whether the semantic conception of truth can indeed be regarded as a precise form of the old, classical con-ception of this notion. . . . As far as my own opinion is concerned, I do not have any doubts that our formulation does conform to the intuitive content of that of Aristotle."[19]

Tarski is very reluctant to affirm that his definition is more than *for-mally* similar to the notion of correspondence: he carefully avoids saying that it establishes a relation between a sentence and the state of affairs satisfying it. Indeed, neither sentence represents a state of affairs external to language: "We have seen that this conception essentially consists in regarding the sen-tence 'X is true' as equivalent to the sentence denoted by 'X' (where 'X' stands for a name of a sentence of the object-language)."[20] Accordingly, "Snow is white" designates a sentence in both its appearances in Tarski's definition: a sentence in the meta-language for ordinary English on its first appearance in the formula and a sentence in the object language for English in its second appearance. It is never used in this definition, as it is in Aristotle, to designate first a sentence, then an extra-linguistic state of affairs. This definition of truth, therefore, is not so much the evocation of correspondence as it is the specification of a mapping relation having sentences in the object language and its meta-language as terms of the relation.

Tarski never exceeds language in anything he says of his definition, nor does he let us do so. He is scathing in response to a critic who argued that the truth relation exceeds language on the side of the state of affairs satisfying a thought or sentence. The critic wanted to amend Tarski's defi-nition to read: "Snow is white" (in the meta-language) is true of "Snow is white" (in the object language) if snow is white. This would have made the sentence in the meta-language true of the sentence in the object language if and only if the sentence in the object language were true of the state of affairs. Tarksi reasonably denies that the truth of the sentence in the meta-language presupposes the truth of the one in the object language: the truth of the sentence in the natural language is incidental to the mapping relation between this sentence and the one in the meta-language.

Now consider this other question: Is this sentence in the object language, "Snow is white," true of the cold, flaky stuff that crunches underfoot? Does it represent an extra-linguistic state of affairs? Tarski has nothing to say of this material question. Why not? Because Tarski was typically careful to say that his formula applies only to the relation of sentences, one in an object language, the other in its meta-language. The answer is different for some interpreters. In their hands, his solution becomes an eclectic montage combining correspondence, identity, and redundancy. They move from one to the other as the interests of exegesis or dialectic require.[21]

There is *identity* in the fact that mind will not let truth be a relation reaching beyond thought or language into the world. This is an intimation of mind's fear that a relation carrying into the world is one that mind cannot itself guarantee. We recall the skeptical argument: truths are to be the body of knowledge, though mind will never be able to guarantee that its claims are true if they reach beyond it into the world; better that all truth should reside in mind as a relation between thoughts or sentences, but also thereby an inspectable qualification of mind itself.

There is *redundancy* in the mapping of sentences: "The term 'true' when occurring in a simple sentence of the form 'X is true' can be eliminated, and the sentence itself, which belongs to the meta-language, can easily be replaced by an equivalent sentence of the object-language."[22] Tarski is here very close to the distinction between sentences appearing in the formal and material modes. This distinction is the analogue to Kant's distinction between transcendental, productive judgments and the objects they create. For the meta-language is not merely a contrivance for reporting on the object language: grammatical formation rules, semantic rules for the use of predicates, and inductive rules for appraising the truth of sentences in the object language are formulated within its extended meta-language. It is within the meta-language that we lay down standards for, then declare what shall count as true within, the object language. Having rules to justify our saying that "Snow is white" is true, we can also suppress the evidence of the formal mode, saying more simply that snow is white.

There is, finally, *correspondence*. Providing for correspondence (or seeming to do so) in a direct and simple way is what makes Tarksi's definition appealing and incontrovertible. For we can use his definition to express every material truth. "Mice roar" is true if and only if mice roar. Well and good, until we discover that the second appearance of the sentence is construed as nothing more than its inscription, not as the reference to little rats with big voices.

Add these three ingredients to one another, and we get a precisely calculated notion of truth, one that avoids commitment to extra-mental states of affairs while giving every impression (like Kantian redundancy) of affirming this commitment.

D. Horwich's Minimalist Definition of Truth

Tarski's formulation is reintroduced, with all these nuances, in a recent book by Paul Horwich. Proposing his "best statement of the deflationary point of view," Horwich proposes this "minimalist" definition: "It is true *that* p if and only if p."[23] This is truth pure and simple: "Truth has a certain purity . . . our understanding of it is independent of other ideas."[24] This is truth separated from such notions as reference and satisfaction. A complete theory of knowledge might require us to introduce these ancillary notions; a comprehensive notion of truth does not.[25]

The separability claimed for truth implies the error of my view that notions of truth are crafted to fit the spaces made for them within value-driven metaphysical theories. Horwich is spartan: his debts to metaphysics and value are mostly ignored or denied. Yet, some assumptions are discernible within his characterization of truth. They locate his version of the disquotational formula within that stripped-down version of the Kantian rubric apparent already in Tarski and Quine, though there are other influences in him, less apparent in them. Citing these other views helps to qualify the claim that truth might stand pure and simple before us, separable from every other notion. It will be apparent that I am using Horwich as a foil. Doing this is easier because he is clear and direct.

Horwich believes that his definition of truth may be used as an axiom within a calculus from which to deduce "explanations" for notions that con-

cern us,[26] knowledge being an example. The system's axoms and rules of
inference are to exhibit the simple basis for whatever complexity is ascribed
to lower-order sentences or ideas. Complex notions are to be derived from
formalized systems, because our understanding of them is otherwise obscure:
we are not sure what a notion includes or how it relates to others. Reconstructed ideas show their proper parts and relations, hence their structural
affinities to one another. Their derivation exhibits the formal relations obtaining among all the concepts susceptible to reconstruction within a system.
I infer that this is, for Horwich, the paradigm for philosophic explanation,
with nothing more or better to be asked of it.

   One thinks of Descartes. He argued, in his "Rules for the Direction
of the Native Talents,"[27] that we discover, then use, simple ideas as axioms
within the deductive systems where ideas of other, more complex phenomena
are derived or constructed. This procedure is said to have these two effects:
it eliminates obscurities from our ideas, while bringing the welter of ideas
into an order that exhibits their essential relations. The mind possessing a
calculus is said to have clear and distinct, simple and complex ideas of all
phenomena arrayed in a single continuous skein, all of it inspectable. Is it
Procrustean to insist that a notion of truth formulated in accord with good
analytic practice be described as the expression of this ancient paradigm?
What other interpretation might we give to Horwich's preference for definitions, formal systems, and the promise that all descriptions (definitions or
constructions) not counted among the axioms will be deduced from them?
There does not seem to be an alternative interpretation. Nor are we much
impelled to look for one after recalling that this is the method revived and
recommended to analytic philosophers by Carnap and Goodman.[28] They,
like Descartes, suppose that philosophy should have a method of its own,
one that distinguishes it from practice and science. They have little patience
for the fallibility and contention of the method requiring both hypotheses
about matters of fact and the dialectical interplay of contending theories. I
prefer this hypothetical method, because I believe that philosophical procedure should be continuous, as regards both its subject matters and method,
with practical and scientific thinking. Horwich prefers the method of Cartesian reconstructions.

   The alleged separability of a system's axioms — what Descartes would
have described as their simplicity — is another expression of Horwich's Cartesian bias. For consider his claim that truth is separable from reference and

180

satisfaction.[29] This is odd if 'Snow is white' is a set of marks or sounds. In themselves and unconstrued, they would refer to, and be satisfied by, nothing. Words refer to or signify something only as we learn or invent rules for construing them. But more, the sentence comprised of these now meaningful words is not true unless something—namely, white snow—satisfies it. Truth of the sort invoked by Horwich's definition is inexplicable without essential, intrinsic appeal to both reference and satisfaction.

Horwich evades this charge at cost to his ontology. He doesn't agree that the vehicles of truth are thoughts or sentences. Those two are just the instruments for expressing the actual bearers of truth: namely, propositions. What propositions are, how they relate to other things in the world, and how they are known are questions Horwich defers.[30] He merely exploits their virtues. Propositions may, for example, be described as the content common to sentences of different languages. More important to Horwich, we don't need reference or designation rules to bring propositions into line with the things that would satisfy them. This is the beauty of propositions: they are self-aligning. *Snow is white* is a proposition embodying both its own rules of reference and its satisfaction conditions. Accordingly, propositions defend the separability of truth by saving Horwich from having to tell how a thought or sentence achieves reference and satisfaction—hence the simplicity of truth and the fulfillment of the Cartesian demand, accepted by Horwich, that axioms be simple and adequate.

There are also some other, more contentious affinities between Horwich and Descartes. Descartes too supposed that ideas, not any particular linguistic expression of them, stand before the mind, taking their place within the calculi from which complex ideas are derived. Horwich's propositions are the correlates of Descartes' ideas. Like them, propositions are truth-bearers and intentional objects. They are intelligible entities set before our inspecting minds, supplying us with information about those states of affairs which do, or merely can, obtain in the world.

Horwich never declares, with Descartes, that knowledge is not achieved without rational intuition of ideas (Horwich's propositions). Yet, it would be odd to favor propositions and the calculus in which propositions are ordered without having some expectation that we shall achieve philosophic understanding only as we grasp these propositions. Horwich is tantalizingly close to endorsing this intuitionist program:

According to the advocate of propositions, whenever anyone has a belief, a desire, a hope, or any of the so-called propositional attitudes then his state of mind consists in there being some relation between him and a special kind of entity: namely, the *thing* that is believed, desired to be the case, hoped for, etc. Thus if Oscar believes that dogs bite, this is alleged to be so in virtue of the obtaining of a relation, *believing*, being Oscar and a certain proposition: namely, *that dogs bite* [31]

I conclude that a compelling argument for the existence of propositions may be built on the premise that they participate in an adequate account of the logical form of belief attributions and similar constructions. Moreover, the required premise appears to be correct. Therefore, despite their peculiarities, we should not balk at propositions and should not object to their use in a theory of truth. [32]

We might be curious about Horwich's commitment to propositions. Are they useful only for defending his claim that the notion of truth is simple, without essential implications for reference and satisfaction? Could they have been introduced to solve this problem, while providing objects, barely mediated by thought and language, for intellectual apprehension—that is to say, for rational intuition?

Horwich invokes propositions and the Cartesian calculus without subverting his own allegiance to the Kantian ideas apparent in Tarski and Quine. His affinities to them are plainest in his remarks about correspondence. It requires that there be a satisfaction relation connecting a thought or sentence to the state of affairs satisfying it. Horwich acknowledges this fact about correspondence without endorsing it. Nor does he agree that there might be states of affairs owning neither their existence nor their character to our ways of thinking or talking about them. "Admittedly," he says, "minimalism does not *explain what truth is* in any such way. But it does not deny that truths *do* correspond—in *some* sense—to the facts." [33] Horwich never tells what sense that is.

There is also this more extended remark meant to show that everything vital to a correspondence relation is encapsulated in the minimalist formulation:

In mapping out the relations of explanatory dependence between phenomena we naturally and properly grant ultimate explanatory priority to such things as basic laws and the initial conditions of the universe. From these facts we deduce, and thereby explain, why, for example

Snow is white.

And only then, given the minimal theory, do we deduce, and thereby explain, why

'Snow is white' is true.[34]

This passage shows Horwich's reason for not committing himself to the view that a sentence is true "because something in the world is a certain way—something typically external to the sentence or proposition."[35] The reason is indicated in the statement of his example, the sentence 'Snow is white.' This sentence implies, *because it appears in the text without inverted commas*, that Horwich is referring to an extra-mental, extra-linguistic state of affairs. Horwich encourages this interpretation by omitting the inverted commas. But this reading is mistaken. 'Snow is white' (in its first appearance in the quotation above) is a sentence deduced from a formalized theory, *not* a state of affairs, it being sentences, not states of affairs, that are deduced and explained. We have only the appearance of materiality, not the extra-mental, real-world term for the correspondence relation.

All reality is now reduced to language, as extended to include propositions as they are expressible in the sentences of a language. On the left side of Horwich's definition is a sentence in the meta-language for ordinary language, and on the right side that same sentence, though without quotation marks, as it occurs in the object language of a natural language. Horwich never exceeds thought or language in the direction of the world, except to the point where he argues that it is propositions expressed by thoughts and sentences, not mere acts, utterances, or inscriptions that are truth vehicles.

My objection is clearer, perhaps, when expressed as a question. What is p in its second appearance in Horwich's definition: It is true *that* p if and only if p? Let us grant Horwich the interpretation of his definition which he prefers: the p occupying the first position in his definition is a proposition. What is p in its second appearance in this formula? Horwich encourages us to read the sentence in this way: It is true that "Snow is white" is true if and only if Snow is white. Realists may dissolve with pleasure, until they notice that p in its second appearance is, for Horwich, just a sentence in the object language, English. We know it is a sentence (not a state of affairs), because it is only sentences that are deduced from formal systems. Accordingly, the sentence *p* appearing first in Horwich's formula is true, because its truth condition — the sentence in the object language — is validly derived from higher-order sentences.

It is plainer now that sentences in the object language, or the propositions expressed by them, are as far into the world as Horwich is prepared to reach. There is to be no exit from language (propositions aside), hence no access to an extra-linguistic world in which sentences signify something other than sentences or their quasi-linguistic shadows (propositions).

We get from Horwich exactly what there is in Tarski (with the addition of the Cartesian emphases mentioned above): a sentence in the meta-language maps a sentence in the object language. Speaking in the meta-language, we report the results of a deduction. Speaking in the object language, we dispense with such formal niceties, forsaking "Snow is white" is true for Snow is white. We get this Cartesian interpretation of the difference between sentences in the transcendental, or formal, mode and those in the empirical, or material, mode: axioms and sentences derived from them are read in the material mode; these same sentences considered as they satisfy the system's rules of inference — as when they are called true — are read in the formal mode.

Sentences in the material mode have all the appearance, but none of the substance, implied when we speak of those states of affairs whose existence and character are independent of thought and language. Why should Horwich want to obscure the difference between sentences in the object language and states of affairs independent of language? There is no evidence in his book that he endorses the idea that states of affairs are merely the effects of productive judgments. Why, then, does he produce a result that so exactly recreates the linguistic version of Kant's distinction between the transcendental (formal) mode and the empirical (material) mode? This might be happenstance, with nothing at all required to explain it. Or it may be — and this seems more likely to me — that his formulation is steeped in Cartesian and Kantian themes. We make Kantian assumptions about the world's essential dependence on thought and Cartesian assumptions about the formally reconstructed languages claimed as thought's instruments. We do all this without having to justify or even acknowledge these assumptions. These are the penumbral assumptions when the sentence 'Snow is white' is shorn of inverted commas in the passage from Horwich quoted above. Does it represent an extra-linguistic state of affairs? Or is it understood that we are to regard these words as a sentence only? The issue is undecided and undeclared, because Kant is our example. He shuffles back and forth between the transcendental and empirical modes. We have his permission to leave the matter equally vague, intimating materiality while never referring beyond the object language into the world.

This is my reason for saying that Horwich's theory, like Kant's, is an expression of the metaphysical theory requiring that truth be identity. Skeptical mind will not tolerate the idea that we represent states of affairs by those mental or linguistic signs which mediate our knowledge of them. Naturalist realists encourage us to trust the signs at least to the point of using them to make testable hypotheses about their objects. Kant prefers this other tack: deny the existence of a world independent of mind, or at least the possibility that such a world could be known. Insist that the world be reconstructed within experience. Only then can mind dwell within its world, comfortable that its knowledge claims do not exceed mind's power for managing the rules used to create the experience of a world.

It is this psycho-centric ontology, this site for world-making, that is home ground for truth as identity. Everything significant for truth, sentences in both the object language and its meta-language, are present within mind. Neither has any status apart from our determination to create and apply the linguistic rules from which they are generated. These sentences, like the experiences schematized by Kant's transcendental ego, are the mind's own qualifications. Horwich's theory of truth is, I infer, the mix of Descartes' *more geometrico* coupled to Kant's determination that everything vital to truth have its inception in mind's own activities.

Much of the foregoing is my surmise. Horwich might disclaim every part of it that is interpretation. One other point is less speculative. Horwich argues that disputes between realists and anti-realists are entirely incidental to the notion of truth.[36] But is this so? Our sun is independent of quarrels between Ptolemy and Copernicus. Truth is, in that respect, independent of disputes among philosophers. Still, the issues dividing them are not at all incidental to either the dialectical history or the adequacy of our notions of truth. Historically, the correspondence idea was dished when philosophers worried that the existence and character of the extra-mental term in the correspondence relation could not be ascertained: the thing might exist, but it might not. Either way, we could guarantee neither access to it nor the adequacy of our representations of it. Conceptually, this argument between realists and idealists drives every version of the coherence, redundancy, and identity theory currently proposed. They are reactive, as each proposes to reconstitute the idea of truth when correspondence commits us, speculatively and unverifiably, to the existence of a world to which truth-confirming access cannot be guaranteed or conceived.

Horwich's minimalism is an elegantly disguised version of this reaction. Like every echo of Kantian epistemology, it gives the appearance of correspondence, but not the substance—though here, at least, world-making is subtle. There is no grand talk of language or culture schematizing its world. Moving from the formal to the material mode, we let the meta-language posit its object language. We get Snow is white merely by dropping the predicate and inverted commas from "Snow is white" is true.

E. Values that Motivate the Idea of Truth as Redundancy

What value motivates the idea that truth is redundancy, where aversion to realism and a desire for certainty sponsor the metaphysical theory promoting it?

One motive is conceptual economy. We require no additional assumptions about truth when Kant's metaphysics of experience has truth's redundancy as its implication: there is no point in saying that a judgment is true if this is the transcendental judgment that creates its object. We explain, hereby, Kant's near silence on the subject of truth.

There is also this related motive: namely, the struggle among Kantians to hide the subjectivist, idealist consequences of their psycho-centric metaphysics. We assume that truth in its classic formulation, truth as correspondence, has no application, for it makes no sense to ask about the adequacy of representations if the world that was to be represented is exiled to the limbo of noumena. This leaves mind to synthesize all the contents of experience and knowledge. But then truth is easy, for the judgments creating experience are self-certifying: "This is an apple is true" if this sentence or thought gives propositional expression to the act which has created the experience of an apple. Have I used some rule to schematize this very experience? Then of course my experience has just the content signified when this rule is expressed as the thought or sentence representing it. The circle inscribed by this Kantian argument is very small.

Kant acknowledges experiences having an objective content that we cannot alter, as the river goes a certain direction and the house has a certain fixed character whichever way we walk around it. Truths about these extra-mental objectivities are implied in Kant; but they are marginalized in the first Critique and later by the internal realism of Carnap and Putnam. It is better that we forget about truth. Back to the facts, we say, thereby distracting attention from the theory which supposes that judgment has created the facts. Accept this invitation, and we lapse naively into the empirical mode of experience and the material mode of linguistic expression. We forget that all the strings are pulled from the side of the transcendental and formal modes. This, to be sure, is an artful forgetting; mind is to forget what mind has done.

It seems to me that all current talk about disquotation requires a fast shuffle between the formal and the material mode, and that all of it is designed to hide the evidence of transcendental world-making. Nothing fishy here: just the facts.

V Behaviorist Notions of Truth

The idea of truth here called *behavioral* comprises three distinct motions: the idea that uses of 'truth' are performative; the view that we use 'truth' in response to stimuli, with truth conditions included among the conditions for asserting that a thought or sentence is true; and the Jamesian pragmatic conception of chapter 1. This third notion sometimes dominates current discussions of truth, the second one having passed the zenith of its plausibility, and the first now mostly a piece of conceptual shrapnel appropriate to a time past.

A. Truth as a Performative

That was an era when we imagined playing language-games, a time when much space was devoted to the various ways in which language is used. Imagine an elderly Egyptian professing his geocentric view of things to a faculty that shouts encouragement: "Right on"; "Tell'em the way it is"; "That's true." Grateful Ptolemy orders beer and sausages for the crowd. Here is a case where *truth* is a performative, where the value motivating us is concern that behaviors be appropriate to our circumstances. Seeing rain-clouds, we gather in the laundry; feeling lonely, we look for company. Hearing Ptolemy, we cheer. It doesn't matter that he is right or wrong if we are hungry and the cheering earns us a free lunch.

These examples are misleading only for implying that behaviors were to be counted appropriate because they secure or satisfy us. It might be incidental that behavior is satisfactory in this way, though it was required that conduct be the commonly learned response to circumstances. Why this emphasis on learning and routine? Because of the concern for communication between an actor and those observers who know his intentions and competence by seeing him respond in circumstances they share.[37] Observers, too, have learned the rules requiring or permitting certain locutions in particular circumstances. He who repeats "That's true" when no one has said or written anything to him leaves them confused, for there is no rule correlating this locution with appropriate circumstances. Bystanders can't make sense of what is said or why he should be saying it.

The priority given to communication makes it urgent that behaviors be ritualized. Only as I learn the rules, while supposing that others learn them too, am I able to turn the rule directing my behavior into a criterion for judging what others do. But more, I must have this criterion if I am not to be lost, confused, or out of control in the company of other people. What are they doing? Is it safe for me to be among them? I cannot be sure that it is if I do not know the significance of what they do because of not knowing the rules they observe. Ritual learning, wherein we learn the same response or range of permissible responses, is the condition for both my understanding and the conviction that I am secure among my fellows.

Each of us might be anxious about our security, so that desire for the uniformity of behavior is reinforced by the desire to control the behavior of other people. One is reminded again of Thrasymachus and of this emended version of Glaucon's remark: that what men find useful, they call true.[38] So do tyrants, employers, and parents find it useful that certain things be called true in particular circumstances. Though surely this performative account of linguistic usage would risk self-parody were it to require that ascriptions of truth express nothing more than the subjugation of a people who say "True!" to satisfy someone else's interests. Is the truth claimed for the performative theory no more than deference to someone's power?

There is, accordingly, this choice of justifications for the performative notion of truth: we learn rules for using various locutions, 'truth' included, in order that we may act and judge uniformly; or we enforce uniformity in the use of various expressions, 'truth' included, for our own purposes. Is either explanation plausible? Only, I suggest, if we persistently confuse hypothesis with construction.[39] Performatives serve the purposes of construction, as saying "I promise" creates a relationship that was not present before. This is thought as it supplies all the terms required for the thing it makes (e.g., a contract). Compare hypothesis. It is deficient where construction is powerful, as when thought cannot guarantee the truth of its speculations. No hypothesis is made true by calling it true, whatever the advantage to us. This vulnerability to error explains the desire that mind have the power to create the other, uncontrolled term of the truth relation. Equally, it explains the behaviorist proposal that truth be reconceived as a performative; for then there is no term that might go missing, 'truth' being merely a word we use in appropriate circumstances. But this formulation is inadequate to the truth of many claims, including the assertion "I am." That truth is always and only a performative is not tenable.

B. The Assertibility Conditions for 'Truth'

The second of these behaviorist accounts also supposes that a sentence is true when its utterance is appropriate to its circumstances; but now the reading of *appropriate* is different. The two versions agree that an utterance is appropriate when its assertibility conditions are satisfied. They disagree about the conditions. Where truth is a performative, the conditions for asserting it are as various as our learned habits for using the word: we may express affection for a friend, irony in debating some thesis, agreement with a book, or support for a speaker's words, all of them called true. The second behaviorist account emphasizes assertibility conditions having a narrower focus: they are or include, it says, the truth conditions for a sentence. Having learned to say the one in the presence of the other, we affirm truly that "The sky is blue" when the sky is blue.[40]

This is neat, but quixotic: we repudiate or ignore the idea that truth is correspondence, only to assume it when specifying the assertibility conditions for an utterance. Notice also that this solution is too fragile to carry all the burden of truth. We do learn to say "Red!" in the presence of red things, though assertibility conditions are not identical with truth conditions for most of the utterances alleged to be true. Seeing smoke, we say "Fire!," not "Smoke!" Seeing the evidence to a crime, we say that Smith did it, though we are careful not to hang him if guilt is not entailed by the assertibility conditions for claiming that he did it. In these examples, assertibility conditions are different from truth conditions, as smoke is not fire but only evidence for the hypothesis that there is a fire causing the smoke. We do learn to say "Fire!" when we see smoke; but we also learn to be careful when saying that inferences like this, from effect to cause, are true.

Another reason for denying that truth conditions are necessarily present within assertibility conditions is the universality claimed for some truths. We say, for example, that something looks blue, where the assertibility conditions include the truth condition—that it does look blue. But now we add that things of this sort always look blue; they will in the future, as they did in the past. This may be true, though nothing we observe, and probably nothing within any specifiable set of assertibility conditions, would be sufficient to confirm it.

These inferences from effects to causes and from particular observations to truths alleged to be universal exhibit this more general point: truth conditions for most of the thoughts or sentences alleged to be true are not included among their assertibility conditions. Still more disconcerting is the observation that every set of assertibility conditions might, in principle, justify the assertion of an infinity of disparate truth-claims, each with truth conditions that do not appear among the assertibility conditions. The simple behaviorist solution, that we learn to say what is true when presented with it, does not explain the many situations when assertibility conditions do not supply a sufficient basis for choosing among the many possible assertions, some of them contrary and all of them having truth conditions distinct from their assertibility conditions.

Suppose, however, that we ignore these counterexamples: we restrict ourselves to observation sentences having assertibility conditions which do include their truth conditions—we say "Red" only when seeing red. Behaviorists who argue for this notion of truth restrict the domain of their examples so that the paradigmatic instances of truth telling are just those satisfying the instinct for rigorous verification and correspondence. This version of behaviorism is the promise that we can have the important truths—observation reports—without the correspondence machinery of words and sentences construed as signs and satisfied by actual states of affairs, whether concrete and particular or nomological and general. Carefully tailoring the domain of assertibility conditions, we roll the disreputable correspondence baby through the behaviorist front door—with this difference: we are to suppose that true observation sentences are not so much true reports as they are cogent reactions.[41]

Why not make the same point while saying that thoughts or sentences — some of them at least — represent extra-mental, extra-linguistic states of affairs? Because words or thoughts construed as signs, hence referring to their objects, are a sticking point for behaviorists constricted by their antimentalist origins. This reaction may be temporary, however, for there is a lag in behaviorist thinking about signs. Abhorring Cartesian mentalism, behaviorists respond with a sketchy physicalism. It requires only that there be bodies in, or capable of, motion and that human bodies should have innate predilections or learned capacities for situation-appropriate behaviors. But this explains too little of intelligent activity, less than can be explained using the intrapsychic cognitive models available to us in computer science, cognitive psychology, engineering, and physiology.

Behaviorism founders when our descriptions of mind are enriched to include the powers required for making and using signs. Talk about bees is meaningful in the respect that 'bee' is construed as a sign having the constitutive and distinguishing properties of bees as its sense. Sentences about bees are true when they are addressed to circumstances where bees do what these sentences represent them as doing. The sentences may be very complex, so complex that we who hear them test ourselves by asking questions or making observations to confirm our understanding. None of this requires that mind be understood as a great circus tent, everywhere illuminated by beams of intentional light.

All the activities vital for making and using signs are likely to be explicable in terms of hierarchically organized associative networks having exclusively physical properties. Reference, even the reference of theoretical terms, is no longer mysterious if signs (e.g., "This is a peach") achieve it by dint of having places within associative networks that terminate, like Aristotle's commonsensibles, in multiple, co-ordinated empirical confirmations. Many theoretical terms are not so directly tied to confirming observables, as 'cousin' and 'quasar' are not. Yet terms like them may also be formulated and used referentially, as we abstract and extrapolate from observables on the way to formulating a notion, before reversing direction to check for evidence of the observable differences which would be perceived if the thing signified did exist. Intrapsychic activities of the sort required for making and using signs are not currently understood in any comprehensive way, though we have an inkling of powers and activities nowhere acknowledged in the black-box physicalism that behaviorists favor.

One prisoner tells another of his family and home, or he explains the physical theory for which the Inquisition has jailed him. Where in their bare cell are the assertibility conditions that make these speeches meaningful and true? We have no use for the behaviorist answer when we acknowledge mind's powers for construing signs, then formulating and testing hypotheses.

What values motivate this second version of behaviorism? Only those generated within the dialectic of philosophic theories. Where should we put our confidence: in verificationism and the aversion to intrapsychic mental activity; or in thoughts or sentences having intracranial origins and truth conditions that may not be directly observable? Behaviorists make their choices, then formulate a theory to satisfy them. We remark that assertibility conditions designed to include truth conditions, even to the point of being coextensive with them, are no progress beyond the correspondence theory which behaviorists reject. Assertibility conditions that do not include truth conditions are a reversion to the behaviorism of performatives. Behaviorists may go either way, but not to the advantage of their claims about truth.

C. Instrumentalism

Behaviorism of the third sort is remote from the versions just described. This notion of truth is known as "instrumentalism" or "pragmatism" and is favored by literary critics, historians, social scientists, and even architects. Emphasizing the instrumental side, we say that our place in the world is determined by the instruments used to alter or create our circumstances. Answering to the theory's pragmatism, we resist dogmatism in plans, values, and beliefs. We credit no thing with a fixed identity or essence. Things known, things affecting us, even we ourselves, are to be flexible, revisable, protean. Confounded in some ways, we are encouraged to succeed in one or many others.

Why call this attitude *behaviorist?* Because *praxis* is the conduct which makes the world livable and comprehensible. These behaviors are the bones and sinews of our accommodations to other people and things. Driven by thought and desire, secured by our relations to other agents, we establish an order appropriate to our desires, loyalties, and freedoms. Valuing success, we call an idea true if the actions it impels have results fulfilling the desire that motivates us. This is the world significant for us, a world we have made.

There are, to be sure, some different kinds of instruments and actions and two different places where action may occur. Instruments differ, as a conceptual system is different from a spade. Actions differ, as using a conceptual system to schematize sensory data is different from using a plan of action to direct a sequence of physical behaviors, and different again from using the spade to dig a hole. The two venues for action are correlated with these different kinds of action. One venue is conscious mind. Behaviorists of this sort are unembarrassed by the idea that actions often transpire within our minds; indeed, many of those described here as behaviorists are Cartesians: they think of mind as an ample place, endowed like a theatre with special facilities for mounting productions unique to consciousness. The other venue is the physical world. An intelligently self-directing body engages some part of the world in ways that may secure and satisfy it.

There is also this difference among the instruments used as we make our way in either place: it is beliefs or utterances, sentences, conceptual systems, and plans, never spades, that count as true. How do instrumentalists explain this difference? They never do explain it, though probably they would say, if asked, that the truth claimed for mental states or artifacts is a relic of the time when truth was thought to be the appropriate virtue of the mental states or entities allegedly corresponding to differences in the extra-mental world. These instrumentalists have no patience for the realist, representationalist view. We recall this observation quoted above: "Pragmatists think that the history of attempts to isolate the True or the Good, or to define the word 'true' or 'good,' supports their suspicion that there is no interesting work to be done in this area."[42] Truth, as contemporary pragmatists describe it, is efficacy. It might suit them to alter ordinary usage so that we might speak of "true spades," as we speak of "true friends." Or we might learn to replace 'true' with 'efficacious', perhaps reserving 'true' for special honorific uses, as when rewarding conceptual instruments for their efficacy by calling them "true."

Thoughts or sentences deemed true because of their utility have their place within two, different metaphysical theories, one deriving from Kant and Fichte, the other naturalistic without being self-consciously physicalistic.

The Kantian-Fichtean theory, described in chapter 1, supposes that a conceptual system is the instrument required for making experience, hence a world. Where Kant argued that one set of categories is presupposed by every possible synthesis of sensory data, this modern emendation affirms that there are myriad possible conceptual systems, each consistent one qualifying for the task of ordering sensations. Kant would have acknowledged this diversity of systems, treating them as subject matter for philosophic anthropology.

Each system prefigures a distinctive experience and world, though every experience schematized exhibits quality, quantity, and relation, these being the transcendental conditions for any possible experience.

Kant would have agreed that the only worlds knowable—or even thinkable—are those created by using rules to organize symbols, thoughts, or percepts. He might have conceded that these worlds have spread, but no depth: that they stretch before us in two dimensions when the phenomena connected within them are differentiated and related in the ways prescribed by some theory or interpretation. These worlds may have a third dimension phenomenologically, but not in reality. For they do not overreach us on a vector that passes beyond us into a world where the existence and character of things are independent of our syntheses. There is, as Rorty has said, no "Beyond."

This instrumentalist metaphysics is reminiscent of the effect created when we restrict ourselves to the material mode, saying that truth and the formal mode are redundant. Limiting ourselves to the facts, all the while knowing that mind has itself created them, we concede that the story is only half complete. We have the product, but not the agent and activity that have produced it. We feel lobotomized. This instrumentalist metaphysics is not complete, or even coherent, until we provide for the mind which hovers everywhere about the experience it creates. Still, instrumentalists are rarely forthcoming about the transcendental status claimed for mind by these stories of its world-making. Carnap's description of the ego as a product of the conceptual framework used for thinking about it is not significantly different from Kant's description of the empirical ego as a continuous sense of self present within schematized experience. Ego, on either telling, is incapable of the schematizations that both of them require; though Kant also affirms what Carnap judiciously denies:[43] that schematization presupposes the activity of a transcendental subject. Certainly, Foucault, Derrida, and Rorty never conceded that their world-making commits them to a world-maker or that an agent having this power must somehow live apart from all worlds as it chooses or creates the conceptual schemas for making particular worlds. Only Putnam concedes that his internal realism seems to entail a difference between the self internal to a world and the self responsible for making it. Even Putnam dismisses the difference as an "image."

This collective silence is an evasion. Should we suppose that conceptual systems are agents in their own right, that symbols or sensory data are schematized without an agent, with only the rules of a theory or interpretation to organize them? One thinks of the neutral monism favored by James and Russell: [44] data in a neutral medium, neither mind nor matter, are ordered, though not by any thinker. We wait for some contemporary pragmatist to tell us how this system of phenomena might be generated, Russell and James having said nothing to explain it. Kant is explicit where these Kantians are reticent. His transcendental ego is the foundation for his—and their—psycho-centric ontology. All being is drawn into this self-sufficient agent. Like a spider gathering and holding all the strands of its web, this mind has differentiated and ordered, as now it contains and discerns, all being.

Is there one mind, or are there many, each one astride its world? Kant ignores the question. The pragmatists who succeed him avert his precariously solipsist views by insisting that the conceptual system used for creating a world is a public language: we jointly create and live in a world having whatever differentiations and relations are crystallized by this common language. There is this much irresolution: each of us schematizes his or her world, our disparate worlds resembling one another to the extent that each of us has used the same experience-schematizing language; or there is a social mind, perhaps a god, which creates the common world in which all of us participate. Perhaps we are multiple personalities within this creator god, each reflecting the common world from its own perspective. We get Kant's autonomous but finite transcendental minds or Leibniz's infinite but immanent God within whom all the rest of us dwell.

Even a god, presumably, would make a world that suits him—hence Leibniz's view that our world was instantiated because a perfectionist God recognized it as the best one possible. Less exalted world-makers have more pedestrian interests. Should the world satisfy tastes that are ascetic or indulgent? Should it be morally demanding or morally lax, luxuriant or mean? These are differences that world-making minds can effect by their choice of conceptual systems. The transcendental ego making these choices is not obliged by history or context to exhibit any particular attitude or to realize its desire in any particular sort of world. For this is a mind out of time, exempt from the influences occurring within the worlds made.

We might allege that this mind desires its own rationality before any other end. In this spirit, world-making egos might feel themselves compelled to adopt some principled basis for the conceptual systems they choose. There might be a rule of world-making, one that obliges us to use the same language and make the same world so that we may achieve a common end. Equally, transcendental egos might disagree, each one desiring some end consistent with the categorical imperative but different from the ends desired by other minds. Holiness, prurience, detachment: many particular aims satisfy the categorical imperative. Why mind should desire any one of them and why it should rank its desires in any particular way is unexplained. Many or most world-makers may be agitated by nothing more categorial or regularizing than whim. We risk having the anarchy of worlds generated by thinkers for whom difference and diversion are the principal values.

One thinks of Italian films, but also of democratized social orders where everyone declares him or herself a world-maker. We are to acknowledge that each of us is entitled to make and inhabit a world satisfying his or her particular interests. Pride in the thing we have made turns Rorty's "conversation of the West" into a fashion show, each of us talking about—displaying—the world made to soothe us. The mutual accessibility of our worlds may be an illusion, however, for it isn't plain that anyone else has entry to another's world. No one may comprehend any other, except as the other intrudes (somehow) into his or her world. Be it a succession of speeches, a fashion show, or a street fair, Rorty's "conversation" will be more like Babel than it is an exchange of opinions. Perhaps Wittgenstein's aversion to private languages was a reaction to this solipsistic world-making,[45] though we do not alter the essentially idealistic tilt of this view by socializing our constructions.

What value explains the appeal of world-making, whether private or social? Is there a single value, or several, which explains the power of Kantian instrumentalism in our time? I can think of only this consideration mentioned already: that we desire, and dare to claim, the power once ascribed only to gods. We will be world-makers, deciding all the differentiations and relations, even the aesthetics, of whatever world we schematize. Nature and society will not confound us. We shall think our way out of situations inimical to us and into worlds constituted so that our desires may be satisfied. These may be desires for very particular goods; though more fundamental and generic is the desire that we be free to make and dwell within a world of our choosing.

Kant's world-making ego is, I suggest, the essential postulate of a theory contrived so that we may plausibly describe ourselves as autonomous, self-satisfying world-makers. But isn't this the apotheosis of vanity in our philosophical tradition, even if the presumption is out of proportion to our status and powers? Never admitting to such vanity, we renounce world-making pragmatism and its notion of truth. Let transcendental pragmatists soften their claim to world-making. Allow that this same value—the freedom of godhood—may drive a less portentous metaphysical theory.

No longer claiming to explain the differentiations and relations within experience, hence the world, by citing the rules used to schematize it, we apply a parallel argument to the efficacy of our merely human behaviors. The preoccupations of James and Dewey displace those of Kant. Instrumentalism, Kantian style, uses conceptual systems to create experience, if only in the contemporary world, by "interpreting" it. Instrumentalists of this other sort emphasize the plans used to direct human behavior, for it is these actions which remake our world by altering our physical or social circumstances. Needing protection, we build houses, as now these houses alter the sense of our selves by promoting families, property, and stable social relations. We are still world-makers; but only of worlds that are local environments altered by our activity. The motivating value also survives, though it is less grandiose: we want sufficient freedom to liberate ourselves from the constraining effects of nature and other people, but we accept having less power than was celebrated by Kant, then Fichte and Hegel.

The metaphysical theory supporting these reduced claims must allow for both our physical reality and our autonomy as actors; though here the account is vague. What is our relation to the other physical realities of this world? How do they support or constrain our self-directed behaviors? James ignores the question. Scientific claims about nature should be taken seriously, he thinks; but nowhere does he elaborate on the information they provide or tell how limitations in our circumstances and within us restrict our freedom of action. Dewey is only a little more forthcoming. He acknowledges our biological and cultural nature;[46] but he too is mute at the point where metaphysics should describe the possibilities and limits of our powers for altering the world to suit us. Indeed, both James and Dewey turn agnostic about these limits. They sometimes write as if the world were altogether malleable to our human energies and intentions. It must accept, they imply, whatever difference we choose to make there.

Schopenhauerian will overwhelms their pragmatism and good sense at the point where human energy and ingenuity should be constrained by a world having a decided form of its own. This romantic intrusion is supported by a mix of things, including the legacy of Kantian world-making, unembarrassed conviction about the virtue of our desires, and the idea that progress will eradicate the obstacles to human happiness. All this is mere decoration, however, and a context for the propelling force of will. Is there something we do not like or something we prefer? Then we should, and can, organize ourselves to get rid of the one or produce the other. The world in itself poses no obstacles that will cannot bend or obliterate.

Or, as we think again, there are no obstacles but the principle of noncontradiction and the laws of physics, and perhaps our economic circumstances, genes, climate, constitution, and some other assortment of contingencies. These limits on action are never acknowledged in any detailed way, because doing so would mean conceding that the actions launched to satisfy desire are performed in contexts having a shape of their own. James and Dewey are romantics. Ignore the established limits, they say; how many "absolute" constraints have been exceeded when people with sufficient initiative and imagination have put their minds and backs to it? Never admit that we might fail.

This leaves us a choice: shall we be little gods, busy everywhere but admitting that the world has a shape of its own, one we sometimes alter but never eradicate; or shall we be gods of that grander sort who act in a void, without opposition? Shall we be prudent and effective or heroic but confounded? James and Dewey are usually the first, while always imagining that we might be the second. We inherit their indecision and its costs. Human power is the source of most of the things that make our lives satisfying and secure. But there is this other side: we are reckless and oblivious to our place in the world; we sometimes exploit any and everything for our perceived advantage, ignoring the consequences for other things and ultimately ourselves.

VI Conclusion

This survey justifies the three claims made at the start of this chapter: that each of the several notions of truth has its place within one or several metaphysical theories; that each theory is sponsored by one or more values; and that each provides a notion of the world congenial to it. Each of these value-driven systems has historical, conceptual integrity. Still, no one of the four notions of truth considered here—not coherence, identity, redundancy, or the several kinds of behaviorism—explains the fact that we successfully accommodate ourselves to a world we do not make. Where does any of them provide for the maps and plans essential to making our way in nature? We know that the question is begged or turned, as when mind pretends to make worlds to satisfy itself. Is correspondence better? Chapter 5 says that it is.

Chapter Five

I The Rationale for Truth as Correspondence

Metaphysical theories supporting the coherence, identity, redundancy, and behaviorist notions of truth were merely sketched in the preceding chapter. More elaborate formulations were not demanded, because these ideas of truth are subsidiary or wrong. My procedure in this chapter is different. I suppose that correspondence is the best hypothesis about truth as it occurs in practice, science, and philosophy. Detailed exposition of the metaphysical theory supporting this notion of truth is therefore required.

My thoughts about correspondence and the theory embedding it are responses to the following question. Which metaphysics do we propose if the value directing inquiry has this complex objective: proximately, of discovering where we stand in the world the better to secure and satisfy ourselves there; more remotely, of knowing where we stand so as to achieve a certain closure as regards our self-understanding? [1] All modern philosophy inspired by Kant diverts attention from this question by substituting a different one: namely, how shall we provide for the impression of a world separate from us when nothing we might know is independent of mind's productive activity?

Kantians do tell what and where we are when they declare that we make the only worlds known to us. Still, my question has an implication that is never satisfied by their solutions. They affirm that the world is somehow in us, only seeming to be "outside" because we project differentiations and relations into the void by way of the theories we use to schematize sensory data or symbols. My question has this contrary implication: that we are creatures living in a world we affect but do not create. Kantians celebrate our freedom and the exuberant pleasure we feel when living in worlds congenial to our interests. My question voices our foreboding that we share a world with things that resist us. Driving in fog, sometimes tripping on chairs in the dark, we reflect that nothing is true merely because we desire that it be so. Truth is, all the while, our miner's lamp. It flashes beyond us onto surfaces and obstacles that are better anticipated than kicked. Discovering ourselves in a world having a form of its own, one that is not pliable to every human desire, we make our accommodations to it.

We also describe the conditions for these adaptations, as creatures having neither innate ideas nor rational intuition use signs to represent the things around them. The signs that represent states of affairs are the natural ones of perception and the conventional ones of thought and language— though it is only propositional signs (thoughts or sentences meeting conditions discussed below) that count as true. More, this is truth as correspondence: thoughts or sentences are true when the states of affairs they signify do obtain. Truth of this sort is a necessary condition if maps and plans are to direct our behaviors in a world we inhabit and alter, but never make.

There are two claims to make and justify if truth is to be described as correspondence: first is a dialectically defensible characterization of the correspondence relation; second is a realist psychology and ontology adequate to both our circumstances and this notion of truth. This is pragmatism of the sort scorned by contemporary textualists but close to the activism encouraged by Dewey and James. They would have resisted my emphasis on accommodation, though realism of the kind sponsoring truth as correspondence accepts this demand without implying that we have only the choice of stubborn mastery or capitulation. Are we acquiescent in circumstances we inherit or determined that they be altered to our advantage? Realism of the sort proposed here does not justify a sullen adaptation to our circumstances, whatever they may be. But this is the easy part: tripping on chairs, we move them.

Details of my realist theory come in three stages. First (sections ii– v) is the preliminary statement of a realist ontology which supports the correspondence of thoughts or sentences about singular existents (e.g., this grasshopper, that tree). We then recall the variety of thoughts and sentences (e.g., generalities and counterfactuals) that might be true because of corresponding to things of a more perplexing sort (e.g., generals or conditional relations). Is it also the case that representations such as these are true because they correspond to states of affairs? I shall argue that this is so; though saying it requires that we elaborate on the realist ontology, making it provide for these more arcane states of affairs (sections VI and VII). Finally, when this variety of thoughts and sentences is accommodated within an amplified realist theory, I shall propose one further elaboration (sections VIII and IX). It deepens the realist theory while supplying more plainly articulated referents for problematic kinds of thoughts and sentences. This final addition is the claim that our actual world is the instantiation of an eternally possible world, one that is replete with internal differentiations and relations. Anyone repelled by talk of possible worlds can ignore this third part of the argument without cost to the view that truth is correspondence: that idea of truth will have been justified before the introduction of claims about possible worlds. Still, the recognition of eternal possibilities is defensible logically and (in an extended sense) empirically. Reference to these possibles is, moreover, clarifying. Some of the thoughts and sentences problematic for the idea that truth is correspondence—especially those representing "negative facts"—are best explained within an ontology that acknowledges possibilities.

Someone hostile to realism will ask if there is anything for which one cannot find a place in my realist metaphysics. Will I succeed only in pushing the "Fido"–Fido theory of truth to its silliest extreme? One thinks of the ontological sobriety that one should have learned from Mill: "Mankind in all ages have had a strong propensity to conclude that wherever there is a name, there must be a distinguishable separate entity corresponding to the name; and every complex idea which the mind has formed for itself by operating upon its conceptions of individual things was considered to have an outward objective reality answering to it."[2] Many features of our thinking (e.g., the contrasting grammars of English and Chinese) have no parallel in the complexity of things represented. But skepticism wants carte blanche for saying that no form of thought or speech is representational. With Hume and Kant as our models, we are to purge our ontologies of all things having an existence and a character independent of the ways we perceive, think, or talk about them. Physical objects, laws, space and time, modalities: there is to be nothing in the world that we have not put there.

Possibilities help to quash that vanity. Where possibilities are the primordial reality (existing because they embody no contradiction) and where the actual world is the instantiation of a possible world, we justify these four claims: that there is a domain of realities we have not made; that it supplies terms for the worldly side of the correspondence relation; that this world independent of mind has layers of intrinsic differentiation and structure; and that mind's responsibility for making the world intelligible is reduced, because the world itself supplies the differentiations and relations that make it thinkable. These are four reasons for saying that possibilities, whether instantiated or not and with the articulations founded within them, support our representations. Thoughts and sentences acknowledge these realities; we do not invent them.

One issue still rankles when correspondence and its supporting realist theory have been detailed. I shall need to tell why the question is not begged when the metaphysical theory which includes the idea of correspondence is itself said to be true because it represents (corresponds to) things as they are. This is circular. We want to be convinced that the circularity is innocuous.

II Abductive Inference

Every elaboration of the ontology supplying a real-world ground for correspondence is an abductive inference. Starting from empirical data or a conceptual problem, we ask about the conditions that need to obtain if the data are to be explained or the problem resolved. An astronomer's photographic plates show that light has disappeared at some places in the heavens; or we are befuddled by the anomaly created when the evidence of empirical regularities is set against Hume's claim that anything may follow anything, though typically it does not. Why does the light disappear? What are the likely conditions for empirical uniformities? Should we ignore the uniformities, out of respect for an argument which implies that they are unlikely to persist. Or do we scuttle the argument because of wanting to identify conditions for uniformities which do persist? The questions are equivalent when the conditions at issue are those for truth. We have theories which deny that truth is correspondence while favoring some alternative account of it; but then we also have the repeated, effective use of maps and plans. Should we ignore the evidence of their effective use? Or do we make these successes our point of reference, inferring from them to the conditions for the truth of our representations?

Abductions specifying those conditions are hypotheses. They are speculative inferences moving to some alleged condition from whatever empirical data or conceptual problem is assumed. They propose that one or another factor explains a problematic phenomenon because of being, for example, its constituent, cause, reason, or constraining law. Conditions may be necessary, sufficient, or both for the matter at issue, as we infer from smoke to fire (a sufficient condition) and from motion to space and time (its necessary conditions). Conditions inferred may themselves be observable, as fire is perceived, or unobservable, as black holes and causal laws are inferred but not observed.

Hume protested that inference should never carry beyond sensory data to conditions which are not themselves observable.[3] His reasoning was straightforward: extra-phenomenal entities do not exist; or, conceding that they exist, they cannot be known if knowledge is acquaintance and these alleged states of affairs are not directly observable. Reality, insofar as we can know it, is limited to the plane of awareness; nothing but impressions and the ideas copying them are to count as real. But now the bizarre inferences justified by these claims begin to multiply; for even the mind to which these things are given and which then inspects them isn't included in Hume's inventory of realities. Why? Because every reflection on it reveals only one or another of the impressions or ideas currently inspected. The result is a crippled psycho-centrism, one in which we acknowledge the things inspected but not the agent to whom they are presented.

Prohibiting inferences to things that are not directly observable is confounding. It guarantees that we shall not explain the data, as Hume could not explain either their presentation, their uniformities, or the efficacy of maps and plans. He responded that anything can produce anything. The myriad, sustained regularities observed (and presumably the success of behaviors directed by maps and plans) are accidents or miracles. Nothing can explain them. Deeper still, there is nothing to explain: anything distinguishable is separable so that there is no reason either in nature or in metaphysics why anything separable should not be self-sufficient. This includes impressions and ideas: it is no contradiction that they should occur in the luminous mental void, with no supporting mind to receive and inspect them. Rather like barnacles registering the passing effects of things, we can only inspect and relate the impressions and ideas occurring within us. We can never estimate or even imagine the conditions for this experience—though, as Hume might have said, there are only the effects, not even the barnacle.[4]

The idea of *explanation* is reduced to the scale of Hume's phenomenalist intuitionism.[5] We might naively suppose, as the use of abduction confirms, that we sometimes explain phenomena by inferring beyond them to their causes or grounds, even when the referents of our inferences are not themselves directly observable. Hume eliminates inferences of this sort, only seeming to provide for them on those many occasions when the condition inferred is itself observable (e.g., as the inference from smoke to fire is confirmed when we see the fire). Cases of this sort are reparsed: rather than describe them as abductions confirmed empirically, we rethink our notion of explanation. We say that a phenomenon is explained when it is subsumed under the law predicting this effect in the presence of some others. Explanation is never to exceed the plane of phenomena set before the mind's eye. Seeing whiskers and an arched back, we infer to the likely appearance of bared teeth and a curved tail, not to the hostile cat that is the cause of these impressions. But this is much less explanation than we plausibly require. As above, it leaves us with no explanation for the presentation and inspection of sensory data, for their regularities, or for the efficacy of maps and plans—all this because of Hume's fastidious skepticism.

Even very simple inferences exceed the Humean limits for thinking about the world, as happens when we infer from an effect to its cause—from the appearance of smoke to smoke itself. Hume would object that the inference from smoke as it appears to smoke itself is speculative and illegitimate. But many inferences breech this standard, most dramatically as we infer from the absence of sensory evidence to the existence of something that is not observable in itself or by way of its effects. Every phenomenalist would once have scorned this pattern of inference, though it is accepted without challenge when illustrated by the inferred disappearance of light into black holes. Do we accept this inference because we have lost our wits; or rather because it has the additional support of the abduction—the physical theory—which predicts and explains the possibility of gravitational collapse in bodies so dense that no light can escape their gravitational fields? Notice that little or nothing alleged by this theory is directly inspectable.

This is a surprising case, one that surpasses the mystery of the dog which did not bark. In the latter, we infer from an absent bark to its perceiv-

able cause; in the former, from the absence of effects to something not per-
ceivable directly or indirectly (ignoring some observable effects of black holes).
Surely, these examples are a caution to anyone who avers that nothing shall
count as real if it is not observed or observable. For why should we suppose
that unobservability is tolerable only as it is explained by some particular
account of matter in motion, as the unobservability of black holes has physical causes only? Why should the inference to unobservables be endorsed in
cases like this one, but not in circumstances where inference runs from the
specification of an act to the specification of its conditioning disposition or
from a uniformity in the sensory data to a causal law? Any inference from
sensory data to their conditions might extend our knowledge of the world if
the inference can be embedded within an otherwise cogent theory which tells
why the inferred entity is necessary to the generation of the data at issue, as
no one walks in the absence of the disposition that qualifies him for walking.[6]

How far can we extend these abductions before our claim to responsible inference turns hollow? Surely, there is no fixed limit to credible inferences once we have exceeded inspectable impressions and ideas; probably
Hume knew that, and fixed the standards narrowly because of it. Anyone
abjuring his rules is free to introduce any factor that is plausibly alleged to
be the condition for something assumed. There will often be objections that
an abduction extends the list of conditions beyond the point where anything
is explained by introducing them, as Molière objected to dormative powers.
Still, we shouldn't strangle the abductive process out of fear that we must
submit to every dubious hypothesis proposed. Someone favoring an inference
is obliged to show, first, that something needs explaining, then that some
alleged condition explains it. Better still, we may ask him or her to convince
us that the sensory data or phenomenon assumed would not be as they are
or would not exist in the absence of the thing inferred.

Abduction exploits this precious opportunity without being able to
confirm, by itself, that its hypotheses accurately represent particular conditions for the things assumed. Having sensory affects within us, we infer speculatively to the existence and character of alleged conditions for these affects.
But much is left undecided. Does the alleged condition actually obtain? We
shall need empirical data confirming predictions made by the hypothesis to
confirm that it does. Is the skein of things requiring explanation infinite, so
that we shall never exhaust the opportunity for one more abduction? This
may be so, but what if it is? Why assume that the sequence of conditions

has, and must have, some fixed limit? Why shouldn't abductions be made responsibly throughout a denumerably infinite succession of effects when each term in the series provokes explanation because, incomplete in itself (meaning that it is not self-sufficient), it has conditions.

Certainly, these hypotheses may only approximate the character of the things represented. They may distort is severely. But hypotheses, even successfully tested ones, are revisable, with improved accuracy coming in fits and starts. It is sufficient, at any one time, that we are accurate to some degree and able to determine where representations and predictions can be further refined. That an allergy causes my sneezing is no less true for being an incomplete specification of the cause. The hypothesis identifying the cause may be true of its extra-linguistic referent, irrespective of improvements introduced into subsequent hypotheses.

What shall we say of entities represented so confusedly as to make us wonder what referents these are. The wavelike particles or particlelike waves postulated by quantum theory are an example. Should we welcome them to the reality required if truth is to be correspondence? The answer is appropriately cautious. Having no coherent model for these entities, we set this disadvantage against experimental evidence confirming the extraordinary mathematical accuracy of quantum theory. Joining these considerations leaves us some distance from a comprehensive specification of quantum phenomena. Yet, we are not altogether ignorant about the character of the things represented by quantum theory, as the discreteness of energy states at the quantum level seems to be a correct inference.

There is, of course, this other possible response to contentious theories. We might respond to current uncertainties about quantum phenomena by proposing that the only sober philosophic task is the one of reconstructing words such as 'atom' or 'quantum' by listing the sensory affects that supply their only material sense. That would be retrograde. For why be purists demanding either a comprehensive, anomaly-purging representation or the skeptical solution that there is nothing beyond the sensory data to represent? We may tolerate, here and everywhere, the ambiguity or inaccuracy of representations less than perfectly adequate to their objects. Why not exult that we, who lack rational intuition and innate ideas, can skillfully refine our hypotheses after thinking about the experimental evidence used to test them. Truth as correspondence requires nothing more than these approximations, as we believe correctly that sugar dissolves in tea without knowing the kinetic and molecular reasons.

It may seem that I beg the question put to realists while minimizing the particular difficulty of confirming that arcane, but confirmed, hypotheses have referents. Is realism merely postulated, then assumed to be true, so that our only problem is the one of formulating accurate descriptions of its worldly referents? No, realism is itself an abductive inference, meaning a hypothesis about the world and our place in it. We speculate that there is a world extending beyond us, a natural world in which we live as natural creatures. We suppose, too, that sensory data are the evidence of our relations to other things and that hypotheses are the more or less accurate, but empirically testable, estimates of the things causing these effects in us. Hypothesis allied to sensation and hypothesis-directed action is, we hypothesize, our only means for testing the reality about and within us.

This realist hypothesis is not mere dogmatism. It is the best sense we can make of our circumstances, a sense tested by the internal coherence of the hypothesis, coupled to the myriad empirical confirmations of the more specific hypotheses formulated to direct behaviors or explain various sensory affects. And certainly, we cannot do better in defense of the abductive method than to add that there is no shortcut to our knowledge of the external world: no innate ideas of specific matters of fact and no rational intuition of them or of being altogether. We shall never grasp things-in-themselves, never address them by stepping out of thought or language to confront them directly. Knowledge of them will always be mediated by sensory data and our conceptualizations. This is contact enough, when conceptual imagination enables us to formulate, revise, and integrate an ever extended network of empirically tested hypotheses.

How accurate must abductions be? Is there a canon of rules for responsible abduction? Yet and no. Responsible abductions satisfy familiar rules of thumb. They are grammatically well formed and logically consistent. They are cogent within the body of accepted hypotheses about the conditions for some domain of sensory data or for sensory data in general. We test these hypotheses against the data, by requiring that they specify a condition or conditions necessary or sufficient for generating the data. Abductions to entities not shown to have this bearing on sensory data may not be mistaken, though we have no reason for believing that they are true. We are suspicious, finally, of any definitive codification of the rules for making or appraising abductions. For there is no alternative but dogmatism to this principle of tolerance: let everyone proceed in any consistent way he or she can to make hypotheses which reveal some previously unsuspected condition for sensory data or the phenomena perceived. Nothing in this principle stops us from rejecting all that is obscure, irrelevant, inconsistent, or empty in the hypothesis proposed. We who defend theory and the world from gratuitous inflation are, on our side, inhibited from saying that reality is exhaustively described already, with no place in it for whatever is specified by some new hypothesis.

III A Preliminary Realist Ontology

Very little is required of a realist theory formulated abductively to supply an extra-mental, extra-linguistic ground for one of the terms of the correspondence relation.[7] Realism of this modest kind need only hypothesize that there exists something whose existence and character are independent of perception, thought, language, feeling, and will. This something may be physical or spiritual, ephemeral or eternal, in or out of space and time, conscious or not. It may be particularized and discrete or continuous and pervasive within its medium, accessible to mind or separated from it by an impenetrable barrier. We could also ignore these refinements, saying only that there is one thing at least whose existence and character are independent of mind and its activities. Thoughts or sentences would be true if they rightly characterize this thing, false otherwise.

Realism of this sort is, however, too meager to support the detail and complexity of experience. For we seek the conditions of our natural signs (i.e., sensory affects) and the referents of our conventional signs (i.e., thoughts and words). Ears ringing with the sound, we infer to thunder. Following the way laid down by a guidebook, we expect that the next building, picture, or street on the left will be the one described. Realism is the hypothesis, the abduction, that there are things affecting and affected by us, things that cause our percepts or satisfy our descriptions. The realism sketched above is too simple, because there is nothing in it to explain the diversity of affects in us.

We elaborate on that first hypothesis after asking this other question: what is the least we need say of things existing apart from us in order to explain these affects? Imagination may have created all of them, or there might be some demon affecting us; but how shall we explain the many affects if explanations of these two sorts are ignored? There is also this other requirement: it isn't enough that we hit the bull's-eye without knowing it, describing things as they are without having evidence to confirm the truth of what we think or say. The abduction specifying the things existing independently of perception, thought, and language should also specify the manner by which we acquire the evidence that falsifies or confirms our particular claims about matters of fact.

There might be several hypotheses that satisfy both requirements. The hypothesis I propose declares that we are located within an ensemble of things related spatially, temporally, and dynamically. We speculate that each thing has several or many properties. Indeed, each is presumably constituted of nothing but its properties, including magnitude, mass, configuration, inertia, and particular spatiotemporal relations. We suppose that these properties are organized so that each thing is a more or less stable structure. Never inert (as the more familiar notion of substance has sometimes implied), motion is regularized and constrained within it. It is important, too, that every stability is a continuant and that differences in structure explain the specificity and range of each thing's functions. Finally, we propose, and experience confirms, that structures are altered in the course of their transformations and interactions and that these changes are notably uniform, hence lawful and repeatable: caterpillars become butterflies; the seasons come and go. This is a universe in which continuity, stability, transformation, and interaction are so many ways of regularizing and constraining motion and energy.

We might emphasize any one of these features when the things postulated by this realist hypothesis are named. I prefer describing them as plastic but stable structures, "stabilities" for short. These are, we speculate, things which survive change. Persistent structure, with its dispositions and behaviors, defines a thing through the epoch of any particular identity. Alter the structure beyond a certain (often vaguely specified) point, and we get a different thing. Nor is this a merely conventional difference: cut flowers may bloom, but they do not grow. There are, nevertheless, many changes that leave a structure unaltered, and many others that express its natural plasticity (e.g., painting a house or bending an arm). Speaking of things as stabilities implies this integrity over time, though we also acknowledge the cataclysmic changes which terminate a structure, hence the epoch or lifetime in which it has a particular identity.

We have evidence of these evolving, interacting structures, because we too are stabilities, with dynamic relations to many others. We are affected by our interactions with them, as by the behaviors internal to us. Differentiating among these affects, we speculate about their causes. Abduction probably starts just here, in the moment of supposing that affects in us occur as we engage other stabilities. We speculate too that these structures are resistant, reactive but also malleable; that their mutual relations are spatial and temporal; and in addition that these things are space- and time-filling. These are some of the hypotheses made as we push things in directions opposed to their current heading. Resisting both deformation and whatever changes of motion are impressed on them, they have, we surmise, an inertia of their own. Slipping or falling, jammed or frustrated by things unexpected or opposed, we infer that the reality engaging us is dynamic and plastic, but stable, disparate, and predictable. It is, we learn, never more than partially controllable.

IV Natural and Conventional Signs

We also learn some things that distinguish us from other stabilities. Our bodies, too, seem to be continuants, though with the difference that we are conscious, as most other things seem not to be. Percepts qualify our consciousness, presumably as the things perceived affect our eyes or ears. We know that the affects are in us, not in the things perceived, because we can remember and imagine them even when their causes are unavailable or destroyed.

These reflections are the basis for two important discoveries. First is the inference that percepts are the natural signs of their causes, correlating with, or corresponding, to them. We might infer that this correlation is also a similarity, as the round look of a thing might imitate its actual shape. Perhaps the actions engaging us in the world are more precise and effective— they have greater survival value—if our percepts do exhibit the properties of their causes. The similarity of a percept and its cause is, nevertheless, incidental to the relation of a sign to its object, as apples that look red are not red in themselves. Second is the observation that causes and their effects may very independently of one another. Changes in a cause are not always echoed in our percepts, as, equally, percepts may vary for reasons (including light and the condition of one's eyes) that are independent of the things perceived. There is also the further evidence of this independence when percepts remembered and imagined are associable with other percepts in ways that have no parallel in their causes, 'golden mountain' being an example.

The independence and variability of natural signs, when compared to the stability of their causes, establish them as precursors of the signs used in thought and language. These other signs are all the more exempt from the constraining effects of their referents: we regularly alter the sense of thoughts or words or combine them in ways having no correlates in the things represented. We explain this license by remarking that these conceptual and linguistic signs are conventional, not natural. Nature, we say, constrains the order of natural signs, at least with respect to our original experience of them. Mind is free to use its conventional signs in whatever way it pleases. So relations among percepts map the relations of their causes, just as the sequence of notes we hear is usually isomorphic with the sequence of notes played. Relations among the conventional signs of thought and language may have no equivalent within the things represented, as there is nothing in nature to justify the English rule that adjectives precede their nouns.

Some differences between these types of signs are also worth remarking—for example, that natural signs are reactive, conventional ones anticipatory. We see or hear the things affecting us; we use conventional signs to signify possibilities which may not yet be realized. Where the independence of natural signs from their objects is a first clue to the independence of conventional signs, this point can now be invoked to emphasize the difference between them. The variability of natural signs is relatively slight; they are anchored, by and large, in their causes. Conventional signs are never so rigidly constrained by their referents. Variations in them are always justifiable pragmatically, by saying that something is more effectively signified because of alterations in the signs themselves, in their relations, or in our use of them.

The relative invariance of natural signs is vital for co-ordinating the behaviors of people allied. You see what I see, thereby establishing that we have this common object of thought and perception. We talk about this thing, agreeing as a common education enables us to do about the conventional signs to be used for signifying it. We also consider what to do with it, using conventional signs to designate possibilities not yet realized. There is reaction, anticipation, and reaction again: talk about something perceived, then talk about the possible things to do with or about it, then more talk representing the circumstances newly revised by our behavior. The cycle of our responses to the thing perceived and signified, considered, altered, and perceived again expresses the pendulumlike movement between natural and conventional signs. But always, we suppose, there is this thing provoking us. It correlates to a natural sign, then to a conventional sign, then again, when behavior has altered it, to a natural sign.

This is a first approximation to a realist metaphysics biased to the conclusion that truth is correspondence. Stabilities with their properties, relations, and changes are independent of thought and language as regards their character and existence. There are also the natural and conventional signs that do or may represent these things. We require that these signs be true, or capable of being true or false. But this needs further clarification, since not every sign can be true or false, as percepts and traffic signs are sometimes misleading, but never false. Correspondence of the sort relevant to truth cannot be the mere pairing of two things under an interpretation that makes one the sign, the other its referent. Signs must earn truth or falsehood by satisfying some further conditions.

Here again, the greater independence of conventional signs from their referents is critical. This is apparent when one of the conditions for truth or falsity is the well-formedness of the sign. We have no way of requiring that natural signs satisfy a normative format, though we are free to demand that conventional signs satisfy formation rules. But which rules? Moves in a game, recipes, and taxi rides all satisfy rules without being true or false. What is it that qualifies sentences satisfying grammatical rules for truth or falsity? There are two considerations. First, a sentence must be syntactically well formed by virtue of having either a subject term of which existence is predicated or denied or one or more subject terms to which some predicate or relation is ascribed (e.g., 'fogbound' is predicated of 'Alderney'; 'Fred', 'Spot', and 'Edith' are bound by the relation "x gave y to z"). Second, the sentence must be semantically consistent, as it is not if the predicate term is anomalous as regards the subject (e.g., "It is raining numbers") or if predicates ascribed to a subject are exclusive of one another (e.g., "Something is both red and green all over at the same time"). Syntactic inconsistencies are fairly easy to spot using general rubrics: for example, 'not both p and $-p$.' The rules barring semantic inconsistencies are less general and are rarely formulated. We typically learn them only as we learn to use the individual terms.

We are closer now to the sufficient conditions for truth and falsity, though there are two further steps to go. First is the requirement that a well-formed sentence be declared: it must be affirmed or denied; for no sentence is true or false merely as entertained. This might seem a mistake, as a student considers a sentence but is uncertain whether to declare it or not. "Do it," says his teacher: "That's true," implying that the sentence is true already, whether or not the student affirms it. We get the impression that there is a truth or falsity already established, because we assume that it is a proposition which is true or false, where declaring the sentence-token serves only to express its truth or falsehood. Suppose, however, that no propositions are expressed by thoughts or sentences standing apart from them as *universalia ante rem* might stand apart from their instances. This leaves truth and falsity to sentences, and more particularly to specific declarations of sentences. It implies, too, that an individual sentence is not true or false until it is pointed and discharged, so to speak, its demonstrative and descriptive terms engaged by our use of it. The teacher who has encouraged the student to declare his sentence should now revise his own assumption that the sentence is true already when undeclared. For the most he could reasonably suppose is that sentence-tokens of this type have been, or would be true, if declared.

There is only this one condition for truth or falsity still to cite: the well-formed sentence declared is true or false according as the state of affairs signified obtains or not. A positive sentence is true if its referent is qualified as the predicate specifies, or if the stated relation obtains. A negative sentence is true if things are not qualified or related as the sentence affirms they are not.

Each of the sentences declared is a hypothesis, a speculation that things are as we represent them. How do we confirm or falsify these claims? By way of the relation between truth-bearing, conventional signs and the natural signs of perception. The one represents the world as it may be; the other is evidence of the world as it is. We make the second relevant to the first by way of ostensive definitions and inductive rules. So "This looks red" is true if the thing specified does look red, while "This is an apple" is likely to be true if the thing has the shape, color, and texture of an apple.

V Truth as Correspondence

Realism proposes that a thought or sentence is true if the state of affairs it represents does obtain, false if it does not. This is obscure, for we haven't yet explained the way that representation is achieved. How do the conventional signs of thought or language represent worldly states of affairs?

A. Austin on Truth

I rely on J. L. Austin's formulation:

> When is a statement true? The temptation is to answer (at least if we confine ourselves to "straightforward" statements): "When it corresponds to the facts." And as a piece of standard English this can hardly be wrong. Indeed, I must confess I do not really think it is wrong at all: the theory of truth is a series of truisms. Still, it can at least be misleading. If there is to be communication of the sort that we achieve by language at all, there must be a stock of symbols of some kind which a communicator ("the speaker") can produce "at will" and which a communicatee ("the audience") can observe: these may be called the "words," though, of course, they need not be anything very like what we should normally call words—they might be signal flags, etc. There must also be something other than the words, which the words are to be used to communicate about: this may be called the "world." There is no reason why the world should not include the words, in every sense except the sense of the actual statement itself which on any particular occasion is being made about the world. Further, the world must exhibit (we must observe) similarities and dissimilarities (there could not be the one without the other): if everything were either absolutely indistinguishable from anything else or completely unlike anything else, there would be nothing to say. And finally (for present purposes—of course there are other conditions to be satisfied too) there must be two sets of conventions: *Descriptive* conventions correlating the words (= sentences) with the *types* of situation, thing, event, etc., to be found in the word. *Demonstrative* conventions correlating the words (= sentences) with the *historic* situations, etc., to be found in the world. A statement is said to be true when the historic state of affairs to which it is correlated by the demonstrative conventions (the one to which it "refers") is of a type with which the

sentence used in making it is correlated by the descriptive conventions.[8]

Austin supposes, and I agree, that talk is more than a current of babble or song coursing among us. Our conversations are more than patterns of give and take, speeches and reassurances, as you carry on, while I nod or respond soothingly that, yes, I understand. Talk is practical and cogent, because it answers to circumstances where interests are engaged and actions performed. These are the contexts where information is exchanged by way of sentences that have achieved correspondence: we talk of things as they are.

Austin's notion of truth is the one that I want to situate within the naturalistic metaphysics sketched above. He supposes that two kinds of words are especially significant for truth: those used descriptively to signify types of things, properties, or events; and those used demonstratively to specify the things that satisfy our descriptions. "(I'll have) This loaf, please" has words of both sorts, organized in a way that satisfies English grammar. The descriptive words signify possible properties, entities, or events; demonstratives lock on to the actual circumstances in which these things may be present. What conditions need to be satisfied if words are to have one or the other of these roles? Austin doesn't tell us, though the answers seem plain enough.

The use of demonstratives, including 'this', 'that', 'he', 'she', and 'it', presupposes these four conditions. First is context. "Watch out," someone shouts to a fellow pedestrian. These same words might be used to warn of flying golf balls or a plunging stock market; but just now, it is the car running a nearby traffic light that provokes them. A second condition is the presence within this situation of discriminable things or features, with the complementary ability in us to perceive or infer these differences, as we see the car. Third is the attention of those to whom we speak or write. Attention is safely assumed if my discourse is a private rumination. Doing my taxes, disgusted by this year's first estimate of the money owed, I know very well what is signified by "this" number. Attention is problematic, however, if one is trying to communicate with someone else. "Let's do that," I say to a distracted partner; but what does "that" signify to someone who pays no attention either to this speech or the contextual clues? Fourth is the ability to coordinate the use of indexicals (Austin's demonstratives) among speakers or writers having more or less divergent perspectives.

Fulfillment of all four conditions seems required for the use of demonstratives, though behaviorists and anyone suspicious of mentalism will want to find some alternative for attention. Wittgenstein, with no confidence that attention might some day have an exhaustively physicalist explanation, is a prominent example. He supposed that mental activity should bear no responsibility for the fact that demonstratives achieve reference. The words should achieve it themselves, it being a contradiction that a logically proper name not have its object.[9] But there seem to be no logically proper names, hence no way that demonstratives could pick out the relevant features of a context by themselves. We are the only ones qualified to make those discriminations. We do that by using indexical words or other clues (we pick something up or point a finger, saying "This" or "That") to fix the attention of auditors. Often, we let other people establish the context in which our words have application: I answer "Sarah" when asked my daughter's name.

Davidson and Quine, writing in the spirit of Wittgenstein's *Philosophical Investigations*, have made us suspicious of reference, especially as it depends on private acts of intention.

> Perhaps someone . . . will be tempted to say, "But at least the speaker knows what he is referring to." One should stand firm against this thought. The semantic features of language are public features. What no one can, in the nature of the case, figure out from the totality of the relevant evidence cannot be part of meaning. And since every speaker must, in some dim sense at least, know this, he cannot even intend to use his words with a unique reference, for he knows that there is no way for his words to convey this reference to another.[10]

Davidson would have us believe that there is no demonstrative use of words if one cannot convey their reference to other people, hence no meaningful private act in the absence of a public criterion. A speaker's private, uncommunicated (perhaps incommunicable) intentions must be irrelevant to the use of words as demonstratives: the beetle drops out of the box. But is this right? We prove that it is not merely by citing a single case or class of cases in which demonstratives have their inception in private intentional acts — for example, the pet names coined secretly for significant things in one's life. Think of the wife who discovers the name of a mysterious woman in her husband's journal, only to learn that, for a long time, this has been his name for her. We often take pains to learn the demonstratives that are familiar already to other people, especially people with whom we share interests or a public space. But neither Wittgenstein nor Davidson has established that demonstratives cannot be introduced by way of private intentions and then sustained by the aggregated intentions of the many people who use them for communicating about their common world.

Nor are demonstratives subverted when Quine remarks that one group's demonstratives may be "inscrutable" to people who do not speak their language. Where references to President Adams are vague for Americans, we readily extrapolate to the difficulties that someone of a different language or merely a different culture would have with the nouns and pronouns of everyday speech. But that is no evidence that we do not have and use demonstratives, as Quine agrees:

> Within the parochial limits of our own language, we can continue as always to find extensional talk clearer than intensional. For the indeterminacy between "rabbit," "rabbit stage," and the rest depended only on a correlative indeterminacy of translation of the English apparatus of individuation—the apparatus of pronouns, pluralization, identity, numerals, and so on. No such indeterminacy obtrudes so long as we think of this apparatus as given and fixed. Given this apparatus, there is no mystery about extension; terms have the same extension when true of the same things. At the level of radical translation, on the other hand, extension itself goes inscrutable.[11]

Suppose that these objections are put aside. Our use of demonstratives achieves their effect: singly or together, we use a word or words to signify some thing. This is the place where descriptive terms come into play. I want to tell you something about this thing: it is green and froglike, or loud, too loud, for me and the neighbors. Two conditions are satisfied by these descriptive terms, both of them common to demonstratives. Things in the world must stand apart because they differ in regard to some property or properties, while we discern (by perception or inference), then specify, these things. Interlocutors must be able to co-ordinate their descriptive terms, so that speakers and writers having different perspectives are able to confirm the suitability of a descriptive term applied from standpoints different from their own. Doing this is commonplace: we regularly take up another perspective, or imagine that we do by extrapolating to the things that would then be perceived from those which are perceived or inferred.

These two sets of conditions are easily and often satisfied: demonstrative and descriptive terms are used innumerable times in the course of any day by everyone. Still, there are some difficulties with words of both sorts. Demonstratives never lose their ambiguity: I assume that I know the thing signified when you say "This" or "That," but I may be mistaken. Descriptive terms may be applied mistakenly, though we agree about their applicability, as juries often agree erroneously about a finding of guilt or innocence. There is also the fact that descriptive terms may be shallow in their characterization of a thing, with later terms superseding earlier ones. Describing something as gold, we ignore, because we may not know, its molecular structure. But description, as much as the use of indexicals, is contextual as regards the interest motivating us: the descriptive terms we use may convey only as much information as circumstances and interest justify. For I may not care about a thing's molecular properties: my motive for confirming a description may be only the concern that I not pay the price of gold for gilt or brass.

B. Demonstrative and Descriptive Terms are Conventional Signs

Austin insists that demonstratives and descriptives are related only conventionally to the states of affairs they represent. This is risky, because it guarantees that the connection of signs to their objects is fragile, as it is if we are struck by amnesia, forgetting how to construe our signs. Suppose this happens, with the result that the conventional relations binding signs to their objects come unstuck: won't the objects fall into limbo, beyond the reach of thought and its signs, hence of knowledge? Wittgenstein may have felt this anxiety when he explains his view, in the *Tractatus*, that sentences represent states of affairs, first, because the form of an atomic sentence is isomorphic with the form of configured objects;[12] second, because the constituent words of an atomic sentence are the logically proper names of the objects configured. This account would explain the intelligibility of the world and its accessibility to knowledge — though we have no examples of the atomic sentences it postulates and no reason for believing that sentences require either sameness of form or logically proper names to represent states of affairs. Thinking or saying that Polly wants a cracker is not at all like Polly wanting a cracker.

C. Evidence for the Conventionality of Signs

The conventionality of representations is all the more apparent when we alter some usually unexamined assumptions. Three are relevant here.

The Complexity of Signs. One is the notion that a complex state of affairs requires a complex representation, with as many articulations in the sign as there are differences and relations in the thing represented. The representation maps the state of affairs; mind need only survey the one to perceive the complexity of the other. Notice, however, that a simple sign, *a*, is an adequate representation for a complex state of affairs if mind construes the simple sign in some complex way appropriate to diversity and relation in the state of affairs. We might, for example, repeat the letter *a*, raising or lowering our voices, ululating sometimes, barking it staccato at other times. Or we might say nothing at all, merely interpreting the single letter cerebrally in the way prescribed by a rule: *a* on its first iteration = 'duck'; second, *a* = 'your'; third, *a* = 'head'; fourth, *a* = '!'. Plainly, this rule, no less than the choice of signs, is a convention without essential affinity to the state of affairs represented.

Reference is Always Conventional. The second of these unexamined assumptions is the restriction of conventionality to marks and sounds, though anything referential in our thoughts is conventional. I am assuming that each thought is a complex neural phenomenon, that it is linked to other thoughts in ways that satisfy an internal grammar,[13] that the semantics and grammar of learned languages are mapped onto the sentences of the language of thought (perhaps as the determinate is to the determinable); and that sentences of a learned language, whether voiced or not, are linked by way of an associative network to those percepts which are effects of the things signified. The unvoiced thought sentence, like sentences uttered, signifies by referring beyond these effects to their cause.

How does any one thought or word refer beyond the associative network in which it is located to something not in the network, as neutrons are not in thought or speech though we do refer to them? A parallel question concerns words in a dictionary: how does 'manatee' refer beyond the words that define it to something extra-linguistic? Or more generally, how do we refer beyond the fabric of words when they are all defined in terms of one another or defined in the case of observation terms, by reference to sensory effects?

One solution supposes that reference exceeds language just because we think or use words while imagining or intending some extra-linguistic referent. This would answer the question only if our imaginings or intendings were acts of rational intuition, hence apprehensions of the things intended. But surely there is no evidence whatever that mind has these unmediated apprehensions of things in themselves. No brain can have them, as matters considerably if mental activities are only the behaviors of a physical system. But more, the point is moot if we can and do use words in this referring way without having these intentions or without deferring to the times when we have them.

Reference is accomplished without rational intuition and without these lambent imaginings, because of this other way of confirming that our signs pick out their objects. We start by conceding that words are used to explicate one another, with exits into the world only at the point of sensory data. The domain of our associative neural networks reaches no farther than that. There is, however, evidence of this other sort confirming that thoughts and words do regularly signify real differences in the world. We are perpetually active, in large ways and small. Anticipated sensory affects regularly occur when thought or language directs the behaviors which engage us in the world. This happens repeatedly as I fumble about my desk; but also when astronomers predict an empirical difference. Observers having that sensory affect when they use a telescope or inspect a photographic plate do plausibly believe that their thoughts and words signify something independent of the associative network in their heads.

What is the sanction for believing that our signs touch ground beyond the array of sensory affects? Consider the possibilities: there is rational intuition; there are innate ideas with God's guarantee of their cogency; or there is skepticism about everything lying beyond thought, language, and our sensory states. With only these three as our options, we properly despair of using thought or language to signify anything beyond themselves or the sensory data. Happily, there is also this fourth option: we infer abductively from the sensory affects generated when signs, in thought and language, effectively direct the behavior engaging us in the world to the things correctly identified by our signs. These things are, we infer, causal conditions for the sensory data. Predicting smoke if fire and seeing smoke, we infer that there is a fire. Arguing as phenomenalists, we might say that the fire is itself only a congeries of sense data, though now our causal abduction is subverted, for there is no dynamic relation (but only the Humean one of conjunction) between the sensory appearance of smoke and that of fire. Accordingly, this fourth explanation for reference requires something stronger than the phenomenalists allow: namely, the abduction from sensory data to their extra-mental conditions (e.g., from the look of smoke to an extra-mental fire). The look of smoke is, we infer, the effect of the interaction engaging these two stabilities: ourselves and the thing burning. What should we say of phenomenalists who remark the conjunction of smoke data, fire data, and water data? That they describe these effects without explaining them.

Thoughts and sentences used referringly often direct our interactions with other things, with the result that predicted sensory affects occur. How shall we explain these successes? We infer that conventional signs achieve their reference, first, because we co-ordinate the use of our words; second, because there is a domain of objects whose existence and character are independent of the fact that we successfully represent them. Words calibrated with one another successfully refer beyond the circle of thought or language when behaviors directed by these words lead first to sensory affects, then to further honings of our referring and descriptive words. Like gunnery officers revising our aim after watching the effects of earlier shots, we refine our use of conceptual and linguistic signs. But all this is only propaedeutic to one more vital point: that successive refinements tested against the world help us to locate referents more accurately, with subsequent experiments to confirm this greater accuracy.

More plausibly now, the idea of correspondence depends for all its credibility on this abduction: the signs which effectively direct our engagements in the world have objects that satisfy their descriptions; otherwise, the manipulations we perform would not have their predicted effects. Even intrapsychic correspondences accord with this description, as "I am in pain" might be satisfied by my headache, then obviated when I take an aspirin. Only this abduction, from sensory affects to their conditions, explains the extension of reference beyond thought, language, and sensory data into a world whose existence and character are independent of the ways we represent it.

Signs are Construed. The conventionality of our signs also has this third consequence: it entails that no word signifies or refers to anything until someone construes it as the sign of an actual or possible property, object, or state of affairs. There are, furthermore, no truths, even where conventions for interpreting words have been established, if there are no thoughts or sentences affirmed or denied, hence no thoughts or sentences related in these conventional ways to the states of affairs represented. The states of affairs are there to be represented; there are rules for formulating sentences that would be true; yet there are no truths. Why? Because truth is *essentially* a *three*-termed relation. There is the thought or sentence (both of them conventional signs), the state of affairs represented, and the act of rule-governed construal whereby the one is taken as the sign of the other.

We typically ignore the act of construal because there are rules for interpreting sentences, because we suppose that the integrity of the sentence as sign implicates these rules, and because making contrual essential to the truth relation is anathema to behaviorist scruples. Behaviorists are happier with rules than ever they could be with the intrapsychic acts directed by them. But plainly the rules have no use but that of directing construal and no disembodied existence apart from the thinking or the habits of sign-users. Antipathy to Cartesian mentalism is, therefore, no defense against having to acknowledge that rules are applied intrapsychically. But more, this bogeyman is vanquished: thinking machines remind us that intrapsychic behaviors do occur with no taint of Cartesian mentalism to make them elusive.

It might seem that this stern requirement — no truths in the absence of this three-termed relation — is compromised immediately by the acknowledgment that each of us has many true beliefs, most of which are at any moment dispositional only. My belief that Lincoln was president was, until this moment, true but not affirmed. Does this subvert the claim that truth, in its essential formation, is a three-termed relation? Not at all, if unexercised dispositions are true only by extension from the truths they qualify us to think or utter.

Careless talk about standing truths in the absence of particular construings also implies neglect of truth vehicles — namely, conventional signs. Truth as a relation is then conflated with truth conditions. There are, for example, mathematical "truths" obtaining in all possible worlds, hence in our own, prior to the time when there are people using signs to represent them. Yet there are no such truths; we describe as "truths" things that are better characterized, without using that word, as formal properties of those worlds. Truth, we insist, is just the relation described above; it requires a state of affairs, whether necessary or contingent, the thoughts or sentences representing it, and the act construing one as sign of the other. Subtract one or more of these terms from the relation, and there are no truths.

Those who speak of truths present in a world prior to thought and language assume that there are standing sentences eternally available as the terms for a truth relation. But are there? Is there some god who establishes conventions of reference and signification that would enable us to think or speak about a world were we to learn its language? Does this god perpetuate truths by constantly reiterating thoughts or sentences that invoke these conventions? Having no evidence of this universal language and none that this god is perpetually using his language to utter his truths, I infer that there are no eternal truths, no truths that abide when no one is uttering or thinking them. The mathematical properties or structures said to inhere in any possible world are "truths" in only this derivative sense: it is always possible that there be an actual language in which to represent them.

I am not suggesting that mind creates matters of fact as it establishes the syntactic and semantic rules used for construing descriptive and demonstrative terms. I simply repeat the claim affirmed above: truth is a relation, a relation which fails to obtain if one of its terms is missing. We lack two of the conditions for truth if the extra-mental world merely has entities and characteristics that could be represented. There are no truths unless all three conditions obtain: there are semantically and syntactically well-formed thoughts or sentences; the world has its features; thinkers or speakers use one to signify the other.

Consider the effect achieved when conventions are established and thoughts are formulated or sentences uttered. Now we have many truths: "Dinner is burnt," "All the neighbors are taller than I am," "Their dog is biting our cat." Each true sentence is conventionally associated with the state of affairs it represents, first by way of indexicals which establish reference (e.g., "*Their* dog . . . "), then by way of descriptive terms signifying the sentence's truth conditions (e.g., their dog biting our cat). Nothing in the world beyond thought and language may have changed; but now there are truths because we have supplied the otherwise missing terms of the relationship.

D. Warnock's Elaboration of Austin's Notion of Truth

G. J. Warnock qualifies his support for Austin's proposal by saying that it is statements, not sentences, which are to count as true: French and English speakers, he notes, use different sentences to make the same statement.[14] Warnock's use of 'statement' is synonymous with 'proposition', not with 'utterance'. There is, however, no place in the naturalistic metaphysical theory sketched in section III for propositions. What is more, we don't need them if we allow that a diversity of sentences in various languages can be used to signify the same state of affairs, as utterances of "Ça c'est rouge" signifies the same thing as "This is red." Propositions, like Platonic Forms, are introduced so that variety may be resolved in favor of identity. Better that we avert this ontological hypothesis when the easier solution acknowledges that different conventional signs may be used to signify the same state of affairs. Even learning is simplified. Discovering that English and French sentences express the same proposition requires that one learn both English and French, before apprehending, comparing, and discovering identity in the propositions expressed by sentences in the two languages. The nominalist, inscriptionalist solution dispenses with this second step. We learn the two languages, where learning includes a specification of the truth conditions for using a sentence.

We also avoid self-inflicted confusion. For it is probably a mistake to suppose that elementary observation reports, with their common referent, are the standard for differences among the sentences of two languages. Red spots are distinguishable and separable as other states of affairs usually are not. Talk about home, work, or politics will probably have many nuances in one language that are absent from sentences in other languages, however much their referents are similar. Should we devote ourselves to locating whatever "essential propositional content" these sentences may share? Why not say instead that the sentences have similar, but different, truth conditions, as people fluent in the two languages can testify.

Warnock wrote as Austin's friend, but not as someone sharing all his views. For Austin was no friend to propositions, if only for the pragmatic reason that they complicate ontology, psychology, and learning for no theoretical advantage: disparate thoughts and utterances calibrated to the same phenomena do as well. Austin supposes that nothing stands between properly construed thoughts or sentences and the things they represent. Warnock's "statements" (meaning propositions) introduce an unnecessary mediator into that relation. His reading to Austin's use of 'sentence' and 'statement' is to be resisted, partly for this historical reason, partly because it unnecessarily complicates the naturalistic metaphysics sketched above.

Propositions are important in this other way, however: they intimate something about the world without correctly identifying it. Propositions are introduced into a metaphysical theory to represent possible states of affairs: yet it is propositions, not possibles, which are nominated for a place in being. I shall argue later in this chapter that we do better to acknowledge possibles, while expunging propositions. We thereby satisfy Warnock's impulse to seek the one in the many, but find that one beyond thought and language in possibilities that are multiply instantiable, as the possibility for red has many instances. Sentences of the same or different languages may signify the same possibility, as every utterance of "Is this red?," "This is red," and "Ça c'est rouge" represent one possibility. Every additional complexity and nuance makes it more likely that the possibilities represented by two or more sentences are different; but this is nothing to fear if there are already an infinity of possibilities available for signification and if we can distinguish among the thoughts and sentences that signify them. This complicating ontological postulate is irrelevant to the argument developed here until section VII.

E. The Argument to This Point

We grant that the rules establishing conventions for the use of demonstrative and descriptive thoughts or words are sometimes ambiguous, changeable, and different from thinker to thinker and language to language. The same rule may be applied differently as contexts vary; and, worst of all, the rules may be so complicated that we can't formulate them well enough to decide whether or not they are properly used. These obstacles and embarrassments are real; but none of them confounds us. Nor is there any puzzle in the assumption that the world may have an existence and character independent of mind and language but representable by our well-formed signs. Skeptics may deny that we have access to the world, or even that a world independent of thought and language exists. But they have no explanation for the evident success of behaviors directed by signs. There is no direct proof for the abduction that behavior works because signs have objects. The indirect proof— untold numbers of predictions confirmed—is not a derisory basis for saying that this realist hypothesis is confirmed. There is no foundation whatever for the suspicion that correspondence is mysterious indeed.

VI Thirteen Kinds of Truth-Claim

Something is awry; but it may be nothing that we cannot fix. Why is it that all the truths used to illustrate the correspondence notion are categorical utterances representing current states of affairs? One of the examples above concerns a particular thing: namely, dinner. Another represents all the members of a class: my neighbors. A third is causal. All are current. There are no examples of the other kinds of things we think and say—none is negative, general, counterfactual, or probabilistic. My reason for neglecting these other kinds of sentences is not that they are never true; but only that the realist metaphysics sketched above is not yet qualified to support truths about negative or general facts, counterfactuals, or probabilities. The one waits on the other.

Remember Strawson's remark that the correspondence notion is deficient because it restricts itself to the truth of categorical thoughts and sentences. Nothing is said, he implies, to support the claim that sentences of these other kinds may also be true by correspondence. The discussion that follows speaks to his point. I shall be saying that sentences of many kinds are true by correspondence, and that our realist metaphysics requires ad hoc additions, then systematic integration, as provision for these referents is incorporated within it.

There is also this counterweight: we do not assume that sentences of every kind should send us rushing to enhance our realist metaphysics. We may not need a distinct worldly referent for every informative thought or sentence. Talk about values is a case in point, with emotivists arguing that claims about them are expressions of attitude, not statements which are true or false. We proceed case by case, adding to our metaphysics only when it seems that thoughts or sentences of a certain grammatical kind or those making a particular material claim do represent a thing or relation which can be acknowledged responsibly within a realist theory.

There are twelve of these problematic inferences (I may have neglected some others) to entities, properties, and relations in addition to the abduction that characterizes stabilities. Add the less contentious truths about actual particulars, and we have thirteen kinds of thoughts or sentences that may be true by correspondence. These thirteen are truths about material entities and truths that are conjunctive, disjunctive, about the past or future, general (lawful), dispositional, counterfactual, mathematical, intentional, valuational, probabilistic, possible, and negative. I must specify the real-world difference supporting each of these truths by correspondence. Several of the differences are not anticipated in the elementary realist theory sketched above, so that we require a summary restatement of the theory. But then the aggregate of these partial solutions justifies a last restatement of the realist theory in sections VIII and IX. Here are the twelve problematic cases preceded by the one defended already.

1. Truths about material entities.   Someone removing a painful shoe sees what looks like a stone. He or she infers that a stone is causing both the pain and these visual data. Our realist theory provides for enduring things of this sort, calling them "stabilities," thereby giving us referents independent of thought and language.

Stabilities may be larger or smaller than those conspicuous to perception. We regularly infer from sensory affects to stable systems as variant in scale as atoms and galaxies. 'Atom' and 'galaxy' are theoretical terms, but they are only somewhat more speculative than 'stone'. Each may be used in sentences that are true, because they accurately report that one or another of the things they signify has the properties ascribed to it. I am supposing that the speculative gap separating 'atom' from 'stone' is narrower than we typically assume. 'Atom' might be a word having no referent; but this risk is not peculiar to words signifying entities that are large or small: 'Santa Claus', 'Reepicheep', and 'Brer Rabbit' are evidence of that.

What is the special difficulty with theoretical terms? That we know their referents, if any there be, by way of the theories introducing them, not through our ordinary engagements in the world. This is an important difference, but one that is quickly overcome when we realize that our every considered engagement with the world is mediated by one or, more likely, an integrated system of hypotheses. 'Stone' no less that 'atom' is a term in one or more such abductions. Each of them is, or should be, testable empirically, each one confirmed or not when its predictions about the likely sensible effects of the things signified are tested against the empirical data. The experiments may be inconclusive; we may be uncertain after interpreting them whether phlogiston, caloric, atoms, or the ether exist. But none of this is peculiar to claims about entities that are large or small. Experimental confirmation of ordinary-sized objects is not always more assured, as we know from disputed sightings of the yeti.

Details are different, but the problem of making and testing representations is the same when the entities at issue vary qualitatively from the discrete particulars—such as stars and stones—familiar to perception. Heuristic similarity—particular as perceived, particular in reality—is less assured when we rely on graphic analogies to represent phenomena other than these particulars: comparing dissipating gossip to the entropic properties of electromagnetic radiation is not very informative about either term of the analogy. Nor are we better informed about changes occurring within fieldlike phenomena when they are compared to waves propagated over the surface of a stretched membrane. Metaphysical characterizations of systems like these are crude: describing them, perhaps, as stabilities of a kind is not so much mistaken as vapid.

This is awkward for our realist metaphysics, but irrelevant to the larger point at issue: for we have reason to believe that there are physical systems having fieldlike properties. Our reason is just the fact that abductive hypotheses characterizing these systems generate testable, confirmed predictions. Realism settles for these scientific descriptions, while waiting for the time when satisfactory metaphysical characterizations are formulated, then integrated into that naturalistic synthesis which replaces the Aristotelian one.

2. Conjunctive truths.   Conjunctive truths have been problematic since Wittgenstein argued in the *Tractatus* that the logical terms used for connecting atomic sentences have no referential sense of their own: "My hands are warm, and my feet are cold" says nothing beyond what is said when the two independent clauses appear as separate sentences.[15] There are rules for determining that molecular sentences using 'and' are tautological, contradictory, or true or false contingently; but never, on this telling, does 'and' signify or communicate information about a material relation.

We avert this conclusion by asking if there is ever a reason for saying that conjunctive truths signify a material difference. For it does not follow from the syntactic use of 'and' that there is no other use. There are, indeed, several different sorts of relation signified by 'and', all of them no less familiar than the use Wittgenstein emphasizes. *Conjunction*, for example, may be spatial or temporal. If "You are standing on my foot" is one truth, then "My foot is here, and you are standing on it" is another. There is also the conjunction of temporal succession or simultaneity, as a musical chord is a conjunction of notes. Sometimes we have spatial and temporal conjunction at once, as when people are stuffed into a subway car at rush hour. *Causation* (e.g., getting bruised because someone stands on one's foot) is a different sort of conjunction, the cause being one term in the relation, the effect the other. A dispute with Hume is formulated in these terms: is causality only contiguity; or is it contiguity plus something else? Either way, 'and' is not merely a logical constant: there is a state of affairs about which our true sentences report. *Aggregation* (e.g., having Harriet, Adelaide, and India as sisters) is also conjunction, one that in this example derives from contiguity in space and time, together with the causal conjunction of their parents. *Seriality* is aggregation under an ordering principle, as numbers, words in a dictionary, or a succession of causes and effects are ordered serially. Seriality may be the generic notion distinguishing all the various sorts of conjunction, as even the aggregation of things in space and time requires satisfaction of the ordering principles intrinsic to space and time. Still, we suspend that conclusion, observing merely that there are these several, nonvacuous sorts of conjunction.

Many things are conjoined in one or more of these several ways, including places and positions, properties, bodies, events, and ideas. Why agree that individual truths conjoined represent particular ("atomic") states of affairs, while denying that conjunctions of truths represent the spatial, temporal, causal, or serial relatedness of the things signified, as there are cats and mats on which they sit. There is, perhaps, only one motive for denying this: the logical atomism inspired by Wittgenstein, then elaborated by Russell.[16]

This was a project for reconstructing our experience and knowledge claims from atomic observation reports; for example, "This, here, now is red," joined by logical constants such as 'and', 'or', 'not'. This proposal is testable: let someone construct all of space, time, causality, and seriality (as of numbers or the moves in a game), and let this story include a chapter about our place in such a world. Surely, the story will be that space, time, causality, and seriality are, so to speak, in us, in the respect that we have constructed them. From this it follows that we have declined to acknowledge the extra-mental reality of space, time, atemporal seriality, and causality in order to celebrate mind's power to construct these matrices. Abjuring this psycho-centric ontology, remarking that none of the proposed reconstructions is ever completed, we may want to think again about the extra-mental reality of space, time, causality, and seriality. These four are better represented than constructed. Though some uses of 'and' are syncategorematic, it is no blunder to speculate that many others signify one or other of these four conjunctive relations among things.

3. *Disjunctive truths.* Disjunctive truths are more problematic than conjunctive truths, though the issues are similar. We have Wittgenstein's claim that all uses of 'or' are syntactic—though here again, there are material considerations signified by uses of 'or'. Three are conspicuous: the mutual exclusion of bodies from places in space, mutually exclusive behaviors, and the mutual exclusion of contrary properties. Disjunctive truths about phenomena of these three kinds are anticipated by our realist theory. Looking at a very small chair and two children struggling to occupy it, we say truly, "Either of you can sit there, but not the two of you at once." Disjunction expresses the fact that the possible occupants are competitors: occupation by one typically precludes occupation by others. This much is plain from even a rudimentary description of things in space.

Space is often described as a system of relative positions; but equally, we may infer that space is a system of separate or overlapping and nested places. Both position and place are exclusionary, though for different reasons. Each position is exclusive of those others from which this one is specified: it is different from, hence exclusive of, them, as *here* is a discriminable position because it is different from and exclusive of *there*. Position is spatially relational, but not necessarily space-filling, as it may consist (ideally) in dimensionless points. Place is space-filling, as a physical body establishes the boundary of a space while occupying it. Places that are unbounded, because they and neighboring places are unoccupied, pass into one another, creating a continuous region. But space is not empty, so that eventually a region is limited by a place or system of places bounded by its occupants. Of course, there may be no empty spaces, with the implication that places are everywhere well defined. We may nevertheless differentiate places by citing the presence or absence of specific properties, as some of the spaces on a canvass might be colored, thereby establishing regions of space which are empty in this respect. Overlapping and nested places are also best understood by citing properties which establish a boundary because they are present in one place but absent from contiguous places. We get overlap where ocean currents merge, and nesting, as in Chinese boxes, where a place is incorporated into successively larger places.

Why is it that places defined by their occupants are usually exclusive? Does their mutual exclusion express some property intrinsic to individuated places, or is it the consequence of a property peculiar to the occupants, as intermolecular forces exclude two bodies from the same place? Perhaps the differentiability of places is just the fact that their occupants typically exclude one another. This is no less than half the answer, but maybe not all of it. For places would be differentiable from one another if the masses occupying them were themselves only "warps" in space resulting from motions occurring in a geometrized space-time. The occupants supplying boundaries for places would owe their inception to a dynamic, physical property intrinsic to space(-time) itself. Space(-time) would be essentially self-differentiating.

We now have these three bases for the disjunctive character of spatial relations: the differentiation of any one position relative to those other positions from which it is specified, the mutual exclusion of physical bodies, and the intrinsic difference of places, as the relative position among pieces within a jigsaw puzzle is complementary to, but not a substitute for, the separate places they occupy. It follows that disjunctive truth has a secure basis in the mutual exclusion of spatial positions and places. We speak truly of the world when we say that only one person or other can occupy a chair.

There is, oddly, no parallel feature of time. The "same time," applying universally from every perspective, is problematic in terms of relativity theory, so we avert this difficulty by restricting ourselves to one frame of reference. But now there is no limit to the number of things that may occur at the same time, as the notes of a musical chord are simultaneous relative to a point of reference, not mutually exclusive.

Behaviors are a second candidate for disjunction. "You can sit, or you can stand," we say, "but you can't do both at the same time." This is not explained by the incompatibility between, say, the capacity for sitting and that for standing: someone lying down has both capacities at once. Is it, perhaps, only perspective that creates the apparent opposition? Moving left or right may be a merely perspectival opposition if someone in motion is seen from opposed standpoints as moving left and also as moving right. Yet this cannot be the whole story, for the one in motion is not observed to be moving left and right simultaneously if we restrict ourselves to a single perspective. Can we explain this recalcitrant opposition in linguistic terms, by citing the grammatical rule that contraries cannot be true concurrently? This gets us closer to the issue, though not close enough, because the question is not linguistic: standing and sitting are physical states, so that any contrariety between them is more than linguistic.

We need to tell, better than the current formulation of our realism enables us to do, why the contrarieties operating in nature are an exceptionless constraint on the things occurring there. We speculate that there is some explanation for them *in nature*. What explanation this might be is not plain, so this is a first example of a problem that is better solved by the final restatement of this metaphysical theory in section IX.

A final set of material disjunctions is intimated by the salesman who tells us, "Sorry. We have it in red or in green; but you cannot have it in a version that is red all over and green all over at the same time." Why not? Again, the linguistic reason—that semantic rules preclude the affirmation of contraries—does not cut deep enough. We speculate that the grammatical rule expresses exclusionary relations intrinsic to states of affairs. Nor is this an untestable inference, when the mutual exclusion of bodies, spatial positions and places, behaviors and properties confirms it. Disjunctions of thoughts and sentences are sometimes true, because they signify alternatives set apart and opposed by these exclusionary relations. 'Or', as used on these occasions, does have material reference.

4. Claims about past and future events. Such claims are problematic, because our first sketch of a realist theory provides for time in too restricted a way. It describes stable things as continuants, thereby implying their stability over time; it also acknowledges time-consuming causal relations, as burning takes time. But nowhere does it provide explicitly for the remote past and the distant future.

We acknowledge times past by hypothesizing that current states of affairs are the successors to antecedents transformed by their interactions. The times past to which we refer are, more accurately, those antecedent, dated states of affairs. Thoughts or sentences about the past are true when they accurately report that and when these things occurred. The more difficult questions about time itself are not considered here. Their solution waits on the formulation of a more comprehensive theory about some fundamental natural variables. Such a theory should do two things: it should characterize space-time, energy, matter, and motion, then explain the generation within a geometrized, dynamic space-time of those material circumstances transformed by the interactions occurring there.

This more ample account of change, hence of time, would also address the curious notion that time is nothing apart from the human experience of time. 'Times past' could signify only, were that true, times earlier in my experience or, by extrapolation, the experiences of other conscious beings — though notice that this extrapolation is illegitimate. For we should be unable to say that other existences are temporally antecedent to our own, short of assuming that there is a god in whose experiential time these successive births and deaths are observed. Surely, this is unsatisfactory: first, for the intrusion of this deus ex machina, and second, because many things seem to have happened before anyone could notice and remember them. Our notion of remote times past requires, therefore, that we locate the basis for time in something other than our experience of it. This is the point of saying, as above, that we shall not have the final word about time short of a comprehensive theory of space-time, motion, and matter. It is sufficient in the meantime that we acknowledge times past as the referents of sentences that use tense, a date, name, or description to signify them. These occasions within the spatiotemporal network of material transformations are, I infer, the truth conditions for sentences about the past.

Present and past events are, or were, determinate as regards properties and their relations (e.g., that Caesar had a certain weight, height, and posture). Claims about *future* events are more problematic because the future, unlike the past, is not entombed within us; it is determinable, not determinate. Those events are still to be created from the interactions and transformations of things present. Claims about events still future cannot, therefore, be true; they lack one term of the correspondence relation: namely, the states of affairs which would satisfy our truth-claims.

Classically there are three ways of providing for the truth of hypotheses about future events. One view concedes that these thoughts and sentences are neither true nor false until the time when the circumstances predicted are to occur. Only those events are suitable terms for a correspondence relation, but their occurrence is a contingency. They may happen; they may not; we can only wait to observe the one or the other. Claims about the future, therefore, are neither true nor false. Alternately, we say that claims about the future are true or false right now, for the reason that this is a block universe where everything is already decided, whether past or future. Predictions are already true or false, though our perspective within time prevents us from knowing that they are the one or the other. Notice that this second position does not affirm the unreality of time, only that our relative position within it prevents us from observing the transformation or sequence of events already accomplished. Time is here construed on the analogy of space. As someone in a valley cannot see beyond the nearby hills, so we are isolated from a future whose character is already settled. Our sense of time, of events passing and still to occur, misleads us about time: it is the sense of time passing, of time not yet complete, that is faulty. We suppose ourselves to be waiting for or anticipating the occurrence of events predicted; but this is mistaken, because they exist or not already. The problem is one of knowledge: our position in time disables us from observing other things that already have positions and places within it.

The third option denies some principal assumptions of the first and second ones. The future, it says, is altogether determinate right now, even if we cannot know its specific character; or it says that probabilistic causal laws sharply limit the possible transformations or successors to our current circumstances. Becoming is real: change is not merely an appearance consequent on our perspective within a completed time. All the conditions for future events, including actual circumstances and laws constraining their transformations, exist at every moment. Changes occur as circumstances are transformed by their interactions; but the transformations or sequences are lawful, so that someone knowing both the initial conditions and the relevant laws can predict either the particular changes that will occur or the array of outcomes to which our causal laws fix a certain array of probability values. There is, however, this divergence between the future and our knowledge of it. Sufficient conditions for future occurrences, including material circumstances, their dispositions, and causal laws, are in place; but our information about the future is partial, for we do not know all the circumstances that will be pertinent to events occurring then. Observing current circumstances and knowing or estimating what causal laws are relevant, we may speculate about the future, though we can never claim that our predictions are more than probably true or probably false. There is, according to this third view, something to know such that knowing it would make our predictions true. But then we rarely or never do know it. The web of circumstances is too dense, the causal laws often too obscure. Our estimates of the future are well-informed guesses, because our representations of the relevant conditions are never or rarely comprehensive.

Consider our choices. The first view denies us a worldly referent for saying that predictions about the future are true or false in advance of the time when the predicted events are to occur. The second and third proposals supply referents in the world for the correspondence relation: either there are events which appear future to us, though they exist already in the block universe where the course of time is completed (so that all events are, in a sense, contemporaneous); or those referents are the conditions, including circumstances and laws, from which future events will be generated.

All three options supply *some* extra-mental or extra-linguistic referent for claims about the future. They differ only as regards the sufficiency of these conditions. The first option says that current circumstances and causal laws may be determining, but are never sufficient to fix the character of future events. The second and third alternatives say that circumstances obtaining in the world are sufficient to determine future events: either they are accomplished already in the block universe, or the events will occur as current circumstances are transformed, deterministically or probabilistically, in law-governed ways. Each of these choices affirms that there are worldly referents for the truth of claims about future events. The only question is this: are the conditions sufficient to generate a specific, determinate effect?

5. Truths about generalities.   Generalities require no amendment to the realist account of particulars (i.e., stabilities) sketched above if the generalities are distributive (e.g., all rocks, any squirrel, every wave). These are claims about members of a denumerable, if infinite, class. The claims are true if each of the particulars in the class signified has the property ascribed to it, false if any single one does not. Generalities of this sort do not signify anything distinct from the aggregate of instances having a property.

There are, however, some generalities that are normative, not distributive, as we say truly that "Anyone born in America or naturalized is a citizen." One might hope to discredit the realist implication of examples like this one by calling them stipulations: the normative demand that someone be treated as a citizen is sponsored by our rule, not by a normative property inherent in citizens. The point is granted; but why infer from this stipulated generality to the claim that generality is merely conventional in mathematical and physical laws? This seems implausible when normative generalities are substantive (e.g., $F = ma$, or the internal angles of a triangle in a plane of no curvature equal 180 degrees). These do seem to be claims about normative features inherent in matters of fact, not prescriptions having no force apart from our determination to enact the rules expressing them. Why should we insist that every instance of the one be construed as an instance of the other? Only because we start with an extensionalist bias and a vast antipathy to the idea of intensional properties *in rebus*.

Didn't Hume establish, after considering the issue to all reasonable depth, that there are no intensional properties—that is, no essences or natural kinds, hence no regulative, nondistributive generalities?[17] Hume did nothing of the sort, though he did show that one cannot support the attribution of normative generalities if one limits oneself to his assumptions. Four of them are vital to his anti-intensionalist conclusion: that impressions are particular; that ideas are only the less forceful and vivacious copies of impressions; that reason has no capacity for inventing ideas but only an ability for comparing them and making simple (e.g., causal) inferences; and that general ideas are merely habits for attaching a word to a class of impressions and ideas—for example, 'triangle' to the impressions and ideas of triangles. Triangularity is, on these assumptions, only the class of relevant impressions and ideas. Anyone imputing normative power to the idea of triangularity ascribes to it a force that belongs only to the habit and the word. We may elaborate on the nature of triangles observed, emphasizing and comparing their details; but nothing in this could justify our saying that any future triangle must have a list of specifiable properties.

But consider: do we intend the implications of this last claim? Or do we affirm it merely as the florid coda to an argument intended to sweep away everything before it, all bizarre implications excused? Might there be a triangle which does not have three sides? We avert the possibility of being surprised by mutant triangles by moving one step beyond Hume, with his emphasis on ideas abstracted from percepts and words used to signify a class of percepts and ideas. We elevate the idea of triangularity to the empyrean where it is exempt from empirical disconfirmation; we turn the idea into a definition, giving it the status sometimes claimed for physical law sentences such as $F = ma$. 'Triangle', we stipulate, signifies a three-sided closed figure. This assures normative standing for 'triangle' by expressing our determination not to recognize as a triangle anything that does not have these properties.

Should we be satisfied when the normative character of generalities lies only in us, not in things themselves? Doesn't this entail that the normativity of stipulated definitions does not apply beyond thought and language to things themselves? Actual triangles should be exempted from whatever is normative in our definition of triangularity; a right one might not satisfy the Pythagorean theorem, when it, too, is a stipulation of ours. Generalize this principle, suppose that natural laws are also stipulations, and we exempt nature from their constraint. The world would be as Hume supposed: anything might happen when things interact; no change would require an antecedent cause. Mass or velocity might increase exponentially and spontaneously, only to diminish at a rate that is different on every occasion, whatever the circumstances—all this for the want of normative generalities intrinsic to nature.

Too often we defer to Hume's strictures about the limits of inference, as if every question reasonably asked of the world must be answered within the horizon of sensory data and the washed-out ideas that copy them. These are resources too feeble to explain what Hume remarks but never explains: namely, the endlessly recurring uniformities in our sensory data, and presumably in their causes. Things don't accelerate spontaneously to infinite velocities; pigs don't fly. There is something amiss in the idea that normative constraints have no application within things themselves, but derive all their force from our insistence that definitions be used criteriologically. 'Horse', 'triangle', and $F = ma$ are all susceptible to this treatment; but always at the cost of drawing normative force from the world in order to locate it within our ways of thinking or talking.

Suppose that we withdrew a bit from this dispute and reflect instead upon some process or event, such as keys opening locks. What are the conditions for this outcome? Several things are significant: people want to get in and out of their houses; security is important; locks and keys hold their shape. All this is relevant, but none of it is sufficient to explain this remarkable behavior; that people carry little metal spears in their purses and pockets, differentiating and securing themselves by virture of these little tools. What justifies our confidence in them? Should we worry that there might be a general key failure such that no lock opens to its key? No one worries that this might happen. But we *should* worry if normative generality has been reduced to the force of our stipulations; for then normative force has been stripped from the things themselves. Anything or nothing might happen when a key is inserted and turned in a lock of complementary shape.

We save the appearances with one of those abductive inferences abhorrent to Hume. It requires that we exceed sensory data on the way to identifying their conditions. Looking for a sufficient condition, we propose this one: there is, we speculate, a geometry intrinsic to the fabric of space, more accurately of space-time; the geometry of locks and keys is one expression of the geometrical relations which are normative in nature. It is no accident that triangles don't alter their properties or that rigid keys continue to open and close their rigid locks. Nature, on this hypothesis, is pervaded and informed by its immanent geometry. The details of this geometry, like the rules of a game, set the terms for interactions in our world, though with the difference that these intensions are intrinsic to nature itself: they are not stipulations introduced by someone concerned to manipulate players or pieces. Where within nature are these generalities located? In the shapes and geometrical relations of particular individuals and regions of space-time. Locks do, and will continue to, open as long as this structure persists. How long will it endure, and why? We don't know. Perhaps we shall have an answer when there is a theory that better integrates space-time, motion, matter, and energy. We may learn that the structure of space-time is, and must be, stable; though equally, space-time might be self-energizing, transforming itself in accord with its immanent, possibly evolving geometry.

Aristotle believed that every natural kind is distinguished by an essential form having normative force upon its instances. *Dog* and *cat*, as much as *triangle*, were thought to be normative kinds. Every particular of a kind would have the appropriate form immanent within it, so this individual would necessarily have the properties and behaviors determined by the form. We are not obliged to endorse every part of Aristotle's essentialism, though we have this much reason for subscribing to its claim that normativity is intrinsic to the material world: there are, we speculate, normative forms immanent within nature, the geometry of space-time being one of them. Even this single example—and there may be others—justifies our saying that general thoughts and sentences are true because they represent pervasive constraints in nature.

6. Truths about dispositions.   These are truths using words such as 'can', 'could', 'habit', and 'capacity', as we say of someone sitting that he or she can walk, and of someone whose eyes are closed that he or she can see. Dispositional talk is rife in speech about ordinary things and common, too, in scientific theory. Yet dispositions are nowhere apparent in the things perceived; as we cannot tell from the look of someone what language he or she speaks. Nor is this a problem merely because the insides of people's heads are closed to us. All the qualities pertinent to keys are conspicuous on the outside; but where is the capacity for opening locks?

This looks to be a question about perplexing matters of fact, though we avert searching for dispositions, habits, or capacities by showing that ontologically misleading disposition words can be replaced by counterfactual conditionals, as 'can bark' translates as 'would bark if . . .'. Eliminating language that implies a referent for 'can', we put in its place a sentence telling what would happen if specified conditions were satisfied: dogs would bark.

This counterfactual analysis has some odd implications. It would have us say that 'can see' is to be analyzed as 'would see if . . .'; though this alters the sense of 'can see' in the following way. We usually translate 'can see' as meaning 'is able to see'. Yet neither phrase appears in our finished analysis of dispositional language: 'can see' and 'is able to see' are superseded by 'seeing when . . .'. We might rephrase this, saying that 'can see' means nothing more than 'seeing when . . .'. But this is odd, for what shall be said of an imagined subject when relevant conditions are not fulfilled, and he or she does not see? This is a problem, because we have eliminated all reference to some current enabling state within a nonseeing subject. There is, we imply, no referent for these dispositional words: the capacity for seeing is just the fact of seeing when . . . . More than having his eyes closed, perhaps because he is asleep, this man should be incapable of seeing, because he has no internal qualification for seeing—because he is blind.

This reductionist account has saved the legitimacy of dispositional talk by translating it into the language of events—of what would happen if relevant conditions were satisfied. But this success is balanced by our inability to distinguish, when these conditions are not satisfied, between those who are not seeing but can see from those not seeing because they cannot see. The counterfactual analysis of dispositional language leaves this difference unexplained: we are to believe that most people see in appropriate circumstances, though nothing within them counts as a sometimes unexercised capacity for seeing.

Is there some demystifying way to provide for dispositions? I propose this one. We distinguish the current, constituent properties of a thing from the relationships for which it qualifies because of one or more of these properties. Keys can open locks because they have a geometrical structure complementary to the structure of the locks they open. Citing these structural properties is not sufficient by itself as a specification of the key's dispositions, because dispositions are not themselves structural properties. They are, instead, qualifications for relatedness present in a thing because of its structural properties, as a key qualifies for opening one or another lock because of its shape. Where properties of one sort are geometrical-structural properties and properties of the other kind are dispositions, we say that a thing's dispositions are distinguishable from, but founded in, its structural properties. Physical objects have properties of both sorts, with the further difference that a single structural property may qualify a thing for myriad relationships.

Also problematic are the dispositions that qualify a thing for an internal state, not for relatedness to something beyond itself — giddiness or depression, for example. We might regard one or more of these states as a suffusion of feeling to which relatedness is incidental; though, probably, this is mistaken. Internal states are typically, perhaps always, relational, as depression may disguise an anger too dangerous to express. The depression or anger is relational, even if its object is only the idea of something external to us, not the thing itself. Dispositions for these internal states are, therefore, like the ones described already: they qualify a thing for the state or activity appropriate to a relationship. The thought or sentence ascribing a disposition is true if the thing signified is qualified for this relatedness, false if not.

Describing first-order properties as geometrical-structural properties may be too restrictive for a thorough accounting of all the dispositions ascribed to stable systems, from shovels and giddy people to bureaucracies. But this is a plausible basis for many dispositions, given the claim of general relativity theory that mass is only the function of motion in curved space-time. Where materiality is itself founded in the spatiotemporal continuum, we speculate that geometrical-structural properties are a basis for many or all material dispositions. Still, we are far from being able to analyze physical systems in these terms. Unable to prove that all the dispositions of molecules and keys are founded in their geometry, we are even less able to prove this for such higher-order systems as state governments and string quartets. Still, we do have referents for truths about disposition: namely, the qualifications for relatedness founded in the constituent structures of things.

7. *True counterfactuals expressing natural laws.*   Counterfactuals were to save us from the realism claimed for dispositions, but counterfactuals are themselves notoriously problematic.[18] This is because of the rules for interpreting material implication: a sentence is true if its antecedent and consequent are

true and if its antecedent is false whatever the truth-value of its consequent. It is true that a match would light if struck, even though it is not struck and does not light, and true that Ohio would be French if Toronto were tropical. Plainly, these truth conditions for counterfactuals are not formulated with any special regard for causal laws, both examples being true by the rules of material implication (true because the antecedent and consequent of both are false). Still, no one doubts that the second example is not a causal law. It successfully predicts no conjunction of sensory data; there is no empirically well-confirmed theory from which to deduce it. Causal law sentences are distinctive among counterfactuals because they satisfy both conditions.

Perhaps there is no urgency for distinguishing among counterfactuals, thereby separating plausible causal laws sentences from the others. Nature isn't confused about the causal laws operating within it. It doesn't wait on our logical rules for deciding what shall or shall not count as a causal law. Nor does it accept the burden of finding a place within itself for every bit of nonsense certified by our logical rules. Why the rush of anxiety when the truth conditions for material implication certify as true sentences that are true accidentally or true of nothing? There is an infinity of counterfactuals satisfying only the syntactic test for truth, but most of them are unlikely candidates for the role of natural laws; and anyway, the required deducibility from a well-confirmed theory saves us from this excess of true counterfactuals.

Too bad that these controls on profligacy have no force in the context of Humean and Kantian reflection. Why? Because Hume and Kant would have us suppose that there are no causal laws in nature to exploit as a control on empirical inquiry. The world, they say, is either nothing at all or an unknowable thing-in-itself, so that thoughts or sentences called "natural laws" are used merely to report or differentiate and organize sensory data. No wonder that bastard counterfactuals satisfying the logical criteria for truth are awkward: there is no acknowledged referent independent of thought and language against which to measure the counterfactuals for which we claim material truth. Nor can we insist that deducibility from a well-confirmed, formalized theory (the second empty justification from the paragraph above) is the basis for choosing the real causal law counterfactuals. Aren't there an infinity of formal systems, hence a home for every possible counterfactual? Add that empirical data are underdetermined so that the data are invariably schematized and organized in the terms prescribed by some theory. We hereby guarantee that each one of the infinity of consistent possible systems shall have confirming empirical data and that any consistent counterfactuals derived from one of them will have both validity and all that counts as empirical truth. Our disappointed conclusion should be that deducibility from a formalized, empirically confirmed theory is no solution to the problem of distinguishing bogus from true counterfactuals.

The sheer complexity of this assault is meant to paralyze us. But it does not if we can penetrate its fortified skepticism and then locate an immanent constraint within nature.

Skeptics suppose that talk of causes and causal laws is only the residue of a time when nature seemed to be the diversion of a god whose reasons or whims become his rules and our laws. Metaphysics secularized this rhetoric. What is the ontological status, it asks, of the causal law reported by our theory-embedded, empirically confirmed causal law sentence? Hume and Kant refused to take the bait. We are bewitched, they said, by the idea that nature is an orderly game, though there are no causes or causal laws within it or, at any rate, none that we can know. We think otherwise because of misdescribing, or over-describing, the constant conjunctions present within experience.

Someone who defends this skeptical view in contemporary terms observes that we have nothing but successfully predicted observations by which to identify the successful abductions. But how do we tell which of the correlations is the expression of an extra-linguistic, extra-mental causal law if there are an infinity of conceptual systems able to supply reliable predictions of correlated data? Everyone else breathes if I breath. Why isn't this a successful abduction when deduced from a well-ordered hypothetico-deductive system and confirmed by the always available evidence for it? Or, more scrupulously, why claim that any one of the many confirmed conditionals is a successful abduction, while all the rest are significant but false or merely false and contrived?

We make that distinction because this scenario is false to all of practical life and science—to diagnosing illness, solving crimes, or predicting rain. For we never have a case where data are characterized in more than a few ways, then derived from different conceptual systems. Talk of infinite possible characterizations and an infinity of systems from which to derive them is just talk. We choose our explanations from one or a few characterizations of the data, then from a small set of cogent theories. Locating the best explanation—the correct abduction—is by no means daunting when our choices are restricted to this small set of alternatives.

Suppose that keys open locks. Several causal laws are pertinent to this result; but one at least is founded in the geometry of lock and key. The key opens the lock because of their complementary shapes, other things being equal (e.g., lock and key are rigid). So does every key of this shape open locks of a complementary shape. This is the generalization of a plausible explanation, one that does not seem to have a large or even a small number of plausible alternatives. This abduction identifies a law or constraint intrinsic to nature in just the respect that the geometry intrinsic to space constrains the changes occurring there. Here, as in all successful abductions, our inference explains the correlation of data by identifying a condition—a cause, constituent, or law—for the data. In this case, the spatial constraint is apparent on the surface of the observed correlation. Other times, abduction specifies a condition that is not apparent in the correlated data, as radio waves are inferred, not observed, in the phenomena they explain.

There are, of course, the many constant conjunctions regarded as causal though the relations of their terms are not geometrical. There may be no ontological glue to sustain such conjunctions; they might come unstuck at any moment. But equally, we may find that conjunctions not apparently founded in the geometric complementarity of their causes do have that bond, as pharmacology and neurology repeatedly discover that certain effects are consequent upon the geometry of their causes. Unlikely though it does seen, we may speculate that everything normative within nature is founded in geometric constraints. Even the statistical regularities to which geometry seems irrelevant—in economic activity, for example—may have a basis in activities to which it is critical, as would be true if the neural behavior impelling us to buy things has causes to which geometry is essential. The statistical description of our buying habits is not phrased in geometrical terms, though material conditions for these behaviors would be geometrical. This may not be the case, so that normative constraints are geometrical sometimes, but conventional or mythic other times. This will do for our purposes, because it acknowledges that there are some natural laws—those founded in a geometrized space-time—having a foundation that is independent of thought and language.

Not every law is causal, as the laws of motion are not. Still, laws of this sort, too, are clarified by the inherence of a particular geometry in space and time. Suppose, for example, that the Pythagorean theorem represents a structural constancy in the right triangles inscribed in Euclidean space. This makes the Pythagorean theorem a law of nature in a world whose space is Euclidean. Perhaps the laws of motion have this same origin: they may be complex relationships invariant to nature because of their foundation in the geometrical structure of our space-time. The counterfactuals representing these laws would also count, were this so, among the truths having real-world referents.

One problem is still to be solved before we can say that any law is traced to its origins in nature: we have to tell how a normative principle can be immanent in a class of particulars. Why must every camel have a hump? How do we explain the rare lapse when some camel isn't humped. If there is normative force to being a natural kind, if causal laws are normative, then particulars must somehow embody this normative effect. How does generality survive in particulars, even to the point of having prescriptive force upon or within them? This was Aristotle's problem when he supposed that universals have a normative effect on individuals, while having no existence (unlike Plato's Forms) apart from substances.[19] Aristotle was never able to tell how the humanity instantiated within us works prescriptively upon us; nor could he specify the basis within particulars for the causal laws determining their relations. Fire burns, though supposing it to have some different effect is not a contradiction: there are possible worlds in which fire does not burn. Where is the basis for the *must* in "Fire must burn," other things being equal, in our world?

There is a site within particulars for the normative force of laws or kinds: namely, in the dispositions considered above. These are the second-order properties that qualify things for relatedness. But more, things of the same structure—keys of the same shape—have the same dispositions. It is dispositions and the structures in which they are founded which limit or direct the effects of interaction. They are the basis for all that is normative in natural laws and kinds.

But still the answer is uncertain, for why are dispositions normative in the way that universals are alleged to be? If one instance of a disposition has one consequence, why shouldn't a different instance have a qualitatively different effect, as one lump of sugar might be disposed to dissolve in coffee, while another would turn coffee into tea? Think again of locks and keys. We infer that a space having a particular, intrinsic geometry has limited tolerances for relatedness. Any key of a specific shape embodies a particular restricted capacity. A geometrized space-time serves, therefore, this additional explanatory role: it gives us the normativity expressed as uniformity.

There is only this concession: I have again located the basis for all that is normative and natural in the geometrical-structural features of things. Here, as before, this does not explain the many laws and dispositions which are normative, but not geometrical. Their normativity is baffling, (when convention is discounted) hence the motive for locating normativity in the geometrical character of things, that being a source of clear examples and a plausible basis for the normativity of some natural relations. The generality of my analysis is incidental, however, to the purpose at hand, for the realist aim is modest. Skeptics insist that no counterfactual does, or can, represent an extra-mental, extra-linguistic natural law having normative force. The realist point is made if there is a single counterfactual that is materially true because it represents a normative relation in nature. That there is more than one such counterfactual, I do not doubt.

8. Mathematical truths.   Mathematics acquires its content in several ways. Some of it is discovered (with Plato); some is the product of analysis (with Descartes and Hilbert); some is constructed (as Wittgenstein supposed when he tacitly invoked Kant's *Critique of Judgment* and its discussion of the rules used in aesthetic or abstract play). We discover the properties of natural numbers and of Euclidean or Riemannian space. We analyze proofs. We construct transfinite numbers.

Mathematical truths are also a mixed lot. Some earn description as truths because of their derivation within formalized systems—better call them "valid" than "true." Others are formally valid, but also materially true; for example, "The two (apples) here, with the two (apples) there, are four (apples)." Truth as correspondence limits our concern to the mathematical truths having truth conditions within actual or possible worlds, each having an existence and a character independent of thought and language. Nominalism and skepticism subvert this application of the correspondence notion: one denies that there are normative generalities of any sort, mathematical ones included, in the extra-linguistic world; the other that there is an external world. Together, they imply that there are not, and could not be, extra-mental or extra-linguistic truth conditions for normative mathematical claims.

Suppose, for the moment, that we accept the skeptic's point. How shall we explain the application of the necessary and general truths of mathematics to the contingent particularities of experience? Kant solved this problem by displacing worldly states of affairs from a region independent of mind to the space and time redescribed as forms of intuition. The world so far as we can know it, he said, is the array of sensory data presented to intuition and schematized by the categories of understanding. There are mathematical properties and relations within every experience, because the transcendental categories used to schematize experience introduce mathematical features into it.

These categories are quality, quantity, and relation. Each prefigures some mathematical aspect of experience, though none can be made applicable to sensory data until it has been converted into a rule, called a "transcendental schema."[20] It is these schemas which render the categories applicable to the pure forms of intuition, space, and time.[21] Mathematical truths are generated as the schematized categories differentiate and organize these pure forms of intuition, thereby creating objects for synthetic a priori mathematical truths.

Quality requires that every datum within experience have a degree of intensity; it is, for example (with sensory data and empirical schemas added), a particular shade of red, yellow, or blue. Quantity may be expressed in any of several ways, including magnitude, unity, or plurality. Mathematically interesting relations include ordinality, spatial or temporal aggregation and configuration, ratios, and functions. Should Kant suppose that each of these features is present in every possible experience? Or is it consistent with his views that mathematical features might vary among experiences, some having one or a few of these features, others having all of them? This variability could be explained only by reference to the two factors which Kant acknowledges as variable: namely, sensory data and empirical schemas. Notice that each of them is empirically determined and contingent, so that no a priori necessity of the sort claimed for mathematicals could depend on them. There is, I infer, no variability, across experience, in the mathematical features intrinsic to it. Color patches may differ as regards their intensity; but each is saturated to some degree. We have, more generally, a set of mathematical properties and relations exhibited at every moment of experience. All are introduced transcendentally as mind schematizes sensuous data. Any different origin would, for Kant, preclude the universality and synthetic a priori necessity claims for mathematical truths.

We now have Kant's answer to the question of how mathematical necessities apply to contingent particulars. We are to say that any possible experience will have all the mathematical properties or relations prefigured by the transcendentally schematized categories. They are a network of geo-metrical and algebraic relations woven into the fabric of space and time. Every schematized manifold of sensory data exhibits these mathematical fea-tures within itself. Mathematical truths are either the rules that create these effects or, in propositional form, the reports that detail the properties and relations intrinsic to a schematized space and time.

Notice that this transcendental basis for mathematical truths takes priority over the formal systems used to prove that some particular claims are true. Formal systems are the product of that logic which Kant describes as "general."[22] It supplies the rules required for constructing formal systems, then for proving a mathematical hypothesis by deducing it from the axioms or higher-order theorems of a system. Someone whose notion of mathemat-ical truth is restricted to this idea of proof will have difficulty explaining (or explaining away) the fact that mathematical truths have application to sensi-ble experience. This, of course, is no mystery to Kant: the empirical appli-cability of mathematical truths is guaranteed by the transcendental condi-tions for experience. This is not a consideration that waits upon, or requires, confirmation by formal proof.

Kant's dictum, "Mathematical knowledge is the knowledge gained by reason from the *construction* of concepts,"[23] is the point of reference for many contemporary views about mathematics. There is, for example, this remark from a paper by Charles Parsons: "By the 'structuralist view' of mathematical objects, I mean the view that reference to mathematical objects is always in the context of some background structure, and that the objects involved have no more to them than can be expressed in terms of the basic relations of the structure."[24] Parsons refers us to a remark of Michael Resnik's: "In mathe-matics, I claim, we do not have objects with an 'internal' composition ar-ranged in structures, we have only structures. The objects of mathematics, that is, the entities, which our mathematical constants and quantifiers denote, are structureless points or positions in structures. As positions in structures, they have no identity or features outside of a structure."[25]

A principal source for this view of mathematics is Carnap's "Empiri-cism, Semantics, and Ontology":

The system of numbers. As an example of a framework which is of a logical rather than a factual nature let us take the system of natural numbers. This system is established by introducing into the language new expressions with suitable rules. . . . Here again there are internal questions, e.g., "is there a prime number greater than hundred?" Here, however, the answers are found, not by empirical investigation based on observations, but by logical analysis based on the rules for the new expressions. Therefore the answers are here analytic, i.e., logically true.[26]

Carnap shared Kant's skepticism about the extra-conceptual reality of mathematicals. But more important here is the implied elision of two issues which Kant separated. He distinguished the transcendental legitimacy of mathematical properties and relations from the formal proofs that general logic could provide for them. Kant's constructivist successors are skittish about his transcendentalism, for they have no transcendental way of legitimizing the schemas used to generate the mathematical properties and relations which are subject matters for mathematical proof. Instead, they depend on the systems constructed to do these two things at once: first, to introduce mathematical terms and relations; second, to provide the operations for testing mathematical claims. This conflation is explicit in Carnap:

> The system of natural numbers . . . is established by introducing into the language new expressions with suitable rules: (1) numerals like "five" and sentence forms like "there are five books on the table"; (2) the general term "number" for the new entities, and sentence forms like "five is a number"; (3) expressions for properties of numbers (e.g., "odd", "prime"), relations (e.g., "greater than"), and functions (e.g., "plus"), and sentence forms like "two plus three is five"; (4) numerical variables ("m", "n", etc.) and quantifiers for universal sentences ("for every n, . . .") and existential sentences ("there is an n such that . . .") with the customary deductive rules.[27]

This says, I suggest, that we rely on a system of conventional rules for both the entities, properties, and relations of mathematics and the deductive rules critical for proving any theorem.

How self-sufficient shall such a system be? Is there no support for it in the mathematical properties of the world itself, so that everything mathematical is internal only to some conceptual system? One sees the plausibility of this program as regards numbers, including the reals and rationals, derived from the natural numbers; for they may have only as much reality as the operations performed first on expressions signifying the natural numbers, then on their successive derivatives. But why make this a universal claim, one appropriate to all mathematical entities, properties, and relations, the natural numbers included?

The answer we get is only the one Kant himself has already provided: the world is unknowable, even unthinkable, in itself; all we can think or know are the experiences and "worlds" differentiated and ordered by the predicates and objectificatory apparatus of our conceptual systems (e.g., languages). This implies an easy solution to questions about the applicability of mathematical notions to reality, for all properties, not only mathematical ones, originate only in our conceptual systems. Where any consistent, empirically interpreted system may be used to differentiate and organize sensory data, we add the stipulation that no world is thinkable if it does not have such mathematical properties as are ascribable to it when the vocabulary and rules pertinent to mathematics are integrated into that system whose theoretical and descriptive language is more recognizably material and empirical. It is this integrated system that enables us to think of quarks in terms of group theory or to say of a cup that it is both half full and half empty. Does any part of this apparatus refer beyond itself to things whose mathematical properties and relations are independent of the theory itself? It does not. That place "beyond" theory is noumenal and unthinkable.

Constructivists writing in the shadow of Kant hardly doubt that all mathematical reality is introduced or generated, conventionally, by rules. Kant disagreed only because he thought that Euclidean geometry is a metric or form intrinsic to any possible space, not merely to space as we have learned to think of it. Yet Kant made this assumption largely because he was ignorant of alternative geometries. Knowing of them, he might have said that spaces vary—that, indeed, we require some empirical schema or convention (either one a rule) to constitute the metric for whatever space supplies the external form for experience.[28] Saying this would eliminate space as a source of mathematical form independent of, and logically prior to, the rules introduced to differentiate and organize it. It would further confirm the constructivist view that all mathematics is founded in the choice of rules for introducing mathematical entities, proving theorems, or generating entities of new sorts. Why should we want or expect any other view when the products of mathematical construction and proof, including even the square root of negative-one, are so plainly useful for schematizing sentences and even sensory data?

One answer—the best one, I think—is that Kant's ideas about reality and the constitution of experience are mistaken. Mind is not responsible, all by itself, for schematizing a thinkable experience. The experience it creates is not all of the world, or all of the world so far as we can know it. Experience is a window into that world whose existence and character are independent of our thought and talk about it. The opening may be small. The glass may obscure the things observed. It is, nevertheless, our point of entry into the world. Sensory data are the first rush of information when the shade is drawn. We speculate that they are affects in us resulting from our physical engagement in the world. Our hypotheses identify their likely causes, as we are burned by touching hot stoves. Do these causes and effects have mathematical properties and relations? Surely, we distinguish number, magnitude, configuration, and aggregation in the sensory effects. We plausibly infer their presence in the things causing these sensations. We also infer that there are mathematical properties and relations in things whose causal relations to us are vastly mediated, as we estimate the magnitude and structure of things which are never observed but only inferred, including leptons and black holes. That such things have mathematical properties in their own right is every bit as plausible as Kant's skeptical claims about the external world and his constructivist view of mathematics.

Which arithmetic and geometrical properties and relations are discovered rather than made? My list includes unity and plurality hence number, magnitude, ordinality, hierarchy, ratios, functions, configurations, transformations, and probabilities. These are some of the mathematicals plausibly ascribed to the extra-mental world on the basis of our perceptions of, and inferences about, it. Some of these items are familiar as mathematical properties or relations (e.g., unity and plurality); some others are phenomena having mathematical properties (e..g., transformations of matter). Why not concede that either discipline, mathematics or physics, may study constancies that survive particular kinds of deformation, some imaginary, others actual. Surely the division of labor is sometimes arbitrary. Constancies through change allow for mathematical representation without being, more narrowly, topics for mathematics. Knot theory, by comparison, is a discipline of pure mathematics, though its physical applications are apparent. The distinction between mathematical entities, properties, or relations and the phenomena having mathematical features is sometimes very fine.

Mathematicians and physicists would agree that the difference between them is plain enough, where only some of the abstract structures described by the one are instantiated in the physical world described by the other. Yet this emphasis is misleading, given the concession that both investigate the mathematical structures which are (incidentally in the one case, significantly in the other) exemplified in the behaviors and relations of material systems. Where mathematics and physics share this common subject matter, it is other features that distinguish them. Physics is bounded by its concern for the constitution and behavior of matter in space-time; mathematics considers this domain and also the mathematical properties of possible worlds that are nowhere instantiated. This difference is important, but not important enough to eradicate what was, and remains, the first domain of mathematical interest—the domain of things in our natural world. The property represented by "four" in "Arthur has four goats" is a property of that sort. Reporting correctly that Arthur has this number of goats or that one remains after three have been sold is a truth about him and his herd, but also a truth about the mathematical properties of things.

Can we also explain the truth of those material claims that turn upon entities, properties, or relations generated when operations are performed on our representations of the natural numbers, as the square root of negative-one is useful to physics. This is a surmise, nothing more; perhaps the higher numbers prove applicable to our world only because they are generated from numbers which are so plainly fundamental to the mix of unity and plurality in nature. Some of the higher numbers introduced on the basis of the natural numbers—the square root of zero squared, for example—do not seem to have this efficacy. Some others do have it, perhaps by reason of proportions within nature itself, proportions that we may not fully comprehend. It is also reasonable that much of mathematics should not be true of our world, as when geometries true of possible worlds other than our own are not true here. Or, as we might also explain it, alternative geometries cannot be true of any one state of affairs in our world if they are contraries.

Is mathematics compromised if this actual world is a principal subject matter for our mathematical thinking? For how can mathematical truths be founded in actual states of affairs without losing their normative force—that is, their necessity? We risk having to say with Mill that mathematics is reduced to contingency because, like physics, it is an inductive science.[29]

This is a false alarm. Consider that there are an infinity of possible geometries. It is a contingent, not a necessary, fact that our world instantiates one or another of them; it is not a contradiction that space here might have been Euclidean, not Reimannian. Whether space in our world is Euclidean or not is an inductive fact, not an a priori one. It does not follow that geometric relations in our world are contingent in that other sense in which the contingent is the changeable. The rules of chess don't change from game to game. Nor do we suppose that the geometry of our world is intrinsically unstable. The rules of the game prescribe what moves are proper within it; equally, the geometry intrinsic to the space of our world is, so far as we can tell, a stable, normative limit on whatever changes occur here. This geometry may be transitional; it might change despite our having no evidence of change. But geometry, changeable or not, is normative at any moment, constraining every motion in way appropriate to itself. Far from being evidence for the contingency of mathematics, the mathematization of the physical world is evidence that there is necessity, hence normativity, in nature.

The recognition of normativity in mathematics is by no means universal. Constructivists acknowledge it, though only after reducing it to syntactic form. The Frege–Russell notion of number[30] dispenses with it altogether, every number being identified with the set of its instances (e.g., the number 3 is identical with the set of triples, in thought, language, the physical world, everywhere). This is a notion of number founded on both an actual difference in the world and on our powers of discrimination. The normativity of number is, so far, irrelevant to it. Though now we risk embarrassment, for no matter that "2" and "3" are only the names of collections, we don't want the solution of 2 + 3 to be any more or less than 5. We get this normativity only as Russell and Frege introduce or invoke rules for operating on numbers, including rules for addition and subtraction. These may be, with Frege, rules prevailing within the universe and known to thought; or, with Russell, conventions deriving from Peano's axioms.[31]

It is a conventionalism like Russell's, not Frege's Platonism, that dominates most contemporary thinking about mathematics, though normativity of the sort provided by his rules and constructions is insufficient to explain the naturally occurring phenomena for which normativity in nature is the more plausible explanations. Inevitably finding that two and two are four or that keys of a particular shape open locks of a complementary shape, we reasonably infer to normative relations in nature. Constructivists in mathematics who acknowledge the extra-mental world while denying normativity to it can only wonder at the miraculous uniformities occurring there. Their mixed account—constructivism on the side of mind, independence from mind on the side of nature—is always at risk of falling apart. Constructivism is strong enough to account for normativity in the world only in the hands of Kant or Kantians; for then our a priori constructions are used transcendentally to create a schematized experience or world having these norms as intrinsic determination. There is, we know, a price for this security: we cannot have Kant without also having a world whose only claim on reality is its dependence on the transcendental subject who makes and sustains it. Surely realism, even a normative realism, is not so implausible as that.

Summarily now, we have these surviving notions of mathematical truth and normativity. One is the idea of mathematical proof: a theorem or hypothesis is valid, necessarily, if it is deduced from the higher-order sentences of a formalized system. Truth and necessity of this first sort are syntactic. They compare to the truths and normativities which are substantive, of which there are two. First are mathematical claims that are true in all possible worlds. They represent mathematical properties and relations deriving from those least conditions that need obtain if a world is to be possible. Included among them are the principals of identity, noncontradiction, and excluded middle, together with some content (any content) to which they apply. Some interpretations of quantum logic affirm that the principle of excluded middle is not applicable to quantum states, let alone to all possible worlds. This is questionable, and probably wrong.[32] Assuming these least conditions, hence the constrast of identity and difference, we guarantee the presence of the natural numbers in every possible world.

Substantive but normative truths of the second kind are parochial. These are truths representing necessities of form inherent to a particular world, as Euclidean space and the truths representing relationships within it are restricted to a subset of all possible worlds. We may come to know these necessary truths merely by considering the formalized description of a geometry. But then we have no reason for thinking that this is the geometry of our world. We have evidence that it may be our geometry when we reflect abductively on our experience. Could it be that the invariant applicability of the Pythagorean theorem to right triangles in real space is merely an accident, like getting heads whenever an honest coin is thrown? The cases do seem to be different. But what is the difference? Only this: we infer that geometrical constancies in the structures and relations of things are an instance of the normativities inherent within our space. All the truths representing relationships within the geometry defining a space are, in this respect, laws of nature in that world. Nor is this arcane. Other things being equal, locks open necessarily to keys of complementary shape. Nature is everywhere constrained by its necessities of form. These are, we repeat, the intrinsic and substantive necessities of form current in all or a subset of possible worlds. They are not syntactical in any sense peculiar to language.

Equally, these necessities should not be confused with universality. Nature's intrinsic constraints tolerate no outcomes but those observed or inferred. Still, the uniformities are derivative, as every instance of a kind exhibits its characteristic necessity of forms. So, locks open necessarily to keys of complementary shape, other things being equal, on every particular occasion. Each of these necessities is confirmable by way of a deductive proof, though it is always mistaken when the validity of a demonstration is confused with that necessity of form confirmed by the proof.

Accordingly, we have a three-part thesis that is inimical both to skepticism and to conventionalism: (1) some mathematical properties and relations are current in the natural world as the properties and relations of material systems; (2) the normativity—the necessity—of the mathematical relationship is incorporated in these material systems; (3) thoughts or sentences ascribing mathematical properties and relations to material states of affairs have these actual states of affairs as their truth conditions. How does it happen that a contingent particular is sufficient evidence to confirm the truth-claim about a normative universal? By virtue of embodying within itself whatever constraints are fixed by the universal, as every key embodies all the geometrical constraints required for opening a lock of complementary shape. Each one of a kind provides evidence justifying an abductive inference to all members of the kind.

Mathematical properties and relations are instantiated in the world. Claims to this effect are true because they have these truth conditions.

9. *Intentional truths.* These are expressed in locutions having such forms as 'I believe . . .,' 'I hope . . . ,' 'I regret . . .,' 'I pray . . .,' 'I intend. . . '. The difficulty of counting utterances taking these forms as truths by correspondence is only the one of establishing rules of reference. For it won't do to say "I think this" or "I believe that" is true if we cannot locate the truth conditions for these claims: namely, the persons saying these things. Eliminate this ambiguity by locating the relevant speakers, and the problem disappears: the sentence "I want it" is true if I want it, false if not. Ambiguity in the reference of the indexical 'I' is an embarrassment to us who want to identify its referent, not to the idea of truth as correspondence.

Correspondence is troubled by this other consideration, however: that hoping, wanting, and believing may be tangled in ambivalence. This is not the problem of knowing what I think, hope, or believe, as would happen if my true state of mind were decided though I could not tell what it is. Confusion and indecisiveness are real. Make up your mind, we say; but many of us cannot. This does not imply that we are always confused as regards our beliefs and intentions. It does suggest that intentional states have two stages: first a mulling, then sometimes the ripening or achievement or belief, hope, or intention. Failing to achieve a decided intention is not, therefore, as simple as we imply by insisting that someone answer to the principle of excluded middle: does he intend it, believe it, want it, or not? Surely, we do or do not believe, though not believing can mean either that the reflective process has not yet terminated in belief or disbelief or that it has ended in disbelief. Either way, we have an objective state of affairs corresponding to the true claim "I disbelieve . . .": I disbelieve because the evidence falsifies some candidate for belief, or only in the respect that I do not yet believe, because I haven't made up my mind. Either state of affairs provides the truth condition for a claim about my state of mind.

10. *Truths about value.* Valuing in an intentional attitude. We can say portentously, "I value this," or we can divert attention from valuing by saying more obliquely, "This is good." Emotivism is the theory that judgments about goodness only appear to be statements about matters of fact, being, more accurately, expressions of attitude: "I like (condemn) this." Where values are only value judgments, the world itself is value-free. This subverts the correspondence theory of truth, because it eliminates truth conditions for claims about value; there is nothing "out there" to satisfy our assertions that

something is good or bad. Though we do satisfy the requirements for correspondence in this other way, if we say that the truth condition for a value claim is just the fact that the speaker has some attitude. So, "This is good (awful)" is true when translated "This is good (awful) for me," if I like (or dislike) the thing at issue.

Reinterpreting emotivist claims as self-referential reports about a speaker's attitudes is not, however, all that emotivists would have us do. We are to understand that judgments expressing our valorizing attitudes are not true or false of anything in the world. But then we get this non sequitur: that everything present there is value-neutral. This is surely mistaken. Saying "Tobacco leaf is good for beetles, though beetles are bad for tobacco," I am not expressing an attitude or preference; instrumental relations are good or bad for the things engaged, irrespective of my interests or judgments. These instrumental relations are intrinsic to nature, so that here is a referent to satisfy the correspondence relation when thoughts or sentences about these relations are declared.

Most of the instrumental relations that draw our attention have the simple cause-and-effect structure of the example above; something has a beneficial or malign effect on something else. Some others ramify in ways having special effects: for example, the instrumental relation of a to b, b to c, through the alphabet and around again for z to a. Individual entities or populations within an ecological system may have these relations to one another, so that the welfare of every entity or population in the system is closely linked to the welfare of the others. We say truly that the system is good for all its participants. A different kind of relationship sponsored by instrumental relations, hence a different sort of truth condition, is exemplified by an orchestra. Violinists are not instrumental goods for tuba-players, nor are tubas good for clarinets. All are instrumental to a common objective—namely, the music played. Do they play it well, we ask? They do or do not, with correspondence satisfied when the answer is yes or no.

Participants in an ecological system, like members of an orchestra, may want us to believe that the goods for which they are instrumental are intrinsic goods. One says that things do, or may, have an absolute, unconditioned value: that a book, for example, is the corporate effect of its constituent words and that the book is absolutely good, bad, or somewhere in between. Intrinsic goodness or badness would be a truth condition—independent of thought and language—for truths by correspondence.

I resist this view because other considerations explain everything that would be explained by intrinsic goods. Suppose that something is good as an instance of its kind. It is a good chair or great art, as a Rembrandt or a Hals is good as a painting. We say this without idealizing the kind as a fixed type. The shape—even the function—of chairs might change; we might forsake canvasses in frames for wall painting, laser painting, or holograms. There is, nevertheless, a historically contingent, but current, notion of 'chair' and 'painting' such that these samples are good as chairs or paintings. We add that things which are good *as* instances of their type are also good *for* us: they have instrumental value. The effect of combining these two sorts of good, *good as* and *good for*, is the impression that there is intrinsic goodness in the things "out there." Shakespeare's plays give this impression, though it is only, I suggest, the effect created when these two kinds of good are merged uncritically. This happens when the plays are credited with being good in themselves because good as plays and good for us.

We avert this confusion by distinguishing the two, ingredient goods. We translate good as the instance of a kind into a more detailed specification of the criteria to be satisfied if something is to count as a superior instance of its kind: what is its shape and use? Is it comfortable? and so on. *Good as* then reduces to a high score on the scale for each of these criteria. This is an objective state of affairs, one that supplies truth conditions for the claim that something is good or bad as a painting or a chair. Similarly, there is an objective fact of the matter as regards being *good for* something, as it is a matter of fact that chairs do or do not support the body; they are good or bad for it. Now, where provision is made for *good as* and *good for*, we don't require an additional qualification for intrinsic goodness. It is or is not true that oboes contribute to the performance of a symphony, that they are good for it; and true again that this performance is good as an instance of music. It does not follow that the music is good in itself. We often want to say it is, but that is only an enthusiasm inflated by the synergy of *good for* and *good as*.

Parallel analyses are appropriate to the right and the beautiful. Both have the two components, right or beautiful *as* and right or beautiful *for*. Rightness or beauty *as* translates into the degree to which a thing satisfies the criteria for rightness or beauty. Rightness or beauty *for* is an objective but utilitarian relation. Neither one justifies for further claim that something is right or beautiful intrinsically. This is a case where nothing in the world supports the truth of claims that something is good, right, or beautiful in itself—though someone hearing Schubert songs or seeing justice done can't be blamed for thinking otherwise.

11. Truths about probabilities. Probabilistic sentences are troublesome candidates for truth. But this is a first impression only if we make the distinction classically observed between probability as frequency and the probability that a hypothesis is true. It is only more or less likely, on the basis of the evidence, that z is a crook, though the sentence affirming that z stole the trousers is true or false: he did it or not. Our difficulty in weighing the evidence is incidental to the point, so that probability of the second kind is not an impediment to truth as correspondence. The preliminary sketch of a realist metaphysics supposed that the world is populated by things which are active; no additions are required for admitting probabilistic claims about a suspect's behavior.

It is only truth-claims about frequencies that first seem difficult for realism. Something does or does not happen. What is the referent when we say that the probability for events of a certain kind is one-half? Where is the place within realist ontologies for probability values between 0 and 1? This problem also dissolves, for there is no obstacle to saying that the probability of an event (e.g., of head or tails) is one in two. This is, after all, a matter of fact: tosses of an honest coin converge on this value. Our probabilistic judgment has this run of events and, more specifically, the proportion of heads to tails as its truth condition.

We can also push this objective reference into the structure of the things whose behaviors are at issue. We are taught that frequencies are ascribed only to classes of events, though the probability of heads in a run of tosses is not independent of the fact that the coin has just two faces, a head and a tail. It is this physical condition that grounds the frequency value: the relation of heads to tails is disjunctive; we get one or the other because the design of the coin makes them contraries. The sentence "The coin falls heads up or tails up, the probability of either being one in two," is satisfied by the structure of the coin.

12. Truths about possibilities. Talk of possibilities is curious and troubling to a metaphysics that speaks only of actual particulars related causally in space and time. The possibility of war, peace, deflation, hives: any of these may concern us as we go about our affairs, thinking about our prospects. We talk of possibilities never realized in our world and of possible worlds different from our own because they have different laws as their signature. What are the referents for these various ways of using 'possibility'? Do these possibles, some or all of them, serve as truth conditions for claims about them?

We may deny this, saying that talk of possibilities is lightly disguised extrapolation from talk about actual states of affairs, a personal God being possible on the analogue of finite friends. This understanding is elaborated systematically in the notion of combinatorial possibility:[33] possibilities are described as products that would result if appropriate operations were performed on actual ideas, words, or things. There is, for example, the infinity of possible sonatas in the style of Haydn because notes may be combined in the ways characteristic of him. All we need do to realize these possibles is to identify the forms common to the musicians of Haydn's time, alter them in his distinctive ways, then set the computer to generating scores. The scores are possible; performing these operations would make them actual. Possibility extends, but never exceeds, the domain of actuals.

There is nothing so far to justify our saying that this storehouse of music was possible, in some other sense, before the discovery of these operations and before the invention of musical notation, computers, and Haydn himself. Our realist ontology carries on, unmodified in its resolutely Aristotelian ways, though it does supply extra-mental, extra-linguistic truth conditions for claims about possibility: namely, things to combine and operations for combining them. Someone denying the feasibility of a proposal may have nothing more in mind. It isn't possible, he says; we don't have the technique or resources.

This analysis is viable as far as it goes, but provisional. Possibility is more than this proposal allows, and more than our current realism can sustain.

13. Negative truths.   These are the final obstacle to correspondence theories. They are its severest test; for there is nothing to which we might refer them. It is not that the world is a void, only that the truth of a negative thought or sentence cuts the referential ground from under itself: *this* is not, it says.

Where are the referents, the truth conditions, for negative truths? The only answer permitted by our Aristotelian ontology is brief and effective: negative truths are second-order truths. We tell what is missing from the world after a more or less extensive inventory of all that is present in the domain at issue. The demonstratives of a thought or sentence have localized its reference, so we survey only a part of the world, not all of it; it is true and important that Pierre is missing from the café, not that he is missing from the cosmos. Accordingly, negative truths are shorthand for the much longer specification of all that is present in some domain, with the additional claim that the thing significant for us is not one of these things. There are no negative facts; or better, negative facts are derived from positive facts in the way just described.

Our realist ontology already supports assertions about the things present in a situation. Negative truths add nothing to this inventory, so no addition is required to support them. But this is clumsy, requiring in principle an infinite specification of all that is present before we can say truly that something else is not present. We need a simpler formulation.

VII The Realist Ontology Amended

This completes my survey of thoughts and sentences not falling easily to the notion that truth is correspondence. None of these thirteen types resists the idea that truth is correspondence, though we have needed to amend the realist theory to include things required as truth conditions by one or another of them. This is the moment for collecting these additions within a unitary statement of the amended realist theory.

My first statement of the theory in section III proposed that the world is comprised of mutually engaged structures, each one at some moment in the course of stabilizing itself or disintegrating. These structures together are a soup characterized by tensions internal and external to the many stabilities. There is nature naturing and nature natured, where stability in the systems generated is the regularizing of motion, not stasis. Individual stabilities are material systems having an inside, an outside, and a more or less stable equilibrium. Each has a developmental history that engages it causally and spatiotemporally with other stable systems. Each is distinguished from the others by its qualities, its internal organization, its place and relative position in space-time, and by the relations it propagates into the world beyond itself. Systems are related in one or another of three ways: they are mutually independent, overlapping, or related hierarchically. Thus, your right hand and mine are mutually independent; intermarried families are overlapping; the relation of the City of New York to the State of New York is hierarchical. The broth in which these stabilities emerge is always heated to a low or rolling boil. No contingent order endures there forever, though the geometry immanent within this space-time may be fixed and eternal.

Providing for the thirteen kinds of truths requires that we amend this complex hypothesis in one principal way: by adding normative generalities. We do this by supposing that nature, including all that is dynamic within it, is set within a geometrically structured space-time, with every change constrained by this geometrical order. The laws of motion are, perhaps, just the expressions of this geometry as it operates to constrain motion, hence matter and energy. $F = ma$ and $e = mc^2$ are, this implies, the progressively more accurate specifications of the universal constraint native to our world. (The constraint is universal within our world but does not extend to space-times structured by different geometries: it is universal, but parochial.) There are also the several force laws, each one a more determinate expression of the universal constraint as it operates within some particular domain. We speculate that everything normative in them is also founded in the geometry of space-time.

It is important to this hypothesis that we not confuse normative with distributive generalities. We do not exhaust or even capture the regulative force of, say, the Pythagorean theorem by remarking that every right triangle satisfies the theorem. For it is no contingency that all right triangles observed do, by chance, satisfy it; nor is this uniformity the effect of our determination that nothing shall be considered a right triangle if it fails the test. This uniformity is a necessity of form, one rooted in nature itself. The normative relations having this source are everywhere, as keys of the appropriate shape necessarily open locks of a complementary shape when other material conditions (e.g., the rigidity of lock and key) are satisfied.

Geometrical properties may not suffice to explain the normativity of all natural laws. The hierarchical organization of stable systems, each level establishing a domain where events may be constrained by distinctive laws, makes it likely that successive orders of normativity, not all of them geometrical, occur in nature. The laws of thermodynamics once seemed to be an instance of this higher-order normativity. Their subsequent replacement by the laws of statistical mechanics does not so much refute the idea of distinct levels of organization as establish that thermodynamical phenomena are not a distinct level within the hierarchy. Nor is there a refutation of the claim that normative generalities inherent in the geometry of space-time have a pervasive effect on phenomena at every level. Their effect is expressed, first, as normativities in the motion and assembly of elementary particles, hence in every higher-order organization having these particles as constituents; second, in higher-order domains having their own geometrical constraints. We have an example of the first effect when neurological behaviors having geometrical constraints express themselves in the overt physical behaviors described in the aggregate by statistical generalities. I am assuming, perhaps not gratuitously, that a constraint upon the neural activity of each person makes a difference in the character of an individual's behavior and then in the aggregated or reciprocal behaviors of people. Equally, there is evidence that geometry is a constraint on the organization of higher-order domains, as the design and efficacy of DNA molecules is the consequence of their geometry. We are a long way from confirming the hypothesis that normativity is pervasive in nature, but a longer way from identifying a basis alternative to the geometrical one for whatever is normative and natural (not conventional) in higher-order phenomena. These considerations are incidental here. Failure to identify the basis for normativity throughout nature is not so important as the discovery that normative generalities—at least some of them founded in the geometry of space-time—are present there.

There is, however, this final point: how are normative generalities located in the broth where stable systems are generated, sustained, and dissolved? The reference to space-time is a first step on the way to locating the basis for these generalities, though we avoid the implication that space-time is separable from the processes and stabilities that fill it. We need to provide for both these considerations: the normative force of a geometrized space-time and its local, particular expressions.

Both requirements are satisfied by invoking the dispositions described above. Dispositions are qualifications for relatedness founded in the structural properties of actual particulars. Included among these structural properties are a thing's geometrical properties (amplified by motion and its consequences—in particular, mass—they may be the foundation for all its structure). There are locks that open to their appropriate keys and molecules that affect animal nervous systems by fitting particular sites in animal brains. Does quantum mechanics refute the hypothesis that motion and its effects have conditions which are essentially local? Not knowing how to reconcile localizability with quantum theory—with Bell's theorem, for example—one remembers these other considerations: first, that the geometric character of space-time has a determining effect on every motion, whatever its scale; second, that the geometric structure of space-time is never less than the assembly of local conditions under the force of a possibly global organization. Totality, even a cosmological holism, does not diminish the localizability of motion and at least some of its conditions.

The normative effects in a geometrized space-time are founded in the qualifications for relatedness conditioned by these local geometrical structures. Higher-order domains within hierarchies of stable systems may introduce regulative principles that derive from the corporate organization of those higher levels. Still, all change requires motion, and all motion is constrained by the dispositions founded in the geometrical-structural properties of local conditions. Normativity originates within the geometrical-structural properties that fix these dispositions, as any key of a particular shape qualifies to open locks of complementary shape.

What basis is there in nature for the regulative force of arithmetic, as $2 + 2 = 4$? One imagines the outline of a satisfactory answer: the principle of contradiction applies within nature; plurality and the natural numbers are generated from unity by applications of this principle. The generation of the higher numbers proceeds within our conceptual systems as we operate on representations of the natural numbers, thereby successively deriving the rational, real, and complex numbers.

These last paragraphs are stronger on speculation than argument. Assume, however, the normative generalities proposed in section VI under the heading *Generalities*, and we have the required counter in nature for the truth, by correspondence, of generalities, counterfactuals, claims about dispositions, and the part of mathematics which is geometry.

VIII A Final Elaboration of the Realist Ontology: Eternal Possibilities

Suppose that our realist metaphysics is enhanced to the point of supporting the truth by correspondence of all thirteen kinds of thoughts or sentences. It doesn't follow that this realist hypothesis is good enough. Some explications of the thirteen in section VI are clumsy; others barely succeed, given the resources there.

Negative truths are a case in point. I argued that their truth is second-order: we tell what is not the case after remarking, then discounting, all the relevant things that obtain. Seeing Ernie and Bert but no one else, we say that Pierre is absent. This is a misrepresentation of negative judgments. It must be so, for these judgments could never be made or confirmed on the conditions cited. Why? Because the inventory of things present is at every moment infinite, in principle; so we could never complete the inventory or survey all the things present to confirm that something is missing. Suppose, however, that we avoid this difficulty by saying that the inventory need only include those things pertinent to the question at issue. Even now, this first account is mistaken, because I do not list, then discount, everything present before concluding that my glasses, keys, or wallet are not among them. Knowing what I am looking for, I announce, without reference to anything else, that it is not here. Often, I'm right: the thing wanted is missing. A correspondence of some sort is achieved.

Someone defending the other view may say that it does have explanatory value, as the sheer burden of making ourselves responsible for the inventory of our circumstances, of the finite things relevant or the infinitude of things present, should deter us from making negative judgments. And indeed, there seem to be many fewer negative than positive claims. We can also explain some absences merely by citing the things present, if those things are contraries, as something cannot be red and green all over at once. But contrariety, though rife in nature, explains only a subset of the absences supporting negative truth-claims. It does not explain cases where the thing or things absent would be compatible with those present, as when Pierre is missing from a circle of friends. How can we reformulate our account of negative truths so that their reference does not depend on the prior citation of positive truths?

I propose this alternative: a negative statement is true if the possibility it signifies is uninstantiated. "There are no ghosts in the closet" is true if the possibility represented does not obtain. This formulation also supplies a necessary and sufficient condition for the truth of positive statements. They are true when the possibilities signified are instantiated: "Your goose is cooked" and $F = ma$ are true if the possibilities they signify are realized in the places to which demonstrative conventions assign them.

This is the whole story about truth but for two additional considerations: we need an account of the possibilities here invoked, then one that tells how our conventional signs (our thoughts and words) can have these possibles, first, as their objects (their senses), then, instantiated or not, as their truth conditions. The explication and defense of possibilities, including their role as objects of sense and as truth conditions, is the topic for this section; the utility of possibilities as real-world counters for truth-claims is considered in section IX.

It was proposed in section VI, item 12, that we identify possibilities with counterfactuals, as some result is possible if it would occur were current actuals combined in a specified way. This emphasis on combinations of, or extrapolations from, current actualities is deficient because it ignores the fact that the possibilities concerning us are unconditioned by anything actual, whether past, present, or future. All Shakespeare's plays and all the bids in every card game ever played were possible before the Big Bang, whether "before" signifies a relation that is temporal or logical. Ths is so because these are *logical, eternal* possibilities, not *material* ones. Material possibles are things or events that could be generated from the states of affairs current at some moment, as tomorrow's weather is materially possible given the weather conditions prevailing today. Logical, eternal possibilities are unaffected by material circumstances. They would obtain in the absence of every material condition.

The existence of eternal possibles is established by way of a simple argument. It starts by affirming the *principle of plenitude:* whatever is not a contradiction is a possibility. From this it follows, by the principle of excluded middle, that something is either a contradiction or a possibility. Something embodying no contradiction is, therefore, a possibility. What is more, it is necessarily a possibility, since there are only the two choices: contradictory or possible.[34]

Plenitude itself begins as a tautology: whatever is not a contradiction is not a contradiction. 'Possibility' is then substituted for the second appearance of 'not a contradiction'. These logical considerations justify the familiar saying that possibles sanctioned by this principle are logical possibilities only: they earn the status of possibles only because they embody no contradiction.

Still, this cannot be all that there is to say of them. For it is things distinguished by their qualities which embody no contradictions. What are these "things"? Several candidates satisfy this characterization, as distinct sentences and ideas may embody no contradiction. Sentences and ideas are, nevertheless, secondary candidates, because they have the primary satisfiers, *properties*, as their constituents. Properties are the elementary constituents of things, whether sentences or their referents, and the attributes of things which are themselves constituted of properties (e.g., cold feet). Where properties are the possibles, everything comprised of them is also possible. It is true of these things, properties simple or complex, that their possibility is entailed by the fact that they embody no contradictions.

'Possibility' is uncontroversial as long as we regard it as only a synonym for 'not a contradiction' and as signifying that which can be, when 'contradiction' is synonymous with 'that which cannot be'. Properties are possible, or not, in this narrowly logical respect. Possibility is contentious only as we speculate that *properties also deserve description as "possibles," because of existing in the first instance as possibilities.* What sort of existence is that? I suggest this answer: possibility is a mode of being, different from, but complementary to, actuality. Properties existing as possibles are available for instantiation, but this is incidental to their existence; it is not a contradiction that possibles are never instantiated.[35]

This modal conception of Plato's Forms proves itself immediately by helping us to resolve issues deriving from Plato's statement of his theory of Forms.[36] Forms can exist *ante rem*, because they are possibilities existing independently of the actual states of affairs which are their instantiations. The problem of the one and the many is also less difficult now, for the one Form is equally distributed among its instances, without diminution of itself, if it is a single possibility and they are diverse particulars giving actual expression to it. This is not the relation of a whole and its parts, but of possibility to actuality. They are distinct but counterpart modes of existence. The third-man argument is assuredly a misconception from this standpoint: the Form for man is not related to every instance of man by way of a third term that is like both of them. There is only the Form and its instances: the one is a possibility; the others are actual particulars that instantiate it. This, like the problem of the one and the many, is resolved as soon as we notice that the terms related have different but complementary modes of existence. Finally, self-predication is not so puzzling here. The possibility for man is not a man; though I am not equally sure that the possibility for good is not itself a good.[37]

Properties existing as possibles are determinable. This is always so with respect to quantity, as the possibility for red may be instantiated one or many times: it is determinable as regards the number of its instantiations.

Some possibilities are also determinable with respect to quality, as the generic possibility for color is determinable as regards its more specific determinations. The possibility for some specific shade of red is, by comparison, qualitatively determinate. Instantiations of a property in space-time are always determinate in quantity and quality, this crimson spot being determinate in both respects. More, this lowest-order, qualitatively determinate individual is the vehicle introducing higher-order qualitative determinables into its actual world, as this spot of crimson is also the locus where possibilities for red and color are instantiated.

Properties existing as possibles (and, when instantiated, as actuals) have three features or marks: quality, quantity, and relation. It is quality that differentiates possibles, as the possibility for yellow is different from that for blue. The marks of quantity are diverse. Each property, whether possible or actual, is a distinct unity. Each property existing as a possible is determinable as regards its magnitude and the number of its instantiations. A property instantiated has some number of instances, each having a determinate magnitude—for example, a size. Relation too is a mark of all properties, as each property may participate in configurations of possibles or actuals. There are limitations, however, on the relations among properties, whether as possibles or actuals. Each may be described as the "name" property of a field, with all other properties arrayed about it in ways appropriate to their associability with it. There are various kinds of relatedness within each field, with every field riven by these differences, as yellow relates to green in a way that differs from its relation to shape. And typically, there are some properties with which a given property is not associable in any way, as it could not be raining numbers.[38]

Possible worlds have their inception in the associability of properties existing as possibles (e.g., the world of golden mountains or of Alice). We also make this other demand of worlds deemed possible: that they have sufficient differentiation and order to be actual. A world comprised only of the possibility for color cannot be actual, for the reason that actual worlds are constituted, at least in part, by properties which are qualitatively and quantitatively determinate—not of spots which are, generically, colored, though not any particular shade. Determinable properties such as color may also be present in such a possible world, but only by way of lowest-order, qualitatively determinate properties, as a crimson spot introduces the possibilities for red and color into a world. Now a question: why should the possibility for color have red rather than yellow or blue for its lower-order expression, and why should red have crimson rather than pink or scarlet as it lower-order expression?

One answer might be that every combination of properties is possible if it embodies no contradiction. Every combination observing the associabilities and incompatibilities prefigured in property fields requires, on this telling, no further explanation. Red squares are possible and might constitute all of a possible world, though the square root of a Peruvian bee is not a possible world, because it embodies a contradiction prohibited by the limits on association prefigured in the property fields of these possibles. This might be described as the Humean view of possible worlds: constituent possibles hang together when their association is not contradictory, though nothing more than contiguity binds them. We add that properties existing as possibles might fall in and out of associations, like bits of glass in a kaleidoscope, the only limits on association being those prefigured in property fields.

Suppose, however, we look for something that tightens the relations of associated properties. Granting that anything might be conjoined with anything else, barring contradiction, might there be something that binds the possibles to one another? For why should it happen, even in possibility, that color has one lower-order expression rather than another? Consider this alternative to the loosely packed worlds just described. We hypothesize that no higher-order determinable possibility achieves lower-order, more determinate expression in the absence of a determining condition. Where the relation of higher- and lower-order properties within a hierarchy is *vertical*, these determining conditions stand in *lateral* relations to the hierarchy in which they have this determining role. The relationship establishing the simplest possible world has, more precisely, these three terms: the determining condition, distinct from a hierarchy, determines that a higher-order determinable within it shall have some lower-order, determinate expression. Square, for example, determines that the determinable property, red, should be some particular shade of scarlet. This is almost a possible world.

It does not yet deserve this honorific status, because a "possible world" should have all the qualitative determinacy that would be present were the possibility instantiated. A possible world is, accordingly, one that is qualitatively determinate and only quantitatively determinable, meaning that it may have one, many, or no instantiations. What is lacking in the three-termed relation described above, such that it does not qualify for being a possible world? Only the fact that the laterally related determining condition may itself be a higher-order qualitatively determinable property, as it might be the possibility for shape or for square which determines that color shall be red or that red shall have some specific shade as its lowest-order determination. We fill out this three-termed relation by specifying that the laterally related determining condition receive qualitative determination down to the lowest-order within its own hierarchy—it is a square of specific dimensions. In the simplest of non-Humean possible worlds, there are two vertical files of qualitatively determinable properties having lowest-order determination. Each file has the same number of vertical orders, and each property in both files is the laterally determining condition for the property to which it is paired in the other file. Every possible world satisfying this condition has no less complexity than this. Many worlds are more complex, as when determinables have two or more laterally related determining conditions (e.g., worlds such that the value of force is determined by the sum or multiple of values for mass and acceleration).

There is also the further condition that no world is possible if it is not embedded in a possible space, time, or space-time. That is so because it is only the instantiation of possibles within a space, time, or space-time that particularizes them, thereby making the properties quantitatively determinate: possible music becomes actual music when played at a particular time and place.

It is time to reconsider the possible worlds described above as Humean. It is possible, because not contradictory, that there be worlds in which relations among properties are only those of chance aggregation, as something is both crimson and a right triangle. This is a world in which these lowest-order determinate properties are the lower-order determinations of higher-order determinables, and also a world such that there are no determining relations between the hierarchies: crimson and right-triangular are related only by the accident of their conjunction. There are also the many other possible worlds in which the lateral relations among possibles are determining. Some of these worlds tolerate accidental conjunctions, though all or some lateral relations in them are the determining relations described above—laterally related conditions determine that higher-order determinables shall have particular lower-order expressions. It is instantiated worlds of this second kind to which causal relations are intrinsic, as pianists make determinable pianos resonate with determinate sounds.

Suppose now that a possible world, with its embedding space, time, or space-time, is instantiated. Is that world one of the Humean possible worlds in which lateral relations are only aggregative? Or is it an actual world having lateral relations which are determining and causal? Remember that this instantiated world may be embedded in a space-time which is itself the source of laterally determining conditions, as when the geometrical-structural properties of things limit and determine causal relations, hence their effects.

How do we decide whether our actual world is Humean and weakly bound, Leibnizian and tightly bound because of having intrinsic, laterally determining relations, or some mix of the two? We might try to settle the question by eliminating one of the alternatives on conceptual grounds alone; we argue, for example, that lateral relations can never be more than, or never so feeble as, those of contiguity. The first alternative is mistaken, because laterally determining relations of greater force are no contradiction. The second appeals tacitly to the principle of sufficient reason: no coupling of properties would occur even in possibility, we surmise, if there were no sufficient condition for it. From this we infer that there must be a laterally related determining condition for the relation of a determinable to its lower-order, more determinate expression.

It seems irrefutable that the principle of sufficient reason does not apply necessarily throughout being, among possibles and actuals too, for we cannot eliminate the possibility of Humean worlds by aggregation. They embody no contradiction and are therefore possible. It does not follow that sufficient reason is not applicable throughout the many other possible worlds in which no determinable achieves lower-order determination without the intervention of a laterally related determining condition. This too is possible. There is no way to eliminate either alternative: some possible worlds are mere aggregates; some others embody functional relations—horizontal and lateral relations—among their constituent properties. Functional relations within possible worlds are the immanent laws of actual worlds. They are its causal laws and the invariances we describe as laws of motion.

The problem stands: do we live in a world of aggregation or in a world such that lateral relations are sometimes or always determining? We have this single way of deciding: we examine an actual world, testing it for evidence that relations among things are determining or not. Do they fall apart or dissolve into chaos, without warning and for no apparent reason? Can we find determining invariances or causes, as locks open to keys of complementary shape? Surely, there is ample reason for believing that the possible world instantiated here is not one of those Humean worlds where aggregation is the sole principle of composition. Imagine a man building a house. He uses an architect's sketch while building within the boundaries of his lot and in ways that satisfy the housing code. The sketch, boundaries, and rules are higher-order determinables. The house planned and built is their lowest-order, fully determinate expression. This owner-builder is the laterally related determining condition. Certainly, we have evidence in our world of many causal agents like him.

One last question brings us to the point of reconsidering the problematic candidates for truth discussed in section VI. What is the relation of possibles and possible worlds to the meaning and truth of words and sentences?

I suppose that descriptive words are signs signifying properties which exist in the first instance as possibles. Words organized to satisfy the grammatical (semantic and syntactic) rules for sentence formation signify a possible state of affairs. The state of affairs is simple or complex according as it has one property or many. The sentence is meaningful because it signifies this possible state of affairs. Where complex itself, the sentence may be unpacked in the way prescribed by Russell's theory of descriptions—as a conjunction of phrases citing each of the properties alleged to comprise the state of affairs.[39] The sentence is true if the possibility is instantiated and if there are demonstratives, whether sentential or circumstantial, that bring this sentence to bear on the state of affairs.

One is reminded of Warnock's emendation of Austin, with propositions substituted for sentences or statements, and of my objections to it. I argued in section V that propositions are a kind of deus ex machina introduced as vehicles for a theory of meaning and truth. There is a whiff of the same motive in my appeal to eternal possibilities: they are described as the objects of our signs—hence as the senses of our words—and, when instantiated, as the truth conditions for claims about the actual world.

There is an affinity between propositions and possibilities, as regards these tasks. I nevertheless prefer that the entities serving as referents for thoughts and sentences comprise a world whose existence and character cannot be ascribed to anything that mind does. Why? Because we will not avert idealism as long as the basis for meaning and existence lies only within our minds. Possibilities earn their status as an extra-mental ground for meaning and existence (as propositions do not) because they are sanctioned by a principle whose content and application are independent of perception, thought, and language: whatever is not a contradiction is a possibility. The eternal possibles sanctioned by this principle are independent of, and prior to, both the thoughts or words signifying them and the actual particulars instantiating them.

There are, moreover, some arguments and evidence for the reality of eternal possibles, but nothing much to say for propositions. We may claim to have rational intuition of them. We may allege that a sentence uttered repeatedly and sentences in different languages express the same proposition. Yet no one would accept a traffic ticket for evidence so feeble. There is no evidence that mind has a power for intuiting anything. Nor are we obliged to endorse propositions in order to explain that a diversity of sentences can signify the same state of affairs. We say, instead, that disparate utterances or inscriptions in the same or different languages may signify the same possibility. The possibility is their sense; its instantiations are their truth conditions. Accordingly, the theoretical role assigned to propositions and possibles is close, though the one is appropriate to an intuitionist idealism, while the other is better suited to the realism I prefer.

We now come to the point for which these ontological claims are preparations: how the theory of properties and worlds existing as possibles helps to establish the truth by correspondence of difficult cases among the thirteen types considered in section VI.

IX The Thirteen Kinds of Truth-Claim, Again

Here are the thirteen types again. There is little to add in some cases, quite a lot in others.

1. Truths about material entities. Things described in section VI as stabilities generated, sustained, and transformed within a dynamic space-time can now be described in this other way: as sets of configured properties embedded in a possible space-time, then instantiated within that space-time as the particulars of our world. Each of these particulars is also the manifest expression of whatever determinables receive lower-order expression by way of their qualitatively determinate properties, as a right-triangular figure embodies the determinable properties triangle and polygon, hence the normative force imposed by those properties on all their lower-order expressions. Finally, this entity is causally related to whatever lateral, determining conditions it may have within the possible world instantiated here. Every actual state of affairs is richly articulated and conditioned. There are many things in it that serve as truth conditions for our thoughts or sentences about it.

2. *Conjunctive truths.* That something is red and square expresses the co-possibility of the two properties. Individuals in a possible world, hence in the actual world instantiating it, are constituted of associable properties. The conjunctions reporting these associations are partial specifications of the property fields mentioned above. For it is within property fields that the limits on, and styles of, association are prefigured. True conjunctions signify that one or another association among possibles is instantiated, or they report the kinds of associability tolerated within property fields.

3. *Disjunctive truths.* Hume supposed that anything may cohere with anything else short of that contrariety which for him is the only one, existence and non-existence.[40] The limits on association among properties existing as possibles, especially as exhibited in the rifts and fissures of a property field, confound this universal tolerance. Discovering these permissions and exclusions as we consider both testable hypotheses and grammar, we map the limits on associability among properties in our world and, more remotely, in logical space.

Limits on the associability of properties are one basis for disjunctive truths; the mutual exclusion of places and positions in space or time is a second; the alternation of causal sequences a third. Some of these exclusions are necessary, some contingent.

Disjunctions founded in limits upon the associability of properties are necessary, for either of two reasons. Some of these mutual exclusions are defenses against contradiction, as in the judgment that "raining numbers" is a solecism. "Hoping for yesterday" and "biting tomorrow" are two more. Misfits such as these are barred already among eternal possibilities. They violate the principles of identity and noncontradiction because of requiring that each property be something other than it is in order that it be associable with the other one. Other necessary disjunctions express contrariety among the lower-order, more determinate expressions of a higher-order determinable, red and green being contrary determinations of color. Probably, spiritualism and materialism are exclusive in one of these ways—as contraries or contradictories—though we think, rather vaguely, that they may somehow be reconciled.

Some incompatibilities of both sorts are quickly discerned and discounted. But mostly, thoughts or sentences marking these deep exclusions are uncommon. We learn not to think or utter them when they seem too obvious and inviolable to deserve attention. Much more common are the true disjunctive thoughts or sentences signifying alternatives which are exclusive only contingently. One can have chocolate or strawberry where having both is precluded for reasons of health, not logic.

Consider, again, the exclusions due to contrariety. It is important that some of them—Euclidean and Riemannian geometry, for example—are not perceived as such. We more often describe one as a limiting case of the other, not as its contrary. We do that because Euclidean geometry is a good approximation to our world if certain parameters—such as curvature—are ignored. The hypothesis is flawed, we say, but good enough for shorter distances, including most of the ones in our middle-sized environment. Set this against my claim that the space, time, or space-time of an instantiated possible world has one organizing form, not several or many contrary forms. There is, I suggest, some actual matter of fact signified by the 'or' in the sentences citing this choice of contraries: the lower-order determination for the determinable, geometry is in our world Euclid's or Riemannn's. We cannot have both at once in the same space any more than the same thing can be concurrently red and green all over.

Disjunctions founded in spatial or temporal places and positions also divide as the necessary or the contingent. So, the difference between two positions plotted from the same points of reference in a flat space is exhibited when they occupy different places. Their difference may be transposed across reference frames by rules which make their mutual exclusion invariant from frame to frame. Two positions, each plotted from different points of references, may occupy the same place. The mutual exclusion of positions from places is therefore contingent on the choice of reference frames and spatial curvature: two positions fixed from the same points of reference in a flat space necessarily occupy different places; two positions, each fixed from different reference points, may occupy the same place.

Places, more than positions, are difficult to individuate. This might seem odd, when positions may be regarded as dimensionless points, hence undifferentiable because identical. Yet positions are differentiable because they are relational and because these relations separate them. Places, I assume, are regions of space, time, or space-time. Individuating places is difficult because differences among them are typically inferred from the numerical difference of their occupants and because places are regions of shifting boundaries which are generated and dissolved by the exfoliation or self-enfolding of a space. Still, places are distinguishable from their occupants even if space-time, as a material medium and generator of material differences, is plastic in itself and inseparable from its occupants. This is so because places are necessarily disjunctive, there being only the exfoliation of places to generate a space, time, or space-time. Folding the places back onto one another dissolves their individuation, at the further cost of shrinking the space asymptotically toward a dimensionless point. Assume an extended medium—for example, space or time—and deny the exclusion of places; we then have the *reductio* that the medium should not be extended because it has collapsed into itself in the direction of the point. We infer that a space, time, or space-time must have disparate places, hence disjunctive places, if it is to be an extended medium. Here is another place where the exclusionary 'or' signifies a difference in things—though not a difference for which we need evoke possibilities.

Some other bases for disjunctive claims about places and positions are contingent, as when bodies exclude one another, though it is no contradiction that there be possible worlds in which bodies occupy the same place. For it is peculiar to our space-time and the force fields generated within it that bodies are mutually exclusive as regards the regions they occupy.

We get this mixed result. It is contingent from the standpoint of possible worlds that bodies within the space, time, or space-time of a world are or are not mutually exclusive: angels occupying the same spiritual places in one world might be restricted to separate places in other worlds. It is necessary within a particular world, however, that the question be resolved in one way or the other. This is so, because laws fix the constraints applying within a world in a way parallel to the effect of rules in a game: what is the game, five-card stud or seven-card draw? So is it that the laws local to a world determine that bodies are or are not mutually exclusive within a place.

Accordingly, the 'or' of disjunctive thoughts or sentences points in either of two ways. Looking at friends, musing that they could occupy the same places or different ones, we compare our world to worlds where laws are different from the ones that operate here. In this case, 'or' has the opposition among worlds as its referent. But then the 'or' of this reflection has no referent as it applies to our world; the thought is false because it implies that the alternation appropriate to possible worlds obtains in our world.

Finally (after truths about disjunctive properties and truths about disjunctive places), possibilities are relevant to four sorts of truths reporting disjunctive causal sequences. First is the presence of intrinsic causal determination in some worlds; not all of them are the aggregative, accidental conjunctions that Hume describes. That possible worlds may be Humean or Leibnizian is a truth about them. Second is the contrariety that sets possible worlds in opposition to one another. The natural laws applying within a world are its signature, one set entailing the absence from that world of whatever sets of laws establish the distinguishing form of other possible worlds. It is these sets of laws, not the individual laws of any set, that are contrary: contrary sets may include some of the same laws. By analogy, the set of rules defining one game is exclusive of every other set of rules, though different games, such as Canadian and American football, may have some of the same rules.

Third is the infinity of possible worlds having the same laws but different initial conditions, hence different histories. Suppose that all these worlds are members of one set, the set having these laws as its signature. Someone considering the members of this set says truly that we may live in one or another of these worlds, but not in two or more at once. The several appearances of 'or' in this truth signify the exclusionary relations among possible worlds. Notice that we cannot tell which world is the one instantiated here short of empirical inquiry, and that, even then, no decisive answer is forthcoming because there is an infinity of possible worlds differing only slightly from our own as regards their initial conditions and current evolution. We shall never be able to sort through the complexity of material conditions in our world on the way to specifying exactly the respects in which the possibility instantiated here differs from those other possible worlds marginally different from it.

Fourth, suppose that we cut into the skein of transformations occurring since the inception of our world (if there was one). Is only one sequence possible, given the circumstances prevailing here (*here* meaning the world altogether or any region of it)? Or could there be any of several divergent transformations from this starting point? The answer depends, in part, on our notion of possibility. Where possibles are the eternal, logical ones, there is an infinity of alternate outcomes for any set of initial conditions, whether cosmological or situational. The answer is more complicated if the possibilities at issue are the material ones appropriate to the circumstances at hand. For then, we look more carefully at the material possibilities current within a situation: is this a rigidly deterministic world or one in which changes or their controlling laws are probabilistic? If the laws are deterministic, there are no alternatives to the transformations that occur. Nothing but the one development is possible; no disjunctive thought or sentence representing opposed options for change is true in these circumstances. Suppose, however, that both change itself and the relevant natural laws are probabilistic. In that event, alternative developments are possible. The 'or' of probabilistic disjunctions signifies a real opposition in things. What exclusionary relation is this? Just that of contrariety. We have one or another of these probabilistic outcomes, each one grounded in current material circumstances; we cannot have more than one.

4. Claims about past and future events. Temporality is implied by the hypothesis that material systems are generated, stabilized, and dissolved by way of successive interactions and transformations. Eternal possibilities add nothing to these claims except the realization that the character of temporality in our world is a contingency having these properties: time is asymmetrical, with the implication that temporal processes are not reversible. The time of our world is integrated with space by way of motion, which presupposes both. But other kinds of time are possible, so there are other possible worlds, even perhaps their instantiated, actual worlds, where time does not have these features. Tensed thoughts or sentences do, nevertheless, have the temporality peculiar to our world as their referent. Where change and transformations are real, there is an extra-mental, extra-linguistic state of affairs for claims representing time as past, present, or future.

5. Truths about generalities. Distributive generalities are unproblematic; each of them may be regarded as a finite or open-ended conjunction of claims about particulars. It is the normative generalities that are difficult, for they imply that a principle, property, or rule has regulative force throughout some domain, though all the things present there are particular. I proposed in section VI that the geometry intrinsic to space-time is paradigmatic of normative generality.

The reference to possibilities extends our understanding of this normative power by introducing the difference between a possibility and its instantiations. Every possibility is general and normative: it is a universal with a distinguishing identity, one that is present in each of its instantiations. Where nothing is actual if it is not first possible, every actual state of affairs is constrained by the possibility it instantiates. What is this constraint? It is not the demand that the possible be instantiated; many or most possibles may never be instantiated. The constraint is more subtle; it is the fact that the character of any actual state of affairs is the character prefigured in the possibility instantiated. This standard operates, though there is no quasi-mechanical influence exerted on the actual by the possible, for one constrains the other merely in virtue of being the possibility instantiated.

Suppose, for clarification, that we distinguish two kinds of possible worlds. One supplies schemas for actual worlds, without anticipating any particular array of individuals or states of affairs. These schemas require, for example, constancies in the relations of certain properties, such as $F = ma$. We might better describe these schemas as blueprints for possible worlds. Possible worlds of the other kind are fully elaborated. They prefigure both the laws of an actual world and the number and organization of its particulars. These possible worlds are determinate to the point of being instantiable as actual worlds. We might think of games played—that is, games as sequences of moves governed by the game-defining rules. Both sorts of possible world and both sorts of game are normative in the respect that is pertinent here. Students of chess might want to replay a classic game, duplicating its every move; or they play afresh, taking care only that their moves satisfy the rules. Possible worlds of both sorts have a regulative effect like that of games: laws prefigured in the blueprint of a possible world are natural laws in the world that instantiates this possibility, whereas the individuals and events of an instantiated world realize all the details prefigured in the possible world. We are reminded that an architect's drawing has a constraining effect on the building constructed, the forms of the one limiting the other.

I supposed in section VI that normative generalities are *universalia in rebus*: there were no resources for treating them in any other way. That is unsatisfactory, because it obscures the difference between normative and distributive generalities: we get likeness among keys of identical shape while losing the regulative demand that every key of this shape have the same efficacy, other things being equal: maybe they will, maybe they won't. Possibilities save us from this dissolving effect, because they enable us to say that normative generality is *ante rem:* possibilities prescribe a form to each of their instantiations. The possibility for triangularity lays down a certain form, one that is realized every time the possibility is instantiated.

The weak link in these claims about normativity, discounting antipathy for the reality of possibles, is the burden implied by their instantiation. For it is here that the normative force of possibles is satisfied in actual particulars. How is the normativity of the one transmitted to the other, if there is, as I allege, no mechanical link between them? I have no answer but this: instantiation is just the realization in space-time of properties existing already as possibles. The one realizes the other in a form that is qualitatively and quantitatively determinate. This is the normativity of the possible in relation to the actual: that everything in the one survives in the other.

I agree that this is a conjecture, one for which the only evidence is its economical rendering of a question near to the limits of speculative inquiry. Does it help if we introduce the idea of a god, assigning to it responsibility for instantiating the possibles, thereby introducing their normativity into the actuals? This only promotes mystification and clutter in a relationship that is better left simple: properties existing as possibles have a certain identity; that identity is normative when the possibles are instantiated.

6. Truths about dispositions.   Dispositions are second-order qualifications for relatedness founded in the structural properties of actuals. Geometrical-structural properties are exemplary foundations for these second-order qualifications, as a key of specific shape is qualified for opening a lock of complementary shape. It would be satisfying if we could generalize from this example and show that all dispositions are fixed decisively by their structural foundations. The reference to possibilities subverts this hope. For most dispositions do not seem to be founded in anything so restrictive as geometrical structure: it is no contradiction that geese should sing *Don Carlo*. Possibility attenuates the relation between structural and dispositional properties because it allows, short of contradiction, that any particular kind of structure may have, in possibility, capacities of every sort.[41] Even geometry would not be restrictive from this point of view *if* it were no contradiction that a lock of one shape might open to keys of any and every shape. Hume would favor this view, though it seems mistaken to me. For it is contradictory, given a geometric form, that we have an effect which requires that the form should have a character other than the one assumed: it is a contradiction, not merely a contingent truth, that square pegs don't fit round holes, when the diagonal on the face of the one is greater than the diameter of the other.

We also need to correct the impression encouraged by saying that the character of a thing's dispositions may not be fixed, in all cases, by the character of its structural properties. For it does not follow that dispositions are not always founded in the structural properties of the thing. Dispositions are not free-floating. These qualifications for relatedness have no footing in reality except that provided by the structures having these capacities.

We have still to face this other question: if structures are not competent to fix the identity of their capacities, what is? Geometrical-structural properties do it for locks and keys. Other behaviors—the resonances of a piano—may be the large-scale effects of geometrically based dispositions and behaviors. What substitutes for geometry in other cases? Inability to think of an alternative is my reason for wanting to show that even some unlikely dispositions have their ground in the geometry of things. But this leaves many dispositions still to be explained: how are those capacities for relatedness decided by the structures they qualify? I don't know.

How have possibilities been helpful to the explication of dispositions? Only by enforcing a mystery: we cannot, yet, generalize from the case of dispositions founded upon and determined by geometrical-structural properties to all dispositions.

7. *True counterfactuals expressing natural laws.* I argued in section VI that counterfactuals counted true merely because they satisfy the rules for material implication are unimportant for a realism tailored to the notion of truth as correspondence. The counterfactuals that concern us are those representing natural laws. Does this difference represent a difference in reality? Possibilities argue that it does: the difference is prefigured in two kinds of possible worlds.

In one, possibles are associated randomly, every property being associable with every other one, contradictions apart. These are possible worlds appropriate to Hume's dictum that anything may follow anything else. Possible worlds of the other sort restrict the associability of properties. This limitation is expressed by the relation of a higher-order determinable to the laterally related property which determines its lower-order expression (e.g., air temperature determines that precipitation shall have rain, sleet, or snow as its lower-order, more determinate expression). This relationship of possibles is instantiated as a causal law. Or an ensemble of functionally related possibles—including, for example, force, mass, and acceleration—is a law of motion within the actual worlds instantiating it.

Which of the two kinds of possible worlds is realized in our world? I suggested in section VIII that we settle this issue by asking if our actual world gives evidence of being one or the other. We remark the conspicuous order of things, then we emphasize the chronic disorder that should everywhere intrude if no laws are immanent here. Why couldn't our world be an instance of those remarkable statistical possibilities such that an honest coin comes up tails on every next throw? This could be a Humean world, though successive tails makes this hypothesis more unlikely. We begin looking for a better explanation, one that cites conditions sufficient for the regularity observed. Chance (meaning that Humean worlds are possible) is one explanation, but increasingly, as the string of coincidences is extended, an implausible one. A different explanation proposes that our world instantiates one of the possible worlds having invariant ensembles of functionally related properties. Natural laws are immanent, we speculate, within our world.

Counterfactuals represent these laws by signifying the effects that would occur if particular causes were assembled or if, say, the relation of force, mass, and acceleration were a pervasively determining invariant in our world. We may interpret the counterfactuals in either of two ways. On one reading, a counterfactual represents a law; on the other, it represents the law's application by specifying a relevant case or class of cases. The counterfactual may be true under both headings, though it may also be true under one but false under the other, as laws signifying the mating behaviors of sabre-toothed tigers are—in one sense—true of our world while having no instances.

8. Mathematical truths.   What we call mathematical truths fall into three categories: truths deduced from formalized systems, as demanded by mathematical proof; truths resulting from an operation (e.g., a line is divided without limit, or definitions are introduced so that the rationals are generated from the natural numbers); and truths representing mathematical features, including unities, pluralities, magnitudes, and relations, as they exist in all or some possible worlds, hence in our world.

Constructivists in mathematics emphasize proof and rules for introducing or constructing mathematical entities, properties, and relations. They deny that mathematical truths might represent entities, properties, or relations independent of our constructions. Their reasons are learned from Kant: nothing can supply truth conditions for thought and language while standing apart from it.

Eternal possibilities help defeat this prejudice because there are three marks common to every possibility: quality, quantity, and relation. Every property or complex of properties existing as a possible is, for example, the possibility for a certain intensity, shape, or size. It may be a term in relations that are spatial, temporal, or relational. These marks are constitutive of the possibility and of the actual states of affairs instantiating it. Every expression of each of the marks, in possibility and actuality as well, is denumerable, has magnitude, and is engaged in one or many relationships implicating order, proportion, or functional relations. Every property has these marks, so that all possibility and actuality, hence all being, is essentially the topic for mathematical representation.

Some mathematical properties are specific to one or several possible worlds, though others apply within all possible worlds. The parochial mathematical necessities of a space having one among the infinity of possible immanent geometries are set against the universal necessities of arithmetic. The truths of Euclidean geometry are local; $7 + 5 = 12$ is not. Properties of both sorts are represented, not made.

9. Intentional truths.   The factual ground for the truth of intentional claims is the mental activity of those who make them, as the claim that I believe or intend some thing is true or false of me. It does not follow from this emphasis on the act of belief or intending that *what* I believe, hope, or desire is incidental. We are unlikely to ignore the intentional object when the belief is true or when the intention is serious and its object important. We are likely, however, to credit the intention, but merely acknowledge its object if the thing is remote and beyond the agent's ability to realize it. "Just so much talk," we say dismissively. Eternal possibilities help to explain the power of phantom objects; for these are ideals existing as possibles. We set these things before us as objects of desire; then we organize ourselves so that they may be achieved. There is the suitor of James's story: never believing that he will not be loved, he remakes his circumstances so that he shall be loved. Instantiating the possibility, he realizes the ideal.

10. Truths about value. Possibilities extend the domain of objective values. For the water good for thirst in our world is good for an infinity of other things in the possible worlds to which they are native. There are also the objectives valued — meaning possibles dignified as ideals. The justice we value may be an eternal possibility, not merely a portentous idea. But there are differing ideas of justice, each one signifying a different possibility. Is any one of them good in itself? Or do we concede that justice of every sort is good only because we desire it? We are reminded of Socrates' question to Euthyphro: do the gods love something because it is good, or is it good because they love it?[42] The role of possibilities is analogous: are they ideals to be realized or merely the objects of glorification and desire? Either way, these possibles are the referents and truth conditions for our claims about them, it being true on either notion of value that health is desirable.[43]

11. Truths about probabilities. Nothing is probable if it is not logically possible. Probability is, however, the estimate of material possibility — that an effect or event will occur because one or more of the things qualified to produce it obtain. Or we say that material possibility is the possibility that the instantiation of an eternal possible will be contemporaneous with or consequent upon the instantiation of one or more others.

Where the possible world instantiated is Humean, the estimate of probabilities is confounded. We may have a gambler's strategy, and it may afford us good predictions of things to come; yet we could never be confident of our inductive policy. How could we trust it when anything of one kind is infinitely unlikely to be coupled repeatedly with instances of another kind if there is an infinity of equally likely alternatives? The world is intrinsically ordered so that Hume is mistaken, or he is right and we should tremble.

Possible worlds of a non-Humean sort afford a different opportunity for the estimate of probabilities. Some have pervasively determining lateral relations, meaning that every possible is a determining condition for the lower-order expression of determinables not in its vertical file: any shade of blue and every other difference is a (nearly) universal cause. Other possible worlds

are more loosely bound: concurrent determinations in them are not determinants for one another, as geological properties are concurrent with, but
not usually determining of, social properties. These are worlds having
separate causal chains. There are, in addition, possible worlds that mix
determinist structures with the chance aggregation of Humean worlds. Finally, there are worlds in which there is only a certain probability that a
higher-order determinable will have one, rather than another, lateral determining condition and only a certain probability when having a lateral determining condition that it will have a particular lower-order expression. Worlds
of this sort can also be mixed with each of the kinds of world described
above.

The epistemic problem is straightforward: what sort of world is ours?
Without a priori illumination or innate ideas, we have the advantage only of
knowing the alternatives just described. We look for evidence of the disorder
that is ever more likely if ours is everywhere a Humean world. Not finding
it, we try to identify conditions—be they causes or invariants like Newton's
laws—for events occurring here. The result is equivocal. We find evidence
of causes and evidence that causal chains are often mutually independent.
This world is not, it seems, pervasively overdetermined, as it would be were
each one's breathing caused by every other. How tightly determined is it?
We cannot yet say.

Finding nothing but chaos, inferring that this is a Humean world, we
wouldn't bother to estimate probabilities. Finding many constant conjunctions and many apparently independent causal chains, we speculate that this
is a world having an immanent structure of determining relations. This hypothesis is our leading principle. Never telling us what the regularities may
be in particular cases, it shapes our expectation that there will be some regularities in a world of structures interacting in ways constrained by immanent
laws. We estimate the probabilities on the basis of this hypothesis and the
evidence of regularities observed.

12. Truths about possibilities.   The idea that some possibles are material (e.g.,
that rain is possible given the cloudy sky) has its complement in the hypothesis that other possibles are logical and eternal. Thoughts and sentences about
possibilities of both kinds may be true because they represent entities whose
existence and character are independent of thought and language.

13. Negative truths. True assertions about that which is not actual are, with disjunctions, normative generalities, and truths about possibles, the principal beneficiaries of this hypothesis about eternal possibilities. 'No' and 'not' are operators indicating the noninstantiation of a property or complex of properties: a negative sentence is true if the possibility signified is not instantiated. There is no more use for the idea that negative truths are second-order claims presupposing an inventory of first-order positive truths. We don't explain that someone is missing by first listing those who are present.

This ends my survey of the thirteen kinds of true thoughts and sentences having referents independent of thought and language. Correspondence is not restricted to the truth of categoricals signifying actual particulars. It seems to me that the realist metaphysics supporting correspondence is deepened by hypotheses about logical, eternal possibilities. Readers deterred by the high ontological price for these advantages may revert to the naturalistic theory of sections III, VI, and VII. Most of the ontology required to support the motion of truth as correspondence is available there.

X The Uses of the Coherence, Identity, and Redundancy Notions of Truth

Preferring correspondence to coherence, identity, redundancy, and behaviorist notions of truth does not mean that these other notions are useless. None of them renders correspondence dispensable, but some of them are useful as adjuncts to it.

    Coherence, especially, is important to us. We use it as a criterion for truth, though coherence alone is not a sufficient condition for truth. How could it be sufficient when equally coherent theories are contraries, so that all could be false, while no more than one could be true? Coherence is, however, a necessary condition for truth; an incoherent alibi or scientific theory is not true, even if its parts are true. What do we require of coherence, when logical consistency is assumed? Two of the familiar standards, one experiential, the other conceptual, were described in chapter 4. The experiential test requires that the montage of thoughts or sentences satisfy standards of coherence abstracted from the empirical data, be they spatial, temporal, or causal. Thoughts or sentences are coherent by this standard if they hang together because of having subject matters related in ways sanctioned by these rubrics. Logic is a sterner requirement, whether it be the logic of demonstration or the more pliable relations of inter-animating sentences. The one holds that a body of thoughts or sentences coheres if it is organized as a deductive system. The other requires that every rule be treated pragmatically: does it produce a coherence satisfying our interest in efficiency, simplicity, or control?

We use these tests with care, as when pleasure in the skein of derived theorems deters us from looking for evidence that a formalized theory is incomplete. Coherence is also blinding when a plan that seems well-knit comes unstuck as we act on it. All the anticipated instrumental relations satisfy causal laws; circumstances seem to be as our map represents them. We act as the plan directs, only to trip or skid on something ignored or misdescribed. But then we carry on as before, ignoring the possible irrelevance of our plan in these circumstances. There is this vulnerable underside to the coherence of consistent theories and well-formed plans: they often distort or ignore significant details in the world represented, though we are fascinated, beyond prudence, by systems more luminous and accessible than the world itself. But there are no perfect signs of truth, so that we lean heavily on this one.

The relation of coherence and correspondence is still more complicated. For we ordinarily suppose that coherence is evidence for correspondence, though we may need some truths by correspondence in order to make the coherences go. There is a question of priority quite equal to that of chicken and egg: which one, correspondence or coherence, is prior in knowledge? Thoughts and sentences are said to be coherent if they are a montage assembled under the control of guiding assumptions about spatial, temporal, and causal relations. These regulative ideas are embodied in our inductive rules—as the symmetry of space and the asymmetry of time are recorded there. We use these rules to control the assembly of thoughts or sentences within a conceptual system, though we do not suppose or intend that information about these relations is a confabulation of ours, one for which imagination supplies the coherence rules. This is to be a true story, one that is true because coherent, though material truth is ascribable to it only because the regulative principles (inductive laws) used to organize thoughts or sentences are, themselves, true of the world, true, that is, because of corresponding to some general features of space, time, or causality. How is coherence the test for truth when the criteria for coherence are only those reported by sentences truly representing, hence corresponding to, these real-world relations?

The air of paradox abates somewhat if we say that the relation between correspondence and the coherences used to test it is dialectical, not simple and direct. A test is simple and direct if it states a rule or condition before asking if the matter at hand satisfies the rule, as a batted ball is fair or foul. The dialectical test is more complicated. Progress is halting, and direction uncertain, but here we are in the middle of things, without innate ideas or rational intuition. We have only these resources: empirical data and a power for making and testing hypotheses about conditions that include their constituents, causes, and laws. There is also our fierce suspicion that many previous hypotheses are likely to be inadequate to their subject matters. Expecting that the predictions of a well-confirmed hypothesis will be successful again, but distrusting the adequacy of the hypothesis, we look for evidence that it says less then needs saying. Like Einstein applying Newton's laws beyond the domain for which he formulated them, we look for the consequences of velocities, densities, or distances exceeding those anticipated by the theory tested. What can it say of them? Is there evidence confirming its forced predictions about them? Often, there is not. We infer that the coherence of Newton's hypotheses about motion is insufficient as the test of their truth. Here, as elsewhere, we challenge coherent theories because we suspect that their very tidiness misleads us about the world. Progress in formulating a true and comprehensive theory moves back and forth between these considerations. A coherent theory is successively revised to make it provide for circumstances that were marginal or unintelligible in earlier formulations of the theory. Wanting coherence as the sign of correspondence, we persistently challenge any coherence purporting to be a final, because comprehensive, representation of things as they are. We bootstrap ourselves, fallibly and inconclusively, to truths about the world.

The other three notions of truth are less useful than coherence. We are annoyed with someone who is forever saying "That's the truth" after the truth has been said and heard. This may be all there is to say in defense of *redundancy* when we have rejected the tangle of Kantian views about productive judgment, together with the artful distinction between formal (transcendental) and material (empirical) modes. Everyone who rejects Kantian world-making distinguishes thoughts, judgments, and signs of every sort from the things represented. For it matters considerably whether the possibility signified by a sign is instantiated or not. That a thought or sentence is true is never redundant, though iterating its truth may be annoying to someone who has already assured himself of it.

Identity retains its utility when the focus is social, but not when it carries the implication required by Plato and Hume. It is too late for saying that mind apprehends truths by seizing the objects to be known when we have agreed that thoughts or sentences are true of things whose character and existence are distinct from these representations. *Being in the truth* is a different, more useful version of truth as identity. This idea survives the finding that truth is correspondence by establishing one of the referents for true sentences: namely, the rules and practices of our culture. We feel safer within a group if our right to be there is confirmed by our success at doing the things required of us. These are facts about us. They can be represented.

Being in the truth is nevertheless risky. We lose critical distance and moral autonomy when social recognition and acceptance become our predominant motives. Truth as correspondence first seems neutral as regards these contrary tensions, though it is, on closer inspection, a principal defense against the loss of autonomy. For we can never be unreserved participants in any activity if all our thoughts about it distance us from the event by interposing representations between it and ourselves. We can always withdraw from the activity by reflecting on these signs. What is their origin and use? What are their relations to, and significance for, other signs. We can turn thoughtful in the midst of frantic, vigorous, or dangerous activity. Correspondence speaks, in this way, for that intellectual distance and reflection which is a condition for moral autonomy.

There is, finally, this much to appropriate from the three *behaviorist* notions of truth. We often say "That's true" or "Fine, thanks," with little thought for the implications; which proves that polite speech is not held to the conditions demanded of accurate speech. A behaviorism made responsible for accurate speech, hence for truth conditions, is only the barely disguised version of correspondence: we learn to say "That's a canary" in circumstances where assertibility conditions include the canary.

Behaviorism of the third sort—truth as conceptual world-making—never accedes to the demands of correspondence. The mutual antipathy of these views is fundamental and never compromised. One is romantic; the other dour. World-making celebrates our powers for having things our way. Correspondence implies our accommodation to things that stand apart from us: we address a world we have not made or things not made by the act representing them. Hypothesis is not construction. Why not set one against the other, acknowledging both? We make and alter many things; hypothesis, by comparison, is a way of representing, not of making, things. True hypotheses are like a miner's lamp: they direct our interventions in the world, thereby facilitating the constructions that make life better or worse.

XI Is the Argument for Correspondence Circular?

My defense of truth as correspondence seems flawed in one egregious way. I have surveyed five different notions of truth, asking which is true. But this implies that some notion of truth is invoked criteriologically: one of the candidate notions is to be counted true because it satisfies the criterion. How shall we avoid circularity if this criterial notion is one of the five surveyed? If it is not one of them, we should identify the additional notion, though doing so will not avert the problem; for sooner or later we shall be using one of the considered notions, be it five, six, or more, to appraise each one's claim to be the truth about truth.

There would be no circularity if our problem were that of telling which of five advertisers tells the truth about its product. There would be an agreed sense for 'tells the truth'; identifying the truth-tellers would be the only problem. Our task is different, because the notion of truth is itself in question. Suppose that the possible notions of truth are the five considered above. How can we say that one of the five is true without tacitly making it the criterion of truth, thereby begging the question?

One way of averting the problem denies that being true is required for being the correct notion of truth. Isn't it good enough that a notion proves its utility, the value of justice, beauty, or civility, for example, being only the work it does within the context of thought and action? Tables and chairs need not be true to be useful; no more is truth required of notions used as conceptual instruments. The truth about truth is only this question about its utility: does it help us to get what we want?

This instrumentalism is well and good for artifacts and even for some conceptual systems (e.g., the rules of baseball). It may work for notions of justice and beauty. It doesn't work for truth. Imagine someone who calls true every fantasy that pleases him. Novels, films, daydreams: all of them are true, just to the extent of filling his time with pleasing distractions and evocations. Reading Oz and thinking of Alice, he one day climbs a fence, feels the wind, spreads his arms, and falls from the Brooklyn Bridge. Well, says the pragmatist, there's the exception: notions are true as long as they are useful. This one, pressed too far, didn't work.

We need to be more discerning as regards the circumstances in which fantasies work. I assume that the work done by our notion of truth is not reserved for the luxury of aesthetic contemplation: velvet drapes here, a Monet there, any one of five notions of truth, each one cogent when used in the proper way. All this is romance when action appropriate to our interests and circumstances requires that there be an idea of truth adequate to circumstances where thought directs our accommodations to a world we have not made and do not merely, passively, enjoy. Do thought and language make us effective as we engage other things, working with them to create some effect? Or do they work only in the privacy of our daydreams? The difference is critical for a notion of truth, because fantasies don't test reality; actions do. Could truth be only utility? No, though utility is a measure of truth.

The idea of sentences satisfied by their referents is the idea of truth presupposed when we say that a notion should be adequate to its subject matter, as the notion of truth should be adequate to truth. But this is also the point conceded above: I have assumed throughout this chapter and the last that truth as correspondence is the criterion for evaluating the five notions of truth, correspondence included. This is circular, but not pernicious: we reduce the question-begging aspect of the argument by making the circle larger.

We do this by putting conceptual space between the five notions of truth and the criterial use of one for appraising both itself and the other four. My argument fills that space with the metaphysical theories embedding the five notions of truth. These theories tell a more ample story about knowledge and being, while satisfying the values which impel their formulation. More, these theories divert attention from the five notions of truth, because my procedure is no longer the brazen one of invoking truth as correspondence to appraise, among other things, the idea of truth as correspondence. Instead, we use this notion of truth to appraise the five metaphysical theories. Which of them best represents things as they are? Which is true?

Attention is diverted from the five notions of truth as we enlarge the range of considerations pertinent to choosing among the five embedding theories.

My procedure for evaluating the five theories is dialectical and empirical. Is each theory consistent and coherent? What are its tacit assumptions? Can the theory justify these assumptions, then elaborate and answer the questions that it puts to the world. Can it resolve, if only by implication, the problems to which the other theories respond? This is the dialectical side. The empirical question is equally direct: Is the theory confirmed by its empirical predictions? Are they co-extensive, at least, with the date predicated by the other theories? A theory passing the dialectical and empirical tests is likely to be the best one. We should be able to identify this theory, especially as we start with only these five candidates. For how many good theories of anything are there? One, a few? Surely not the infinity that should be commonplace if every datum is easily subsumed under a consistent theory.

There are only two metaphysical theories supporting the five alternative notions of truth: namely, realism and idealism. Correspondence and some forms of the behaviorist notion presupposes realism; coherence, identity, redundancy, and Jamesian instrumentalism are embedded in one or another version of idealism. The contemporary fulcrum for struggles between idealism and realism is the issue of empirical confirmation, with "underdetermination" and "overdetermination" as the idealist slogans: the data lack intrinsic differentiations and organization (they are underdetermined) until form is imposed by conceptual systems (they are overdetermined). A consistent story can explain anything, where 'explain' means that underdetermined data are differentiated and organized in the style prescribed by a schematizing theory. No wonder that we find ourselves puzzled, awash in the diversity of theories, by the choice of a good or best theory. Yet all of us are familiar with one of the simplest instances of this class: we might explain everything by saying "Fate," though people commending this explanation have even less to say when asked to predict what it is that fate promises or how fate produces it.

Reducing the problem of knowledge to the one of finding a schematization adequate to the data—"curve fitting," it is sometimes called—is Kant's solution to the problem of knowledge. It requires that we find a place within our system for every datum, however recalcitrant (remember Quine's permission to reject as "hallucination" any datum that resists schematization). I wonder if anyone claiming to do this can shake off the mix of skepticism and grandiosity that clings to this view. Unwilling to make hypotheses about the extra-mental, extra-linguistic conditions for the data, we are to make worlds for ourselves, creating simulacra within the schematized data for everything denied to the world itself—including modalities, objects, and laws.

Abductions are bolder. They specify the conditions which may have produced the data perceived, hence what further data there may be if other conditions are satisfied. It is no easy thing to formulate a successful abduction, given the requirement that we both explain and predict variations among the data. But there is no alternative to abductive inference, given that we have neither rational intuition nor innate ideas of our circumstances. Hypotheses about the extra-mental, extra-linguistic conditions for sensory data are obligatory for anyone who wants information about the world as a preliminary to acting effectively within it. This is abduction as it identifies the conditions for sensory data, abduction as it serves the interests of action and control.

Am I prejudicing the question of truth by assuming that there is a world independent of thought and language, but representable by way of their signs? Notice the difference between postulating and acknowledging that extra-mental world. Peirce remarked that the idealist drunk is confuted when he swings out of the barroom door into a lamppost. No idealist theory explains this man's bruised jaw unless we suppose that the world-making transcendental ego sets snares and obstacles to surprise its empirical self. Realism does better by inferring to conditions which are sufficient to explain these effects. Specifying these conditions, then controlling them, is our reason for saying that this is the best explanation for systematic variations among the data. This is a fundamental abduction, for it identifies, if only generically, the extra-mental world of which representations are true or false.

Is realism vulnerable to the fact that there might be an infinity of realist theories? Nothing in this question is pernicious to realism if each variant explains the contact, shock, and bruise of Peirce's example by speculating about the extra-mental, extra-linguistic conditions for the impact of two bodies. Comparing alternative characterizations of space-time or causality, then finding an empirical basis for choosing among them, is subtle, but not so consequential as remarking that our five embedded notions of truth reduce the metaphysical choices to just these two: a psycho-centric ontology for which the known world comprises only mind's productive activities and qualifications (e.g., schematization and its product) and a materialist realism supplemented, perhaps, by claims about eternal possibilities. It seems to me that conceptual and empirical considerations fault the idealism, while confirming the realism, whatever its final details. Alternatives on the realist side are reduced to the hypothesis that we humans know and adapt ourselves to the natural world as creatures born and living in the midst of it. We get this result: that representations are essential to realism because they secure minds' connection to things thought and perceived. We require that sensory data and words be signs and that truth be correspondence: a well-formed thought or sentence is true when it signifies and is satisfied by a state of affairs having an existence and character independent of its representation.

These are considerations that attenuate the circularity of my argument. They are reasons for saying that the circularity is more benign than brazen. Truth as correspondence is vindicated in an argument where truth as correspondence is the criterion used to evaluate the five candidate notions of truth. Yet I have not taken direct aim at these five, using one of them to beggar the others while endorsing itself. Rather, the five have been considered within the context of their supporting metaphysical theories. We ask which of the theories is true (by correspondence) only to learn, half naively, that the theory confirmed is one that includes the very notion of truth used to confirm it. The argument is circular, but not shameless.

XII Paradoxes of Self-Reference

There is one remaining technical detail. It requires attention, only because neglecting it might seem to hide some deep error in the idea that truth is correspondence.

Consider these familiar examples: the Cretan who says "All Cretans always lie"; the sentence "I am lying"; the sentence "This sentence is false." Each of these has been used to make the point that truth-claims may lead to paradox. This happens if the Cretan cannot speak either truly or falsely about all Cretans without speaking, at that moment, to contrary effect: saying truly that all Cretans always lie, he (a Cretan) must be speaking falsely; speaking falsely, he confirms the truth of his own saying.

We get this paradoxical result by dilating on each of the three examples above; but there are two differences among them. The first two are examples of the speaker's self-reference, whereas the third is an instance of self-reference in the sentence itself. More, the first two are elliptical, while the third is not. The first does not tell us that it is a Cretan who says that all Cretans always lie. The complete version of the second reads, "I am lying when I say . . . ," this on the assumption that I cannot be lying or truth-telling either if I am not asserting something. The essential context for the first two, is, therefore, richer than that for the third. Further, the third entails a paradox merely on the assumption that the phrase "This sentence" in "This sentence is false" is self-referential. These differences are incidental to a general solution of the paradoxes they generate. Still, they justify our choice of the third case as the tidier one for analysis. There is nothing of ellipsis in it and nothing in its context, rather than in the sentence itself, that is pertinent to resolving the paradox.

Now this question: is there anything about truth as correspondence, with or without eternal possibilities, which is sufficient to generate these paradoxes? The answer, I suggest, is that correspondence is innocent. Only truth as correspondence *plus self-reference* breeds paradox. So paradox results as we do these three things. First, we interpret the sentence "This sentence is false" as signifying its truth condition: this sentence being false. Second, we construe the phrase "This sentence" as self-referential. Third, we detach the self-referential phrase "This sentence" from its predicate "is false" and join it to the predicate generated when we compare the original sentence to its truth condition. We get this result: "This sentence is false" is true, hence, "This sentence is true"; or "This sentence is false" is false, so that, again, "This sentence is true."

These glosses are mistaken because "This sentence is true" is not a substitute, on the same semantic level, for "This sentence is false." Russell makes this point as he averts paradox by moving to those successively higher levels that we call *meta-languages*.[44] We avert same-level self-reference, hence paradox, by saying that the former is a sentence in the meta-language having sentences of the level below as its object language. Doing this enables us to specify the truth condition for the higher-order sentence without paradox, as we say "The sentence is false" (a sentence in the meta-language) is true if and only if the sentence (in the object language) is false. Summarily, we invoke the difference between levels, together with the idea that truth is correspondence or satisfaction, to eliminate the paradox from self-reference.

For it is only self-reference, not any difficulty with truth as correspondence, that generates these paradoxes.

Does it make a difference to this claim that we invoke eternal possibilities? Just this much. These paradoxes are eliminated by invoking the hierarchical structures of self-reference, as within a theory of levels. But where do we look for evidence of this recursive pattern? Nominalists flatten reality by acknowledging no ontological status for any level but that of substantial particulars. One who insists on the reality of species and genera is told that the only realities are particulars, which are sometimes very much alike. Are there no hierarchies congenial to nominalists? Only these two orders prefigured in language: first, the hierarchical organization of predicates (e.g., 'color', 'red', and 'scarlet'); second, the rules permitting talk about talk. Linguistic hierarchies of the first sort represent the hierarchical organization of properties existing as possibles, as when properties are organized vertically from the more determinable to the more determinate. Hierarchies of the second kind are different, because there is no change of determination from level to level within a hierarchy: "This sentence is false" is not more or less determinate whatever its level within an infinite regress of meta-languages.

What do eternal possibles tell us about hierarchies of this second kind, given that ignorance of them has not prevented us from distinguishing meta-languages from object languages? Only this: that there is nothing in actuality that is not first in possibility. Nominalists respond that hierarchies are generated by a procedure, hence that successive levels do not exist until they are introduced. Logical, eternal possibilities make us suspicious of this claim. Recursion, they imply, is ontological before it is linguistic.

XIII Truth and Value

Value has mostly disappeared amidst the considerations significant for correspondence. This is proper, because value is always irrelevant to the fact that the possibility signified by a thought, sentence, or theory is instantiated or not. It often happens that a value moves us to produce an effect, but then it is true or false, irrespective of value, that the effect occurs. This is the old caution that wishing doesn't make a thing true. Still, it does not follow that correspondence and the realist metaphysics supporting it are not motivated by, and do not satisfy, one or many values.

I have argued that a realist metaphysics, with its notion that truth is correspondence, is motivated principally by the desire for more effective control of, or accommodation to, our circumstances. The next chapter reverses this emphasis, asking how values and attitudes are constrained by truths. Nietzsche made reason a slave to will and the passions. Romantic Kantians, our contemporaries included, follow his example, making truth the function of attitude and desire. Their view is consistent with the democratization of experience, hence with the demand that each of us be free to live in a world of his or her own choosing. This call to perfect freedom, the freedom for world-making, is nevertheless ironic. It barely comports with the fact that all of us are more accommodating than godlike, however privileged and powerful. Nor is this freedom consistent with the reasonable demand that we do not violate other people or the environment we share when pursuing our private satisfactions. Better that we educate attitude and desire about the risks of egoism. Nature or other people will sooner or later do that if we let the issue slide; truths will do it too. They are the benign, preferred instrument for finding our way in a world we alter but never make.

Chapter Six

I Truth Informs Desire

Truth as correspondence is spartan. The possibility represented by a sentence is instantiated or not, making the sentence true or false if the sentence is positive, false or true if it is negative. Value is irrelevant to the question of truth, though correspondence is valuable instrumentally because it is decisive on all those occasions when any creature acts in defense of its interests. Where are we? What are the resources available to us? What instrumental relations are appropriate to these tasks and circumstances? No action will likely succeed if we have not distinguished motives from circumstances. No plan expressing the one is effective if it is oblivious to truths about the other.

This might seem trivial good sense, until we remember that James and Dewey despaired of the caution it implies. Will we ever do anything important if we are forever looking about us, never acting until we have mapped our situation, anticipating every sinkhole and crevice? Better to move ahead, taking responsibility for all that we do and all the plans and instruments used for doing it. Let us make the world behave as we desire it should.

This project, so much in the style of Genesis and Teddy Roosevelt, requires that the ambient world be either a void or so protean as to set no limits on our interventions. Every obstacle is razed as we flatten and excavate a site before constructing a building; or we suppose that the world about us is filled with an infinitely malleable substance that will assume whatever shape we impose. Either way, there is nothing in the world to impede us. A plan can fail only because it is badly composed or executed, because necessary resources are unavailable, or because there is conflict among actors on converging paths. Otherwise, things should go well: the thoughtful, well-prepared actor should realize his objective. His plan should be the blueprint for that part of the world remade to his specifications.

Truth, this says, is no constraint on value. To the contrary, value has determined what sort of experience and world we shall schematize. Truths representing or expressing any part of the world are derivative: they are consequent on those acts of world-making driven by our desires and attitudes. Where attitude is generic and desire particular, these two are beams of light projecting design and detail into the world around us.

Correspondence is a fly in this romantic ointment. Thoughts or sentences are true, it holds, because they represent states of affairs whose character and existence are independent of these signs. The states of affairs are an environment that abides everywhere within and about us. We have made some of them, but always by altering or assembling things that were found, not made. Indeed, we ourselves and all the things we make or engage are the spatially, temporally, causally, and hierarchically organized constituents of a nature having a substantial character and intrinsic forms of its own. Several notions of truth—namely, coherence, redundancy, and identity—encourage the idea that mind need not look beyond itself for the purposes of world-making. But their sense is quixotic: we are to practice our megalomania in the midst of a world to which we accommodate or die.

Someone building a garage at the edge of the cliff is careful that the door opens onto the road, not the abyss. Other choices are less critical, though they always require information about our circumstances. The information may be useful to many people, though one's use of it is decided by particular wants or the tilt of one's cognitive-affective balance. News of an opium shortage is heard differently by addicts and others: the addict anticipates a rise in prices; the policeman counts on fewer addicts and less crime. Both parties subordinate information to desire, but neither can have his wish by ignoring the pertinent truths.

Desire is joined to reality testing: *truth informs desire.* Learning where we are and what we might hope to do there, we shape, as much as satisfy, our desires. There are these two things operating within us: the equilibrium (however idiopathic and precarious) of an established cognitive-affective balance and the internal conversation in which desires provoke hypotheses, while hypotheses falsified or confirmed educate desires. The cognitive-affective balance has an inertia of its own; yet it too is altered by the situational changes to which this conversation is sensitive. Inhibitions that were critical in the past may be dispensable now; impulses that were safely expressed in some other place may be inappropriate here. The Jamesian (Nietzschean) bias is reversed: rather than say that truth is indebted to value, we require that values be shaped by truths. Wanting to fly as birds do, but never succeeding, we revise our desire. We desire to do what circumstances, including our innate limits and capacities, qualify us for doing. The desire is framed now by truths telling what and where we are. It has become a *rational desire.*

Rationality in this context is not the demand of Kant's categorical imperative for a principle or procedure that is noncontradictory and universalizable. This is rationality contextualized by the specificity of our desires and the particularity of our circumstances. We have this choice: act impulsively in order to have or do the thing desired or deliberate on this objective and its execution, asking ourselves the benefits of doing something or nothing and our capacity for doing it. Deliberation is the opportunity to take the measure of our circumstances, to ask what consequences there will likely be for ourselves and others if we act as desire prescribes. This is deliberation about means and ends. There are truths appropriate to each of them, as when thoughtless desires are redirected by truths about interests that would be harmed were the desires satisfied. The rationality appropriate here is just this situation-sensitive deliberation. Truths, as much as desires, are its material.

Not everything that might be counted a desire requires or deserves this consideration: we rightly distinguish desires from whims. Whims are transient and trivial. Spontaneity, with indifference to their conditions and consequences, is important to the satisfaction of having them. Desires are different, because they are proper objects of justification. The gravity of one is inappropriate to the other, though even the whims of someone deliberate may be informed by prior reflection, as when he or she knows the times and behaviors appropriate to spontaneity. Certainly, things of which we are rightly heedless in one situation are topics for the most careful deliberation in others. Still, there are some questions: How shall we know that an impulse is one and not the other? When is it safe that desire in one of us be thoughtless whim in another? These are serious questions that I shall ignore.

My concern is the relation between truths cogent to the circumstances where things are desired and the impulse itself. My thesis is that particular desires are modified by deliberating on the things desired and their likely consequences, given these truths. Truths, I allege, are the vital condition for self-regulation: thinking about them, we alter desires so that we may have or avert particular consequences. What are the mechanics of impulse control? Punishment and reward are only part of the story: addictions are not always extinguished after causing pain. Attention to those consequences, perhaps allied to a vivid imagination, may do as much. My concern is the deliberation that makes this control conscious, flexible, and principled.

I shall be saying that desires are made reasonable in an intraphysic context defined by the following considerations. First are the particular desires at issue: which one shall direct us? Second is a hierarchically organized network of other desires and attitudes. Some of the constituent desires and attitudes and the relations among them are ephemeral: they change as our circumstances change. Some others are more enduring: these, typically, are attitudes more or less fixed within an agent's cognitive-affective balance. I assume that any candidate desire, whatever its order within this hierarchy, must be congenial to, consistent with, or tolerated by higher-order desires and attitudes. At worst—and this will make for trouble within us—there is disassociation within this network, a place being made for some candidate attitude or desire by isolating it from attitudes that would otherwise preclude it.

Third are salient truths. Calling them "salient" means that they are relevant to the situation where a desire would be enacted. They identify one or more of our interests or they represent some feature of the terrain, apposite moral laws, or statutes, or they specify the mechanics or consequences of the actions considered. One thinks of tax codes salient for accountants and truths about the skills of his team salient for a manager thinking bunt or steal.

All three factors—current desires, the network of attitudes and desires, and salient truths—are critical for the discussion that follows. Salient truths are its focus. Why emphasize them? Because proponents of worldmaking want us to believe that truths and the existences they prefigure are creatures of thought. This has many important consequences, but my concern is only the effect on deliberation and action if we suppose that truths are evidence of our value-driven interests, not representations of the extramental, extra-linguistic things to which we accommodate ourselves. Deliberation without these truths is better described as fantasy. We know this difference well enough. The one suffices for daydreams; the other is critical for reality testing and a condition for our well-being. Salient truths are the required baseline for anyone who cares to satisfy his desires by engaging other people and things.

Consequentialist deliberation exhibits a certain pattern. We start, I assume, with particular needs or interests keenly felt: "desires," we call them. But now it is important that we have an inventory of our circumstances, with an estimation of what would happen were we to act on some particular desire. For we shall not choose this objective if we do not want its effects, its costs included. Wanting them or not, or uncertain about the mix of costs and benefits, we express the network of our hierarchically organized desires and attitudes. Choice, or the possibility of it, resonates with them. Lunch, even an expensive lunch, may pass muster. A poisoned one does not.

It is most important to this sketch of deliberation that no list of pertinent truths is sufficient in itself to determine what object of desire we should pursue. The complex reasons for saying this are considered below, but we see enough of them already. For consider any particular truth. It sanctions certain objects for desire, eliminating some others. "Stealing from the poor is evil" would be a truth like that if it represented a natural moral law or even if it expressed an accepted convention. It does not follow that this option is foreclosed to someone who thinks of stealing. For that person would also have some other salient truths at hand—that he or she is poorer than anyone and desperately needy. What should the person do when salient truths have this effect: they establish an array of objects appropriate for desire, though some are contraries?

Deliberation points us, inconclusively, in several directions at once. We who choose minimize the contention by reflecting as best we can on the relations among our hierarchically organized attitudes and desires. What do they tolerate or encourage? We want direction. Where these attitudes are vague or ill formed, we make them authoritative and determining by applying them to specific tasks. The dieter tempted by things he shouldn't eat imagines himself at a particular weight and size. The politician tempted equally by candor and obfuscation details the idea of himself as forthright. Each of us is necessarily didactic as we formulate a more detailed ranking of our relevant attitudes and interests, with a scaling of attitudes and interests within each rank of the hierarchy. We also juggle our calculations of the likely consequences of acting in an assortment of possible ways, all by way of comparing the various orders of cost and benefit were these several choices to be pursued.

In the end, we formulate a more or less accurate cost–benefit analysis, with cautionary warnings everywhere that estimates of the likely consequences of action are provisional. We concede that predictions about the consequences of possible actions may be mistaken; and also that we have probably failed to discern all the complexities and conflicts among our associated attitudes and desires. Even choices made with the greatest care may turn out to violate some attitude or interest, as we agree when the bride or groom fails to appear at a long-planned wedding. Do we conclude that deliberation was a failure, where successful deliberation determines the one best thing to do, given salient truths and the hierarchy of our interests and attitudes? No. For the deeper we go, the plainer the realization that there are several or many choices that might equally be made in particular circumstances. Does it follow that deliberation is pointless, that we would do as well to act impulsively? No; it follows only that deliberation, however prudent, is inconclusive.

This is my sketch of the situation before us. My suggestion is that deliberation tells us three things: what is true of our circumstances; what are the likely consequences of acting on particular desires; and what objects for desire are appropriate because of having consequences acceptable within the network of our attitudes and desires. Where salient truths alone are insufficient to determine what choice to make among the range of objects appropriate for desire (given the truths), it is some other attitude or desire or relation among them which makes the choice. But plainly now, the use of truths within deliberation is potent and cogent too. The student or pilot, with a test to pass or a plane to fly in the morning, is better advised to spend the night sleeping than drinking. Are some students more relaxed when drunk? Perhaps. Do some pilots manage to complete a flight when drunk? Apparently. Is either behavior advisable given the possible or likely consequences? One doesn't think so. Does deliberation make us boring, but safe and effective? That is its aim.

My account of deliberation is idealized. It makes no references to the turmoil and urgency that are often its context. More important, it says too little of one factor determining the salience of truths: namely, the attitudes and desires established already in an agent's cognitive-affective balance. This affective posture is the valorizing lens through which information—meaning salient truths about our circumstances and interests—must pass. Being cautious, the baseball manager doesn't notice or care that the other side would be weakly defended against initiatives he could take. Truths that would be salient for another are irrelevant to him. This is disabling: no one wants to overlook truths that would be useful to him were he to know how to use them. The point is conceded, but no place is made for it because doing that would require that my notion of "salient" truths be qualified by each person's aptitude for using particular truths. We would have to speak of truths which are salient for one but not for another, where the difference is an individual's habits and inhibitions, established attitudes and desires. I usually ignore this variable condition for the salience of truths in order to make the argument simpler. Abstracting from our differences, I suppose that the truths salient to us are all the ones pertinent to our circumstances and generic interests—in health, safety, morality—whatever our personal bent. This has the effect of making us seem more uniform than we are, but that impression is easily corrected when we acknowledge this other condition for the salience of truths. There is also this offsetting point: that attitudes and desires excluded as conditions for the salience of truths are included when it comes to deciding which of the objectives sanctioned by truths should be pursued. Why credit these established attitudes and desires for making this choice when they are neglected as conditions for salience? Because salient truths are not sufficient to make the determination and because nothing else is left to make it.

There is also this residual question: why make so much of truths if passion, in the form of higher-order attitudes, is the final arbiter of choice? For surely, the insufficiency of truths as determinants of choice is even balder than acknowledged. What we call "truths" are only the objectification of an ideology, as truths about free-market economies are applicable only because society has organized itself to create those markets. Why do we have free markets, given the choice between them and systems of barter or centrally managed economies? That might sometimes be a historical contingency; but we do have some choices in these affairs. Having open markets is evidence that some or many people want them. It follows that truths defining the range of objects appropriate to desire—in this case, truths about the operations of the free market in which we live—are themselves the disguised expressions of value, our own or someone else's. Now consider: what is the virtue of disqualifying and repressing one or many desires out of regard for truths that serve the interests of those who profit most from the circumstances represented by the truths?

There might be no benefit whatever to this deception. But this story about truth is mistaken in one respect and misguided in another. It is mistaken for implying that there are no truths untainted by ideology, as truths of physics and physiology (truths, not the pseudo-truths of ideologists) are free of it. The argument is misguided, because it implies that the truths relevant to our circumstances are less obdurate and relevant to choice because they represent states of affairs sponsored by values. For no matter that we are distressed because exploited: the truth acknowledging our distress is significant information. We are not better off for ignoring it or the companion truths that represent its causes and directing values. This only guarantees the perpetuation of whatever control is exercised upon us. Surely, it is better for intelligent choice and autonomy that we know what and where we are. We shall never make choices appropriate to our well-being if we don't know that.

II Salient Truths

Making desire rational would seem to be a good thing, though doing it can work against us; too severe a dose of reason can be disabling. We don't want to murder initiative out of concern for prudence and "the facts." We cannot fly as birds do, though it was also plain for a long time that we could not fly in any way. Was the desire for flight irrational before the invention of balloons and airplanes? Surely, it was not feasible, given our information and resources (hence irrational in this respect); though denouncing the aim—as contradictory—would have been mistaken (and irrational in a different respect), given the results subsequently achieved. Never assume that all the salient truths are against us, that all doors are closed to our initiative. Dewey and James would have us remember this when surveying the truths that constrain us.

Wanting to identify the kinds of salient truths, we find these six: truths about natural laws; truths about states of affairs in the part of the

world where action is to be performed; truths about the moral principles and
sensibilities incumbent in these circumstances, whether natural or conventional; truths about an agent's information, abilities, and determination; truths
about the agent's interests, whether essential and common (e.g., health) or
acquired and distinguishing (e.g., piano playing); and truths about the hierarchically organized network of the agent's attitudes and desires, especially
as they defend these interests.

These are the kinds of truths that limit choice by establishing a domain of objects appropriate for desire in the circumstances at hand (though,
as mentioned above, truths about distinguishing interests are ignored here).
Desire can flout these limits, but not without cost to the well-being of the
agent or those other things for which he or she is responsible. Equally, the
vulnerability ensuing if we neglect these truths is relative. Most of us cannot
climb Everest walking backwards on our hands; we might think anyone crazy
to try. But no one will be more than very surprised by the news that someone
has done it. Mindful of James and Dewey, we don't want people deterred
from doing the things they might usefully and successfully do. Still, truths of
all six kinds represent states of affairs to which many or most of us can only
accommodate ourselves.

We invoke these truths to educate attitude and desire. Six questions,
shadowing the six kinds of truths, direct us. Is it possible in principle, given
the laws of nature, that a particular objective might be achieved? How will
we or others be affected by the probable consequences if the objective is
achieved? Does it satisfy our interests? Is it defensible morally? Is the objective feasible, given the combination of objective circumstances and our information, abilities, and determination? Is it congenial to the network of attitudes and desires established within us? No desire is rational if the first
condition is not met or desirable if the consequences are not moral, and, on
balance, beneficial, given our interests. Where these conditions are satisfied,
all the burden falls on the side of feasibility and attitude. Is this something
that *I* (or *we*) may reasonably desire, because *I* (or *we*) could do or get it?
Is it something *I* (or *we*) want to do, given my (or our) hopes and concerns?

These last two questions express the uncertain, particularized, and
perspectival character of rational choice. Truths about our circumstances may
stymie most of us, but they are a goad to action for some others. Actions

306

unthinkable for one may be appropriate to the talents and attitudes of another. Behavior is not irrational if your ability to produce a desired result justifies ignoring the caution of people less innovative or vigorous than yourself. It would have been irrational for most people, though not for Amundsen, to mount dogsleds for the South Pole. Truths about actual circumstances were coercive for those stay-at-homes, but not for him. Not all the salient truths were against him: those describing his character and equipment were not.

We are reminded that rational desire is less coercive than arithmetic, but more constraining than the freedom to do what we please. There is the triangular space for rational choice mentioned above. It is defined by contingent and necessary truths about our circumstances, by established attitudes and desires, and by the real limits of our intellectual and physical power. What are we capable of doing? How determined are we to do it? Rational desire does not eliminate the role of impulse or passion. It merely restricts them to the boundaries established by truths about natural laws and morals, our situation, and ourselves. It will be hard, we say; but you could do it. Do you want to do it, knowing the obstacles? Some things would never be done if we knew the costs in advance. It may be our good luck that many choices are impulsive. Yet many things tried are not accomplished because, given our character and circumstances, they could not have been. Probably, it would have been better had these things never been tried. Doing them was irrational, though we can never be sure that someone more determined or resourceful could not have succeeded.

III Deliberation and its Subject Matters

Deliberation has several tasks. One, just discussed, is the supply and appraisal of objects suitable for desire. Another is the systematic pursuit of aims considered achievable and appropriate. This is reason directing the achievement of ends fixed by desire. Acting deliberately, repressing impulse, we formulate the map and plan that will guide behavior. The action itself is directed by reason and desire together: the one as we apply and revise the plan, the other as we carry on through frustration or exhilaration to our goal.

There is also this third task: we acknowledge, then choose between, self-interest and the general good. It is incidental to this difference that we pursue self-interest impulsively or with forethought. Both attitudes express our narrow self-concern, the one by the urgency of its desires, the other in its calculation of personal advantage. The principal models of economic behavior and the puzzles of rational decision making (how shall we reconcile mutually exclusive benefits to our advantage?) assume this second point of view, with little or no regard for the well-being of the community at large. Or they cite communitarian interests, but only to the point of calculating behaviors which make the communal good instrumental to our own.

Deliberation moderates, or even transforms, this perspective. It makes us sensitive to the truths that define our situation, truths reporting that the space in which we live and move is larger than that defined by our self-interest. For it is true that other people reasonably want for themselves some of the things that we want, and true that they may have as much power for getting them or as much right to them as we ourselves. Ignoring these truths makes desire irrational in the sense of making it stupid: we deprive ourselves of information relevant to our situation, hence information significant for deciding whether particular objects for desire are appropriate or not.

The use of such information is also interesting in this other way: that learning truths about our place in the world, as one among many like ourselves, alters some of the attitudes which determine the choice of objects for desire. Egoism is transformed into attitudes more plainly communitarian as we are obliged by salient truths to consider the relevant objects for desire: we feed the hungry because doing that is feasible and appropriate.

I assume that egoism is an attitude or complex of attitudes and that these attitudes are revised, because educated, when we find ourselves located within a network of reciprocally related, mutually affecting agencies. Suppose that hammering planks makes a terrible noise, scaring away the only birds which carry and plant the seeds that become the trees from which the boards are cut. Being active carpenters, we cut down all the trees, putting ourselves out of work. Our calculations have been too narrowly self-interested. We have ignored the fact that relations called instrumental for the purposes of human desire are also consequential and reciprocal. Things are mutually engaged and mutually affecting. We concede that every living thing has its self-interest, even that nonliving things are stable systems with a sustained character, hence an integrity. We acknowledge our place among these disparate things, perceiving their interests and the sometimes binding mutual interest among us. We set all this against the perspective of narrow self-concern. We do, or can do, all this without acknowledging that many of the agents to which we are reciprocally related are people like ourselves.

How shall we choose between self-interest and a communitarian good? Probably, we would never choose the latter were there not evidence that this choice is, by and large, the one more favorable to our own well-being. But we want evidence—meaning truths—that this is so. Egoism has its point, with some hardly disputed truths to define and defend it. But egoism is mute about those relations which are mutually consequential for the people they engage. Reciprocal relations include not only those of friendship and family life, but also all those which bring us into mutually consequential relationships with nature at large. One imagines a jigsaw puzzle with every piece but one in place. The relations of the other pieces define the one remaining empty space, as the piece filling it helps define the spaces of the pieces contiguous to it. Like these pieces, we take up places and roles in settings where each participant has both an interest of its own and consequential relations to the other agents or stable systems.

It is easier to perceive this reciprocity and the common interest it generates when the agents engaging us are other human beings; for they can be counted on to let us know that their wants and objectives are no less urgent than our own. Reasoned desire, here called *morality*, is the demand that we subordinate the perspective of self-interest to that of reciprocity. We make ourselves responsible for knowing and responding to the truth that each of us, however self-preoccupied, is reciprocally engaged with some or many others. Unwillingness to shape desire with regard for this truth is often or usually the evidence of stupidity, savagery, or wickedness.

Think of the mythic farmer. He considers many of his personal desires within the context of his work. Living on and by the land, he must not damage this asset. Of course, farmers do harm their land through carelessness or ignorance; but that is not typically their aim. A tacit bargain is struck: the farmer takes care of the land, and the land rewards him for his effort. He abstains from some things that might gratify him—such as quick, profitable crops that leach the soil—not only because of concern for his own long-term interests, but also because of desiring that he, his family, and fellow workers may effectively occupy a niche in an environment of mutually affecting, mutually supporting agencies.

Someone living high in a tower within a big city, someone who sleeps late, hates grass, and spends most nights in a bar, does not feel that he misses anything for having no place in nature. Most of us living in cities, unfamiliar even to our neighbors, resemble this man more than we do the farmer. We are located, nevertheless, within a network of mutually consequential relations. Hearing every radio and sink in the building, solicited and petitioned by cults and sects unimagined, sharing the subway and streets with people more exotic than an MTV video, we know that we are not alone. Nor do we pretend to be. Neighbors organize, and we participate. Someone unknown needs help, and we sometimes give it. Here where people are thought to be most self-concerned, we may be sensitive as a trip-wire to those affecting or affected by us.

How is attention diverted from hypnotic self-interest to the reciprocities that engage us? A dominating self-concern makes it seem as if all the world is constructed of the bits and pieces energized by individual desires. Philosophy, with its respect for the arguments of skeptics and solipsists, tolerates this bias, especially when modern-day Kantians present it rigorously as a "pragmatic" theory of action. Theirs, however, is a specially cultivated, intellectual taste. People out of touch with the arguments of philosophers, people who are disappointed, frustrated, or confounded, do not share the illusion of world-making. They are engaged, every moment, in mutually consequential relations with people or things that resist them.

Resolute oblivion to people and things is unreasonable. Why? Because truths about our circumstances, including truths about the integrities of the things that engage us, are pertinent information for one who appraises his or her desires. What will be the effects of my conduct on others? What will they do to me? Surely, these questions are relevant; though, equally, this information is ignored if we persist in the illusion that the world has no character apart from the montage constructed in service to our interests. This conceit is false to our circumstances, inimical to other things, and bad for us.

We may acknowledge that other people are right to demand that their welfare be considered when a plan is enacted. Isn't it equally reasonable that we consider the integrity of other stable systems, from earthworms to the Earth itself, unable to plead for themselves? Desire is rational when we anticipate the effects incurred as we act on them. Desires are insufficiently reasonable when we ignore the consequential relations which they promote. This consideration for other things does not entail that we prefer their well-being to our own, only that we are willing to see their interests considered.

Our regard for them might be casual and transitory, as no one cares very much that kitchen lights bother pigeons roosting on windowsills. There is, however, a point of prudent sensibility, for we may only begin to care about other things, living or not, when our behaviors alter the environment to our disadvantage, as polluted air is bad for us.

We ponder the idea that there is a natural order of things, perhaps a system of mutually consequential relations in which we have a place. One thinks of Augustine:

> The peace of all things is the tranquility of order. Order is the distribution which allots things equal and unequal, each to its own place. And hence, though the miserable, in so far as they are such, do certainly not enjoy peace, but are severed from the tranquility of order in which there is no disturbance, nevertheless, inasmuch as they are deservedly and justly miserable, they are by their very misery connected with order. They are not, indeed, conjoined with the blessed, but they are disjoined from them by the law of order. And though they are disquieted, their circumstances are not withstanding adjusted to them, and consequently they have some tranquility of order, and therefore some peace. But they are wretched because, although not wholly miserable, they are not in that place where any mixture of misery is impossible. They would, however, be more wretched if they had not that peace which arises from being in harmony with the natural order of things.[1]

The fixed places of Plato's *Republic* are here extended to all being. It should follow that desire in each of us is sensitive to knowledge of our proper place. Knowing what space I occupy, I should know better what to desire.

There is also this corollary: that the creature fitting a particular place will have an intrinsic nature that suits it to its place and role. This is reason enough for considering the truths about me before acting on those uninformed desires which express my unconsidered passions. Knowledge of my proper place and qualifying habits (whether learned or innate) should determine what I want. Desire uninflected by the knowledge of the roles I am qualified to play can lead only to self-perversion. There is the implied dictum of the phrase "my station and its duties": we are encouraged to identify that place, then to prepare ourselves to fill it. Desires expressing our self-concern are to be transformed by the recognition of our duties and qualifications, then by accommodation to our proper role.

This is an ancient solution, one voicing the hope that all our troubles would dissolve if we could return to the system of fixed places from which we have strayed. Never mind the evidence of evolution and technology as they refute the idea that there are fixed places for us humans. This Augustinian view is, nevertheless, a critical point of reference. For there is a question to answer: how far have we evolved from a fixed biological, if not cosmological, niche? Is it safe to jettison every truth about those places and our qualifications for them on the way to satisfying desire?

IV Is Our Place in the World Fixed?

The idea that we live within, and qualify for, a set of cosmological, biologically, or socially fixed places is barely credible to us. Niches disappear and environments change, so that creatures qualified for one place find their innate or acquired abilities inappropriate to their new circumstances. It may be a disadvantage in the new place that we have a nature qualifying us for the other place. The less there are of natural ecology and innate qualifications, the more we require the support of a surrogate culture. But now, as creatures of a world we have made for ourselves, we may be more remote than ever from the peace that an established order was said to provide. Why should I want the place that the political order has created for me if I truly believe that this order has been conceived and organized for the advantage of others, without regard for its cost to me? Accommodating myself to a place within this system might only be evidence that "education" has disabled me for appraising my circumstances and best interests. I may have no recourse: there may be no political choice, as there is no state of nature to which I might return. Either way, I may feel and be displaced.

We assume that natural ecology is the most likely paradigm for Augustine's myth, though the character of our biological inheritance is not always so plain. We humans are not like some moss or bird having a biological niche with stable reciprocal relations to other things. We did have a fixed, if plastic, nature and an ecological niche (or several of them) millions of years ago; but there is all the history of the practical arts to separate us from that niche. We no longer cleave self-consciously, as other things relate instinctively, to natural places within an ecological system. With technology as the engine of transformation, we remake ourselves so as to use and enjoy the new systems of places that we invent to secure us. However damaging our effects on other things, we are ever more successful at protecting ourselves from them.

But notice this other side. Having reduced the exposure to our natural place by leaving or transforming it, we are vulnerable to all the effects, expected or not, of the new places we create for ourselves. We typically look ahead, not behind, when it is exigent that we sensitize ourselves to opportunities and risks in the spaces newly created or transformed. That anxiety too often blinds us to continuities in ourselves and our circumstances. We are too much obsessed by the contexts and qualifying natures that we successively make for ourselves, as if nothing of our original place in nature still constrains us. Yet surely, we do retain a fixed, if generic, nature, even when partially exiled from the natural places for which it suited us. The natural order invoked by Augustine is never less than the warp on which we string the more detailed, cultural patterns of our lives.

These continuities are apparent when determinable natural abilities (being able to work with other people) achieve specific expression in our learned behaviors (working as fishermen, teachers, or miners). Our complex, determinable nature is sometimes hard to discern, because so many behaviors appear to have nothing but convention as their sponsor. Yet, we are rarely or never in the position of being unconstrained by a natural determinable as it receives more determinate, conventional expression. We speak one or another language, but always, if Chomsky is believed,[2] a language giving more determinate expression to the biologically founded grammar common to us. The possibilities for cooperation among people and the kinds of interchange possible between humans and other things are also limited and determinable. Every particular activity, be it work, friendship, or war, gives expression to one or another of these natural modes of reciprocity.

V Truth-Informed Attitudes and Desires as Determinants of Choice

Desire is made reasonable by directing it in ways that are appropriate to truths obtaining at two levels: first is the mix of truths representing natural and innate, but determinable, roles and relations; second are truths representing the historically contingent expressions of these determinables. Maternity is biologically fixed; but there are differences among practices for bearing and rearing children. Women educate themselves by identifying the natural roles for which they are suited and the historically conditioned, conventional ways of filling those roles. The mother-to-be assumes or considers the salient truths before surveying and appraising the choices appropriate to her.

A contentious example makes the point. That children are born to women is a natural determinable; that women think or feel any particular way during pregnancy is a contingency. That women may happily anticipate the birth of their children in reasonable, because sensitive to a woman's actual relation to the child she carries. Many of the hopes for her baby are affected by her culture. Wanting for him or her what the culture promises or approves, she looks for direction in the established attitudes of her people. Getting an education, marrying well, finding work appropriate to one's talents: these things are good for us, the culture says. And this is true, because the culture rewards these behaviors. Wanting these things for one's children, waiting for the time when the children want these goods for themselves, is another case of desire educated by truths.

Suppose, however, that a woman affirms her natural power for bearing children, while renouncing the things valued by her culture. She wants different things for her children, preferring, for example, that they never learn the interdependence favored by the culture she rejects. Truths once affirmed are renounced, thereby changing the possible options for desire. These renunciations and substitutions are all the more dramatic if we suppose that a woman reflecting on her natural power regrets the dependence it forces on her, however temporarily. She gladly renounces maternity because she wants the freedom promised by molecular biology. Human children, it speculates, may someday be cultivated, like oysters on a string, in some appropriate solution. Once "born," they may be raised and educated, even to responsible adulthood, in suitably mechanized environments. The traditional role of women—indeed, of parents and their sexuality—is superseded by technological advances only a little beyond our present competence. Why should it be unreasonable for women and men to desire that this possibility be realized?

Here is a situation where the choice of objects for desire is made by one or a complex of attitudes and desires within the network of attitudes and desires. Truths may represent our generic biological inheritance and the conventional ways learned for expressing it. They may specify the likely penalties for ignoring these conventions. But equally, truths establishing a domain of appropriate objects for desire, some of them contraries, are not sufficient to decide which one we should want. Accordingly, there is a question about the sufficiency of truths; or rather, we need to confirm that reflection upon truths is not, and cannot be, sufficient to determine an object for desire, Augustine notwithstanding.

We might have supposed that truths alone would be sufficient to define the domain of appropriate objects for desire, though several points confirm that this is not so. First is the infinity of truths relevant to every situation, hence to any deliberation regarding the desires appropriate to it. No one could know all these truths; consequently, no one could ever identify the restricted domain of objects rendered appropriate by them. Second is the contrariety of some of the objects for desire qualified as appropriate by salient truths: you may have a car, but it will have a steering wheel on the right or left, not usually both at once. Third is the fact that salient truths are not a calculus for deriving some maximally appropriate object for desire. These truths can only limit the range of appropriate choices. With all the information before us, it remains for us to decide. Fourth, and decisively, the range of appropriate objects for desire is determined by the combination of salient truths and the network of shifting, but hierarchically organized, values and desires. Attitudes that dominate from one perspective are subsidiary from another, sometimes for reasons that are independent of truths. The differing calibrations of these attitudes guarantee that truths can never be sufficient in themselves to determine the array of objects appropriate for desire.

Suppose I am driving a car. I know all the traffic rules, all there is to know about the streets and roads, everything about the design of the car, and everything about current traffic flow and the other contingencies, including all the facts of my history. All this information may affect me causally as I choose my destination; but none of it entails that I ought to choose some particular destination. Truths tell me the possible destinations and the likely consequences of choosing one or another of them. But that is all they do. It remains for me to determine, first, which of these possible objectives is appropriate to me, relative to the set of my higher-order attitudes and desires, then which choice shall be mine.

It may seem implausible to ascribe this power to attitudes, given our vague notions of faculty psychology: attitudes seem too vague for the task of making choices. But this is not quite right, given some things we know or surmise, including the network of hierarchically organized attitudes and desires within us, some of them ephemeral, others founded in our cognitive-affective balance; our immediately preceding history, with its effects on the configuration and relative dominance of attitudes within the network; and, finally, the process of deliberation itself. Deliberation is fact-finding in service to attitude. For attitudes relate to one another rather like the aperture of a camera. Deliberation focuses the attitudes by supplying the information which fixes the relations among them. There is some critical point at which the inhibitions on action are released or, alternatively, where a stolid agent is roused to move itself in the direction that attitude prescribes. Nothing in this account identifies the mental activity which earns description as "attitude choosing among the appropriate objects for desire." This citation of conditions and activities only pretends to specify, crudely, the activities and conditions having this effect.

Suppose we accept, if only provisionally, this metaphorical rendering of the relevant affective and cognitive functions. How do we reduce the slippage between the truths defining a situation and the network of attitudes and desires left responsible for choosing among the objectives judged appropriate because of the truths? Granting that truths can only shrink the domain of appropriate desires, what is to count as a rational way of informing attitudes as they determine what options to pursue? I propose this historical-dialectical solution.

VI Aristotle, Nietzsche, and Dewey on Truth and Choice

Aristotle, Nietzsche, and Dewey define our position. The first two are antitheses, the third a synthesizing, sober middle ground.

People of every time may think of themselves as living in the wake or at the brink of something grand. If this claim has sometimes been inflated, ours is not. We are the last generation of humans obliged to accept their biological nature because the first able to change its genetic inheritance. Truths that were once no less necessary in practical terms than those of mathematics now seem plastic and contingent.

Truths establishing regions of appropriate choice have always been a mix of some that are revisable and others that are fixed. Truths about local conventions, learned abilities, and our moral and civil laws might change, but truths about physical and biological determinables could not. Lower-order determinations vary—we are vegetarians or carnivores—but higher-order determinables are settled. Things sent aloft might be rocks or rockets, but the laws of motion don't change. Citing these fixed truths about us was comforting, because it established a kind of Augustinian peace: unable to change natural laws or the course of natural transformations, we could agree that our only choices were those left open by them. No matter, then, if biology and climate were beyond our control; we could live within the constraints they establish.

Our situation is transformed, because determinables once thought fixed have submitted to our understanding and control. It has been true for a long time that someone disliking the shape of his nose or chin can change it. Now we imagine altering them before birth. This is hopeful but frightening: we cannot depend on being forever the creatures we have been. Molecular biology, most conspicuously, has introduced truths which transform the domain of appropriate choices. Our generic and personal identity begins to fall within the circle of reasonable objects for desire. Do we understand the consequences of this power? We, as a species, are the viable outcome of aeons of biological evolution. Will we do as well for ourselves when tinkering with our genes is commonplace?

Many things that occurred before Aristotle (Plato or Augustine) alienated us from our ecological niche, but nothing we had done or could do was sufficient to alter our character to the point of making us unrecognizable to ourselves over a few generations or less. That was an invisible possibility, one hidden by the perception of an ample, vastly elaborated set of physical, biological, and social stabilities within and around us. This settled order guarantees that, even today, a substantial part of all we do is fixed in ways that we cannot, so far, alter. Change is real; the physical constitution of individuals and species is perpetually transformed. It is, nevertheless, pap that everything about us is plastic and revisable if only we will intrude on nature, altering it physically or using some different conceptual system to think it. There are many truths about us humans which apply almost universally over many generations. That we are tool- and language-users, impulsive but consciously self-regulating, sometimes reckless but susceptible to feelings of guilt: these are qualities of no creatures but ourselves, whatever our circumstances.

This is Aristotle's congenial view. He steadies us, while Nietzsche everywhere disrupts our confidence in the established order and rhythm. His "will to power" is the impulse to remake us and our circumstances in whatever way seems appropriate to a vision of our transfigured selves. Nietzsche believed that many people are animated by these overreaching desires, though only a minority have the persistence and self-conviction to satisfy their ambitions. Everyone else settles for the inert, uniform ways of a culture, complaining sometimes, but never daring to violate the boundary between imitation and originality.

These are people enfeebled by dread of their vulnerability. They escape into faceless, socially approved routine. Their standard practices are canonized as rules and truths, so that conformists everywhere describe themselves as "typical" or "correct." These imitators, the "herd," believe that predictability is the expression of good learning. But more, their practices are to define the choices appropriate to anyone's desire; each of us is to mimic them. We who do the "right" things are recognized for "being in the truth." Other behaviors are "distortions" of these "standard," recommended practices. They are "inappropriate," "irrelevant," or "new." Law-abiding citizens despise and fear the nonconformists among them, perhaps because they want to believe that there is something natural or exalted about their own behavior. They will do anything they can, always in the name of public order and morals, to eradicate the radical, transvaluing few.

These renegades are threatening because they prove, merely by being different, that nothing in our standard practices is correct by dint of being constrained by significant truths. Or better, the standard practices do not win their adherence merely because they are prescribed as truths that should direct their behaviors. Nietzsche might have been reluctant to say that there are no truths relevant to our choice of objects for desire. He surely was contemptuous of typical behaviors redescribed as normative truths.

Aristotle supposed that truth is often, if not always, a sufficient directive to desire. Perceiving what is good or right or appropriate in our circumstances should be enough to make us desire that thing. Nietzsche is not bound by this citation of the facts incumbent on us. Obdurate facts are a delusion—one often sponsored by the self-protecting interests of the herd—if will is an engine for transforming objective circumstances. For there are few, or no, absolutely relevant truths and, equally, no objects for desire that are absolutely obligatory because appropriate to these truths.

We reduce the cogency of truths as a guide for desire by saying that all the truths in the world can define the world exhaustively only as it has existed up to the current moment. They cannot prescribe either means or aims to an agent wanting to gratify his immanent, impelling will. This act of self-determination is, for Nietzsche, spontaneous. There are no sufficient conditions for it among the truths representing any or all the states of affairs currently or previously obtaining. How could our knowledge of them be the appropriate limit on desire when that knowledge is always retrospective — hence a specification of the conditions that have prevailed — while desire is forever prospective? Truths could limit desire only by crippling it.

How shall we address the future if there are no truths to direct us? Nietzsche's answer seems to me to derive from Kant's *Critique of Judgment:*[3] the route pursued as we act on a value expresses an intrinsic, ordering form, though the rule directing us is not formulated or is subject, when formulated, to an infinity of interpretations. We observers cannot tell exactly what schema or interpretation someone else is using when desire drives him or her to remake part of the world. We cannot be certain that his or her way of interpreting the situation is right, reasonable, cogent, or even consistent. There are many ways to skin a cat and many ways to live, even here in the midst of practices that once seemed settled and uncontroversial. We who are mystified or offended by some particular accommodation should be chastened by the memory of other times when practices considered deviant and intolerable were accepted and aped as the new orthodoxy. We, too, should not object when someone who has no direct, deleterious effects on us follows the thread of his or her own life. He or she is an artist of a sort, developing the form that is immanent already in the bias of his or her cognitive-affective balance.[4]

Nietzsche sometimes illustrates this point with tightrope-walkers: they jump or turn when we expect them to go forward. Tightropes make risk emphatic; but they are straight and too constraining. Consider, instead, a dancer playing a role for which there are established steps. This is a virtuoso. Her phrasing and speed, posture and execution, are all her own. Her audience knows the role and knows what she must do next; but they sit transfixed because they do not know what she will do. What is more, she doesn't know. Feeling strong, hearing the music, challenged by the tension in the house, she pushes the limits of her agility. Taking these risks, she remakes the role. The audience weeps and roars; but no one can tell exactly what she has done. There were no truths sufficient to direct her. No one will formulate a rule that others could teach or learn.

Someone asks later if the dancer had imagined what she would do, giving herself reasons, including truths, for doing that particular thing. She has often practiced and thought about the role; but, no, she answers: the impulse to dance as she did was not rehearsed or deliberate in that classic way. It was the expression of her strength in the moment. There was nothing more reflective than this, nothing to be generalized or argued or taught. The desire that moved her was not rational in Aristotle's sense, though surely it was rational in the spirit of Kant's *Critique of Judgment*. The dance was elaborated continuously and coherently. It had order, development, and proportion. There was form, and one might call that form a rule—though the rule and all that was rational in the dance was immanent in the steps, having no separate expression or justification.[5]

Will, embroidering on the materials available to it, creates something new. Nietzsche puts no store in settled conditions or intrinsic forms. Everything of worth is our creation: we have desired, then made, it. We are self-valuing and self-creating. We live beyond ourselves, acknowledging no truths that would constrain us as we transform ourselves and our situation. Where is the energy for this creative act? In will. Like Samson feeling the pillars, we take the measure of our circumstances; not so that we may limit the will, but only so that our exertions may be directed more effectively. Are these creations appropriate? Who is to say? What is the measure? Like the dance, the thing is good as it is done. It shows its value to those who can see it. It is self-justifying and appropriate in being itself.

What are the principal instruments for creating values? Remember Nietzsche's complaint: that it is the will of those who are intellectually adroit but physically lame that is most powerful. They create the conceptual systems, the interpretations, that determine how the world shall be made over, in thought and action. There is, however, no standpoint in Nietzsche from which to adjudicate disputes about the conceptual systems to be used for remaking some part of the world: only the raw power of wills in conflict settles these disputes. Fighting one another for the right to say that the world is as *we* see it, we have little opportunity to enjoy the worlds remade so that desire is satisfied.

Is there an alternative way of deciding what to think, what to desire, what to do? The one alternative at hand is Aristotle's view that we inhabit a world of plainly differentiated, fixed places. Knowledge of our proper place, coupled to knowledge of the abilities that qualify us for it, is sufficient to teach us what objects are appropriate to desire. Compare this with Nietzsche's dictum that we must be perpetually self-transcending: no one is to concede that the place he occupies is his final, settled condition. We could resolve this quarrel by choosing one of the sides, but that would be costly, because both are required for understanding value and truth as goads and limits to action. These are the carrot and the stick: there is desire focused on an object that comes to be articulated only as we are moved to possess it; equally, there are truths that limit both the content and execution of our desires.

Dewey provides for both. He is sometimes two thinkers tangled in one: the pragmatic idealist for whom reality is the outcome of inquiry and the world-engaged pragmatist for whom inquiry is the discipline that solves real-world problems. Dewey the idealist inveighs against the correspondence theory of truth.[6] This side of him obscures the difference between constructions and hypotheses, the one as we make a difference, the other as we represent differences already made. This is Dewey, in alliance with James, cutting away the dead weight of a nature opposed to human will.

There is also the Dewey turned inquisitorial, the Dewey aroused by threats to our well-being. What has gone wrong? Who and where are we? What might we do, given our circumstances and the resources available to us? What are the likely effects if we do one or another of these things? Surely there is some historical record of the steps taken by people as troubled as we are. What are the interests implicated and the strategies most likely to do them justice? Each of these questions is a request for information—for truths—about our situation. We necessarily defer to them, because problem solving is only a delusion if it carries on without regard for the circumstances where problems are solved.

Gathering information takes time, so that impulse control is a necessary adjunct to inquiry. Inhibition is the effect of deliberation as it mediates between frustration and the reaction that occurs unthinkingly as we act to clear the way before us. We buy time, thereby averting a more expensive, less effective solution. Notice, too, that there is no categorical imperative, no principle that abstracts from our situation, justifying the neglect of its specificities. Dewey prefers that our situation be seen in its particularity. We are to consider specific obstacles, confusions, and afflictions as we strike a productive accommodation to the people and things that engage us.

Dewey in this other mode is unfailingly judicious, tough, and practical. What is more, he is a metaphysical realist as regards the existence and character of a world we alter, but do not make. Dewey is also sober, neither fecklessly sanguine nor morose about our prospects for finding a way through the problems that beset us. These are sometimes the trivial hiccoughs in a system that works. Other times, the breakdown is more fundamental, as in

American cities today. Or technological developments—including bionic engineering and molecular biology—encourage us to transform ourselves in ways that were previously unimagined. But what are we to do in circumstances with no history, hence no truths or even well-founded probabilities to define the region of choice?

We solve a problem by first diagnosing it: something has broken down; a system which did work works no longer. Or we propose transforming present circumstances so that an interest may be satisfied. Either way, we shall want to know the circumstances that currently obtain. Has the car stopped working? Is there anyone to whom we can give the cat? These are questions about material circumstances. Complementary to them are some different, but equally critical, matters of fact. What have we been trying to do? What is the reigning conceptualization? How is it challenged by new empirical data or a different theory? Is the inequity among us the acceptable outcome of our freedom, or is some of it the consequence of inefficiency and collusion?

We add these cerebral considerations because circumstances alone do not create a problem. It is only our way of appraising situations that has this effect: heart attacks in human beings are a problem; those in mice are not. Caring about the one, we are mostly indifferent to the other. Calling a situation problematic is a judgment, one that we express after surveying pertinent, but disappointing, truths.

There is a difference in the gravity of a problem and in the strategy and resources required for solving it, when problems are, as I shall call them, Aristotelian or Nietzschean. Tires go flat, and we fix them. Wanting the car to go, understanding why it does not, we do what is required to restore the previous state of affairs. This is an Aristotelian problem. Constant in our desire, knowing the pertinent truths, having the skills required, we repair the damage and carry on as before. Or we change some things in order to get the effect we desire; though we make only those changes that are typically made in situations like this one. So, getting to work is always a problem, but usually one that has an established solution. Or our working hypothesis is confounded, but only in a way that leaves a predictable alternative: expecting sunny weather, we get rain, though we know how to protect ourselves from it. Each of these problems disrupts a current equilibrium, but only for as long as it takes us to adjust our behavior in a standardized way. Having relevant truths and constantly held values to frame the situation, we use well-honed skills to solve the problem.

These are examples appropriate to Aristotle's notion that we occupy stable places in nature and society. Instinct and training enable us to do whatever we need to do in order to restore the equable flow of things and our place among them. Even Nietzsche would take no exception to these examples. Herd morality requires a social order of settled, safe places. Prizing stability, wanting uniformity and predictability, we hurry to restore the old order.

Nietzschean problems are forward-looking. They occur as circumstances are transformed so that we may realize an idealization having, perhaps, no prior instances. Utopian social practice is problematic in this respect; but so is it problematic when any of us tries to do something that we have not done before. Other people may have the experience and habits appropriate to solving the problem, but we beginners do not. Baking an apple pie is, for us, a step into the void. There is a resolute will and maybe some estimates of the likely outcome; but there are no truths known to us that limit the domain of appropriate actions.

Our philosophic problem, but everyone's real-life task, is that of joining Aristotle to Nietzsche. How shall value be linked to truth in ways that limit the array of objects appropriate for desire? Their relation is apparent wherever the truth specifying a thing also expresses our values, without the need for saying that this state of affairs is desirable or not. Someone ill has only to mention his health, temporarily lost, for us to know that he values it. The problem becomes severe only as "pertinent" truths seem less and less constraining, to the point where a recitation of the facts, even supposing them to be undisputed, has no limiting effect on our choices. We would certainly approve a prenatal dental treatment that guarantees no cavities for life, with no side effects. Should we also approve the bionic part-replacement that would allow us humans to carry on forever, like Neurath's boat? Consequentialist reasons, founded on truths or probable truths, justify the dental project; but there seem to be insufficient truths limiting our views on the program for perpetuating individual lives. In the one case, desire informed by truths makes its choice. In the other, desire is still confused, not because of insufficient information, but rather because of conflicting attitudes. If one attitude would have us go on forever, another takes solace in our finitude. How shall we determine the appropriate objectives, or decide among them?

Dewey invokes the idea of deliberation:

I am convinced that contemporary discussion of values and valuation suffers from confusion of the two radically different attitudes — that of direct, active, non-cognitive experience of goods and bads and that of valuation, the latter being simply a mode of judgment like any other form of judgment, differing in that its subject-matter happens to be a good or a bad instead of a horse or planet or curve. But unfortunately for discussions, "true value" means two radically different things: to prize and appraise; to esteem and to estimate; to find good in the sense described above, and to judge it to be good, to *know* it as good.[7]

Experiencing health as good, we prize it. Later or concurrently, we appraise the condition, finding reasons to justify the desire. What sorts of reasons are these? They are truths telling what we are and do when healthy and also what effects we have on other things. It is the consequentialist estimation of these truths which prompts us to say that, yes, health is better than sickness. But notice that this estimate of the consequence adds nothing evaluative to them: we merely report that certain things cause health whereas others cause sickness and that people have good consequentialist reasons for preferring the one to the other: being sick, they can't work or play. Value is already assumed as the value favoring health.

Still, this linkage is not identity. The citation of truths is not always the specification of a value. This is apparent when someone cites a litany of truths, describing wealth, beauty, and power, before adding that he or she does not want these things for him or herself. The conjunction of truth and value is synthetic in this and every case: one may know the truths but deny the value of whatever they represent. The linkage seems tighter than it is only when the judgment concluding our survey of relevant truths is almost universally shared. Then the mere recitation of salient truths seems to be the incantation of an allied value. A similar effect occurs in anyone who regularly and unselfconsciously satisfies himself; there are, he assumes, relevant truths justifying (perhaps entailing) his values.

Aristotelian problems invite this conflation of truths and values. Living in circumstances that we have stabilized for our own good reasons, having views widely shared as to the desirability of many things — including taxes, debt, and toothaches — we have only to recite the truths applying to a situation before invoking their habitually coupled values. Desire might be decoupled from these truths: we might ignore the effects of disease on our ability to live and thrive. But this is so contrary to the bias of desire as to seem paradoxical: expressing our freedom to choose the objects of desire, we would at the same time be wanting something that would subvert the freedom. Still, we acknowledge contingency in the relation of truth and desire. We could perversely, but consciously, subvert our well-being—though it violates the spirit of Aristotelian deliberation that anyone comprehending his or her situation would do that.

We get, in this Aristotelian way, a justification and excuse for doing such things as please us. We create stable systems, then fix those that break down. Where all the neighbors live in houses like our own, we have a vast stock of shared, crossed, and overlapping truths. We also have consensus about their use. Everyone knows immediately that a neighbor is dismayed by water in the basement or a hole in the roof. Each can help the other, because everyone is somewhat skilled at doing and getting the things appropriate to the desires they share. Given the linkage of the truths and desires that characterize us, we are collectively in the truth.

Many things prized unreflectively are valued all the more keenly after reflection has shown that their consequences are beneficial. It is not surprising that we should work to sustain systems having these benefits (e.g., cities) or that we should often resort to instrumental relations having a desired effect (e.g., educating children). Much more difficult are those occasions when an established instrumental relation is no longer viable or when change has made a previous stability irretrievable. An estuary silts over, killing a port; violence destroys business and civility in a city. Unable to recover the old values, we create new ones. These are Nietzschean problems. Truth's relation to value is more uncertain in them. For what truths are salient when we propose doing what we have not done before or salient when the world has come unstuck? What are the values appropriate to the context established by these truths? We may not know. One thinks again of the dancer. Excitement and pleasure are our first responses to her. We like what she has done, and we let her know it. But then we wait for the review of a thoughtful critic: what did happen? A good critic tells us, by locating this performance within its historical context. Why was it good, musicality and technique apart? Does it extend the line of developments previously seen or open possibilities not previously exploited? The critic supplies a considered opinion.

We are closer now to a procedure for reducing the uncertainty in situations where attitude is left to choose an object for desire from among those established as appropriate by salient truths. How does this procedure carry us beyond the characterization proposed above? Only by extrapolation: objectives appropriate for desire are those falling within the space defined by truths representing what is and has been, coupled to estimates of what might be. It is this consequentialist reflection that informs attitudes, though it never displaces the power of choice from attitudes to truths. Someone driving over a cliff at full speed knows well enough what the consequence will be. Pathological, we say. Yes, but evidence that the autonomy of the passions is not altogether compromised by the information which informs and controls them. Nor could it be in the circumstances stressed by Nietzsche, where there is a scarcity of salient truths or of salient truths known to us.

We know, for example, the conditions for, and consequences of, sexual reproduction. There are truths pertinent to both. Suppose, however, that someone proposes to liberate us from the burdens of natural reproduction and parental responsibility. We are to create synthetic fertilized eggs, bringing them to term in fish tanks. The infants produced are to be raised in Skinner boxes, even to the age of thirty. Justice is done to the children; the adults are liberated—but not liberated, perhaps, for sexual license. Someone far-sighted proposes that we alter human genes to eliminate sexuality, since it is vestigial and distracting in our new circumstances. Better that we do without it: better for efficiency, better for health. What shall we say?

Dewey's proposal is general, but cogent: "Nietzsche would probably not have made so much of a sensation, but he would have been within the limits of wisdom, if he had confined himself to the assertion that all judgment, in the degree in which it is critically intelligent, is a transvaluation of prior values."[8] This transvaluation of values is just the rethinking of old values in circumstances altered so that one cannot have either the old truths or the old values.

There is, nevertheless, the basis for continuity within deliberation. We locate it with a question: is this a break with the past or its transformation? Can we tell, with hindsight, how this change has occurred and what aspects of former things are preserved in it? Truths about our history and circumstances are the essential ground for extrapolations to future truths and values. What is, or would be appropriate, for us in these revised circumstances? There is no handle on this question if we do not *start* by asking about previous consequences of the matter at issue. What are the appropriate objects for desire? The ones extrapolated from objectives found appropriate in the past. Those were objectives appropriate both to truths about our circumstances and to the informed attitudes that directed our choices. What does "appropriate" signify here? Just the fact that these were objectives consistent with, or congenial to, the attitudes dominating our choices in previous circumstances. There was, for example, the calculation that something or other would be no threat to health or public order, when one or the other of these was a higher-order desire. Dewey, after Aristotle, supposed that information about times past is appropriate to current circumstances when the costs to health or civility are relevant, but unknown. But nothing in our regard for truth is reactionary. We get risk and safety too: even Columbus used a navigator.

This formulation is problematic, however. Here are two examples, one to show its strength, the other its weakness.

Suppose that genetic engineers were able to devise people tailored to a function. We could realize the ideal of Plato's *Republic* by creating people who are distinctly aggressive, intelligent, or smart enough only for manual labor. The people themselves would be happy and productive. The society they comprised would be harmonious and efficient. Is this an appropriate objective? These consequences are valued; but this is not reason enough for approving the strategy. Even Plato had his doubts: the first soul to select a next life in the myth of Er chooses the greatest tyranny. Having come down from a well-ordered state, he had learned virtue by habit, not wisdom.[9]

We infer that extrapolations from our historical condition are speculative but constraining: the mix of freedom and responsibility is a condition for moral judgment in our world and also, so far as we can anticipate, a condition for it in successor worlds. Genetic engineers can hardly know what to create if they have no information about the consequences of things, hence no reasons (no relevant truths) to consider as they decide what things are worth retaining or improving. Still, we cannot be certain that truths limiting the range of appropriate choices in our current world are relevant to that new world. Having a class of contented, but narrowly talented, workers may not have consequences that are deleterious to the welfare of citizens in the new order, these workers included. It is principally our historical experience that makes us suspicious of this promise. Relying on this experience as the basis for extrapolations to odd cases, we are conservative.

The second example requires that our present circumstances be altered so radically as to make extrapolation impossible. Suppose that Earth is struck by a comet, annihilating all life as we have known it, though a few people survive. Little that we have known seems appropriate to them. They would have to thrash about for as long as it takes to learn the consequential relations in their altered circumstances. There would be a period of trial and error, of wanting something only to regret having it, of trying again so as to refine or enlarge some uncertain benefit. Deliberation on truths about the past would have little or no advantage. Every decision regarding the appropriate objects for desire would depend on discoveries about unpredictable, consequential relations in the new circumstances.

We summarize the difference between these two examples by saying that extrapolation from the past to the future is possible in the one case, but not the other. A useful figure represents this difference. Suppose we are asked to draw a line through a point. What direction should it go? If truths representing current circumstances are the point, then truths about relevant history are an anterior point. The direction of the line to be drawn is plain. We have both points, hence a vector into the future in the case of planning for Plato's ideal state. But there is no second point—there are no significant historical truths—in the event of drastic, apocalyptic changes on Earth. This deprives us of the information required for choosing a second point, hence a direction for the line.

The implication is dismaying and dangerous. It was conceded before that truths are never sufficient to decide any particular object of desire: truths can only define a space of objectives appropriate to the circumstances they signify. Now the link between truth and value is weaker still. Situations of the first kind (e.g., breeding a class of human drones) anticipate a breach separating our past from a radically different future. There are truths about the past, though we don't know how constraining they should be. Are they pertinent to the unforeseeable consequences of acting in the novel way proposed? They might not be, though, equally, someone who discounts the salience of information about our history too much resembles the man driving at high speed on a wet road in the dark. Still, our situation is not altogether bleak. We have interests to conserve, and we are not obliged to do the new thing. We can proceed more cautiously, even in the direction of this more radical proposal, or we may decline to do anything that would upset the established order.

Situations of the other (end of the world) sort leave us disoriented, feeble, and probably ineffective. Having agreed already that truth is not sufficient to fix values, we admit that an impoverished set of truths (no information about the past) disables us from establishing a set of appropriate objectives. Worse, and finally ruinous, we don't know the consequences of anything done in these new circumstances. We want to secure and satisfy ourselves; but in these circumstances we don't know how to do it. All our navigating lights are extinguished. This is the Apocalypse.

Should we turn our backs on the past, as this second example requires? Even Nietzsche would necessarily have distinguished the two sorts of cases just considered, had he imagined them. For no one supposes that will alone, however self-convinced, could secure us in the radically altered circumstances of this second example. Let us put aside, therefore, the drastic implications of a future altogether out of joint with our past. We consider just those cases for which the past supplies useful information in contexts where the future diverges radically from it.

How would Nietzsche have us bridge this gap? We should act, he would say. Scorning deliberation because it makes the future hostage to the past, we should do whatever a noble impulse moves us to do. Why not restrain this impulse long enough to appraise it or consider the truths relevant to our situation? Nietzsche would probably decline to do either one. Don't cripple passion, he would say, by making it reflective. But surely, things done in ignorance, like action in the dark, are likely to be insensitive to our nature, circumstances, and well-being.

Regard for the welfare of ourselves and other things makes desire cautious. We are responsive to the truths that inform us about our circumstances, our prospects, and ourselves. Nor are we forced to choose between being reckless and inert. Hoping to be neither, we require a middle way. Nietzsche would despise our caution: stodgy, he might say, is just this side of dead. But no one proves his spontaneity by walking blindly into a jet engine; though ignoring, almost spitefully, all the truths about past and present has only this effect.

Nietzsche mistakes every moment in life as a choice made in ruptured time and circumstances, as if every moment were the beginning of time. But that is not our situation. We have both a past and some information about it. The line we draw through the present is a decided vector. It begins in historical truths before running through our present circumstances into a future of restricted possibilities. The exact orientation of the line expresses the judgment that some aspects of our past are more salient than others as regards our present and future. This orientation is not so easily decided, since we are often mistaken in the choice and characterization of our history. But assume that a decision about the relevant past is made. A line is drawn, and a domain of objects appropriate for desire is established.

These are the circumstances where Aristotle, Nietzsche, and Dewey instruct us. We have Aristotle's caution, his respect for continuity, and the truths that carry us some way into the future on the basis of our information about what did or did not work in the past. We also have Nietzsche. We don't save him for those occasions when our backs are turned on truth before we act upon a desire. Reflection on salient truths is never, we agree, sufficient to determine what we shall do. It is always and only the affective side of us that makes this determination. Yet — and now we have Dewey — we curb impulse so that choice may be as well informed as time and circumstances enable us to make it. We do so not in order to murder spontaneity, but merely so that the attitudes sponsoring choice may be well informed. Does it follow that we *know* what to do when presented with alternative, but appropriate, choices for desire? No, we say only that facing ahead, having some idea of where we are going and why, is usually better for us than backing in with eyes closed, all the while telling ourselves that the future is always better than the past.

VII Truth's Debt to Value

The use of truths to educate attitude and desire is no sure thing: deliberation is no cure for people who are not moved by the truth. Value-driven ideologies, with their contempt for truth and for truths inimical to their aims, are proof of that. Fire by truth is, nonetheless, our one alternative to blundering error. Add that truth is the discipline of thought and that mutual confidence, hence all voluntarily co-ordinated behavior, is founded in the belief that we are truth-tellers.

Alasdair MacIntyre lists truth telling as one of the three cardinal virtues.[10] This is exactly right when telling others and ourselves who and where we are is vital to our collective well-being. That we do not make the world, but can only alter it for better or worse, is an important truth to declare. This is the only debt of truth to value: caring for other people, things and ourselves, having to know some truths as we act in their behalf and our own, we are not reckless about truth or truths.

Notes

•

Introduction

1   The idea of world-making is common to many of the writers considered below. The phrase "world-making" is Nelson Goodman's. See his *Ways of Worldmaking* (Indianapolis: Hackett, 1978).

2   Willard V. O. Quine, *Pursuit of Truth* (Cambridge, Mass.: Harvard University Press, 1990), pp. 20, 81, 95, 98, 99.

3   Immanuel Kant, *Critique of Pure Reason*, trans. Norman Kemp Smith (New York: St. Martin's Press, 1965), pp. 92–296. See also Johann G. Fichte, *Gesamtausgabe der Bayerischen Akademie der Wissenschaften*, ed. R. Lauth, H. Jacobs, and H. Gliwitzky, (Stuttgart-Bad Cannstatt: Frommann, 1964). I, 5, 77: "Our freedom *itself is a theoretical determining principle of our world.*" Also ibid., 1, 4, 332: "the practical I is the I of original self-consciousness . . . a rational being perceives itself immediately only in willing . . . it would not perceive itself—and, consequently, would not perceive the world—and would not even be an intellect if it were not a practical being." These passages from Fichte are cited by Daniel Breazeale, "Why Fichte Now?," *Journal of Philosophy* 88, no. 10 (Oct. 1991): 526.

4   See also Plato's notion that the Good is the highest Form, every other quality and relation having been created and made visible by it: Plato, *Republic*, in *The Collected Dialogues of Plato*, ed. Edith Hamilton and Huntington Cairns (New York: Pantheon, 1961), 508C, p. 743. See also David Weissman, *Hypothesis and the Spiral of Reflection* (Albany: State University of New York Press, 1989), pp. 223–26.

5   Hilary Putnam, *Reason, Truth and History* (Cambridge: Cambridge University Press, 1981), p. 137.

6   Donald Davidson, "The Structure and Content of Truth," *Journal of Philosophy* 87, no. 6 (June 1990): 326.

7   "I have been reproached . . . for defining the power of desire as the *power of being the cause, through one's presentations, of the actuality of the objects of these presentations.*" Kant reaffirms this claim while explaining the apparent exception that wishing is not sufficient to create its objects: Immanuel Kant, *Critique of Judgment*, trans. Werner S. Pluhar (Indianapolis: Hackett, 1987), p. 16, n. 18.

8   Johann G. Fichte, *The Science of Knowledge*, trans. Peter Heath and John Lachs (Cambridge: Cambridge University Press, 1982), p. 231. There is also this remark: "The above-mentioned original *duality* in the self—of striving and reflection—is thereby intimately unified. All reflection is based on striving, and in the absence of striving there can be no reflection. . . . And so here then there appears once more in its fullest light the principle: no ideality, no reality, and *vice versa*" (ibid., pp. 258–59).

9   Kant, *Critique of Judgment*, p. 16.

10 Ibid., p. 38.

11 "To give men back the courage to their natural drives": Friedrich Nietzsche, *The Will to Power*, trans. Walter Kaufmann and R. J. Hollingdale (New York: Random House, 1968), p. 76.

12 William James, "The Will to Believe," in *The Writings of William James*, ed. John J. McDermott (New York: Modern Library, 1968), pp. 717–35.

13 Rudolf Carnap, "Empiricism, Semantics, and Ontology," in *Semantics and the Philosophy of Language*, ed. Leonard Linsky (Urbana: University of Illinois Press, 1952), pp. 208–28.

14 Carnap did worry about the need for making these practical matters responsible. See Paul Schilpp, ed., *The Philosophy of Rudolf Carnap* (La Salle, Ill.: Open Court, 1963), p. 862: "Many problems concerning conceptual frameworks seem to me to belong to the most important problems of philosophy. I am thinking here of both theoretical investigations and of practical deliberations and decisions with respect to an acceptance or a change of frameworks, especially of the most general frameworks containing categorial concepts which are fundamental for the representation of all knowledge."

15 Richard Rorty, *Contingency, Irony and Solidarity* (Cambridge: Cambridge University Press, 1989), pp. 141–88.

16 Richard Rorty, *Consequences of Pragmatism* (Minneapolis: University of Minnesota Press, 1982), p. 141.

17 Ibid., p. 149.

18 Ibid., pp. 150–51.

19 Ibid., p. 153.

20 Ibid., p. 154.

21 Ibid., p. 153.

22 Ibid., p. 152.

23 Ibid., p. xliii.

24 See also Thomas Kuhn on Rorty's reading of him: ibid., p. 153. We are to infer that the choice of the paradigm used to organize a science is, like every novel, value-driven. See Kuhn, *The Structure of Scientific Revolutions* (Chicago: University of Chicago Press, 1962).

25 Immanuel Kant, *Critique of Practical Reason*, trans. Thomas K. Abbott (London: Long-mans, 1873), p. 51.

26 Nietzsche, *Will to Power*, p. 10.

27 Hilary Putnam, *Meaning and the Moral Sciences* (London: Routledge and Kegan Paul, 1978), pp. 124, 130.

28 Davidson, "Structure and Content of Truth," p. 304.

29 Peter Strawson, "Truth," in *Truth*, ed. George Pitcher (Englewood Cliffs, N.J.: Prentice-Hall, 1964), p. 52.

30 David Weissman, *Eternal Possibilities* (Carbondale: Southern Illinois University Press, 1977).

1 Peirce and James

1 Charles Sanders Peirce, "What Pragmatism Is," in *Collected Papers of Charles Sanders Peirce* (Cambridge, Mass.: Harvard University Press, 1934), 5:276–77.

2 James, "Will to Believe."

3 Edward Craig, *The Mind of God and the Works of Man* (Oxford: Clarendon Press, 1987), pp. 2–10.

4 C. S. Peirce, "The Fixation of Belief," in *Collected Papers*, 5:223–47.

5 René Descartes, "Rules for the Direction of the Native Talents," in *René Descartes: The Essential Writings*, trans. John J. Blom (New York: Harper and Row, 1977), pp. 22–98.

6 The *cogito*'s alleged self-confirmation is an exception to these remarks: the claim acknowledging it is not a universal truth, though its negation is a contradiction.

7 C. S. Peirce, "Questions concerning Certain Faculties Claimed for Man," in *Collected Papers*, 5:135–55.

8 C. S. Peirce, "The Categories Continued," in *Collected Papers*, 5:52.

9 David Hume, *A Treatise of Human Nature*, ed. L. A. Selby-Bigge and P. H. Nidditch (Oxford: Clarendon Press, 1978), p. 275.

10 Ibid., p. 79.

11 Warner Wick, "The 'Political' Philosophy of Logical Empiricism," *Philosophical Studies*, 11, no. 4 (1951): 51–52.

12 Helen Longino, *Science as Social Knowledge* (Princeton: Princeton University Press, 1990), p. 4, introduces the notions of *constitutive* and *contextual* values. Her constitutive values are "the source of the rules determining what constitutes acceptable scientific practice or scientific method." Her contextual values are those belonging "to the social and cultural environment in which science is done." The values described in my text as *regulative* include both the constitutive and contextual values described by Longino. The values that I describe as *constitutive* function in this other way: they determine what properties and relations shall be ascribed to things, or they determine which inductive rules shall be applied as we decide the thoughts or sentences that are to be counted as true. It is value's constitutive role that is implied by the slogan *truth is a function of value*. Longino argues that the rules of scientific practice and method are sometimes abused, with the effect that values do have the role implied by calling them "constitutive" in my sense. For then we pretend to formulate and confirm hypotheses about an alledged state of affairs, though more careful examination shows that we have used the trappings of honest inquiry to misrepresent or alter circumstances in service to some attitude or desire. On these occasions, but not otherwise, there is a convergence in the application of Longino's use of 'constitutive' and my own, though we use the term differently.

13 This qualifying phrase, "in the moment of," allows that I may subsequently alter things represented in ways determined by my values. We may do so even in the moment of representing things, as happens if we make or change an item while thinking or talking about it. The point at issue survives: that representing a thing in thought or speech is not, by itself, a value-sponsored way of remaking it. James exploits the apparent exceptions to this point (see the discussion below), but even they are its examples: one might redescribe defeat as victory, but then it remains to justify the redescription with thoughts or deeds that confirm the new description.

14 James, "Will to Believe," p. 723.

15 Ibid., p. 720.

16 Ibid., p. 730. Also see Fichte, *Science of Knowledge*, p. 270: "We have already pointed above to a determination of the self's ideal activity by means of the drive, which must constantly effect as much as it can. In consequence of this determination, the activity must serve to *posit*, in the first place, *the ground of limitation*, as an object determined, moreover, entirely by itself; for which very reason, such an object neither comes, nor can come, to consciousness. And besides, a drive to mere determination has just come to light in the self; and in virtue thereof the ideal activity must at least begin by striving to set about *determining* the object posited." And ibid., p. 264: "Here lies the ground of all reality. Only through that relation of feeling to the self, which has now been demonstrated, is the reality either of the self, or the not-self, possible for the self. Anything which is possible solely through *the relation of a feeling*, without the self being

conscious, or able to be conscious, *of its intuition thereof, and which therefore appears to be felt,* is *believed.* As to reality in general, whether that of the self or the not-self, there is only a *belief."*

17 William James, *Pragmatism and the Meaning of Truth* (Cambridge, Mass.: Harvard University Press, 1975), p. 123.

18 Craig, *Mind of God,* p. 263, cites the last quotation above, and then explains: "Within these limits, it is up to us to create that system of beliefs which will afford us maximum satisfaction; and in so far as we succeed we have both grasped the real and made it." Craig then quotes this passage from James, *Pragmatism and the Meaning of Truth,* p. 123: "No one can deny that such a role would add both to our dignity and to our responsibility as thinkers. To some of us it proves a most inspiring notion. Signor Papini, the leader of Italian pragmatism, grows fairly dithyrambic over the view that it opens up man's divinely creative functions."

19 Rorty, *Consequences of Pragmatism,* p. xliii.

20 Putnam, *Reason, Truth and History,* p. 128.

21 Ibid., p. 130.

22 Ibid., p. 201.

23 Ibid., p. 137.

24 Carnap, "Empiricism, Semantics, and Ontology," pp. 219–20.

25 Michel Foucault, *Power/Knowledge,* ed. Colin Gordon (New York: Pantheon, 1977), p. 131. Also see Michel Foucault, *The Archaeology of Knowledge,* trans. A. M. Sheridan Smith (New York: Pantheon, 1972), p. 68: "Neither the relation of discourse to desire, nor the processes of its appropriation, nor its role among non-discursive practices is extrinsic to its unity, its characterization, and the laws of its formation. They are not disturbing elements which, superposing themselves upon its pure, neutral, atemporal, silent form, suppress its true voice and emit in its place a travestied discourse, but, on the contrary, its formative elements."

26 Gilles Deleuze and Felix Guattari, *Nomadology: The War Machine,* trans. Brian Massumi (New York: Semiotext, 1986), p. 43.

27 Rorty, *Consequences of Pragmatism,* p. xviii.

28 Martin Heidegger, *Being and Time,* trans. John Macquarrie and Edward Robinson (New York: Harper and Row, 1962), p. 191.

29 Ibid., p. 133: "Why has recourse been taken to the phenomenon of value when it has seemed necessary to round out such an ontology of the world?" Heidegger did not publish the essay in which the intimated role of value as ground for the ontology of things ready-to-hand was to be elaborated.

30 Friedrich Nietzsche, *On the Genealogy of Morals and Ecce Homo*, trans. Walter Kaufmann and R. J. Hollingdale (New York: Random House, 1969), p. 161: "in us the will to truth becomes conscious of itself as a problem."

31 Karl Marx, *The Communist Manifesto*, ed. Samuel H. Beer (New York: Appleton, Century, Crofts, 1955), pp. 30–31.

32 Jacques Derrida, *Speech and Phenomena* (Evanston, Ill.: Northwestern University Press, 1973), pp. 129–60.

33 Martin Heidegger, "Metaphysics as the History of Being," in *The End of Philosophy*, trans. Joan Stambaugh (London: Souvenir Press, 1975), pp. 1–54.

34 Richard Rorty, *Philosophy and the Mirror of Nature* (Princeton: Princeton University Press, 1979), pp. 389–94.

35 Wittgenstein would not have taken this possibility seriously: he would have said that people show by their conduct that they have learned the same forms of life. Their private valuings cannot be known even to themselves (they lack a public criterion to make them intelligible); or they do not exist. It is not plain that James, Heidegger, Foucault, Putnam, Carnap, Derrida, or Rorty would concede these points. Certainly, Rorty's "conversation of the West" would seem to tolerate desires and attitudes peculiar to each of many interlocutors. See Ludwig Wittgenstein, *Philosophical Investigations*, trans. G. E. M. Anscombe (New York: Macmillan, 1953), para. 580, p. 153.

36 Rorty, *Consequences of Pragmatism*, p. xliii.

37 Ibid., pp. 86–87.

38 Ibid., p. xlii.

39 Ibid., pp. xlii–xliii.

40 Fichte is the critical source for views of this sort, whether in Sartre or Rorty. Fichte, *Science of Knowledge*, pp. 222–23: "The self posits itself absolutely, and without any other ground, and *must* posit itself, if it is to posit anything else: for what does not *exist*, cannot posit; but the self exists (for the self) solely and absolutely through its own positing of itself. The self cannot posit the not-self without restricting itself. For the not-self is completely opposed to the self; what the not-self is, the self is not; and thus insofar as the not-self is posited (or the predicate of 'being posited' is ascribed to it), the self is not posited. If, say, the not-self were posited without quantity, as infinite and unlimited, the self would not be posited at all and its reality would be utterly annihilated, which contradicts what was said above. . . . The expressions *to posit a not-self* and *to restrict the self are completely equivalent.*

41 Johann G. Fichte, *The Vocation of Man*, ed. Roderick Chisholm (Indianapolis: Bobbs-Merrill, 1956), pp. 35–82.

42 George W. F. Hegel, *Hegel's Logic*, trans. William Wallace (Oxford: Clarendon Press, 1975), pp. 44–54.

43 Gilbert Ryle, *Dilemmas* (Cambridge: Cambridge University Press, 1954).

44 G. E. Moore, "A Defense of Common Sense," in *Philosophical Papers* (London: George Allen and Unwin, 1959), pp. 32–59.

45 Heidegger, *Being and Time*, p. 236.

46 Rorty, *Consequences of Pragmatism*, p. 86.

47 Willard V. O. Quine, "Two Dogmas of Empiricism," in *From a Logical Point of View* (New York: Harper and Row, 1961), p. 43.

48 Kant, *Critique of Pure Reason*, pp. 294–96.

49 Nietzsche, *Genealogy of Morals*, p. 35.

50 C. S. Peirce, "Some Consequences of Four Incapacities," in *Collected Papers*, 5:187.

51 Rudolf Carnap, *The Logical Structure of the World*, trans. Rolph A. George (Berkeley and Los Angeles: University of California Press, 1967), p. viii.

52 Peirce, "What Pragmatism Is," p. 287. Notice the effect of reading a pragmatist, or pragmaticist, whose views about pragmatist doctrine are exactly opposed to the ones declared by James's successors. There are, e.g., Rorty's claims in *Consequences of Pragmatism*, p. xiv: "Pragmatists think that the history of attempts to isolate the True or the Good, or to define the word 'true' or 'good,' supports their suspicion that there is no interesting work to be done in this area." And ibid., p. xxxviii: "Pragmatism denies the possibility of getting beyond the Sellarsian notion of 'seeing how things hang together.' " Compare Peirce, "What Pragmatism Is," p. 282: "Pragmaticism is a species of prope-positivism. But what distinguishes it from other species is, first its retention of a purified philosophy; secondly, its full acceptance of the main body of our instinctive beliefs; and thirdly, its strenuous insistence upon the truth of scholastic realism." Who speaks *ex cathedra* for pragmatism? Plainly, no one does; though Peirce, at least, had the right to think he did.

53 Peirce, "What Pragmatism Is," p. 392.

54 Putnam, *Reason, Truth and History*, p. 147.

55 Putnam, *Meaning and the Moral Sciences*, pp. 123–38.

56 Carnap, "Empiricism, Semantics, and Ontology," pp. 218–21.

57 Putnam, *Reason, Truth and History*, p. 201. Putnam wants Peirce's support for internal realism: *Meaning and the Moral Sciences*, p. 125: " 'Verified' (in any operational sense)

does not imply 'true', on the metaphysical realist picture, even in the ideal limit. It is this feature that distinguishes metaphysical realism, as I am using the term, from the mere belief that there *is* an ideal theory (Peircian realism)." And ibid., 130: "Metaphysical realism collapses just at the point at which it claims to be distinguishable from Peircean realism—i.e., from the claim that there is an ideal theory . . . Peirce himself . . . always *said* metaphysical realism collapses into incoherence at *just* that point."

This is a contentious reading of Peirce, one unsupported by reference to his words. Peirce was surely a metaphysical realist, as confirmed by the passages cited in my text, and a fallibilist. He hypothesized that there is a world whose existence and character are independent of the ways we think about it, i.e., independent of our standards of rational acceptability; but he did believe that this general hypothesis, like every more particular one, may be mistaken. Indeed, "The perfect truth cannot be stated, except in the sense that it confesses its imperfection": Peirce, "Truth," in *Collected Papers*, 5:396.

58 Putnam, *Meaning and the Moral Sciences*, pp. 123–24.

59 Ibid., p. 125.

60 Ibid.

61 Ibid., p. 126.

62 Ibid.

63 Putnam's argument is somewhat complicated when he uses 'model' in these two ways: we are to map a model onto THE WORLD, yet the entire notion, "*any* correct theory to all or part of THE WORLD," is also described as a model. Ibid., p. 123.

64 Ibid., p. 139, n. 4.

65 Ibid., p. 126.

66 Alfred Tarski, "The Semantic Conception of Truth," in *Semantics and the Philosophy of Language*, ed. Leonard Linsky (Urbana: University of Illinois Press, 1952), pp. 33–34. For a reading of Tarski that anticipates my own, see John Etchemendy, "Tarski on Truth and Logical Consequence," *Journal of Symbolic Logic*, 53 (1988):51–79. Putnam implies, contrary to Tarski's warning, that truths satisfying Tarski's convention have material consequences. Donald Davidson also ignores Tarski's assertion that his semantic notion of truth does not have material import: Davidson, "Structure and Content of Truth," p. 299: "In his appeal to convention-T, Tarski assumes, as we have seen, a prior grasp of the concept of truth; he then shows how this intuition can be implemented in detail for particular languages. The implementation requires the introduction of a referential concept, a relation between words and things—some relation like satisfaction." This remark is odd when the only satisfaction relation acknowledged by Tarski is that of a sentence in the object language and its name in the meta-language. There is, perhaps, only this Kantian way to explain the use that Putnam and Davidson make of Tarski: we are to suppose that the sentence in the object language reports the schematization, hence the objectification and presentation, of a "material" state of af-

fairs. Both the sentence in the object language and the "objective" state of affairs it reports (any distinction between them is only notional) satisfies the sentence in the meta-language.

67 Putnam, *Meaning and the Moral Sciences*, pp. 137–38.

68 Kant, *Critique of Judgment*, pp. 16–17, n. 18.

69 Putnam, *Meaning and the Moral Sciences*, p. 137.

70 Ibid., pp. 133–35.

71 Ibid., p. 135.

72 Ibid.

73 Ibid., pp. 130–33.

74 Ibid., p. 131.

75 Peirce, "Truth," p. 397.

76 Franz Brentano, *Psychology from an Empirical Standpoint*, trans. A. C. Rancurello, D. B. Terrell, and L. L. MacAlister (New York: Humanities Press, 1973), p. 324.

77 C. S. Peirce, "Letters to Lady Welby," in *Charles Peirce: Selected Writings*, ed. Philip P. Wiener (New York: Dover, 1958), pp. 391–93.

78 Quine, *Pursuit of Truth*, p. 29.

79 Ibid., pp. 97–99.

80 Ibid., p. 3.

81 Idid., p. 5.

82 This conclusion is contrary to the view, sometimes implied, that sensory data have no discriminable character of their own, *all* the features ascribable to them being the product of the theory under which the data are subsumed. How cleanly should we distinguish raw empirical content from the characterizations supplied when data are subsumed under a theory? Quine says plainly, *Pursuit of Truth*, p. 7, that sensory data do have a character distinct from our descriptions of them: "Seen holophrastically, as conditioned to stimulatory situations, the sentence is theory-free; seen analytically, word by word, it is theory-laden." This same ground is covered, in *Word and Object* (Cambridge, Mass.: MIT Press, 1960), p. 33, with significantly less space allotted to the pretheoretic character of sensory data, as when "ocular irradiation" is immediately superseded for the purposes of characterizing the data by (Ibid., p. 36) a subject's "evolving dispositions to assent to or dissent from a sentence." The suggestion that sensory data are inextricably caught up in theory, without any way of acknowledging their pre-theoretic character, is reminiscent of Carnap, *Logical Structure of the World*, p. 109: "In choosing

as basic elements the elementary experiences, we do not assume that the stream of experience is composed of determinate, discrete elements. We only presuppose that statements can be made about certain places in the stream of experience, to the effect that one such place stands in a certain relation to another place, etc. But we do not assert that the stream of experience can be uniquely analyzed into such places." Putnam would seem to be closer to the earlier Quine and to Carnap than to the later Quine.

83 David Weissman, "Mental Structure," *Ratio* II, no. 1 (June 1969), pp. 14–37.

84 Putnam, *Meaning and the Moral Sciences*, p. 138. Also see Foucault, *The Archaeology of Knowledge*, pp. 113, 183, 192, 202–05.

85 Carnap, *Logical Structure of the World*, p. 286.

86 Kant, *Critique of Pure Reason*, pp. 297–300.

87 Carnap, *Logical Structure of the World*, p. 286.

88 Kant, *Critique of Pure Reason*, pp. 653–65.

89 Ibid., pp. 629–52.

90 Quine, *Word and Object*, pp. 270–76.

91 Peirce, "What Pragmatism Is," p. 278.

92 For a discussion that resolves these issues in favor of relativism and internal realism, see Joseph Margolis, *Pragmatism without Foundations* (Oxford: Basil Blackwell, 1986), pp. 281–307.

93 Sidney Hook, *John Dewey* (New York: John Day, 1939), p. 35.

2 Two Kinds of Thinking: Hypothesis and Construction

1 Ernest Nagel, *The Structure of Science* (New York: Harcourt, Brace and World, 1961), pp. 494–95.

2 David Weissman, *Intuition and Ideality* (Albany: State University of New York Press, 1987), pp. 17–52.

3 Kant, *Critique of Pure Reason*, pp. 95–97, 111–13. Also see Foucault's remarks about "The Formation of Objects," *The Archaeology of Knowledge*, pp. 41–42, 184–92. Foucault claims for discourse powers that are startlingly similar to the ones the Carnap ascribes to semantical frameworks. See his "Empiricsm, Semantics, and Ontology."

4 Ibid., p. 654.

5 "The pure form of sensible intuitions in general, in which all the manifold of intuition is intuited in certain relations, must be found in the mind *a priori*": Ibid., p. 66.

6   Ibid., p. 98. Also see Foucault, *The Archaeology of Knowledge*, p. 234. He credits dis-
    course with "the power of constituting domains of objects, in relation to which one
    can affirm or deny true or false propositions."

7   Ibid., p. 97.

8   Ibid., p. 221.

9   Ibid., p. 654.

10 Kant, *Critique of Judgment*, pp. 13–15.

11 Kant, *Critique of Pure Reason*, pp. 167–68.

12 George W. F. Hegel, *Phenomenology of Mind*, trans. J. B. Baillie (New York: Harper
    and Row, 1967), pp. 514–58.

13 Wittgenstein, *Philosophical Investigations*, paras. 1–23, pp. 2–12.

14 G. W. Leibniz, *Monadology, Monadology and Other Essays*, trans. P. and A. M. Schrecker
    (Indianapolis: Bobbs-Merrill, 1965), p. 148. For a discussion of social rules as the con-
    tent of self-knowledge, see Peter Winch, *The Idea of a Social Science and its Relation to
    Philosophy* (London: Routledge, 1965).

15 Rorty, *Consequences of Pragmatism*, p. 140.

16 Ibid., p. 139.

17 Ibid., p. 141.

18 Ibid., p. 143.

19 Ibid., pp. 92–93.

20 As Kant explains this failure, *Critique of Judgment*, p. 419, n. 50: "The power of desire
    can also be determined in such a way that it contradicts itself."

21 Putnam, *Reason, Truth and History*, pp. 134–35.

22 See, e.g., Hegel, *Hegel's Logic*; and Francis H. Bradley, *Appearance and Reality* (Oxford:
    Clarendon Press, 1969).

23 Leibniz, *Monadology*, p. 153.

24 Putnam, *Meaning and the Moral Sciences*, p. 137. There is also this passage from Quine
    in *Dear Carnap, Dear Van*, ed. Richard Creath (Berkeley and Los Angeles: University
    of California Press, 1990), p. 66: "When we adopt such a syntax, in which the *a priori*
    is confined to the analytic, every true proposition then falls into one of two classes:
    either it is a synthetic empirical proposition, belonging within one or another of the
    natural sciences, or it is an *a priori* analytic proposition, in which case it derives its

validity from the conventional structure, or *syntax*, of the language itself—'syntax' being broadly enough construed to cover all linguistic conventions."

Where semantic truths as much as analytic ones are syntactic and where syntax is a priori because of being conventional, we are very much closer to synthetic a priori truths (of a kind) than Quine here allows.

25 Carnap, *Logical Structure of the World*, pp. 103–06.

26 This *ontological* foundationalism is an answer to some startled questions. See Breazeale, "Why Fichte Now?", p. 525: 'Why Fichte now? Or, more specifically, what can philosophers who pride themselves on their 'anti-idealism,' their 'antitranscendentalism,' and their 'antifoundationalism' possibly hope to gain from an acquaintance with Fichte's *Wissenschaftslehre?*" and ibid., p. 524: "It would be difficult to imagine a paradigm of philosophical inquiry more completely at odds with those of the late twentieth century. Nevertheless, to the consternation of some and the bewilderment of others, a world-wide revival of interest in Fichte's thought is currently underway, a revival . . . giving rise as well to dramatic claims on behalf of the intrinsic merits and contemporary value of Fichte's transcendental philosophy." The interest in Fichte is less surprising if his transcendentalism is one of the styles that dominates twentieth-century thinking, down to and including some of its principal analytic philosophers. We are slow to realize the power of Fichtean transcendentalism among us.

27 Immanuel Kant, *Foundation of the Metaphysics of Morals*, trans. Lewis White Beck (Indianapolis: Bobbs-Merrill, 1959), pp. 64–83.

28 Arthur Schopenhauer, *The World as Will and Idea*, trans. R. B. Haldane and J. Kemp (London: Routledge, 1964); and Nietzsche, *Will to Power*.

29 This is the topic of chap. 5, sec. VIII.

30 Weissman, *Eterenal Possibilities*, pp. 237–90; idem, *Hypothesis and the Spiral of Reflection*, pp. 161–69.

31 Longino, *Science as Social Knowledge*, pp. 83–133.

3 The Cognitive-Affective Basis for Value

1 Benedict Spinoza, *Ethics* (with *On the Improvement of the Understanding* and *Correspondence*), trans. R. H. M. Elwes (New York: Dover, 1955), p. 173.

2 Ibid., p. 156.

3 Heidegger, *Being and Time*, pp. 102–04.

4 Spinoza, *Ethics*, p. 170: "But desire is each man's nature or essence; therefore desire in one individual differs from desire in another individual, only in so far as the nature or essence of the one differs from the nature or essence of the other."

5   Cognitive-affective balance is also discussed in my *Hypothesis and the Spiral of Reflection*, pp. 179–204, although it is the cognitive role of hypotheses, not value, that is emphasized there.

6   Sigmund Freud, *The Ego and the Id*, trans. Joan Rivière (London: Hogarth Press, 1947), p. 15.

7   Ibid., p. 12.

8   John Stuart Mill, *On Liberty* (New York: Macmillan, 1987), p. 16.

9   Quine, *Word and Object*, pp. 9–13.

10   Weissman, *Eternal Possibilities*, p. 234.

11   Longino, *Science as Social Knowledge*, pp. 162–86.

4 Truth

1   Paul Horwich, *Truth* (Oxford: Basil Blackwell, 1990), p. 26.

2   Carnap, *Logical Structure of the World*, pp. 107–08.

3   Quine, *From a Logical Point of View*, pp. 20–46.

4   Kuhn, *Structure of Scientific Revolutions*, pp. 43–51.

5   Pierre Duhem, *The Aim and Structure of Physical Theory*, trans. Philip P. Wiener (New York: Atheneum, 1962), pp. 295–98.

6   In psychic reality, the 'or' is inclusive, as thoughts are linked to thoughts, sentences to sentences, and thoughts to sentences. We interpret the 'or' exclusively only for the ease of exposition, and because we don't know how to identify or individuate linked thoughts apart from the sentences expressing them.

7   Weissman, *Intuition and Ideality*, pp. 53–108.

8   G. W. Leibniz, *Gottfried Wilhelm Leibniz: Philosophical Papers and Letters* (Dordrecht: D. Reidel, 1969), p. 14.

9   Quine, *Pursuit of Truth*, p. 36.

10   Plato, *Phaedo*, in *Collected Dialogues*, 78b3–84b5, pp. 61–67.

11   George Berkeley, *The Principles of Human Knowledge*, in *The Works of George Berkeley, Bishop of Cloyne* (London: Nelson, 1964), 2:41–42. Hume, *Treatise of Human Nature*, p. 70.

12   Tarski, "Semantic Conception of Truth," p. 15.

13 Kant, *Critique of Pure Reason*, p. 210.

14 Frank Ramsey, "Facts and Propositions," in *Truth*, ed. G. Pitcher (Englewood Cliffs, NJ.: Prentice-Hall, 1964), p. 17; id. *The Foundations of Mathematics* (New York: Humanities Press, 1950), p. 143.

15 Quine, *Pursuit of Truth*, p. 80. Notice the ambiguity in the remark "To ascribe truth to the sentence is to ascribe whiteness to snow." This is incorrect, *pace* Tarski, if it is only a way of citing that sentence in the object language named by the sentence in the meta-language. It is not innocent, but false to Tarski's own restrictions on the interpretation of his semantic definition of truth, if it is the extra-linguistic substance, *snow*, which is inferred to be white when the sentence in the meta-language is declared true. We reasonably infer from Quine's recasting of Kantian themes that the stuff said to be white exists only to the extent of being expressed (formulated, presented) by sentences formulated in the material mode.

16 Quine, *Word and Object*, p. 272.

17 Quine, *Pursuit of Truth*, p. 81.

18 Tarski, "Semantic Conception of Truth," pp. 14–15.

19 Ibid., pp. 31–32.

20 Ibid., p. 30.

21 See chap. 1, n. 66.

22 Tarski, "Semantic Conception of Truth," p. 30.

23 Horwich, *Truth*, p. 7.

24 Ibid., p. 12.

25 Ibid., pp. 121, 125.

26 Ibid., pp. 11, 120.

27 Descartes, "Rules for the Direction of the Native Talents."

28 Carnap, *Logical Structure of the World*; Nelson Goodman, *The Structure of Appearance* (New York: Bobbs-Merrill, 1966).

29 Horwich, *Truth*, pp. 122–25.

30 Ibid., pp. 17–18.

31 Ibid., p. 89.

32 Ibid., p. 93.

33 Ibid., p. 110.

34 Ibid., p. 111.

35 Ibid., pp. 110–11.

36 Ibid., pp. 54–62.

37 Wittgenstein, *Philosophical Investigations*, paras. 2–24, pp. 2–12. J. L. Austin, *Philosophical Papers* (Oxford: Oxford University Press, 1970), pp. 233–52; Strawson, "Truth," pp. 32–53.

38 Plato, *Republic*, 359a3, p. 606.

39 One might also make this point by distinguishing assertive and illocutionary uses of language. See John Searle, *Speech Acts* (Cambridge: Cambridge University Press, 1978), pp. 159–62.

40 Donald Davidson, "Reality without Reference," in *Inquiries into Truth and Interpretation* (Oxford: Clarendon Press, 1990), pp. 215–25.

41 Quine, *Pursuit of Truth*, pp. 40–42.

42 Rorty, *Consequences of Pragmatism*, p. xiv.

43 Carnap, *Logical Structure of the World*, p. 286.

44 William James, "A World of Pure Experience," in *Writings of William James*, pp. 194–214. Bertrand Russell, *The Analysis of Mind* (London: Allen and Unwin, 1971), pp. 287–308.

45 Wittgenstein, *Philosophical Investigations*, paras. 293–95, p. 100.

46 John Dewey, *Logic: The Theory of Inquiry*, in *John Dewey: The Later Works, 1925–53* (Carbondale: Southern Illinois University Press, 1986), 12:30–65.

5 Truth as Correspondence

1 Weissman, *Hypothesis and the Spiral of Reflection*, pp. 202–04.

2 John Stuart Mill, *A System of Logic* (Toronto: University of Toronto Press, 1973), pp. 756–57.

3 Hume, *Treatise of Human Nature*, pp. 1–7, 69–73.

4 For Hume's reductionist argument, see David Weissman, *Dispositional Properties* (Carbondale: Southern Illinois University Press, 1965), pp. 72–82. For an argument defending Hume's realism, see Galen Strawson, *The Secret Connexion* (Oxford: Clarendon Press, 1989), pp. 59–70.

5 Weissman, *Intuition and Ideality*, pp. 82–85.

6 The disposition for walking is, I suppose, that qualification for relation or activity consequent upon, but not reducible to, an agent's structural properties—e.g., skeletal and muscular ones. See Weissman, *Dispositional Properties*, pp. 187–93; "Dispositions as Geometrical-Structural Properties," *Review of Metaphysics* 32, idem, no. 2 (Dec. 1978): 275–97.

7   This formulation is easily amended to provide for truths about states or activities within the mind. I emphasize the extra-mental character of terms for the correspondence relation only because of the Kantian view that there is no thinkable extra-mental term for this relation.

8   J. L. Austin, "Truth," in *Truth*, ed. A. Pitcher (Englewood Cliffs, N.J.: Prentice-Hall, 1964), pp. 21–22; idem, *Philosophical Papers*, pp. 121–22.

9   Ludwig Wittgenstein, *Tractatus Logico-Philosophicus*, trans. D. F. Pears and B. F. McGuinness (London: Routledge and Kegan Paul, 1961), paras. 3.144–3.221, p. 23, and paras. 3.26–3.261, p. 25.

10 Donald Davidson, "The Inscrutability of Reference," in *Inquiries into Truth and Interpretation*, p. 235.

11 Willard V. O. Quine, *Ontological Relativity and Other Essays* (New York: Columbia University Press, 1969), p. 235.

12 Wittgenstein, *Tractatus Logico-Philosophicus*, para. 2.151, p. 15.

13 Jerry Fodor, *The Language of Thought* (Cambridge, Mass.: Harvard University Press, 1979).

14 G. J. Warnock, "A Problem about Truth," in *Truth*, ed. G. Pitcher (Englewood Cliffs, N.J.: Prentice-Hall, 1964), pp. 54–67.

15 Wittgenstein, *Tractatus Logico-Philosophicus*, para. 4.0312, p. 43.

16 Bertrand Russell, "The Philosophy of Logical Atomism," in *Logic and Knowledge*, ed. Robert C. Marsh (London: Macmillan, 1964), pp. 177–281.

17 Hume, *Treatise of Human Nature*, pp. 17–25.

18 Nelson Goodman, "The Problem of Counterfactual Conditionals," in *Semantics and the Philosophy of Language*, ed. L. Linsky (Urbana: University of Illinois Press, 1952), pp. 231–46.

19 Aristotle, *Metaphysics*, in *The Basic Works of Aristotle*, ed. Richard McKeon (New York: Random House, 1941), 999a25–999b23, pp. 724–25.

20 Kant, *Critique of Pure Reason*, pp. 180–87.

21 Ibid., pp. 65–91.

22 Ibid., pp. 93–95, 98–99.

23 Ibid., p. 577.

24 Charles Parsons, "The Structuralist View of Mathematical Objects," *Synthese*, no. 84 (1990): 304.

25 Michael Resnik, "Mathematics as a Science of Patterns: Ontology and Reference," *Nous* 15 (1981): 530.

26 Carnap, "Empiricism, Semantics, and Ontology," p. 212.

27 Ibid.

28 Why should the transcendental ego use one rather than another—e.g., Euclidean or Riemannian—set of rules to constitute the a priori form of space? Only for the reason to which Kantians always resort when some variable category receives determination: a valorizing attitude or desire decides among the available alternatives.

29 Mill, *System of Logic*, pp. 75–77.

30 Gottlob Frege, *The Foundations of Arithmetic*, trans. J. L. Austin (Evanston, Ill.: Northwestern University Press, 1968), pp. 67–98; Bertrand Russell, *Introduction to Mathematical Logic* (London: Allen and Unwin, 1967), pp. 7–13.

31 Russell, *Introduction to Mathematical Knowledge*, p. 4.

32 Michael Redhead, *Incompleteness, Nonlocality and Realism* (Oxford: Clarendon Press, 1987), pp. 160–64.

33 D. M. Armstrong, *A Combinatorial Theory of Possibility* (Cambridge: Cambridge University Press, 1989).

34 Weissman, *Eternal Possibilities*, pp. 72–93.

35 For a different notion of possibility, see David Lewis, *On the Plurality of Worlds* (Oxford: Basil Blackwell, 1986). Lewis supposes that worlds deemed possible from our point of view are actual in themselves, "possibility" being only the way of signifying that these worlds are inaccessible and different from our world. Lewis has no notion of possibility as a mode of being, hence none that properties existing as possibles may be instantiated, thereby providing actual particulars for worlds such as ours. Negative truths, as he understands them, have this complex truth condition: necessarily they obtain in no possible (meaning actual) world because they are contradictory; or the state of affairs specified by a thought or sentence obtains in some other possible (read actual) world or worlds, though not in our world. I doubt that we do justice to possibility by requiring that 'possible' be used to signify that which is actual in other worlds. See my review of Lewis's *On the Plurality of Worlds*, in *Review of Metaphysics* 40, no. 3 (Mar. 1987): 585–88.

36 Plato, *Parmenides*, in *Collected Dialogues*, 126a1–166b15, pp. 920–56.

37 The body of this paragraph derives from Weissman, *Eternal Possibilities*, p. 8.

38 Ibid., pp. 86–89.

39 Russell, "On Denoting," in *Logic and Knowledge*, pp. 39–56.

40 Hume, *Treatise of Human Nature*, p. 173.

41 Weissman, *Dispositional Properties*, p. 188.

42 Plato, *Euthyphro*, in *Collected Works*, 10a1–3, p. 178.

43 See Weissman, *Eternal Possibilities*, pp. 237–90, for a theory of meaning appropriate to an ontology of eternal possibilities.

44 Bertrand Russell, "Mathematical Logic as Based on the Theory of Types," in *Logic and Knowledge*, pp. 59–102.

6 Rational Attitude and Desire

1 Augustine, *The Essential Augustine* (Indianapolis: Hackett, 1964), pp. 216–17.

2 Noam Chomsky, *Cartesian Linguistics* (New York: Harper and Row, 1966), p. 35.

3 Kant, *Critique of Judgment*, pp. 251–55.

4 One thinks of Wittgenstein's views about the use of rules: *Philosophical Investigations*, paras. 183–90, pp. 74–77.

5 Dancers asking George Balanchine what to feel or the reasons to consider before doing steps were told, "Just dance."

6 John Dewey, *Essays in Experimental Logic* (New York: Dover, n. d.), pp. 239–40.

7 Ibid., p. 354.

8 Dewey, *Essays in Experimental Logic*, p. 386.

9 Plato, *Republic*, 619c8, p. 843.

10 Alasdair MacIntyre, *After Virtue* (Notre Dame, Ind.: Notre Dame University Press, 1984), pp. 192–93.

Index